BOLLINGEN SERIES XX

THE COLLECTED WORKS

OF

C. G. JUNG

VOLUME 12

EDITORS

HERBERT READ

MICHAEL FORDHAM, M.D., M.R.C.P.

GERHARD ADLER, PH.D.

WILLIAM MCGUIRE, *executive editor*

PSYCHOLOGY
AND
ALCHEMY

C. G. JUNG

SECOND EDITION

TRANSLATED BY R. F. C. HULL

270 ILLUSTRATIONS

BOLLINGEN SERIES XX

PRINCETON UNIVERSITY PRESS

Second edition, completely revised, 1968
First Princeton / Bollingen Paperback printing, 1980
Eighth printing of the revised edition, 1993
9   11   13   15   16   14   12   10

THIS EDITION IS BEING PUBLISHED IN THE
UNITED STATES OF AMERICA BY PRINCETON
UNIVERSITY PRESS AND IN ENGLAND BY
ROUTLEDGE AND KEGAN PAUL, LTD. IN THE
AMERICAN EDITION, ALL THE VOLUMES COM-
PRISING THE COLLECTED WORKS CONSTITUTE
NUMBER XX IN BOLLINGEN SERIES. THE PRES-
ENT VOLUME IS NUMBER 12 OF THE COL-
LECTED WORKS, AND WAS THE FIRST TO
APPEAR.

Originally published in German as *Psy-chologie und Alchemie*, by Rascher Verlag, Zurich, 1944; 2nd edition revised, 1952.

ISBN 0-691-09771-2
ISBN 0-691-01831-6 pbk.
LIBRARY OF CONGRESS CATALOG CARD NUMBER: 75-156
MANUFACTURED IN THE U.S.A.

PREFATORY NOTE TO THE ENGLISH EDITION

To the reader who knows little or nothing of my work, a word of explanation may be helpful. Some thirty-five years ago I noticed to my amazement that European and American men and women coming to me for psychological advice were producing in their dreams and fantasies symbols similar to, and often identical with, the symbols found in the mystery religions of antiquity, in mythology, folklore, fairytales, and the apparently meaningless formulations of such esoteric cults as alchemy. Experience showed, moreover, that these symbols brought with them new energy and new life to the people to whom they came.

From long and careful comparison and analysis of these products of the unconscious I was led to postulate a "collective unconscious," a source of energy and insight in the depth of the human psyche which has operated in and through man from the earliest periods of which we have records.

In this present study of alchemy I have taken a particular example of symbol-formation, extending in all over some seventeen centuries, and have subjected it to intensive examination, linking it at the same time with an actual series of dreams recorded by a modern European not under my direct supervision and having no knowledge of what the symbols appearing in the dreams might mean. It is by such intensive comparisons as this (and not one but many) that the hypothesis of the collective unconscious—of an activity in the human psyche making for the spiritual development of the individual human being—may be scientifically established.

[*Undated*]

C. G. JUNG

From EDITORIAL NOTE TO THE FIRST EDITION

This volume of Professor Jung's *Collected Works* is a translation, with minor alterations made at the instance of the author, of *Psychologie und Alchemie* (Zurich, 1944; 2nd edition, revised, 1952). That work was based on the two lectures mentioned in Professor Jung's foreword, "Traumsymbole des Individuationsprozesses," *Eranos-Jahrbuch 1935* (Zurich, 1936), and "Die Erlösungsvorstellungen in der Alchemie," *Eranos-Jahrbuch 1936* (Zurich, 1937).

The two lectures were previously translated by Stanley Dell and published in *The Integration of the Personality* (New York, 1939; London, 1940) under the titles "Dream Symbols of the Process of Individuation" and "The Idea of Redemption in Alchemy." Professor Jung then considerably expanded them and added an introduction, in which he set out his whole position particularly in relation to religion. These three parts together with a short epilogue make up the Swiss volume.

The translation now presented to the public has been awaited with impatience in many quarters, for it is one of Professor Jung's major works, to be compared in importance with *Psychology of the Unconscious* and *Psychological Types*. It may be said that round the material contained in this volume the major portion of his later work revolves. On this account *Psychology and Alchemy* is being published first, though it is not Volume 1 of the *Collected Works*.

. . . .

EDITORIAL NOTE TO THE SECOND EDITION

For this second edition of Volume 12, technical considerations made it necessary to reset the text, and this in turn made various improvements possible. The translation has been thoroughly revised, and additions and revisions have been made in accordance with the second Swiss edition, 1952. The bibliography and the footnote references have been corrected and brought up to date, particularly in respect of the author's subsequent publications in English. The paragraph numeration has been preserved, but the pagination has unavoidably changed. An entirely new index has been prepared. The late Mr. A. S. B. Glover was responsible for numerous improvements in the translations from the Latin and in the bibliographical references. The illustrations are printed almost entirely from new photographs; consequently the sources have sometimes had to be altered. For valuable assistance in obtaining new photographs the Editors are indebted to Mrs. Aniela Jaffé, Dr. Jolande Jacobi, and Dr. Rudolf Michel; for general editorial help, to Mrs. B. L. Honum Hull.

After the author's death in 1961, the unpublished draft of a "prefatory note to the English edition," written in English, was found among his papers, and this has been added to the present edition. For permission to publish it, the Editors are indebted to the late Mrs. Marianne Niehus-Jung, then acting on behalf of the heirs of C. G. Jung.

A variant of the text of Part II presenting the essay in its *Eranos-Jahrbuch 1935* form appeared as "Dream Symbols of the Individuation Process" in *Spiritual Disciplines* (Papers from the Eranos Yearbooks, 4; New York and London, 1959).

TRANSLATOR'S NOTE

So far as concerns the translation of this and other volumes of these collected works, the primary aim has naturally been to reproduce the straightforward, lively, and often informal language of the author. In an undertaking such as this one, it would indeed be an act of presumption for the translator to ignore the labours of his predecessors, and the present edition does not seek to stress its newness and difference by studiously overlooking the manifold excellences of the existing translations. In general, therefore, the secondary aim has been to establish a standard terminology for all volumes in this series and to reduce them to a uniform style, while making the fullest use of previous work in this field. In preparing the text of the present volume I had frequent recourse to the material already translated by Stanley Dell in *The Integration of the Personality;* I gratefully acknowledge my debt to him, and also to Miss Barbara Hannah, who magnanimously placed her private, unpublished version of *Psychology and Alchemy* at my disposal, as well as giving me every possible help in the correction of the typescripts and the proofs.

FOREWORD TO THE SWISS EDITION

The present volume contains two major studies which grew out of lectures delivered at the Eranos Congress. They were first printed in the *Eranos-Jahrbuch* for 1935 and 1936. The present edition has been augmented by nearly a half through the inclusion of additional material and the full apparatus of documentation. The text has been improved in certain respects and part of it newly arranged. Another new feature is the wealth of illustrations, the large number of which is justified by the fact that symbolical images belong to the very essence of the alchemist's mentality. What the written word could express only imperfectly, or not at all, the alchemist compressed into his images; and strange as these are, they often speak a more intelligible language than is found in his clumsy philosophical concepts. Between such images and those spontaneously produced by patients undergoing psychological treatment there is, for the expert, a striking similarity both in form and in content, although I have not gone into it very deeply in the course of my exposition.

I am particularly indebted to Dr. M. L. von Franz for philological help in translating the Zosimos text, which, besides being corrupt, is hard to construe and controversial. I wish also to thank Miss R. Schärf for information on the Og and Unicorn legend in Talmudic literature and Mrs. O. Fröbe-Kapteyn for obtaining photographic copies of a number of alchemical pictures. Lastly, I should like to express my very warm thanks to Dr. J. Jacobi for choosing and arranging the illustrations and looking after the details of printing.

Küsnacht, January, 1943

C. G. JUNG

TABLE OF CONTENTS

PART I

INTRODUCTION TO THE RELIGIOUS AND PSYCHOLOGICAL PROBLEMS OF ALCHEMY

PART II

INDIVIDUAL DREAM SYMBOLISM IN RELATION TO ALCHEMY

Chapter 1. Introduction

Chapter 2. The Initial Dreams

Chapter 3. The Symbolism of the Mandala

PART III

RELIGIOUS IDEAS IN ALCHEMY   225

Chapter 6. Alchemical Symbolism in the History of Religion

LIST OF ILLUSTRATIONS

References to documentary sources, which are somewhat shortened in the captions to the illustrations, are given more fully in this list. For explanation of the abbreviations and acknowledgment of photographs, etc., see the note at the end of the list (p. xxxv).

xxiii

NOTE OF ACKNOWLEDGMENT

The illustrations are derived from:

(1) Rare books, MSS., and other works in the author's collection at Küsnacht, which have been reproduced by kind permission of Mr. Franz Jung and photographed under the supervision of Mrs. Aniela Jaffé; indicated by the initials "C.G.J."

(2) Rare books in Mr. Paul Mellon's former collection, reproduced by kind permission of him and of the Yale University Library, where the collection has been deposited under the name "Mellon Collection of the Alchemical and Occult"; photographed by Yale University Library; indicated by the initials "M.C.A.O."

(3) Photographs in private collections, in particular that of Dr. Jolande Jacobi, Zurich, and that of the C. G. Jung Institute, Zurich (indicated as "Inst.").

(4) Books, MSS., and other works in various museums, libraries, archives, etc., as indicated; photographed by the institution unless otherwise noted. Commercial photographic agencies are credited.

(5) In a few cases, the blocks used in earlier editions and kindly made available by Rascher Verlag, Zurich.

1. The Creator as Ruler of the threefold and fourfold universe, with water and fire
as the counterpart of heaven.—"Liber patris sapientiae," *Theatrum chemicum
Britannicum* (1652)

I

INTRODUCTION TO THE RELIGIOUS AND PSYCHOLOGICAL PROBLEMS OF ALCHEMY

Calamum quassatum non conteret, et linum fumigans non extinguet. . . .

—Isaias 42 : 3

The bruised reed he shall not break, and the smoking flax he shall not quench. . . . (D.V.)

2. A pair of alchemists, kneeling by the furnace and praying for God's blessing.
—*Mutus liber* (1702)

1   For the reader familiar with analytical psychology, there is no need of any introductory remarks to the subject of the following study. But for the reader whose interest is not professional and who comes to this book unprepared, some kind of preface will probably be necessary. The concepts of alchemy and the individuation process are matters that seem to lie very far apart, so that the imagination finds it impossible at first to conceive of any bridge between them. To this reader I owe an explanation, more particularly as I have had one or two experiences since the publication of my recent lectures which lead me to infer a certain bewilderment in my critics.

2   What I now have to put forward as regards the nature of the human psyche is based first and foremost on my observations of people. It has been objected that these observations deal with experiences that are either unknown or barely accessible. It is a remarkable fact, which we come across again and again, that absolutely everybody, even the most unqualified layman, thinks he knows all about psychology as though the psyche were something that enjoyed the most universal understanding. But anyone who really knows the human psyche will agree with me

when I say that it is one of the darkest and most mysterious regions of our experience. There is no end to what can be learned in this field. Hardly a day passes in my practice but I come across something new and unexpected. True enough, my experiences are not commonplaces lying on the surface of life. They are, however, within easy reach of every psychotherapist working in this particular field. It is therefore rather absurd, to say the least, that ignorance of the experiences I have to offer should be twisted into an accusation against me. I do not hold myself responsible for the shortcomings in the lay public's knowledge of psychology.

3   There is in the analytical process, that is to say in the dialectical discussion between the conscious mind and the unconscious, a development or an advance towards some goal or end, the perplexing nature of which has engaged my attention for many years. Psychological treatment may come to an *end* at any stage in the development without one's always or necessarily having the feeling that a *goal* has also been reached. Typical and temporary terminations may occur (1) after receiving a piece of good advice; (2) after making a fairly complete but nevertheless adequate confession; (3) after having recognized some hitherto unconscious but essential psychic content whose realization gives a new impetus to one's life and activity; (4) after a hard-won separation from the childhood psyche; (5) after having worked out a new and rational mode of adaptation to perhaps difficult or unusual circumstances and surroundings; (6) after the disappearance of painful symptoms; (7) after some positive turn of fortune such as an examination, engagement, marriage, divorce, change of profession, etc.; (8) after having found one's way back to the church or creed to which one previously belonged, or after a conversion; and finally, (9) after having begun to build up a practical philosophy of life (a "philosophy" in the classical sense of the word).

4   Although the list could admit of many more modifications and additions, it ought to define by and large the main situations in which the analytical or psychotherapeutic process reaches a temporary or sometimes even a definitive end. Experience shows, however, that there is a relatively large number of patients for whom the outward termination of work with the doctor is far from denoting the end of the analytical process. It is rather the

case that the dialectical discussion with the unconscious still continues, and follows much the same course as it does with those who have not given up their work with the doctor. Occasionally one meets such patients again after several years and hears the often highly remarkable account of their subsequent development. It was experiences of this kind which first confirmed me in my belief that there is in the psyche a process that seeks its own goal independently of external factors, and which freed me from the worrying feeling that I myself might be the sole cause of an unreal—and perhaps unnatural—process in the psyche of the patient. This apprehension was not altogether misplaced inasmuch as no amount of argument based on any of the nine categories mentioned above—not even a religious conversion or the most startling removal of neurotic symptoms—can persuade certain patients to give up their analytical work. It was these cases that finally convinced me that the treatment of neurosis opens up a problem which goes far beyond purely medical considerations and to which medical knowledge alone cannot hope to do justice.

5   Although the early days of analysis now lie nearly half a century behind us, with their pseudo-biological interpretations and their depreciation of the whole process of psychic development, memories die hard and people are still very fond of describing a lengthy analysis as "running away from life," "unresolved transference," "auto-eroticism"—and by other equally unpleasant epithets. But since there are two sides to everything, it is legitimate to condemn this so-called "hanging on" as negative to life only if it can be shown that it really does contain nothing positive. The very understandable impatience felt by the doctor does not prove anything in itself. Only through infinitely patient research has the new science succeeded in building up a profounder knowledge of the nature of the psyche, and if there have been certain unexpected therapeutic results, these are due to the self-sacrificing perseverance of the doctor. Unjustifiably negative judgments are easily come by and at times harmful; moreover they arouse the suspicion of being a mere cloak for ignorance if not an attempt to evade the responsibility of a thorough-going analysis. For since the analytical work must inevitably lead sooner or later to a fundamental discussion between "I" and "You" and "You" and "I" on a plane stripped of

all human pretences, it is very likely, indeed it is almost certain, that not only the patient but the doctor as well will find the situation "getting under his skin." Nobody can meddle with fire or poison without being affected in some vulnerable spot; for the true physician does not stand outside his work but is always in the thick of it.

6   This "hanging on," as it is called, may be something undesired by both parties, something incomprehensible and even unendurable, without necessarily being negative to life. On the contrary, it can easily be a positive "hanging on," which, although it constitutes an apparently insurmountable obstacle, represents just for that reason a unique situation that demands the maximum effort and therefore enlists the energies of the whole man. In fact, one could say that while the patient is unconsciously and unswervingly seeking the solution to some ultimately insoluble problem, the art and technique of the doctor are doing their best to help him towards it. "Ars totum requirit hominem!" exclaims an old alchemist. It is just this *homo totus* whom we seek. The labours of the doctor as well as the quest of the patient are directed towards that hidden and as yet unmanifest "whole" man, who is at once the greater and the future man. But the right way to wholeness is made up, unfortunately, of fateful detours and wrong turnings. It is a *longissima via*, not straight but snakelike, a path that unites the opposites in the manner of the guiding caduceus, a path whose labyrinthine twists and turns are not lacking in terrors. It is on this *longissima via* that we meet with those experiences which are said to be "inaccessible." Their inaccessibility really consists in the fact that they cost us an enormous amount of effort: they demand the very thing we most fear, namely the "wholeness" which we talk about so glibly and which lends itself to endless theorizing, though in actual life we give it the widest possible berth.[1] It is infinitely more popular to go in for "compartment psychology," where the left-hand pigeon-hole does not know what is in the right.

7   I am afraid that we cannot hold the unconsciousness and

[1] It is worth noting that a Protestant theologian, writing on homiletics, had the courage to demand wholeness of the preacher from the ethical point of view. He substantiates his argument by referring to my psychology. See Händler, *Die Predigt.*

impotence of the individual entirely responsible for this state of affairs: it is due also to the general psychological education of the European. Not only is this education the proper concern of the ruling religions, it belongs to their very nature—for religion excels all rationalistic systems in that it alone relates to the outer and inner man in equal degree. We can accuse Christianity of arrested development if we are determined to excuse our own shortcomings; but I do not wish to make the mistake of blaming religion for something that is due mainly to human incompetence. I am speaking therefore not of the deepest and best understanding of Christianity but of the superficialities and disastrous misunderstandings that are plain for all to see. The demand made by the *imitatio Christi*—that we should follow the ideal and seek to become like it—ought logically to have the result of developing and exalting the inner man. In actual fact, however, the ideal has been turned by superficial and formalistically-minded believers into an external object of worship, and it is precisely this veneration for the object that prevents it from reaching down into the depths of the psyche and giving the latter a wholeness in keeping with the ideal. Accordingly the divine mediator stands outside as an image, while man remains fragmentary and untouched in the deepest part of him. Christ can indeed be imitated even to the point of stigmatization without the imitator coming anywhere near the ideal or its meaning. For it is not a question of an imitation that leaves a man unchanged and makes him into a mere artifact, but of realizing the ideal on one's own account—*Deo concedente*—in one's own individual life. We must not forget, however, that even a mistaken imitation may sometimes involve a tremendous moral effort which has all the merits of a total surrender to some supreme value, even though the real goal may never be reached and the value is represented externally. It is conceivable that by virtue of this total effort a man may even catch a fleeting glimpse of his wholeness, accompanied by the feeling of grace that always characterizes this experience.

8   The mistaken idea of a merely outward *imitatio Christi* is further exacerbated by a typically European prejudice which distinguishes the Western attitude from the Eastern. Western man is held in thrall by the "ten thousand things"; he sees only particulars, he is ego-bound and thing-bound, and unaware of

the deep root of all being. Eastern man, on the other hand, experiences the world of particulars, and even his own ego, like a dream; he is rooted essentially in the "Ground," which attracts him so powerfully that his relations with the world are relativized to a degree that is often incomprehensible to us. The Western attitude, with its emphasis on the object, tends to fix the ideal—Christ—in its outward aspect and thus to rob it of its mysterious relation to the inner man. It is this prejudice, for instance, which impels the Protestant interpreters of the Bible to interpret ἐντὸς ὑμῶν (referring to the Kingdom of God) as "among you" instead of "within you." I do not mean to say anything about the validity of the Western attitude: we are sufficiently convinced of its rightness. But if we try to come to a real understanding of Eastern man—as the psychologist must—we find it hard to rid ourselves of certain misgivings. Anyone who can square it with his conscience is free to decide this question as he pleases, though he may be unconsciously setting himself up as an *arbiter mundi*. I for my part prefer the precious gift of doubt, for the reason that it does not violate the virginity of things beyond our ken.

9   Christ the ideal took upon himself the sins of the world. But if the ideal is wholly outside then the sins of the individual are also outside, and consequently he is more of a fragment than ever, since superficial misunderstanding conveniently enables him, quite literally, to "cast his sins upon Christ" and thus to evade his deepest responsibilities—which is contrary to the spirit of Christianity. Such formalism and laxity were not only one of the prime causes of the Reformation, they are also present within the body of Protestantism. If the supreme value (Christ) and the supreme negation (sin) are outside, then the soul is void: its highest and lowest are missing. The Eastern attitude (more particularly the Indian) is the other way about: everything, highest and lowest, is in the (transcendental) Subject. Accordingly the significance of the Atman, the Self, is heightened beyond all bounds. But with Western man the value of the self sinks to zero. Hence the universal depreciation of the soul in the West. Whoever speaks of the reality of the soul or psyche[2] is accused

2 [The translation of the German word *Seele* presents almost insuperable difficulties on account of the lack of a single English equivalent and because it combines the two words "psyche" and "soul" in a way not altogether familiar to the Eng-

of "psychologism." Psychology is spoken of as if it were "only" psychology and nothing else. The notion that there can be psychic factors which correspond to divine figures is regarded as a devaluation of the latter. It smacks of blasphemy to think that a religious experience is a psychic process; for, so it is argued, a religious experience "is not *only* psychological." Anything psychic is *only* Nature and therefore, people think, nothing religious can come out of it. At the same time such critics never hesitate to derive all religions—with the exception of their own—from the nature of the psyche. It is a telling fact that two theological reviewers of my book *Psychology and Religion*—one of them Catholic, the other Protestant—assiduously overlooked my demonstration of the psychic origin of religious phenomena.

10   Faced with this situation, we must really ask: How do we know so much about the psyche that we can say "only" psychic? For this is how Western man, whose soul is evidently "of little worth," speaks and thinks. If much were in his soul he would speak of it with reverence. But since he does not do so we can only conclude that there is nothing of value in it. Not that this is necessarily so always and everywhere, but only with people who put nothing into their souls and have "all God outside." (A

---

lish reader. For this reason some comment by the Editors will not be out of place.

[In previous translations, and in this one as well, "psyche"—for which Jung in the German original uses either *Psyche* or *Seele*—has been used with reference to the totality of *all* psychic processes (cf. Jung, *Psychological Types*, Def. 48); i.e., it is a comprehensive term. "Soul," on the other hand, as used in the technical terminology of analytical psychology, is more restricted in meaning and refers to a "function complex" or partial personality and never to the whole psyche. It is often applied specifically to "anima" and "animus"; e.g., in this connection it is used in the composite word "soul-image" (*Seelenbild*). This conception of the soul is more primitive than the Christian one with which the reader is likely to be more familiar. In its Christian context it refers to "the transcendental energy in man" and "the spiritual part of man considered in its moral aspect or in relation to God." (Cf. definition in *The Shorter Oxford English Dictionary*.)

[In the above passage in the text (and in similar passages), "soul" is used in a non-technical sense (i.e., it does not refer to "animus" or "anima"), nor does it refer to the transcendental conception, but to a psychic (phenomenological) fact of a highly numinous character. This usage is adhered to except when the context shows clearly that the term is used in the Christian or Neoplatonic sense. —EDITORS.]

9

little more Meister Eckhart would be a very good thing sometimes!)

11   An exclusively religious projection may rob the soul of its
values so that through sheer inanition it becomes incapable of
further development and gets stuck in an unconscious state. At
the same time it falls victim to the delusion that the cause of
all misfortune lies outside, and people no longer stop to ask
themselves how far it is their own doing. So insignificant does
the soul seem that it is regarded as hardly capable of evil, much
less of good. But if the soul no longer has any part to play, religious life congeals into externals and formalities. However we
may picture the relationship between God and soul, one thing is
certain: that the soul cannot be "nothing but." [3] On the contrary it has the dignity of an entity endowed with consciousness
of a relationship to Deity. Even if it were only the relationship
of a drop of water to the sea, that sea would not exist but for the
multitude of drops. The immortality of the soul insisted upon
by dogma exalts it above the transitoriness of mortal man and
causes it to partake of some supernatural quality. It thus infinitely surpasses the perishable, conscious individual in significance, so that logically the Christian is forbidden to regard
the soul as a "nothing but." [4] As the eye to the sun, so the soul
corresponds to God. Since our conscious mind does not comprehend the soul it is ridiculous to speak of the things of the soul in
a patronizing or depreciatory manner. Even the believing Christian does not know God's hidden ways and must leave him to
decide whether he will work on man from outside or from
within, through the soul. So the believer should not boggle at
the fact that there are *somnia a Deo missa* (dreams sent by God)
and illuminations of the soul which cannot be traced back to
any external causes. It would be blasphemy to assert that God
can manifest himself everywhere save only in the human soul.
Indeed the very intimacy of the relationship between God and

---

3 [The term "nothing but" (*nichts als*), which occurs frequently in Jung to denote
the habit of explaining something unknown by reducing it to something apparently known and thereby devaluing it, is borrowed from William James, *Pragmatism,* p. 16: "What is higher is explained by what is lower and treated for ever
as a case of 'nothing but'—nothing but something else of a quite inferior sort."]
4 The dogma that man is formed in the likeness of God weighs heavily in the
scales in any assessment of man—not to mention the Incarnation.

the soul precludes from the start any devaluation of the latter.[5] It would be going perhaps too far to speak of an affinity; but at all events the soul must contain in itself the faculty of relationship to God, i.e., a correspondence, otherwise a connection could never come about.[6] *This correspondence is, in psychological terms, the archetype of the God-image.*

12   Every archetype is capable of endless development and differentiation. It is therefore possible for it to be more developed or less. In an outward form of religion where all the emphasis is on the outward figure (hence where we are dealing with a more or less complete projection), the archetype is identical with externalized ideas but remains unconscious as a psychic factor. When an unconscious content is replaced by a projected image to that extent, it is cut off from all participation in and influence on the conscious mind. Hence it largely forfeits its own life, because prevented from exerting the formative influence on consciousness natural to it; what is more, it remains in its original form—unchanged, for nothing changes in the unconscious. At a certain point it even develops a tendency to regress to lower and more archaic levels. It may easily happen, therefore, that a Christian who believes in all the sacred figures is still undeveloped and unchanged in his inmost soul because he has "all God outside" and does not experience him in the soul. His deciding motives, his ruling interests and impulses, do not spring from the sphere of Christianity but from the unconscious and undeveloped psyche, which is as pagan and archaic as ever. Not the individual alone but the sum total of individual lives in a nation proves the truth of this contention. The great events of our world as planned and executed by man do not breathe the spirit of Christianity but rather of unadorned paganism. These things originate in a psychic condition that has remained archaic and has not been even remotely touched by Christianity. The Church assumes, not altogether without reason, that the fact

---

[5] The fact that the devil too can take possession of the soul does not diminish its significance in the least.

[6] It is therefore psychologically quite unthinkable for God to be simply the "wholly other," for a "wholly other" could never be one of the soul's deepest and closest intimacies—which is precisely what God is. The only statements that have psychological validity concerning the God-image are either paradoxes or antinomies.

of *semel credidisse* (having once believed) leaves certain traces behind it; but of these traces nothing is to be seen in the broad march of events. Christian civilization has proved hollow to a terrifying degree: it is all veneer, but the inner man has remained untouched and therefore unchanged. His soul is out of key with his external beliefs; in his soul the Christian has not kept pace with external developments. Yes, everything is to be found outside—in image and in word, in Church and Bible—but never inside. Inside reign the archaic gods, supreme as of old; that is to say the inner correspondence with the outer God-image is undeveloped for lack of psychological culture and has therefore got stuck in heathenism. Christian education has done all that is humanly possible, but it has not been enough. Too few people have experienced the divine image as the innermost possession of their own souls. Christ only meets them from without, never from within the soul; that is why dark paganism still reigns there, a paganism which, now in a form so blatant that it can no longer be denied and now in all too threadbare disguise, is swamping the world of so-called Christian civilization.

13   With the methods employed hitherto we have not succeeded in Christianizing the soul to the point where even the most elementary demands of Christian ethics can exert any decisive influence on the main concerns of the Christian European. The Christian missionary may preach the gospel to the poor naked heathen, but the spiritual heathen who populate Europe have as yet heard nothing of Christianity. Christianity must indeed begin again from the very beginning if it is to meet its high educative task. So long as religion is only faith and outward form, and the religious function is not experienced in our own souls, nothing of any importance has happened. It has yet to be understood that the *mysterium magnum* is not only an actuality but is first and foremost rooted in the human psyche. The man who does not know this from his own experience may be a most learned theologian, but he has no idea of religion and still less of education.

14   Yet when I point out that the soul possesses by nature a religious function,[7] and when I stipulate that it is the prime task of all education (of adults) to convey the archetype of the God-

---

7 Tertullian, *Apologeticus*, xvii: "Anima naturaliter christiana."

image, or its emanations and effects, to the conscious mind, then it is precisely the theologian who seizes me by the arm and accuses me of "psychologism." But were it not a fact of experience that supreme values reside in the soul (quite apart from the ἀντίμιμον πνεῦμα who is also there), psychology would not interest me in the least, for the soul would then be nothing but a miserable vapour. I know, however, from hundredfold experience that it is nothing of the sort, but on the contrary contains the equivalents of everything that has been formulated in dogma and a good deal more, which is just what enables it to be an eye destined to behold the light. This requires limitless range and unfathomable depth of vision. I have been accused of "deifying the soul." Not I but God himself has deified it! *I did not attribute a religious function to the soul, I merely produced the facts which prove that the soul is naturaliter religiosa,* i.e., possesses a religious function. I did not invent or insinuate this function, it produces itself of its own accord without being prompted thereto by any opinions or suggestions of mine. With a truly tragic delusion these theologians fail to see that it is not a matter of proving the existence of the light, but of blind people who do not know that their eyes could see. It is high time we realized that it is pointless to praise the light and preach it if nobody can see it. It is much more needful to teach people the art of seeing. For it is obvious that far too many people are incapable of establishing a connection between the sacred figures and their own psyche: they cannot see to what extent the equivalent images are lying dormant in their own unconscious. In order to facilitate this inner vision we must first clear the way for the faculty of seeing. How this is to be done without psychology, that is, without making contact with the psyche, is frankly beyond my comprehension.[8]

15   Another equally serious misunderstanding lies in imputing to psychology the wish to be a new and possibly heretical doctrine. If a blind man can gradually be helped to see it is not to be expected that he will at once discern new truths with an eagle eye. One must be glad if he sees anything at all, and if he begins to understand what he sees. Psychology is concerned with the act of seeing and not with the construction of new religious

8 Since it is a question here of human effort, I leave aside acts of grace which are beyond man's control.

truths, when even the existing teachings have not yet been perceived and understood. In religious matters it is a well-known fact that we cannot understand a thing until we have experienced it inwardly, for it is in the inward experience that the connection between the psyche and the outward image or creed is first revealed as a relationship or correspondence like that of *sponsus* and *sponsa*. Accordingly when I say as a psychologist that God is an archetype, I mean by that the "type" in the psyche. The word "type" is, as we know, derived from τύπος, "blow" or "imprint"; thus an archetype presupposes an imprinter. Psychology as the science of the soul has to confine itself to its subject and guard against overstepping its proper boundaries by metaphysical assertions or other professions of faith. Should it set up a God, even as a hypothetical cause, it would have implicitly claimed the possibility of proving God, thus exceeding its competence in an absolutely illegitimate way. Science can only be science; there are no "scientific" professions of faith and similar *contradictiones in adiecto*. We simply do not know the ultimate derivation of the archetype any more than we know the origin of the psyche. The competence of psychology as an empirical science only goes so far as to establish, on the basis of comparative research, whether for instance the imprint found in the psyche can or cannot reasonably be termed a "God-image." Nothing positive or negative has thereby been asserted about the possible existence of God, any more than the archetype of the "hero" posits the actual existence of a hero.

16 Now if my psychological researches have demonstrated the existence of certain psychic types and their correspondence with well-known religious ideas, then we have opened up a possible approach to those experienceable contents which manifestly and undeniably form the empirical foundations of all religious experience. The religious-minded man is free to accept whatever metaphysical explanations he pleases about the origin of these images; not so the intellect, which must keep strictly to the principles of scientific interpretation and avoid trespassing beyond the bounds of what can be known. Nobody can prevent the believer from accepting God, Purusha, the Atman, or Tao as the Prime Cause and thus putting an end to the fundamental disquiet of man. The scientist is a scrupulous worker; he cannot take heaven by storm. Should he allow himself to be seduced

into such an extravagance he would be sawing off the branch on which he sits.

17   The fact is that with the knowledge and actual experience of these inner images a way is opened for reason and feeling to gain access to those other images which the teachings of religion offer to mankind. Psychology thus does just the opposite of what it is accused of: it provides possible approaches to a better understanding of these things, it opens people's eyes to the real meaning of dogmas, and, far from destroying, it throws open an empty house to new inhabitants. I can corroborate this from countless experiences: people belonging to creeds of all imaginable kinds, who had played the apostate or cooled off in their faith, have found a new approach to their old truths, not a few Catholics among them. Even a Parsee found the way back to the Zoroastrian fire-temple, which should bear witness to the objectivity of my point of view.

18   But this objectivity is just what my psychology is most blamed for: it is said not to decide in favour of this or that religious doctrine. Without prejudice to my own subjective convictions I should like to raise the question: Is it not thinkable that when one refrains from setting oneself up as an *arbiter mundi* and, deliberately renouncing all subjectivism, cherishes on the contrary the belief, for instance, that God has expressed himself in many languages and appeared in divers forms and that all these statements are *true*—is it not thinkable, I say, that this too is a decision? The objection raised, more particularly by Christians, that it is impossible for contradictory statements to be true, must permit itself to be politely asked: Does one equal three? How can three be one? Can a mother be a virgin? And so on. Has it not yet been observed that all religious statements contain logical contradictions and assertions that are impossible in principle, that this is in fact the very essence of religious assertion? As witness to this we have Tertullian's avowal: "And the Son of God is dead, which is worthy of belief because it is absurd. And when buried He rose again, which is certain because it is impossible." [9] If Christianity demands faith in such contradictions it does not seem to me that it can very well condemn those who assert a few paradoxes more. Oddly enough the paradox is one of our most valuable spiritual possessions, while

9 Tertullian, *De carne Christi*, 5 (Migne, *P.L.*, vol. 2, col. 751).

15

uniformity of meaning is a sign of weakness. Hence a religion becomes inwardly impoverished when it loses or waters down its paradoxes; but their multiplication enriches because only the paradox comes anywhere near to comprehending the fulness of life. Non-ambiguity and non-contradiction are one-sided and thus unsuited to express the incomprehensible.

19   Not everyone possesses the spiritual strength of a Tertullian. It is evident not only that he had the strength to sustain paradoxes but that they actually afforded him the highest degree of religious certainty. The inordinate number of spiritual weaklings makes paradoxes dangerous. So long as the paradox remains unexamined and is taken for granted as a customary part of life, it is harmless enough. But when it occurs to an insufficiently cultivated mind (always, as we know, the most sure of itself) to make the paradoxical nature of some tenet of faith the object of its lucubrations, as earnest as they are impotent, it is not long before such a one will break out into iconoclastic and scornful laughter, pointing to the manifest absurdity of the mystery. Things have gone rapidly downhill since the Age of Enlightenment, for, once this petty reasoning mind, which cannot endure any paradoxes, is awakened, no sermon on earth can keep it down. A new task then arises: to lift this still undeveloped mind step by step to a higher level and to increase the number of persons who have at least some inkling of the scope of paradoxical truth. If this is not possible, then it must be admitted that the spiritual approaches to Christianity are as good as blocked. We simply do not understand any more what is meant by the paradoxes contained in dogma; and the more external our understanding of them becomes the more we are affronted by their irrationality, until finally they become completely obsolete, curious relics of the past. The man who is stricken in this way cannot estimate the extent of his spiritual loss, because he has never experienced the sacred images as his inmost possession and has never realized their kinship with his own psychic structure. But it is just this indispensable knowledge that the psychology of the unconscious can give him, and its scientific objectivity is of the greatest value here. Were psychology bound to a creed it would not and could not allow the unconscious of the individual that free play which is the basic condition for the production of archetypes. It is precisely the

spontaneity of archetypal contents that convinces, whereas any prejudiced intervention is a bar to genuine experience. If the theologian really believes in the almighty power of God on the one hand and in the validity of dogma on the other, why then does he not trust God to speak in the soul? Why this fear of psychology? Or is, in complete contradiction to dogma, the soul itself a hell from which only demons gibber? Even if this were really so it would not be any the less convincing; for as we all know the horrified perception of the reality of evil has led to at least as many conversions as the experience of good.

20   The archetypes of the unconscious can be shown empirically to be the equivalents of religious dogmas. In the hermeneutic language of the Fathers the Church possesses a rich store of analogies with the individual and spontaneous products to be found in psychology. What the unconscious expresses is far from being merely arbitrary or opinionated; it is something that happens to be "just-so," as is the case with every other natural being. It stands to reason that the expressions of the unconscious are natural and not formulated dogmatically; they are exactly like the patristic allegories which draw the whole of nature into the orbit of their amplifications. If these present us with some astonishing *allegoriae Christi,* we find much the same sort of thing in the psychology of the unconscious. The only difference is that the patristic allegory *ad Christum spectat*—refers to Christ— whereas the psychic archetype is simply itself and can therefore be interpreted according to time, place, and milieu. In the West the archetype is filled out with the dogmatic figure of Christ; in the East, with Purusha, the Atman, Hiranyagarbha, the Buddha, and so on. The religious point of view, understandably enough, puts the accent on the imprinter, whereas scientific psychology emphasizes the *typos,* the imprint—the only thing it can understand. The religious point of view understands the imprint as the working of an imprinter; the scientific point of view understands it as the symbol of an unknown and incomprehensible content. Since the *typos* is less definite and more variegated than any of the figures postulated by religion, psychology is compelled by its empirical material to express the *typos* by means of a terminology not bound by time, place, or milieu. If, for example, the *typos* agreed in every detail with the dogmatic figure of Christ, and if it contained no determinant that went beyond

that figure, we would be bound to regard the *typos* as at least a faithful copy of the dogmatic figure, and to name it accordingly. The *typos* would then coincide with Christ. But as experience shows, this is not the case, seeing that the unconscious, like the allegories employed by the Church Fathers, produces countless other determinants that are not explicitly contained in the dogmatic formula; that is to say, non-Christian figures such as those mentioned above are included in the *typos*. But neither do these figures comply with the indeterminate nature of the archetype. It is altogether inconceivable that there could be any definite figure capable of expressing archetypal indefiniteness. For this reason I have found myself obliged to give the corresponding archetype the psychological name of the "self"—a term on the one hand definite enough to convey the essence of human wholeness and on the other hand indefinite enough to express the indescribable and indeterminable nature of this wholeness. The paradoxical qualities of the term are a reflection of the fact that wholeness consists partly of the conscious man and partly of the unconscious man. But we cannot define the latter or indicate his boundaries. Hence in its scientific usage the term "self" refers neither to Christ nor to the Buddha but to the totality of the figures that are its equivalent, and each of these figures is a symbol of the self. This mode of expression is an intellectual necessity in scientific psychology and in no sense denotes a transcendental prejudice. On the contrary, as we have said before, this objective attitude enables one man to decide in favour of the determinant Christ, another in favour of the Buddha, and so on. Those who are irritated by this objectivity should reflect that science is quite impossible without it. Consequently by denying psychology the right to objectivity they are making an untimely attempt to extinguish the life-light of a science. Even if such a preposterous attempt were to succeed, it would only widen the already catastrophic gulf between the secular mind on the one hand and Church and religion on the other.

21   It is quite understandable for a science to concentrate more or less exclusively on its subject—indeed, that is its absolute *raison d'être*. Since the concept of the self is of central interest in psychology, the latter naturally thinks along lines diametrically opposed to theology: for psychology the religious figures point to the self, whereas for theology the self points to its—theology's

—own central figure. In other words, theology might possibly take the psychological self as an allegory of Christ. This opposition is, no doubt, very irritating, but unfortunately inevitable, unless psychology is to be denied the right to exist at all. I therefore plead for tolerance. Nor is this very hard for psychology since as a science it makes no totalitarian claims.

22   The Christ-symbol is of the greatest importance for psychology in so far as it is perhaps the most highly developed and differentiated symbol of the self, apart from the figure of the Buddha. We can see this from the scope and substance of all the pronouncements that have been made about Christ: they agree with the psychological phenomenology of the self in unusually high degree, although they do not include all aspects of this archetype. The almost limitless range of the self might be deemed a disadvantage as compared with the definiteness of a religious figure, but it is by no means the task of science to pass value judgments. Not only is the self indefinite but—paradoxically enough—it also includes the quality of definiteness and even of uniqueness. This is probably one of the reasons why precisely those religions founded by historical personages have become world religions, such as Christianity, Buddhism, and Islam. The inclusion in a religion of a unique human personality —especially when conjoined to an indeterminable divine nature —is consistent with the absolute individuality of the self, which combines uniqueness with eternity and the individual with the universal. The self is a union of opposites *par excellence,* and this is where it differs essentially from the Christ-symbol. The androgyny of Christ is the utmost concession the Church has made to the problem of opposites. The opposition between light and good on the one hand and darkness and evil on the other is left in a state of open conflict, since Christ simply represents good, and his counterpart the devil, evil. This opposition is the real world problem, which at present is still unsolved. The self, however, is absolutely paradoxical in that it represents in every respect thesis and antithesis, and at the same time synthesis. (Psychological proofs of this assertion abound, though it is impossible for me to quote them here *in extenso.* I would refer the knowledgeable reader to the symbolism of the mandala.)

23   Once the exploration of the unconscious has led the conscious mind to an experience of the archetype, the individual is con-

fronted with the abysmal contradictions of human nature, and this confrontation in turn leads to the possibility of a direct experience of light and darkness, of Christ and the devil. For better or worse there is only a bare possibility of this, and not a guarantee; for experiences of this kind cannot of necessity be induced by any human means. There are factors to be considered which are not under our control. Experience of the opposites has nothing whatever to do with intellectual insight or with empathy. It is more what we would call fate. Such an experience can convince one person of the truth of Christ, another of the truth of the Buddha, to the exclusion of all other evidence.

24   Without the experience of the opposites there is no experience of wholeness and hence no inner approach to the sacred figures. For this reason Christianity rightly insists on sinfulness and original sin, with the obvious intent of opening up the abyss of universal opposition in every individual—at least from the outside. But this method is bound to break down in the case of a moderately alert intellect: dogma is then simply no longer believed and on top of that is thought absurd. Such an intellect is merely one-sided and sticks at the *ineptia mysterii*. It is miles from Tertullian's antinomies; in fact, it is quite incapable of enduring the suffering such a tension involves. Cases are not unknown where the rigorous exercises and proselytizings of the Catholics, and a certain type of Protestant education that is always sniffing out sin, have brought about psychic damage that leads not to the Kingdom of Heaven but to the consulting room of the doctor. Although insight into the problem of opposites is absolutely imperative, there are very few people who can stand it in practice—a fact which has not escaped the notice of the confessional. By way of a reaction to this we have the palliative of "moral probabilism," a doctrine that has suffered frequent attack from all quarters because it tries to mitigate the crushing effect of sin.[10] Whatever one may think of this phe-

[10] Zöckler ("Probabilismus," p. 67) defines it as follows: "Probabilism is the name generally given to that way of thinking which is content to answer scientific questions with a greater or lesser degree of probability. The moral probabilism with which alone we are concerned here consists in the principle that acts of ethical self-determination are to be guided not by conscience but according to what is probably right, i.e., according to whatever has been recommended by any representative or doctrinal authority." The Jesuit probabilist Escobar (d. 1669) was, for instance, of the opinion that if the penitent should plead a probable opinion

nomenon one thing is certain: that apart from anything else it holds within it a large humanity and an understanding of human weakness which compensate for the world's unbearable antinomies. The tremendous paradox implicit in the insistence on original sin on the one hand and the concession made by probabilism on the other is, for the psychologist, a necessary consequence of the Christian problem of opposites outlined above —for in the self good and evil are indeed closer than identical twins! The reality of evil and its incompatibility with good cleave the opposites asunder and lead inexorably to the crucifixion and suspension of everything that lives. Since "the soul is by nature Christian" this result is bound to come as infallibly as it did in the life of Jesus: we all have to be "crucified with Christ," i.e., suspended in a moral suffering equivalent to veritable crucifixion. In practice this is only possible up to a point, and apart from that is so unbearable and inimical to life that the ordinary human being can afford to get into such a state only occasionally, in fact as seldom as possible. For how could he remain ordinary in face of such suffering! A more or less probabilistic attitude to the problem of evil is therefore unavoidable. Hence the truth about the self—the unfathomable union of good and evil—comes out concretely in the paradox that although sin is the gravest and most pernicious thing there is, it is still not so serious that it cannot be disposed of with "probabilist" arguments. Nor is this necessarily a lax or frivolous proceeding but simply a practical necessity of life. The confessional proceeds like life itself, which successfully struggles against being engulfed in an irreconcilable contradiction. Note that at the same time the conflict remains in full force, as is once more consistent with the antinomial character of the self, which is itself both conflict and unity.

---

as the motive of his action, the father-confessor would be obliged to absolve him even if he were not of the same opinion. Escobar quotes a number of Jesuit authorities on the question of how often one is bound to love God in a lifetime. According to one opinion, loving God once shortly before death is sufficient; another says once a year or once every three or four years. He himself comes to the conclusion that it is sufficient to love God once at the first awakening of reason, then once every five years, and finally once in the hour of death. In his opinion the large number of different moral doctrines forms one of the main proofs of God's kindly providence, "because they make the yoke of Christ so light" (Zöckler, p. 68). Cf. also Harnack, *History of Dogma*, VII, pp. 101ff.

25   Christianity has made the antinomy of good and evil into a world problem and, by formulating the conflict dogmatically, raised it to an absolute principle. Into this as yet unresolved conflict the Christian is cast as a protagonist of good, a fellow player in the world drama. Understood in its deepest sense, being Christ's follower involves a suffering that is unendurable to the great majority of mankind. Consequently the example of Christ is in reality followed either with reservation or not at all, and the pastoral practice of the Church even finds itself obliged to "lighten the yoke of Christ." This means a pretty considerable reduction in the severity and harshness of the conflict and hence, in practice, a relativism of good and evil. Good is equivalent to the unconditional imitation of Christ and evil is its hindrance. Man's moral weakness and sloth are what chiefly hinder the imitation, and it is to these that probabilism extends a practical understanding which may sometimes, perhaps, come nearer to Christian tolerance, mildness, and love of one's neighbour than the attitude of those who see in probabilism a mere laxity. Although one must concede a number of cardinal Christian virtues to the probabilist endeavour, one must still not overlook the fact that it obviates much of the suffering involved in the imitation of Christ and that the conflict of good and evil is thus robbed of its harshness and toned down to tolerable proportions. This brings about an approach to the psychic archetype of the self, where even these opposites seem to be united—though, as I say, it differs from the Christian symbolism, which leaves the conflict open. For the latter there is a rift running through the world: light wars against night and the upper against the lower. The two are not one, as they are in the psychic archetype. But, even though religious dogma may condemn the idea of two being one, religious practice does, as we have seen, allow the natural psychological symbol of the self at one with itself an approximate means of expression. On the other hand, dogma insists that three are one, while denying that four are one. Since olden times, not only in the West but also in China, uneven numbers have been regarded as masculine and even numbers as feminine. The Trinity is therefore a decidedly masculine deity, of which the androgyny of Christ and the special position and veneration accorded to the Mother of God are not the real equivalent.

26   With this statement, which may strike the reader as peculiar, we come to one of the central axioms of alchemy, namely the saying of Maria Prophetissa: "One becomes two, two becomes three, and out of the third comes the one as the fourth." As the reader has already seen from its title, this book is concerned with the psychological significance of alchemy and thus with a problem which, with very few exceptions, has so far eluded scientific research. Until quite recently science was interested only in the part that alchemy played in the history of chemistry, concerning itself very little with the part it played in the history of philosophy and religion. The importance of alchemy for the historical development of chemistry is obvious, but its cultural importance is still so little known that it seems almost impossible to say in a few words wherein that consisted. In this introduction, therefore, I have attempted to outline the religious and psychological problems which are germane to the theme of alchemy. The point is that alchemy is rather like an undercurrent to the Christianity that ruled on the surface. It is to this surface as the dream is to consciousness, and just as the dream compensates the conflicts of the conscious mind, so alchemy endeavours to fill in the gaps left open by the Christian tension of opposites. Perhaps the most pregnant expression of this is the axiom of Maria Prophetissa quoted above, which runs like a *leitmotiv* throughout almost the whole of the lifetime of alchemy, extending over more than seventeen centuries. In this aphorism the even numbers which signify the feminine principle, earth, the regions under the earth, and evil itself are interpolated between the uneven numbers of the Christian dogma. They are personified by the *serpens mercurii,* the dragon that creates and destroys itself and represents the *prima materia.* This fundamental idea of alchemy points back to the תְּהוֹם (Tehom),[11] to Tiamat with her dragon attribute, and thus to the primordial matriarchal world which, in the theomachy of the Marduk myth,[12] was overthrown by the masculine world of the father. The historical shift in the world's consciousness towards the masculine is compensated at first by the chthonic femininity of the

11 Cf. Genesis 1 : 2.
12 The reader will find a collection of these myth motifs in Lang, *Hat ein Gott die Welt erschaffen?* Unfortunately philological criticism will have much to take exception to in this book, interesting though it is for its Gnostic trend.

unconscious. In certain pre-Christian religions the differentiation of the masculine principle had taken the form of the father-son specification, a change which was to be of the utmost importance for Christianity. Were the unconscious merely complementary, this shift of consciousness would have been accompanied by the production of a mother and daughter, for which the necessary material lay ready to hand in the myth of Demeter and Persephone. But, as alchemy shows, the unconscious chose rather the Cybele-Attis type in the form of the *prima materia* and the *filius macrocosmi*, thus proving that it is not complementary but compensatory. This goes to show that the unconscious does not simply act *contrary* to the conscious mind but *modifies* it more in the manner of an opponent or partner. The son type does not call up a daughter as a complementary image from the depths of the "chthonic" unconscious—it calls up another son. This remarkable fact would seem to be connected with the incarnation in our earthly human nature of a purely spiritual God, brought about by the Holy Ghost impregnating the womb of the Blessed Virgin. Thus the higher, the spiritual, the masculine inclines to the lower, the earthly, the feminine; and accordingly, the mother, who was anterior to the world of the father, accommodates herself to the masculine principle and, with the aid of the human spirit (alchemy or "the philosophy"), produces a son —not the antithesis of Christ but rather his chthonic counterpart, not a divine man but a fabulous being conforming to the nature of the primordial mother. And just as the redemption of man the microcosm is the task of the "upper" son, so the "lower" son has the function of a *salvator macrocosmi*.

27   This, in brief, is the drama that was played out in the obscurities of alchemy. It is superfluous to remark that these two sons were never united, except perhaps in the mind and innermost experience of a few particularly gifted alchemists. But it is not very difficult to see the "purpose" of this drama: in the Incarnation it looked as though the masculine principle of the father-world were approximating to the feminine principle of the mother-world, with the result that the latter felt impelled to approximate in turn to the father-world. What it evidently amounted to was an attempt to bridge the gulf separating the two worlds as compensation for the open conflict between them.

28   I hope the reader will not be offended if my exposition

sounds like a Gnostic myth. We are moving in those psychological regions where, as a matter of fact, Gnosis is rooted. The message of the Christian symbol is Gnosis, and the compensation effected by the unconscious is Gnosis in even higher degree. Myth is the primordial language natural to these psychic processes, and no intellectual formulation comes anywhere near the richness and expressiveness of mythical imagery. Such processes are concerned with the primordial images, and these are best and most succinctly reproduced by figurative language.

29   The process described above displays all the characteristic features of psychological compensation. We know that the mask of the unconscious is not rigid—it reflects the face we turn towards it. Hostility lends it a threatening aspect, friendliness softens its features. It is not a question of mere optical reflection but of an autonomous answer which reveals the self-sufficing nature of that which answers. Thus the *filius philosophorum* is not just the reflected image, in unsuitable material, of the son of God; on the contrary, this son of Tiamat reflects the features of the primordial maternal figure. Although he is decidedly hermaphroditic he has a masculine name—a sign that the chthonic underworld, having been rejected by the spirit and identified with evil, has a tendency to compromise. There is no mistaking the fact that he is a concession to the spiritual and masculine principle, even though he carries in himself the weight of the earth and the whole fabulous nature of primordial animality.

30   This answer of the mother-world shows that the gulf between it and the father-world is not unbridgeable, seeing that the unconscious holds the seed of the unity of both. The essence of the conscious mind is discrimination; it must, if it is to be aware of things, separate the opposites, and it does this *contra naturam*. In nature the opposites seek one another—*les extrêmes se touchent*—and so it is in the unconscious, and particularly in the archetype of unity, the self. Here, as in the deity, the opposites cancel out. But as soon as the unconscious begins to manifest itself they split asunder, as at the Creation; for every act of dawning consciousness is a creative act, and it is from this psychological experience that all our cosmogonic symbols are derived.

31   Alchemy is pre-eminently concerned with the seed of unity which lies hidden in the chaos of Tiamat and forms the counterpart to the divine unity. Like this, the seed of unity has a trini-

tarian character in Christian alchemy and a triadic character in pagan alchemy. According to other authorities it corresponds to the unity of the four elements and is therefore a quaternity. The overwhelming majority of modern psychological findings speaks in favour of the latter view. The few cases I have observed which produced the number three were marked by a systematic deficiency in consciousness, that is to say, by an unconsciousness of the "inferior function." The number three is not a natural expression of wholeness, since four represents the minimum number of determinants in a whole judgment. It must nevertheless be stressed that side by side with the distinct leanings of alchemy (and of the unconscious) towards quaternity there is always a vacillation between three and four which comes out over and over again. Even in the axiom of Maria Prophetissa the quaternity is muffled and alembicated. In alchemy there are three as well as four *regimina* or procedures, three as well as four colours. There are always four elements, but often three of them are grouped together, with the fourth in a special position— sometimes earth, sometimes fire. Mercurius[13] is of course *quadratus*, but he is also a three-headed snake or simply a triunity. This uncertainty has a duplex character—in other words, the central ideas are ternary as well as quaternary. The psychologist cannot but mention the fact that a similar puzzle exists in the psychology of the unconscious: the least differentiated or "inferior" function is so much contaminated with the collective unconscious that, on becoming conscious, it brings up among others the archetype of the self as well—τὸ ἕν τέταρτον, as Maria Prophetissa says. Four signifies the feminine, motherly, physical; three the masculine, fatherly, spiritual. Thus the uncertainty as

---

13 In alchemical writings the word "Mercurius" is used with a very wide range of meaning, to denote not only the chemical element mercury or quicksilver, Mercury (Hermes) the god, and Mercury the planet, but also—and primarily— the secret "transforming substance" which is at the same time the "spirit" indwelling in all living creatures. These different connotations will become apparent in the course of the book. It would be misleading to use the English "Mercury" and "mercury," because there are innumerable passages where neither word does justice to the wealth of implications. It has therefore been decided to retain the Latin "Mercurius" as in the German text, and to use the personal pronoun (since "Mercurius" is personified), the word "quicksilver" being employed only where the chemical element (Hg) is plainly meant. [*Author's note for the English edn.*]

to three or four amounts to a wavering between the spiritual and the physical—a striking example of how every human truth is a last truth but one.

32   I began my introduction with human wholeness as the goal to which the psychotherapeutic process ultimately leads. This question is inextricably bound up with one's philosophical or religious assumptions. Even when, as frequently happens, the patient believes himself to be quite unprejudiced in this respect, the assumptions underlying his thought, mode of life, morale, and language are historically conditioned down to the last detail, a fact of which he is often kept unconscious by lack of education combined with lack of self-criticism. The analysis of his situation will therefore lead sooner or later to a clarification of his general spiritual background going far beyond his personal determinants, and this brings up the problems I have attempted to sketch in the preceding pages. This phase of the process is marked by the production of symbols of unity, the so-called mandalas, which occur either in dreams or in the form of concrete visual impressions, often as the most obvious compensation of the contradictions and conflicts of the conscious situation. It would hardly be correct to say that the gaping "rift" [14] in the Christian order of things is responsible for this, since it is easy to show that Christian symbolism is particularly concerned with healing, or attempting to heal, this very wound. It would be more correct to take the open conflict as a symptom of the psychic situation of Western man, and to deplore his inability to assimilate the whole range of the Christian symbol. As a doctor I cannot demand anything of my patients in this respect, also I lack the Church's means of grace. Consequently I am faced with the task of taking the only path open to me: the archetypal images—which in a certain sense correspond to the dogmatic images—must be brought into consciousness. At the same time I must leave my patient to decide in accordance with his assumptions, his spiritual maturity, his education, origins, and temperament, so far as this is possible without serious conflicts. As a doctor it is my task to help the patient to cope with life. I cannot presume to pass judgment on his final decisions, because I know from experience that all coercion—be it suggestion, insinuation, or any other method of persuasion—ultimately

14 Przywara, *Deus semper maior*, I, pp. 71ff.

proves to be nothing but an obstacle to the highest and most decisive experience of all, which is to be alone with his own self, or whatever else one chooses to call the objectivity of the psyche. The patient must be alone if he is to find out what it is that supports him when he can no longer support himself. Only this experience can give him an indestructible foundation.

33 I would be only too delighted to leave this anything but easy task to the theologian, were it not that it is just from the theologian that many of my patients come. They ought to have hung on to the community of the Church, but they were shed like dry leaves from the great tree and now find themselves "hanging on" to the treatment. Something in them clings, often with the strength of despair, as if they or the thing they cling to would drop off into the void the moment they relaxed their hold. They are seeking firm ground on which to stand. Since no outward support is of any use to them they must finally discover it in themselves—admittedly the most unlikely place from the rational point of view, but an altogether possible one from the point of view of the unconscious. We can see this from the archetype of the "lowly origin of the redeemer."

34 The way to the goal seems chaotic and interminable at first, and only gradually do the signs increase that it is leading anywhere. The way is not straight but appears to go round in circles. More accurate knowledge has proved it to go in spirals: the dream-motifs always return after certain intervals to definite forms, whose characteristic it is to define a centre. And as a matter of fact the whole process revolves about a central point or some arrangement round a centre, which may in certain circumstances appear even in the initial dreams. As manifestations of unconscious processes the dreams rotate or circumambulate round the centre, drawing closer to it as the amplifications increase in distinctness and in scope. Owing to the diversity of the symbolical material it is difficult at first to perceive any kind of order at all. Nor should it be taken for granted that dream sequences are subject to any governing principle. But, as I say, the process of development proves on closer inspection to be cyclic or spiral. We might draw a parallel between such spiral courses and the processes of growth in plants; in fact the plant motif (tree, flower, etc.) frequently recurs in these dreams and

fantasies and is also spontaneously drawn or painted.[15] In alchemy the tree is the symbol of Hermetic philosophy.

35   The first of the following two studies—that which composes Part II—deals with a series of dreams which contain numerous symbols of the centre or goal. The development of these symbols is almost the equivalent of a healing process. The centre or goal thus signifies *salvation* in the proper sense of the word. The justification for such a terminology comes from the dreams themselves, for these contain so many references to religious phenomena that I was able to use some of them as the subject of my book *Psychology and Religion*. It seems to me beyond all doubt that these processes are concerned with the religion-creating archetypes. Whatever else religion may be, those psychic ingredients of it which are empirically verifiable undoubtedly consist of unconscious manifestations of this kind. People have dwelt far too long on the fundamentally sterile question of whether the assertions of faith are true or not. Quite apart from the impossibility of ever proving or refuting the truth of a metaphysical assertion, the very existence of the assertion is a self-evident fact that needs no further proof, and when a *consensus gentium* allies itself thereto the validity of the statement is proved to just that extent. The only thing about it that we can verify is the psychological phenomenon, which is incommensurable with the category of objective rightness or truth. No phenomenon can ever be disposed of by rational criticism, and in religious life we have to deal with phenomena and facts and not with arguable hypotheses.

36   During the process of treatment the dialectical discussion leads logically to a meeting between the patient and his shadow, that dark half of the psyche which we invariably get rid of by means of projection: either by burdening our neighbours—in a wider or narrower sense—with all the faults which we obviously have ourselves, or by casting our sins upon a divine mediator with the aid of *contritio* or the milder *attritio*.[16] We know of

---

15 See the illustrations in Jung, "Concerning Mandala Symbolism."
16 *Contritio* is "perfect" repentance; *attritio* "imperfect" repentance (*contritio imperfecta*, to which category *contritio naturalis* belongs). The former regards sin as the opposite of the highest good; the latter reprehends it not only on account of its wicked and hideous nature but also from fear of punishment.

course that without sin there is no repentance and without repentance no redeeming grace, also that without original sin the redemption of the world could never have come about; but we assiduously avoid investigating whether in this very power of evil God might not have placed some special purpose which it is most important for us to know. One often feels driven to some such view when, like the psychotherapist, one has to deal with people who are confronted with their blackest shadow.[17] At any rate the doctor cannot afford to point, with a gesture of facile moral superiority, to the tablets of the law and say, "Thou shalt not." He has to examine things objectively and weigh up possibilities, for he knows, less from religious training and education than from instinct and experience, that there is something very like a *felix culpa*. He knows that one can miss not only one's happiness but also one's final guilt, without which a man will never reach his wholeness. Wholeness is in fact a charisma which one can manufacture neither by art nor by cunning; one can only grow into it and endure whatever its advent may bring. No doubt it is a great nuisance that mankind is not uniform but compounded of individuals whose psychic structure spreads them over a span of at least ten thousand years. Hence there is absolutely no truth that does not spell salvation to one person and damnation to another. All universalisms get stuck in this terrible dilemma. Earlier on I spoke of Jesuit probabilism: this gives a better idea than anything else of the tremendous catholic task of the Church. Even the best-intentioned people have been horrified by probabilism, but, when brought face to face with the realities of life, many of them have found their horror evaporating or their laughter dying on their lips. The doctor too must weigh and ponder, not whether a thing is for or against the Church but whether it is for or against life and health. On paper the moral code looks clear and neat enough;

17 A religious terminology comes naturally, as the only adequate one in the circumstances, when we are faced with the tragic fate that is the unavoidable concomitant of wholeness. "My fate" means a daemonic will to precisely that fate— a will not necessarily coincident with my own (the ego will). When it is opposed to the ego, it is difficult not to feel a certain "power" in it, whether divine or infernal. The man who submits to his fate calls it the will of God; the man who puts up a hopeless and exhausting fight is more apt to see the devil in it. In either event this terminology is not only universally understood but meaningf·· as well.

but the same document written on the "living tables of the heart" is often a sorry tatter, particularly in the mouths of those who talk the loudest. We are told on every side that evil is evil and that there can be no hesitation in condemning it, but that does not prevent evil from being the most problematical thing in the individual's life and the one which demands the deepest reflection. What above all deserves our keenest attention is the question "Exactly *who* is the doer?" For the answer to this question ultimately decides the value of the deed. It is true that society attaches greater importance at first to what is done, because it is immediately obvious; but in the long run the right deed in the hands of the wrong man will also have a disastrous effect. No one who is far-sighted will allow himself to be hoodwinked by the right deed of the wrong man, any more than by the wrong deed of the right man. Hence the psychotherapist must fix his eye not on what is done but on how it is done, because therein is decided the whole character of the doer. Evil needs to be pondered just as much as good, for good and evil are ultimately nothing but ideal extensions and abstractions of doing, and both belong to the chiaroscuro of life. In the last resort there is no good that cannot produce evil and no evil that cannot produce good.

37   The encounter with the dark half of the personality, or "shadow," comes about of its own accord in any moderately thorough treatment. This problem is as important as that of sin in the Church. The open conflict is unavoidable and painful. I have often been asked, "And what do you *do* about it?" I do nothing; there is nothing I can do except wait, with a certain trust in God, until, out of a conflict borne with patience and fortitude, there emerges the solution destined—although I cannot foresee it—for that particular person. Not that I am passive or inactive meanwhile: I help the patient to understand all the things that the unconscious produces during the conflict. The reader may believe me that these are no ordinary products. On the contrary, they are among the most significant things that have ever engaged my attention. Nor is the patient inactive; he must do the right thing, and do it with all his might, in order to prevent the pressure of evil from becoming too powerful in him. He needs "justification by works," for "justification by faith" alone has remained an empty sound for him as for so many

others. Faith can sometimes be a substitute for lack of experience. In these cases what is needed is real work. Christ espoused the sinner and did not condemn him. The true follower of Christ will do the same, and, since one should do unto others as one would do unto oneself, one will also take the part of the sinner who is oneself. And as little as we would accuse Christ of fraternizing with evil, so little should we reproach ourselves that to love the sinner who is oneself is to make a pact with the devil. Love makes a man better, hate makes him worse—even when that man is oneself. The danger in this point of view is the same as in the imitation of Christ; but the Pharisee in us will never allow himself to be caught talking to publicans and whores. I must emphasize of course that psychology invented neither Christianity nor the imitation of Christ. I wish everybody could be freed from the burden of their sins by the Church. But he to whom she cannot render this service must bend very low in the imitation of Christ in order to take the burden of his cross upon him. The ancients could get along with the Greek wisdom of the ages: Μηδὲν ἄγαν, τῷ καιρῷ πάντα πρόσεστι καλά (Exaggerate nothing, all good lies in right measure). But what an abyss still separates us from reason!

38   Apart from the moral difficulty there is another danger which is not inconsiderable and may lead to complications, particularly with individuals who are pathologically inclined. This is the fact that the contents of the personal unconscious (i.e., the shadow) are indistinguishably merged with the archetypal contents of the collective unconscious and drag the latter with them when the shadow is brought into consciousness. This may exert an uncanny influence on the conscious mind; for activated archetypes have a disagreeable effect even—or I should perhaps say, particularly—on the most cold-blooded rationalist. He is afraid that the lowest form of conviction, namely superstition, is, as he thinks, forcing itself on him. But superstition in the truest sense only appears in such people if they are pathological, not if they can keep their balance. It then takes the form of the fear of "going mad"—for everything that the modern mind cannot define it regards as insane. It must be admitted that the archetypal contents of the collective unconscious can often assume grotesque and horrible forms in dreams and fantasies, so that even the most hard-boiled rationalist is not immune from shattering nightmares and haunting fears. The

psychological elucidation of these images, which cannot be passed over in silence or blindly ignored, leads logically into the depths of religious phenomenology. The history of religion in its widest sense (including therefore mythology, folklore, and primitive psychology) is a treasure-house of archetypal forms from which the doctor can draw helpful parallels and enlightening comparisons for the purpose of calming and clarifying a consciousness that is all at sea. It is absolutely necessary to supply these fantastic images that rise up so strange and threatening before the mind's eye with some kind of context so as to make them more intelligible. Experience has shown that the best way to do this is by means of comparative mythological material.

39   Part II of this volume gives a large number of such examples. The reader will be particularly struck by the numerous connections between individual dream symbolism and medieval alchemy. This is not, as one might suppose, a prerogative of the case in question, but a general fact which only struck me some ten years ago when first I began to come to grips with the ideas and symbolism of alchemy.

40   Part III contains an introduction to the symbolism of alchemy in relation to Christianity and Gnosticism. As a bare introduction it is naturally far from being a complete exposition of this complicated and obscure subject—indeed, most of it is concerned only with the *lapis*-Christ parallel. True, this parallel gives rise to a comparison between the aims of the *opus alchymicum* and the central ideas of Christianity, for both are of the utmost importance in understanding and interpreting the images that appear in dreams and in assessing their psychological effect. This has considerable bearing on the practice of psychotherapy, because more often than not it is precisely the more intelligent and cultured patients who, finding a return to the Church impossible, come up against archetypal material and thus set the doctor problems which can no longer be mastered by a narrowly personalistic psychology. Nor is a mere knowledge of the psychic structure of a neurosis by any means sufficient; for once the process has reached the sphere of the collective unconscious we are dealing with healthy material, i.e., with the universal basis of the individually varied psyche. Our understanding of these deeper layers of the psyche is helped not only by a knowledge of primitive psychology and mythology, but to an even greater extent by some familiarity with the history of our

modern consciousness and the stages immediately preceding it. On the one hand it is a child of the Church; on the other, of science, in whose beginnings very much lies hid that the Church was unable to accept—that is to say, remnants of the classical spirit and the classical feeling for nature which could not be exterminated and eventually found refuge in the natural philosophy of the Middle Ages. As the "spiritus metallorum" and the astrological components of destiny the old gods of the planets lasted out many a Christian century.[18] Whereas in the Church the increasing differentiation of ritual and dogma alienated consciousness from its natural roots in the unconscious, alchemy and astrology were ceaselessly engaged in preserving the bridge to nature, i.e., to the unconscious psyche, from decay. Astrology led the conscious mind back again and again to the knowledge of Heimarmene, that is, the dependence of character and destiny on certain moments in time; and alchemy afforded numerous "hooks" for the projection of those archetypes which could not be fitted smoothly into the Christian process. It is true that alchemy always stood on the verge of heresy and that certain decrees leave no doubt as to the Church's attitude towards it,[19] but on the other hand it was effectively protected by the obscurity of its symbolism, which could always be explained as harmless allegory. For many alchemists the allegorical aspect undoubtedly occupied the foreground to such an extent that they were firmly convinced that their sole concern was with chemical substances. But there were always a few for whom laboratory work was primarily a matter of symbols and their psychic effect. As the texts show, they were quite conscious of this, to the point of condemning the naïve goldmakers as liars, frauds, and dupes. Their own standpoint they proclaimed with propositions like "Aurum nostrum non est aurum vulgi." Although their labours over the retort were a serious effort to elicit the secrets of chemical transformation, it was at the same time —and often in overwhelming degree—the reflection of a parallel psychic process which could be projected all the more easily into the unknown chemistry of matter since that process is an uncon-

[18] Paracelsus still speaks of the "gods" enthroned in the *mysterium magnum* (*Philosophia ad Athenienses*, p. 403), and so does the 18th-cent. treatise of Abraham Eleazar, *Uraltes chymisches Werk*, which was influenced by Paracelsus.
[19] Cf. Sanchez, *Opus morale*, Decalog. 2, 49n., 51; and Pignatelli, *Consultationes canonicae*, canon ix.

34

scious phenomenon of nature, just like the mysterious alteration of substances. What the symbolism of alchemy expresses is the whole problem of the evolution of personality described above, the so-called individuation process.

41   Whereas the Church's great buttress is the imitation of Christ, the alchemist, without realizing it and certainly without wanting it, easily fell victim, in the loneliness and obscure problems of his work, to the promptings and unconscious assumptions of his own mind, since, unlike the Christians, he had no clear and unmistakable models on which to rely. The authors he studied provided him with symbols whose meaning he thought he understood in his own way; but in reality they touched and stimulated his unconscious. Ironical towards themselves, the alchemists coined the phrase "obscurum per obscurius." But with this method of explaining the obscure by the more obscure they only sank themselves deeper in the very process from which the Church was struggling to redeem them. While the dogmas of the Church offered analogies to the alchemical process, these analogies, in strict contrast to alchemy, had become detached from the world of nature through their connection with the historical figure of the Redeemer. The alchemical four in one, the philosophical gold, the *lapis angularis,* the *aqua divina,* became, in the Church, the four-armed cross on which the Only-Begotten had sacrificed himself once in history and at the same time for all eternity. The alchemists ran counter to the Church in preferring to seek through knowledge rather than to find through faith, though as medieval people they never thought of themselves as anything but good Christians. Paracelsus is a classical example in this respect. But in reality they were in much the same position as modern man, who prefers immediate personal experience to belief in traditional ideas, or rather has it forced upon him. Dogma is not arbitrarily invented nor is it a unique miracle, although it is often described as miraculous with the obvious intent of lifting it out of its natural context. The central ideas of Christianity are rooted in Gnostic philosophy, which, in accordance with psychological laws, simply *had* to grow up at a time when the classical religions had become obsolete. It was founded on the perception of symbols thrown up by the unconscious individuation process which always sets in when the collective dominants of human life fall into decay. At such a time there is bound to

35

be a considerable number of individuals who are possessed by archetypes of a numinous nature that force their way to the surface in order to form new dominants. This state of possession shows itself almost without exception in the fact that the possessed identify themselves with the archetypal contents of their unconscious, and, because they do not realize that the role which is being thrust upon them is the effect of new contents still to be understood, they exemplify these concretely in their own lives, thus becoming prophets and reformers. In so far as the archetypal content of the Christian drama was able to give satisfying expression to the uneasy and clamorous unconscious of the many, the *consensus omnium* raised this drama to a universally binding truth—not of course by an act of judgment, but by the irrational fact of possession, which is far more effective. Thus Jesus became the tutelary image or amulet against the archetypal powers that threatened to possess everyone. The glad tidings announced: "It has happened, but it will not happen to you inasmuch as you believe in Jesus Christ, the Son of God!" Yet it could and it can and it will happen to everyone in whom the Christian dominant has decayed. For this reason there have always been people who, not satisfied with the dominants of conscious life, set forth—under cover and by devious paths, to their destruction or salvation—to seek direct experience of the eternal roots, and, following the lure of the restless unconscious psyche, find themselves in the wilderness where, like Jesus, they come up against the son of darkness, the ἀντίμιμον πνεῖμα. Thus an old alchemist—and he a cleric!—prays: "Horridas nostrae mentis purga tenebras, accende lumen sensibus!" (Purge the horrible darknesses of our mind, light a light for our senses!) The author of this sentence must have been undergoing the experience of the *nigredo,* the first stage of the work, which was felt as "melancholia" in alchemy and corresponds to the encounter with the shadow in psychology.

42   When, therefore, modern psychotherapy once more meets with the activated archetypes of the collective unconscious, it is merely the repetition of a phenomenon that has often been observed in moments of great religious crisis, although it can also occur in individuals for whom the ruling ideas have lost their meaning. An example of this is the *descensus ad inferos* depicted in *Faust,* which, consciously or unconsciously, is an *opus alchymicum.*

36

43   The problem of opposites called up by the shadow plays a great—indeed, the decisive—role in alchemy, since it leads in the ultimate phase of the work to the union of opposites in the archetypal form of the *hierosgamos* or "chymical wedding." Here the supreme opposites, male and female (as in the Chinese *yang* and *yin*), are melted into a unity purified of all opposition and therefore incorruptible. The prerequisite for this, of course, is that the artifex should not identify himself with the figures in the work but should leave them in their objective, impersonal state. So long as the alchemist was working in his laboratory he was in a favourable position, psychologically speaking, for he had no opportunity to identify himself with the archetypes as they appeared, since they were all projected immediately into the chemical substances. The disadvantage of this situation was that the alchemist was forced to represent the incorruptible substance as a chemical product—an impossible undertaking which led to the downfall of alchemy, its place in the laboratory being taken by chemistry. But the psychic part of the work did not disappear. It captured new interpreters, as we can see from the example of *Faust*, and also from the signal connection between our modern psychology of the unconscious and alchemical symbolism.

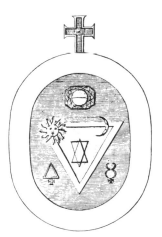

3. Symbol of the alchemical work.
—*Hermaphroditisches Sonn- und Mondskind* (1752)

LE
TABLEAV
DES RICHES
INVENTIONS
Couuertes du voile des feintes
Amoureuſes, qui ſont re-
preſentees dans le

SONGE DE POLIPHILE
Desvoilees des ombres du Songe,
& ſubtilement expoſees

PAR BEROALDE

A.PARIS.
Chez MATTHIEV GVILLEMOT, au Palais,
en la gallerie des priſonniers.
Auec priuilege du Roy.
1600

4. Representation of the symbolic process which begins in chaos and ends with the birth of the phoenix.—Title-page, Béroalde de Verville, *Le Tableau des riches inventions* or *Le Songe de Poliphile* (1600)

II

INDIVIDUAL DREAM SYMBOLISM
IN RELATION TO ALCHEMY

A STUDY OF THE UNCONSCIOUS PROCESSES
AT WORK IN DREAMS

> *. . . facilis descensus Averno;*
> *noctes atque dies patet atri ianua Ditis;*
> *sed revocare gradum superasque evadere ad auras,*
> *hoc opus, hic labor est. . . .*
> VIRGIL, *Aeneid*, VI, 126–29

> . . . easy is the descent to Avernus: night and
> day the door of gloomy Dis stands open; but to
> recall thy steps and pass out to the upper air,
> this is the task, this the toil!
> —Trans. by H. R. Fairclough

5. Seven virgins being transformed.—Béroalde de Verville, *Le Songe de Poliphile*
(1600)

1. INTRODUCTION

I. THE MATERIAL

44   The symbols of the process of individuation that appear in
dreams are images of an archetypal nature which depict the centralizing process or the production of a new centre of personality. A general idea of this process may be got from my essay,
"The Relations between the Ego and the Unconscious." For
certain reasons mentioned there I call this centre the "self,"
which should be understood as the totality of the psyche. The
self is not only the centre, but also the whole circumference
which embraces both conscious and unconscious; it is the centre
of this totality, just as the ego is the centre of consciousness.

45   The symbols now under consideration are not concerned with
the manifold stages and transformations of the individuation
process, but with the images that refer directly and exclusively
to the new centre as it comes into consciousness. These images
belong to a definite category which I call mandala symbolism.

In *The Secret of the Golden Flower,* published in collaboration with Richard Wilhelm, I have described this symbolism in some detail. In the present study I should like to put before you an individual series of such symbols in chronological order. The material consists of over a thousand dreams and visual impressions coming from a young man of excellent scientific education.[1] For the purposes of this study I have worked on the first four hundred dreams and visions, which covered a period of nearly ten months. In order to avoid all personal influence I asked one of my pupils, a woman doctor, who was then a beginner, to undertake the observation of the process. This went on for five months. The dreamer then continued his observations alone for three months. Except for a short interview at the very beginning, before the commencement of the observation, I did not see the dreamer at all during the first eight months. Thus it happened that 355 of the dreams were dreamed away from any personal contact with myself. Only the last forty-five occurred under my observation. No interpretations worth mentioning were then attempted because the dreamer, owing to his excellent scientific training and ability, did not require any assistance. Hence conditions were really ideal for unprejudiced observation and recording.

46   First of all, then, I shall present extracts from the twenty-two initial dreams in order to show how the mandala symbolism makes a very early appearance and is embedded in the rest of the dream material. Later on I shall pick out in chronological order the dreams that refer specifically to the mandala.[2]

47   With few exceptions all the dreams have been abbreviated, either by extracting the part that carries the main thought or by condensing the whole text to essentials. This simplifying procedure has not only curtailed their length but has also removed personal allusions and complications, as was necessary for reasons of discretion. Despite this somewhat doubtful interference I have, to the best of my knowledge and scrupulosity, avoided any

1 I must emphasize that this education was not historical, philological, archaeological, or ethnological. Any references to material derived from these fields came unconsciously to the dreamer.

2 "Mandala" (Sanskrit) means "circle," also "magic circle." Its symbolism includes—to mention only the most important forms—all concentrically arranged figures, round or square patterns with a centre, and radial or spherical arrangements.

arbitrary distortion of meaning. The same considerations had
also to apply to my own interpretation, so that certain passages
in the dreams may appear to have been overlooked. Had I not
made this sacrifice and kept the material absolutely complete, I
should not have been in a position to publish this series, which
in my opinion could hardly be surpassed in intelligence, clarity,
and consistency. It therefore gives me great pleasure to express
my sincere gratitude here and now to the "author" for the service he has rendered to science.

II. THE METHOD

48   In my writings and lectures I have always insisted that we
must give up all preconceived opinions when it comes to the
analysis and interpretation of the objective psyche,[3] in other
words the "unconscious." We do not yet possess a general theory
of dreams that would enable us to use a deductive method with
impunity, any more than we possess a general theory of consciousness from which we can draw deductive conclusions. The
manifestations of the subjective psyche, or consciousness, can be
predicted to only the smallest degree, and there is no theoretical
argument to prove beyond doubt that any causal connection
necessarily exists between them. On the contrary, we have to
reckon with a high percentage of arbitrariness and "chance"
in the complex actions and reactions of the conscious mind.
Similarly there is no empirical, still less a theoretical, reason to
assume that the same does not apply to the manifestations of the
unconscious. The latter are just as manifold, unpredictable, and
arbitrary as the former and must therefore be subjected to as
many different ways of approach. In the case of conscious utter-
ances we are in the fortunate position of being directly addressed and presented with a content whose purpose we can
recognize; but with "unconscious" manifestations there is no
directed or adapted language in our sense of the word—there
is merely a psychic phenomenon that would appear to have only
the loosest connections with conscious contents. If the expres-

3 For this concept see Jung, "Basic Postulates of Analytical Psychology," and
Wolff, "Einführung in die Grundlagen der komplexen Psychologie," pp. 34ff.

sions of the conscious mind are incomprehensible we can always ask what they mean. But the objective psyche is something alien even to the conscious mind through which it expresses itself. We are therefore obliged to adopt the method we would use in deciphering a fragmentary text or one containing unknown words: we examine the context. The meaning of the unknown word may become evident when we compare a series of passages in which it occurs. The psychological context of dream-contents consists in the web of associations in which the dream is naturally embedded. Theoretically we can never know anything in advance about this web, but in practice it is sometimes possible, granted long enough experience. Even so, careful analysis will never rely too much on technical rules; the danger of deception and suggestion is too great. In the analysis of isolated dreams above all, this kind of knowing in advance and making assumptions on the grounds of practical expectation or general probability is positively wrong. It should therefore be an absolute rule to assume that every dream, and every part of a dream, is unknown at the outset, and to attempt an interpretation only after carefully taking up the context. We can then apply the meaning we have thus discovered to the text of the dream itself and see whether this yields a fluent reading, or rather whether a satisfying meaning emerges. But in no circumstances may we anticipate that this meaning will fit in with any of our subjective expectations; for quite possibly, indeed very frequently, the dream is saying something surprisingly different from what we would expect. As a matter of fact, if the meaning we find in the dream happens to coincide with our expectations, that is a reason for suspicion; for as a rule the standpoint of the unconscious is complementary or compensatory[4] to consciousness and thus unexpectedly "different." I would not deny the possibility of *parallel* dreams, i.e., dreams whose meaning coincides with or supports the conscious attitude, but, in my experience at least, these are rather rare.

49   Now, the method I adopt in the present study seems to run directly counter to this basic principle of dream interpretation. It looks as if the dreams were being interpreted without the least regard for the context. And in fact I have not taken up the con-

[4] I intentionally omit an analysis of the words "complementary" and "compensatory," as it would lead us too far afield.

6. A maternal figure presiding over the goddesses of fate.—Thenaud, "Traité de la cabale" (MS., 16th cent.)

text at all, seeing that the dreams in this series were not dreamed (as mentioned above) under my observation. I proceed rather as if I had had the dreams myself and were therefore in a position to supply the context.

50   This procedure, if applied to *isolated* dreams of someone unknown to me personally, would indeed be a gross technical blunder. But here we are not dealing with isolated dreams; they form a coherent series in the course of which the meaning gradually unfolds more or less of its own accord. *The series is*

45

the context which the dreamer himself supplies. It is as if not one text but many lay before us, throwing light from all sides on the unknown terms, so that a reading of all the texts is sufficient to elucidate the difficult passages in each individual one. Moreover, in the third chapter we are concerned with a definite archetype—the mandala—that has long been known to us from other sources, and this considerably facilitates the interpretation. Of course the interpretation of each individual passage is bound to be largely conjecture, but the series as a whole gives us all the clues we need to correct any possible errors in the preceding passages.

51   It goes without saying that while the dreamer was under the observation of my pupil he knew nothing of these interpretations and was therefore quite unprejudiced by anybody else's opinion. Moreover I hold the view, based on wide experience, that the possibility and danger of prejudgment are exaggerated. Experience shows that the objective psyche is independent in the highest degree. Were it not so, it could not carry out its most characteristic function: the compensation of the conscious mind. The conscious mind allows itself to be trained like a parrot, but the unconscious does not—which is why St. Augustine thanked God for not making him responsible for his dreams. The unconscious is an autonomous psychic entity; any efforts to drill it are only apparently successful, and moreover are harmful to consciousness. It is and remains beyond the reach of subjective arbitrary control, in a realm where nature and her secrets can be neither improved upon nor perverted, where we can listen but may not meddle.

7. The Uroboros as symbol of the aeon.—
Horapollo, *Selecta hieroglyphica* (1597)

46

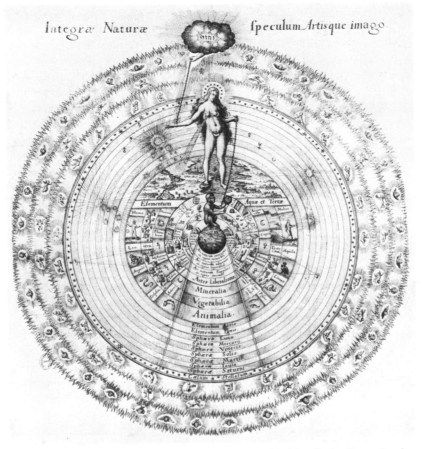

3. The *anima mundi,* guide of mankind, herself guided by God.—Engraving by
J. T. de Bry, from Fludd, *Utriusque cosmi* (1617)

2. THE INITIAL DREAMS

1. DREAM:

52   *The dreamer is at a social gathering. On leaving, he puts on
a stranger's hat instead of his own.*

53   The hat, as a covering for the head, has the general sense
of something that epitomizes the head. Just as in summing up
we bring ideas "under one head" (*unter einen Hut*), so the hat,
as a sort of leading idea, covers the whole personality and imparts its own significance to it. Coronation endows the ruler

47

with the divine nature of the sun, the doctor's hood bestows the dignity of a scholar, and a stranger's hat imparts a strange personality. Meyrink uses this theme in his novel *The Golem*, where the hero puts on the hat of Athanasius Pernath and, as a result, becomes involved in a strange experience. It is clear enough in *The Golem* that it is the unconscious which entangles the hero in fantastic adventures. Let us stress at once the significance of the *Golem* parallel and assume that the hat in the dream is the hat of an Athanasius, an immortal, a being beyond time, the universal and everlasting man as distinct from the ephemeral and "accidental" mortal man. Encircling the head, the hat is round like the sun-disc of a crown and therefore contains the first allusion to the mandala. We shall find the attribute of eternal duration confirmed in the ninth mandala dream (par. 134), while the mandala character of the hat comes out in the thirty-fifth mandala dream (par. 254). As a general result of the exchange of hats we may expect a development similar to that in *The Golem*: an emergence of the unconscious. The unconscious with its figures is already standing like a shadow behind the dreamer and pushing its way into consciousness.

2. DREAM:

54   *The dreamer is going on a railway journey, and by standing in front of the window, he blocks the view for his fellow passengers. He must get out of their way.*

55   The process is beginning to move, and the dreamer discovers that he is keeping the light from those who stand *behind* him, namely the unconscious components of his personality. We have no eyes behind us; consequently "behind" is the region of the unseen, the unconscious. If the dreamer will only stop blocking the window (consciousness), the unconscious content will become conscious.

3. HYPNAGOGIC VISUAL IMPRESSION:

56   *By the sea shore. The sea breaks into the land, flooding everything. Then the dreamer is sitting on a lonely island.*

57   The sea is the symbol of the collective unconscious, because unfathomed depths lie concealed beneath its reflecting surface.[1]

1 The sea is a favourite place for the birth of visions (i.e., invasions by unconscious contents). Thus the great vision of the eagle in II Esdras 11 : 1 rises out

Those who stand behind, the shadowy personifications of the unconscious, have burst into the *terra firma* of consciousness like a flood. Such invasions have something uncanny about them because they are irrational and incomprehensible to the person concerned. They bring about a momentous alteration of his personality since they immediately constitute a painful personal secret which alienates and isolates him from his surroundings. It is something that we "cannot tell anybody." We are afraid of being accused of mental abnormality—not without reason, for much the same thing happens to lunatics. Even so, it is a far cry from the intuitive perception of such an invasion to being inundated by it pathologically, though the layman does not realize this. Isolation by a secret results as a rule in an animation of the psychic atmosphere, as a substitute for loss of contact with other people. It causes an activation of the unconscious, and this produces something similar to the illusions and hallucinations that beset lonely wanderers in the desert, seafarers, and saints. The mechanism of these phenomena can best be explained in terms of energy. Our normal relations to objects in the world at large are maintained by a certain expenditure of energy. If the relation to the object is cut off there is a "retention" of energy, which then creates an equivalent substitute. For instance, just as persecution mania comes from a relationship poisoned by mistrust, so, as a substitute for the normal animation of the environment, an illusory reality rises up in which weird ghostly shadows flit about in place of people. That is why primitive man has always believed that lonely and desolate places are haunted by "devils" and suchlike apparitions.

4. DREAM:

58   *The dreamer is surrounded by a throng of vague female forms* (cf. fig. 33). *A voice within him says, "First I must get away from Father."*

59   Here the psychic atmosphere has been animated by what the Middle Ages would call succubi. We are reminded of the visions of St. Anthony in Egypt, so eruditely described by Flau-

---

of the sea, and the vision of "Man"—ἄνθρωπος—in 13 : 3, 25, and 51 comes up "from the midst of the sea." Cf. also 13 : 52: "Like as thou canst neither seek out nor know the things that are in the deep of the sea: even so can no man upon earth see my Son. . . ."

bert in *La Tentation de Saint-Antoine*. The element of hallucination shows itself in the fact that the thought is spoken aloud. The words "first I must get away" call for a concluding sentence which would begin with "in order to." Presumably it would run "in order to follow the unconscious, i.e., the alluring female forms" (fig. 9). The father, the embodiment of the traditional spirit as expressed in religion or a general philosophy of life, is standing in his way. He imprisons the dreamer in the world of the conscious mind and its values. The traditional masculine world with its intellectualism and rationalism is felt to be an impediment, from which we must conclude that the unconscious, now approaching him, stands in direct opposition to the tendencies of the conscious mind and that the dreamer, despite this opposition, is already favourably disposed towards the unconscious. For this reason the latter should not be subordinated to the rationalistic judgments of consciousness; it ought rather to be an experience *sui generis*. Naturally it is not easy for the intellect to accept this, because it involves at least a partial, if not a total, *sacrificium intellectus*. Furthermore, the problem thus raised is very difficult for modern man to grasp; for to begin with he can only understand the unconscious as an inessential and unreal appendage of the conscious mind, and not as a special sphere of experience with laws of its own. In the course of the later dreams this conflict will appear again and again, until finally the right formula is found for the correlation of conscious and unconscious, and the personality is assigned its correct position between the two. Moreover, such a conflict cannot be solved by understanding, but only by experience. Every stage of the experience must be lived through. There is no feat of interpretation or any other trick by which to circumvent this difficulty, for the union of conscious and unconscious can only be achieved step by step.

60   The resistance of the conscious mind to the unconscious and the depreciation of the latter were historical necessities in the development of the human psyche, for otherwise the conscious mind would never have been able to differentiate itself at all. But modern man's consciousness has strayed rather too far from the fact of the unconscious. We have even forgotten that the psyche is by no means of our design, but is for the most part autonomous and unconscious. Consequently the approach of

9. The awakening of the sleeping king depicted as a judgment of Paris, with Hermes as psychopomp.—Thomas Aquinas (pseud.), "De alchimia" (MS., 16th cent.)

10, 11, 12. Melusina; two-headed Melusina; mermaid with mask.—Eleazar,
Uraltes chymisches Werk (1760)

the unconscious induces a panic fear in civilized people, not least
on account of the menacing analogy with insanity. The intellect
has no objection to "analysing" the unconscious as a passive
object; on the contrary such an activity would coincide with our
rational expectations. But to let the unconscious go its own way
and to experience it as a reality is something that exceeds the
courage and capacity of the average European. He prefers simply not to understand this problem. For the spiritually weak-
kneed this is the better course, since the thing is not without its
dangers.

61   The experience of the unconscious is a personal secret com-
municable only to very few, and that with difficulty; hence the
isolating effect we noted above. But isolation brings about a
compensatory animation of the psychic atmosphere which strikes
us as uncanny. The figures that appear in the dream are feminine, thus pointing to the feminine nature of the unconscious.
They are fairies or fascinating sirens and lamias (figs. 10, 11, 12;
cf. also fig. 157), who infatuate the lonely wanderer and lead
him astray. Likewise seductive maidens appear at the begin-

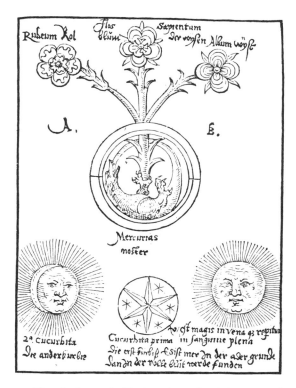

13. The "tail-eater" (Uroboros) as the *prima materia*
of the alchemical process, with the red-and-white rose,
the *flos sapientum*. Below, *coniunctio solis et lunae*,
with the *lapis philosophorum* as the son.—Reusner,
Pandora (1588)

ning of the *nekyia*[2] of Poliphilo[3] (fig. 33), and the Melusina of
Paracelsus[4] is another such figure.

2 Νεκυία from νέκυς (corpse), the title of the eleventh book of the Odyssey, is the
sacrifice to the dead for conjuring up the departed from Hades. *Nekyia* is therefore an apt designation for the "journey to Hades," the descent into the land of
the dead, and was used by Dieterich in this sense in his commentary on the
Codex of Akhmim, which contains an apocalyptic fragment from the Gospel of
Peter (*Nekyia: Beiträge zur Erklärung der neuentdeckten Petrusapokalypse*).
Typical examples are the *Divine Comedy*, the classical *Walpurgisnacht* in *Faust,*
the apocryphal accounts of Christ's descent into hell, etc.
3 Cf. the French edition of *Hypnerotomachia,* called *Le Tableau des riches inventions* or *Songe de Poliphile* (1600), trans. Béroalde de Verville. (See fig. 4.)
[The original Italian edn. appeared in 1499.]
4 For details see Jung, "Paracelsus as a Spiritual Phenomenon," pars. 179f., 214ff.

53

5. VISUAL IMPRESSION:

62   *A snake describes a circle round the dreamer, who stands rooted to the ground like a tree.*

63   The drawing of a spellbinding circle (fig. 13) is an ancient magical device used by everyone who has a special or secret purpose in mind. He thereby protects himself from the "perils of the soul" that threaten him from without and attack anyone who is isolated by a secret. The same procedure has also been used since olden times to set a place apart as holy and inviolable; in founding a city, for instance, they first drew the *sulcus primigenius* or original furrow[5] (cf. fig. 31). The fact that the dreamer stands rooted to the centre is a compensation of his almost insuperable desire to run away from the unconscious. He experienced an agreeable feeling of relief after this vision—and rightly, since he has succeeded in establishing a protected *temenos*,[6] a taboo area where he will be able to meet the unconscious. His isolation, so uncanny before, is now endowed with meaning and purpose, and thus robbed of its terrors.

6. VISUAL IMPRESSION, DIRECTLY FOLLOWING UPON 5:

64   *The veiled figure of a woman seated on a stair.*

65   The motif of the unknown woman—whose technical name is the "anima"[7]—appears here for the first time. Like the throng of vague female forms in dream 4, she is a personification of the animated psychic atmosphere. From now on the figure of the unknown woman reappears in a great many of the dreams. Personification always indicates an autonomous activity of the unconscious. If some personal figure appears we may be sure that the unconscious is beginning to grow active. The activity of such figures very often has an anticipatory character: something that the dreamer himself will do later is now being done in advance. In this case the allusion is to a stair, thus indicating an ascent or a descent (fig. 14).

66   Since the process running through dreams of this kind has an historical analogy in the rites of initiation, it may not be

---

5 Knuchel, *Die Umwandlung in Kult, Magie und Rechtsbrauch.*

6 A piece of land, often a grove, set apart and dedicated to a god.

7 For the concept of the "anima," see Jung, "The Relations between the Ego and the Unconscious," pars. 296ff.

14. Jacob's dream.—Watercolour by William Blake ·

superfluous to draw attention to the important part which the
Stairway of the Seven Planets played in these rites, as we know
from Apuleius, among others. The initiations of late classical
syncretism, already saturated with alchemy (cf. the visions of
Zosimos[8]), were particularly concerned with the theme of ascent,

8 Zosimos lived *c.* A.D. 300. Cf. Reitzenstein, *Poimandres,* pp. 9ff.; Berthelot, *Collection des anciens alchimistes grecs,* III, i, 2.

Mortuis Corporibus remanent spiritus soluti Igitur corporibus morte
vestitis illa equitatis cum Sale et cum ☉ ☽ lumine et 10
stellis fixis

Caput Corvi dicitur

Laton dicitur ista fig.
ra idest principium
artis qui in vase
apparet niger, et
est principium
corruptionis

cala Lapidis
Hermetis

figura nigra Superius est prima materia, quando ponitur in vase
ad ignem, fit ita nigra ascendendo gradatim ad albedinem per
scalam digestionis, et per gradus ignis decoquendos.

15. The *scala lapidis*, representing the stages of the alchemical process.—
"Emblematical Figures of the Philosophers' Stone" (MS., 17th cent.)

i.e., sublimation. The ascent was often represented by a ladder (fig. 15); hence the burial gift in Egypt of a small ladder for the *ka* of the dead.[9] The idea of an ascent through the seven spheres of the planets symbolizes the return of the soul to the sun-god from whom it originated, as we know for instance from Firmicus Maternus.[10] Thus the Isis mystery described by Apuleius[11] culminated in what early medieval alchemy, going back to Alexandrian tradition as transmitted by the Arabs,[12] called the *solificatio,* where the initiand was crowned as Helios.

7. VISUAL IMPRESSION:

67   *The veiled woman uncovers her face. It shines like the sun.*

68   The *solificatio* is consummated on the person of the anima. The process would seem to correspond to the *illuminatio,* or enlightenment. This "mystical" idea contrasts strongly with the rational attitude of the conscious mind, which recognizes only intellectual enlightenment as the highest form of understanding and insight. Naturally this attitude never reckons with the fact that scientific knowledge only satisfies the little tip of personality that is contemporaneous with ourselves, not the collective psyche[13] that reaches back into the grey mists of antiquity and always requires a special rite if it is to be united with present-day consciousness. It is clear, therefore, that a "lighting up" of the unconscious is being prepared, which has far more the character of an *illuminatio* than of rational "elucidation." The *solificatio* is infinitely far removed from the conscious mind and seems to it almost chimerical.

8. VISUAL IMPRESSION:

69   *A rainbow is to be used as a bridge. But one must go under it and not over it. Whoever goes over it will fall and be killed.*

70   Only the gods can walk rainbow bridges in safety; mere mortals fall and meet their death, for the rainbow is only a lovely semblance that spans the sky, and not a highway for

---

[9] The ladder motif is confirmed in dreams 12 and 13 (pars. 78 and 82). Cf. also Jacob's ladder (fig. 14).

[10] *De errore profanarum religionum:* "Animo descensus per orbem solis tribuitur" (It is said [by the pagans] that the soul descends through the circle of the sun).

[11] *The Golden Ass.*   [12] Cf. Ruska, *Turba.*

[13] Cf. "collective unconscious" in Jung, *Psychological Types,* Def. 56.

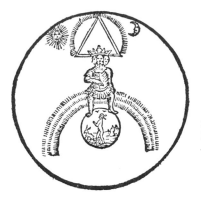

16. *Mercurius tricephalus* as Anthropos. Below, blindfolded man led by an animal. —Kelley, *Tractatus de Lapide philosophorum* (1676)

human beings with bodies. These must pass "under it" (fig. 16). But water flows under bridges too, following its own gradient and seeking the lowest place. This hint will be confirmed later.

9. DREAM:

71   *A green land where many sheep are pastured. It is the "land of sheep."*

72   This curious fragment, inscrutable at first glance, may derive from childhood impressions and particularly from those of a religious nature, which would not be far to seek in this connection—e.g., "He maketh me to lie down in green pastures," or the early Christian allegories of sheep and shepherd [14] (fig. 18). The next vision points in the same direction.

10. VISUAL IMPRESSION:

73   *The unknown woman stands in the land of sheep and points the way.*

74   The anima, having already anticipated the *solificatio*, now appears as the psychopomp, the one who shows the way [15] (fig. 19). The way begins in the children's land, i.e., at a time when rational present-day consciousness was not yet separated from the historical psyche, the collective unconscious. The separation is indeed inevitable, but it leads to such an alienation from that

[14] The direct source of the Christian sheep symbolism is to be found in the visions of the Book of Enoch 89 : 10ff. (Charles, *Apocrypha and Pseudepigrapha*, II, p. 252). The Apocalypse of Enoch was written about the beginning of the 1st cent. B.C.

[15] In the vision of Enoch, the leader and prince appears first as a sheep or ram: Book of Enoch 89 : 48 (Charles, II, p. 254).

17. The artifex (or Hermes) as shepherd of Aries and Taurus, who symbolize
the vernal impulses, the beginning of the *opus.*—Thomas Aquinas (pseud.),
"De alchimia" (MS., 16th cent.)

dim psyche of the dawn of mankind that a loss of instinct ensues.
The result is instinctual atrophy and hence disorientation in
everyday human situations. But it also follows from the separation that the "children's land" will remain definitely infantile
and become a perpetual source of childish inclinations and impulses. These intrusions are naturally most unwelcome to the
conscious mind, and it consistently represses them for that reason. But the very consistency of the repression only serves to
bring about a still greater alienation from the fountainhead,
thus increasing the lack of instinct until it becomes lack of soul.
As a result, the conscious mind is either completely swamped by
childishness or else constantly obliged to defend itself in vain
against the inundation, by means of a cynical affectation of old
age or embittered resignation. We must therefore realize that
despite its undeniable successes the rational attitude of present-
day consciousness is, in many human respects, childishly un-

59

18. Christ as shepherd.—Mosaic, mausoleum of Galla Placidia, Ravenna
(*c.* 424–451)

adapted and hostile to life. Life has grown desiccated and cramped, crying out for the rediscovery of the fountainhead. But the fountainhead can only be found if the conscious mind will suffer itself to be led back to the "children's land," there to receive guidance from the unconscious as before. To remain a child too long is childish, but it is just as childish to move away and then assume that childhood no longer exists because we do not see it. But if we return to the "children's land" we succumb to the fear of becoming childish, because we do not understand that everything of psychic origin has a double face. One face looks forward, the other back. It is ambivalent and therefore symbolic, like all living reality.

75   We stand on a peak of consciousness, believing in a childish way that the path leads upward to yet higher peaks beyond. That is the chimerical rainbow bridge. In order to reach the next peak we must first go down into the land where the paths begin to divide.

11. DREAM:

76   *A voice says, "But you are still a child."*

77   This dream forces the dreamer to admit that even a highly differentiated consciousness has not by any means finished with childish things, and that a return to the world of childhood is necessary.

60

19. The soul as guide, showing the way.—Watercolour by William Blake for
Dante's *Purgatorio,* Canto IV

12. DREAM:

78 *A dangerous walk with Father and Mother, up and down many ladders.*

79 A childish consciousness is always tied to father and mother, and is never by itself. Return to childhood is always the return to father and mother, to the whole burden of the psychic non-ego as represented by the parents, with its long and momentous history. Regression spells disintegration into our historical and hereditary determinants, and it is only with the greatest effort that we can free ourselves from their embrace. Our psychic pre-history is in truth the spirit of gravity, which needs steps and ladders because, unlike the disembodied airy intellect, it cannot fly at will. Disintegration into the jumble of historical determinants is like losing one's way, where even what is right seems an alarming mistake.

80 As hinted above, the steps and ladders theme (cf. figs. 14, 15) points to the process of psychic transformation, with all its ups and downs. We find a classic example of this in Zosimos' ascent and descent of the fifteen steps of light and darkness.[16]

81 It is of course impossible to free oneself from one's childhood without devoting a great deal of work to it, as Freud's researches have long since shown. Nor can it be achieved through intellectual knowledge only; what is alone effective is a remembering that is also a re-experiencing. The swift passage of the years and the overwhelming inrush of the newly discovered world leave a mass of material behind that is never dealt with. We do not shake this off; we merely remove ourselves from it. So that when, in later years, we return to the memories of childhood we find bits of our personality still alive, which cling round us and suffuse us with the feeling of earlier times. Being still in their childhood state, these fragments are very powerful in their effect. They can lose their infantile aspect and be corrected only when they are reunited with adult consciousness. This "personal unconscious" must always be dealt with first, that is, made conscious, otherwise the gateway to the collective unconscious cannot be opened. The journey with father and mother up and down many ladders represents the making conscious of infantile contents that have not yet been integrated.

16 Berthelot, *Collection des anciens alchimistes grecs,* III, i, 2. Cf. also Jung, "The Visions of Zosimos."

13. DREAM:

82
The father calls out anxiously, "That is the seventh!"

83
During the walk over many ladders some event has evidently taken place which is spoken of as "the seventh" (fig. 20). In the language of initiation, "seven" stands for the highest stage of illumination and would therefore be the coveted goal of all desire (cf. fig. 28). But to the conventional mind the *solificatio* is an outlandish, mystical idea bordering on madness. We assume that it was only in the dark ages of misty superstition that people thought in such a nonsensical fashion, but that the lucid and hygienic mentality of our own enlightened days has long since outgrown such nebulous notions, so much so, indeed, that this particular kind of "illumination" is to be found nowadays only in a lunatic asylum. No wonder the father is scared and anxious, like a hen that has hatched out ducklings and is driven to despair by the aquatic proclivities of its young. If this interpretation—that the "seventh" represents the highest stage of illumination—is correct, it would mean in principle that the process of integrating the personal unconscious was actually at an end. Thereafter the collective unconscious would begin to open up, which would suffice to explain the anxiety the father felt as the representative of the traditional spirit.

84
Nevertheless the return to the dim twilight of the unconscious does not mean that we should entirely abandon the precious acquisition of our forefathers, namely the intellectual differentiation of consciousness. It is rather a question of the *man* taking the place of the *intellect*—not the man whom the dreamer imagines himself to be, but someone far more rounded and complete. This would mean assimilating all sorts of things into the sphere of his personality which the dreamer still rejects as disagreeable or even impossible. The father who calls out so anxiously, "That is the seventh!" is a psychic component of the dreamer himself, and the anxiety is therefore his own. So the interpretation must bear in mind the possibility that the "seventh" means not only a sort of culmination but something rather ominous as well. We come across this theme, for instance, in the fairytale of Tom Thumb and the Ogre. Tom Thumb is the youngest of seven brothers. His dwarflike stature and his cunning are harmless enough, yet he is the one who leads his brothers to the ogre's lair, thus proving his own dangerous double nature as a bringer of good and bad luck; in other words.

20. The six planets united in the seventh, Mercury, depicted as the Uroboros, and the red-and-white (hermaphroditic) double eagle.—Thomas Aquinas (pseud.), "De alchimia" (MS., 16th cent.)

21. The seven gods of the planets in Hades.—Mylius, *Philosophia reformata* (1622)

he is also the ogre himself. Since olden times "the seven" have represented the seven gods of the planets (fig. 20); they form what the Pyramid inscriptions call a *paut neteru,* a "company of gods" [17] (cf. figs. 21, 23). Although a company is described as "nine," it often proves to be not nine at all but ten, and sometimes even more. Thus Maspero[18] tells us that the first and last members of the series can be added to, or doubled, without injury to the number nine. Something of the sort happened to the classical *paut* of the Greco-Roman or Babylonian gods in the postclassical age, when the gods were degraded to demons and retired partly to the distant stars and partly to the metals inside the earth. It then transpired that Hermes or Mercurius possessed a double nature, being a chthonic god of revelation and also the spirit of quicksilver, for which reason he was represented as a hermaphrodite (fig. 22). As the planet Mercury, he is

[17] Budge, in *Gods of the Egyptians,* I, p. 87, uses this expression.
[18] *Études de mythologie,* II, p. 245.

65

22. Mercurius in the "philosopher's egg" (the alchemical vessel). As *filius* he stands on the sun and moon, tokens of his dual nature. The birds betoken spiritualization, while the scorching rays of the sun ripen the homunculus in the vessel.—*Mutus liber* (1702)

nearest to the sun, hence he is pre-eminently related to gold. But, as quicksilver, he dissolves the gold and extinguishes its sunlike brilliance. All through the Middle Ages he was the object of much puzzled speculation on the part of the natural philosophers: sometimes he was a ministering and helpful spirit, a πάρεδρος (literally "assistant, comrade") or *familiaris;* and sometimes the *servus* or *cervus fugitivus* (the fugitive slave or stag), an elusive, deceptive, teasing goblin[19] who drove the alchemists to despair and had many of his attributes in common with the devil. For instance he is dragon, lion, eagle, raven, to mention only the most important of them. In the alchemical hierarchy of gods Mercurius comes lowest as *prima materia* and highest

[19] Cf. the entertaining dialogue between the alchemist and Mercurius in Sendivogius, "Dialogus," *Theatr. chem.,* IV.

as *lapis philosophorum*. The *spiritus mercurialis* (fig. 23) is the alchemists' guide (Hermes Psychopompos: cf. fig. 146), and their tempter; he is their good luck and their ruin. His dual nature enables him to be not only the seventh but also the eighth—the eighth on Olympus "whom nobody thought of" (see infra, par. 204f.).

85   It may seem odd to the reader that anything as remote as medieval alchemy should have relevance here. But the "black art" is not nearly so remote as we think; for as an educated man the dreamer must have read *Faust*, and *Faust* is an alchemical drama from beginning to end, although the educated man of today has only the haziest notion of this. Our conscious mind is far from understanding everything, but the unconscious always keeps an eye on the "age-old, sacred things," however strange they may be, and reminds us of them at a suitable opportunity. No doubt *Faust* affected our dreamer much as Goethe was affected when, as a young man in his Leipzig days, he studied Theophrastus Paracelsus with Fräulein von Klettenberg.[20] It was then, as we certainly may assume, that the mysterious equivalence of seven and eight sank deep into his soul, without his conscious mind ever unravelling the mystery. The following dream will show that this reminder of *Faust* is not out of place.

14. DREAM:

86   *The dreamer is in America looking for an employee with a pointed beard. They say that everybody has such an employee.*

87   America is the land of practical, straightforward thinking, uncontaminated by our European sophistication. The intellect would there be kept, very sensibly, as an employee. This naturally sounds like *lèse-majesté* and might therefore be a serious matter. So it is consoling to know that everyone (as is always the case in America) does the same. The "man with a pointed beard" is our time-honoured Mephisto whom Faust "employed" and who was not permitted to triumph over him in the end, despite the fact that Faust had dared to descend into the dark chaos of the historical psyche and steep himself in the ever-changing, seamy side of life that rose up out of that bubbling cauldron.

88   From subsequent questions it was discovered that the

20 Goethe, *Dichtung und Wahrheit*.

23. The mystic vessel where the two natures unite (*sol* and *luna, caduceus*) to produce the *filius hermaphroditus,* Hermes Psychopompos, flanked by the six gods of the planets.—"Figurarum Aegyptiorum secretarum" (MS., 18th cent.)

dreamer himself had recognized the figure of Mephistopheles in the "man with the pointed beard." Versatility of mind as well as the inventive gift and scientific leanings are attributes of the astrological Mercurius. Hence the man with the pointed beard represents the intellect, which is introduced by the dream as a real *familiaris,* an obliging if somewhat dangerous spirit. The intellect is thus degraded from the supreme position it once occupied and is put in the second rank, and at the same time branded as daemonic. Not that it had ever been anything but daemonic—only the dreamer had not noticed before how possessed he was by the intellect as the tacitly recognized supreme power. Now he has a chance to view this function, which till then had been the uncontested dominant of his psychic life, at somewhat closer quarters. Well might he exclaim with Faust: "So that's what was inside the poodle!" Mephistopheles is the diabolical aspect of every psychic function that has broken loose from the hierarchy of the total psyche and now enjoys independence and absolute power (fig. 36). But this aspect can be perceived only when the function becomes a separate entity and is objectivated or personified, as in this dream.

89   Amusingly enough, the "man with the pointed beard" also crops up in alchemical literature, in one of the "Parabolae" contained in the "Güldenen Tractat vom philosophischen Stein," [21] written in 1625, which Herbert Silberer[22] has analysed from a psychological point of view. Among the company of old white-bearded philosophers there is a young man with a black pointed beard. Silberer is uncertain whether he should assume this figure to be the devil.

90   Mercurius as quicksilver is an eminently suitable symbol for the "fluid," i.e., mobile, intellect (fig. 24). Therefore in alchemy Mercurius is sometimes a "spirit" and sometimes a "water," the so-called *aqua permanens,* which is none other than *argentum vivum.*

15. DREAM:

91   *The dreamer's mother is pouring water from one basin into another.* (The dreamer only remembered in connection with vision 28 of the next series that this basin belonged to his sister.)

21 Printed in *Geheime Figuren der Rosenkreuzer.*
22 *Problems of Mysticism and Its Symbolism.*

24. The activities presided over by Mercurius.—Tübingen MS. (*c.* 1400)

25. The fountain of life as *fons mercurialis.—Rosarium philosophorum* (1550)

This action is performed with great solemnity: it is of the highest significance for the outside world. Then the dreamer is rejected by his father.

92   Once more we meet with the theme of "exchange" (cf. dream 1): one thing is put in the place of another. The "father" has been dealt with; now begins the action of the "mother." Just as the father represents collective consciousness, the traditional spirit, so the mother stands for the collective unconscious, the source of the water of life[23] (fig. 25). (Cf. the maternal significance of πηγή,[24] the *fons signatus*,[25] as an attribute of the Virgin Mary, etc.—fig. 26.) The unconscious has altered the locus of the life forces, thus indicating a change of attitude. The dreamer's subsequent recollection enables us to see who is now

23 For water as origin, cf. Egyptian cosmogony, among others.
24 Wirth, *Aus orientalischen Chroniken*, p. 199.
25 "A fountain sealed": Song of Songs 4 : 12.

26. The Virgin Mary surrounded by her attributes, the quadrangular enclosed
garden, the round temple, tower, gate, well and fountain, palms and cypresses
(trees of life), all feminine symbols.—17th-century devotional picture

the source of life: it is the "sister." The mother is superior to the son, but the sister is his equal. Thus the deposition of the intellect frees the dreamer from the domination of the unconscious and hence from his infantile attitude. Although the sister is a remnant of the past, we know definitely from later dreams that she was the carrier of the anima-image. We may therefore assume that the transferring of the water of life to the sister really means that the mother has been replaced by the anima.[26]

93   The anima now becomes a life-giving factor, a psychic reality which conflicts strongly with the world of the father. Which of us could assert, without endangering his sanity, that he had accepted the guidance of the unconscious in the conduct of his life, assuming that anyone exists who could imagine what that would mean? Anyone who could imagine it at all would certainly have no difficulty in understanding what a monstrous affront such a *volte face* would offer to the traditional spirit, especially to the spirit that has put on the earthly garment of the Church. It was this subtle change of psychic standpoint that caused the old alchemists to resort to deliberate mystification, and that sponsored all kinds of heresies. Hence it is only logical for the father to reject the dreamer—it amounts to nothing less than excommunication. (Be it noted that the dreamer is a Roman Catholic.) By acknowledging the reality of the psyche and making it a co-determining ethical factor in our lives, we offend against the spirit of convention which for centuries has regulated psychic life from outside by means of institutions as well as by reason. Not that unreasoning instinct rebels of itself against firmly established order; by the strict logic of its own inner laws it is itself of the firmest structure imaginable and, in addition, the creative foundation of all binding order. But just because this foundation is creative, all order which proceeds from it—even in its most "divine" form—is a phase, a stepping-stone. Despite appearances to the contrary, the establishment of order and the dissolution of what has been established are at

26 This is really a normal life-process, but it usually takes place quite unconsciously. The anima is an archetype that is always present. (Cf. Jung, *Psychological Types*, Defs. 48, 49, and "The Relations between the Ego and the Unconscious," pars. 296ff.) The mother is the first carrier of the anima-image, which gives her a fascinating quality in the eyes of the son. It is then transferred, via the sister and similar figures, to the beloved.

bottom beyond human control. The secret is that only that which can destroy itself is truly alive. It is well that these things are difficult to understand and thus enjoy a wholesome conceal-ment, for weak heads are only too easily addled by them and thrown into confusion. From all these dangers dogma—whether ecclesiastical, philosophical, or scientific—offers effective protec-tion, and, looked at from a social point of view, excommunica-tion is a necessary and useful consequence.

94   The water that the mother, the unconscious, pours into the basin belonging to the anima is an excellent symbol for the liv-ing power of the psyche (cf. fig. 152). The old alchemists never tired of devising new and expressive synonyms for this water. They called it *aqua nostra, mercurius vivus, argentum vivum, vinum ardens, aqua vitae, succus lunariae,* and so on, by which they meant a living being not devoid of substance, as opposed to the rigid immateriality of mind in the abstract. The ex-pression *succus lunariae* (sap of the moon-plant) refers clearly enough to the nocturnal origin of the water, and *aqua nostra,* like *mercurius vivus,* to its earthliness (fig. 27). *Acetum fontis* is a powerful corrosive water that dissolves all created things and at the same time leads to the most durable of all products, the mysterious *lapis.*

95   These analogies may seem very far-fetched. But let me refer the reader to dreams 13 and 14 in the next section (pars. 154 and 158), where the water symbolism is taken up again. The im-portance of the action "for the outside world," noted by the dreamer himself, points to the collective significance of the dream, as also does the fact—which had a far-reaching influence on the conscious attitude of the dreamer—that he is "rejected by the father."

96   The saying "extra ecclesiam nulla salus"—outside the Church there is no salvation—rests on the knowledge that an in-stitution is a safe, practicable highway with a visible or definable goal, and that no paths and no goals can be found outside it. We must not underestimate the devastating effect of getting lost in the chaos, even if we know that it is the *sine qua non* of any re-generation of the spirit and the personality.

27. Life-renewing influence of the conjoined sun and moon on the bath.—Milan,
Biblioteca Ambrosiana, Codex I

16. DREAM:

97   *An ace of clubs lies before the dreamer. A seven appears beside it.*

98   The ace, as "1," is the lowest card but the highest in value. The ace of clubs, being in the form of a cross, points to the Christian symbol.[27] Hence in Swiss-German the club is often called *Chrüüz* (cross). At the same time the three leaves contain an allusion to the threefold nature of the one God. Lowest and highest are beginning and end, alpha and omega.

99   The seven appears after the ace of clubs and not before. Presumably the idea is: first the Christian conception of God, and then the seven (stages). The seven stages symbolize the transformation (fig. 28) which begins with the symbolism of Cross and Trinity, and, judging by the earlier archaic allusions in dreams 7 and 13, culminates in the *solificatio.* But this solution is not hinted at here. Now, we know that the regression to the Helios of antiquity vainly attempted by Julian the Apostate was succeeded in the Middle Ages by another movement that was expressed in the formula "per crucem ad rosam" (through the cross to the rose), which was later condensed into the "Rosie Crosse" of the Rosicrucians. Here the essence of the heavenly Sol descends into the flower—earth's answer to the sun's countenance (fig. 29). The solar quality has survived in the symbol of the "golden flower" of Chinese alchemy.[28] The well-known "blue flower" of the Romantics might well be the last nostalgic perfume of the "rose"; it looks back in true Romantic fashion to the medievalism of ruined cloisters, yet at the same time modestly proclaims something new in earthly loveliness. But even

---

27 Cf. dream 23 of second series (par. 212, also par. 220).

28 Concerning the "golden flower" of medieval alchemy (cf. fig. 30), see Adolphus Senior, *Azoth.* The golden flower comes from the Greek χρυσάνθιον (Berthelot, *Alch. grecs,* III, xlix. 19) and χρυσάνθεμον = 'golden flower', a magical plant like the Homeric μῶλυ, which is often mentioned by the alchemists. The golden flower is the noblest and purest essence of gold. The same name is sometimes given to pyrites. (Cf. Lippmann, *Entstehung und Ausbreitung der Alchemie,* I, p. 70.) The strength of the *aqua permanens* is also called *flos,* 'flower' (*Turba,* ed. Ruska, p. 214, 20). *Flos* is used by later alchemists to express the mystical transforming substance. (Cf. "flos citrinus" in *Aurora consurgens;* "flos aeris aureus" in "Consil. coniug., *Ars chemica,*" p. 167; "flos est aqua nummosa [Mercurius]" in "Allegoriae sapientum," p. 81; "flos operis est lapis" in Mylius, *Philosophia reformata,* p. 30.)

28. Capture of the Leviathan with the sevenfold tackle of the line of David, with
the crucifix as bait.—Herrad of Landsberg's *Hortus deliciarum* (12th cent.)

29. Seven-petalled rose as allegory of the seven planets, the seven
stages of transformation, etc.—Fludd, *Summum bonum* (1629),
frontispiece

the golden brilliance of the sun had to submit to a descent, and
it found its analogy in the glitter of earthly gold—although, as
aurum nostrum, this was far removed from the gross materiality
of the metal, at least for subtler minds. One of the most interesting of the alchemical texts is the *Rosarium philosophorum,* subtitled *Secunda pars alchimiae de lapide philosophico vero modo
praeparando. . . . Cum figuris rei perfectionem ostendentibus*
(1550).[29] The anonymous author was very definitely a "philosopher" and was apparently aware that alchemy was not concerned with ordinary goldmaking but with a philosophical secret. For these alchemists the gold undoubtedly had a symbolic
nature[30] and was therefore distinguished by such attributes as
vitreum or *philosophicum.* It was probably owing to its all too

[29] Reprinted in *Artis auriferae,* II, pp. 204ff. (1593) and *Bibliotheca chemica
curiosa,* II, pp. 87ff. (1702). My quotations are usually taken from the 1593
version.

[30] As the *Rosarium* says: "Aurum nostrum non est aurum vulgi" (Our gold is
not the common gold). *Art. aurif.,* II, p. 220.

obvious analogy with the sun that gold was denied the highest philosophical honour, which fell instead to the *lapis philosophorum*. The transformer is above the transformed, and transformation is one of the magical properties of the marvellous stone. The *Rosarium philosophorum* says: "For our stone, namely the living western quicksilver which has placed itself above the gold and vanquished it, is that which kills and quickens." [31] As to the "philosophical" significance of the *lapis*, the following quotation from a treatise ascribed to Hermes is particularly enlightening: "Understand, ye sons of the wise, what this exceeding precious stone proclaims . . . 'And my light conquers every light, and my virtues are more excellent than all virtues. . . . I beget the light, but the darkness too is of my nature. . . .' " [32]

17. DREAM:

100
The dreamer goes for a long walk, and finds a blue flower on the way.

101
To go for a walk is to wander along paths that lead nowhere in particular; it is both a search and a succession of changes. The dreamer finds a blue flower blossoming aimlessly by the wayside, a chance child of nature, evoking friendly memories of a more romantic and lyrical age, of the youthful season when it came to bud, when the scientific view of the world had not yet broken away from the world of actual experience—or rather when this break was only just beginning and the eye looked back to what was already the past. The flower is in fact like a friendly sign, a numinous emanation from the unconscious, showing the dreamer, who as a modern man has been robbed of security and of participation in all the things that lead to man's salvation, the historical place where he can meet friends and brothers of like mind, where he can find the seed that wants to sprout in him too. But the dreamer knows nothing as yet of the old solar gold which connects the innocent

---

31 "Quia lapis noster scilicet argentum vivum occidentale, quod praetulit se auro et vicit illud, est illud quod occidit et vivere facit."—Ibid., p. 223.

32 "Intelligite, filii sapientum, quod hic lapis preciosissimus clamat, . . . et lumen meum omne lumen superat ac mea bona omnibus bonis sunt sublimiora. . . . Ego gigno lumen, tenebrae autem naturae meae sunt. . . ." Ibid., p. 239. Concerning the Hermes quotations in *Rosarium*, see infra, par. 140, n. 17.

30. The red-and-white rose, the "golden flower" of alchemy, as birthplace of the *filius philosophorum.*—"Ripley Scrowle" (**MS.,** 1588)

flower with the obnoxious black art of alchemy and with the blasphemous pagan idea of the *solificatio.* For the "golden flower of alchemy" (fig. 30) can sometimes be a blue flower: "The sapphire blue flower of the hermaphrodite." [33]

18. DREAM:

102   *A man offers him some golden coins in his outstretched hand. The dreamer indignantly throws them to the ground and immediately afterwards deeply regrets his action. A variety performance then takes place in an enclosed space.*

103   The blue flower has already begun to drag its history after it. The "gold" is offered and is indignantly refused. Such a misinterpretation of the *aurum philosophicum* is easy to understand. But hardly has it happened when there comes a pang of remorse that the precious secret has been rejected and a wrong answer given to the riddle of the Sphinx. The same thing happened to the hero in Meyrink's *Golem,* when the ghost offered him a handful of grain which he spurned. The gross materiality of the yellow metal with its odious fiscal flavour, and the mean look of the grain, make both rejections comprehensible enough —but that is precisely why it is so hard to find the *lapis:* it is *exilis,* uncomely, it is thrown out into the street or on the dung-

[33] "Epistola ad Hermannum," *Theatr. chem.,* V, p. 899.

hill, it is the commonest thing to be picked up anywhere—
"in planitie, in montibus et aquis." It has this "ordinary" aspect
in common with Spitteler's jewel in *Prometheus and Epimetheus,* which, for the same reason, was also not recognized by the
worldly wise. But "the stone which the builders rejected, the
same is become the head of the corner," and the intuition of this
possibility arouses the liveliest regret in the dreamer.

104   It is all part of the banality of its outward aspect that the
gold is minted, i.e., shaped into coins, stamped, and valued. Applied psychologically, this is just what Nietzsche refuses to do in
his *Zarathustra:* to give names to the virtues. By being shaped
and named, psychic life is broken down into coined and valued
units. But this is possible only because it is intrinsically a great
variety of things, an accumulation of unintegrated hereditary
units. Natural man is not a "self"—he is the mass and a parti-
cle in the mass, collective to such a degree that he is not even
sure of his own ego. That is why since time immemorial he has
needed the transformation mysteries to turn him into something, and to rescue him from the animal collective psyche,
which is nothing but a *variété.*

105   But if we reject this unseemly *variété* of man "as he is," it is
impossible for him to attain integration, to become a self.[34] And
that amounts to spiritual death. Life that just happens in and
for itself is not real life; it is real only when it is *known.* Only
a unified personality can experience life, not that personality
which is split up into partial aspects, that bundle of odds and
ends which also calls itself "man." The dangerous plurality already hinted at in dream 4 (par. 58) is compensated in vision 5
(par. 62), where the snake describes a magic circle and thus
marks off the taboo area, the *temenos* (fig. 31). In much the same
way and in a similar situation the *temenos* reappears here, drawing the "many" together for a united variety performance—a
gathering that has the appearance of an entertainment, though
it will shortly lose its entertaining character: the "play of goats"
will develop into a "tragedy." According to all the analogies, the
satyr play was a mystery performance, from which we may as-

[34] This does not mean that the self is created, so to speak, only during the
course of life; it is rather a question of its becoming conscious. The self exists
from the very beginning, but is latent, that is, unconscious. Cf. my later explanations.

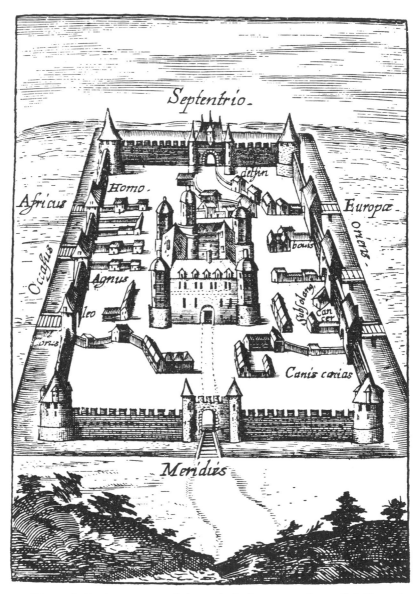

31. The symbolic city as centre of the earth, its four protecting walls laid out in a square: a typical *temenos*.—Maier, *Viatorium* (1651)

sume that its purpose, as everywhere, was to re-establish man's connection with his natural ancestry and thus with the source of life, much as the obscene stories, αἰσχρολογία, told by Athenian ladies at the mysteries of Eleusis, were thought to promote the earth's fertility.[35] (Cf. also Herodotus' account[36] of the exhibitionistic performances connected with the Isis festivities at Bubastis.)

106   The allusion to the compensatory significance of the *temenos*, however, is still wrapped in obscurity for the dreamer. As might be imagined, he is much more concerned with the danger of spiritual death, which is conjured up by his rejection of the historical context.

19. VISUAL IMPRESSION:

107   *A death's-head. The dreamer wants to kick it away, but cannot. The skull gradually changes into a red ball, then into a woman's head which emits light.*

108   The skull soliloquies of Faust and of Hamlet are reminders of the appalling senselessness of human life when "sicklied o'er with the pale cast of thought." It was traditional opinions and judgments that caused the dreamer to dash aside the doubtful and uninviting-looking offerings. But when he tries to ward off the sinister vision of the death's-head it is transformed into a red ball, which we may take as an allusion to the rising sun, since it at once changes into the shining head of a woman, reminding us directly of vision 7 (par. 67). Evidently an enantiodromia, a play of opposites,[37] has occurred: after being rejected the unconscious insists on itself all the more strongly. First it produces the classical symbol for the unity and divinity of the self, the sun; then it passes to the motif of the unknown woman who personifies the unconscious. Naturally this motif includes not merely the archetype of the anima but also the dreamer's relationship to a real woman, who is both a human personality and a vessel for psychic projections. ("Basin of the sister" in dream 15, par. 91.)

109   In Neoplatonic philosophy the soul has definite affinities

[35] Foucart, *Les Mystères d'Eleusis.*
[36] [*Histories,* II, 58; trans. Powell, I, p. 137.]
[37] See *Psychological Types,* Def. 18.

with the sphere. The soul substance is laid round the concentric spheres of the four elements above the fiery heaven.[38]

20. VISUAL IMPRESSION:

110   *A globe. The unknown woman is standing on it and worshipping the sun.*

111   This impression, too, is an amplification of vision 7 (par. 67). The rejection in dream 18 evidently amounted to the destruction of the whole development up to that point. Consequently the initial symbols reappear now, but in amplified form. Such enantiodromias are characteristic of dream-sequences in general. Unless the conscious mind intervened, the unconscious would go on sending out wave after wave without result, like the treasure that is said to take nine years, nine months, and nine nights to come to the surface and, if not found on the last night, sinks back to start all over again from the beginning.

112   The globe probably comes from the idea of the red ball. But, whereas this is the sun, the globe is rather an image of the earth, upon which the anima stands worshipping the sun (fig. 32). Anima and sun are thus distinct, which points to the fact that the sun represents a different principle from that of the anima. The latter is a personification of the unconscious, while the sun is a symbol of the source of life and the ultimate wholeness of man (as indicated in the *solificatio*). Now, the sun is an antique symbol that is still very close to us. We know also that the early Christians had some difficulty in distinguishing the ἥλιος ἀνατολῆς (the rising sun) from Christ.[39] The dreamer's anima still seems to be a sun-worshipper, that is to say, she belongs to the ancient world, and for the following reason: the conscious mind with its rationalistic attitude has taken little or no interest in her and therefore made it impossible for the

---

[38] Cf. Fleischer, *Hermes Trismegistus*, p. 6; also the spherical form of Plato's Original Man and the σφαῖρος of Empedocles. As in the *Timaeus*, the alchemical *anima mundi*, like the "soul of the substances," is spherical, and so is the gold (cf. fig. 209). (See Maier, *De circulo physico*, pp. 11f.) For the connection between the *rotundum* and the skull or head, see Jung, "Transformation Symbolism in the Mass," pp. 239ff.

[39] Cf. St. Augustine's argument that God is not this sun but he who made the sun (*In Joannis Evang. Tract.*, XXXIV, 2) and the evidence of Eusebius, who actually witnessed "Christian" sun-worship (*Constantini Oratio ad Sanctorum Coelum*, VI; Migne, *P.G.*, vol. 20, cols. 1245–50).

32. *Coniunctio solis et lunae.*—Trismosin, "Splendor solis" (MS., 1582)

anima to become modernized (or better, Christianized). It almost seems as if the differentiation of the intellect that began in the Christian Middle Ages, as a result of scholastic training, had driven the anima to regress to the ancient world. The Renaissance gives us evidence enough for this, the clearest of all being the *Hypnerotomachia* of Francesco Colonna, where Poliphilo meets his anima, the lady Polia, at the court of Queen Venus, quite untouched by Christianity and graced with all the "virtues" of antiquity. The book was rightly regarded as a mystery text.[40] With this anima, then, we plunge straight into the ancient world. So that I would not think anyone mistaken who interpreted the rejection of the gold in dream 18 *ex effectu* as an attempt to escape this regrettable and unseemly regression to antiquity. Certain vital doctrines of alchemical philosophy go back textually to late Greco-Roman syncretism, as Ruska, for instance, has sufficiently established in the case of the *Turba*. Hence any allusion to alchemy wafts one back to the ancient world and makes one suspect regression to pagan levels.

113   It may not be superfluous to point out here, with due emphasis, that consciously the dreamer had no inkling of all this. But in his unconscious he is immersed in this sea of historical associations, so that he behaves in his dreams as if he were fully cognizant of these curious excursions into the history of the human mind. He is in fact an unconscious exponent of an autonomous psychic development, just like the medieval alchemist or the classical Neoplatonist. Hence one could say—*cum grano salis*—that history could be constructed just as easily from one's own unconscious as from the actual texts.

    21. VISUAL IMPRESSION:

114   *The dreamer is surrounded by nymphs. A voice says, "We were always there, only you did not notice us"* (fig. 33).

115   Here the regression goes back even further, to an image that is unmistakably classical. At the same time the situation of dream 4 (par. 58) is taken up again and also the situation of dream 18, where the rejection led to the compensatory enantiodromia in vision 19. But here the image is amplified by the hallucinatory recognition that the drama has always existed al-

40 Béroalde de Verville, in his introduction ["Recueil stéganographique"] to the French translation (1600) of *Hypnerotomachia*, plainly adopts this view.

33. Poliphilo surrounded by nymphs.—Béroalde de Verville, *Le Songe de Poliphile* (1600)

though unnoticed until now. The realization of this fact joins the unconscious psyche to consciousness as a coexistent entity. The phenomenon of the "voice" in dreams always has for the dreamer the final and indisputable character of the αὐτὸς ἔφα,[41] i.e., the voice expresses some truth or condition that is beyond all doubt. The fact that a sense of the remote past has been established, that contact has been made with the deeper layers of the psyche, is accepted by the unconscious personality of the dreamer and communicates itself to his conscious mind as a feeling of comparative security.

116   Vision 20 represents the anima as a sun-worshipper. She has as it were stepped out of the globe or spherical form (cf. fig. 32). But the first spherical form was the skull. According to tradition the head or brain is the seat of the *anima intellectualis*. For this reason too the alchemical vessel must be round like the head, so that what comes out of the vessel shall be equally

41 "He said [it] himself." The phrase originally alluded to the authority of Pythagoras.

87

34. The *nigredo* standing on the *rotundum*, i.e., *sol niger.*—Mylius, *Philosophia reformata* (1622)

"round," i.e., simple and perfect like the *anima mundi.*[42] The work is crowned by the production of the *rotundum*, which, as the *materia globosa*, stands at the beginning and also at the end, in the form of gold (fig. 34; cf. also figs. 115, 164, 165). Possibly the nymphs who "were always there" are an allusion to this. The regressive character of the vision is also apparent from the fact that there is a multiplicity of female forms, as in dream 4 (par. 58). But this time they are of a classical nature, which, like the sun-worship in vision 20, points to an historical regression. The splitting of the anima into many figures is equivalent to dissolution into an indefinite state, i.e., into the unconscious, from which we may conjecture that a relative dissolution of the conscious mind is running parallel with the historical regression (a

42 Cf. "Liber Platonis quartorum," *Theatr. chem.*, V, pp. 149ff., 174. This treatise is a Harranite text of great importance for the history of alchemy. It exists in Arabic and Latin, but the latter version is unfortunately very corrupt. The original was probably written in the 10th cent. Cf. Steinschneider, *Die europäischen Übersetzungen aus dem Arabischen.*

process to be observed in its extreme form in schizophrenia). The dissolution of consciousness or, as Janet calls it, *abaissement du niveau mental*, comes very close to the primitive state of mind. A parallel to this scene with the nymphs is to be found in the Paracelsan *regio nymphididica*, mentioned in the treatise *De vita longa* as the initial stage of the individuation process.[43]

22. VISUAL IMPRESSION:

117   *In a primeval forest. An elephant looms up menacingly. Then a large ape-man, bear, or cave-man threatens to attack the dreamer with a club* (fig. 35). *Suddenly the "man with the pointed beard" appears and stares at the aggressor, so that he is spellbound. But the dreamer is terrified. The voice says, "Everything must be ruled by the light."*

118   The multiplicity of nymphs has broken down into still more primitive components; that is to say, the animation of the psychic atmosphere has very considerably increased, and from this we must conclude that the dreamer's isolation from his contemporaries has increased in proportion. This intensified isolation can be traced back to vision 21, where the union with the unconscious was realized and accepted as a fact. From the point of view of the conscious mind this is highly irrational; it constitutes a secret which must be anxiously guarded, since the justification for its existence could not possibly be explained to any so-called reasonable person. Anyone who tried to do so would be branded as a lunatic. The discharge of energy into the environment is therefore considerably impeded, the result being a surplus of energy on the side of the unconscious: hence the abnormal increase in the autonomy of the unconscious figures, culminating in aggression and real terror. The earlier entertaining variety performance is beginning to become uncomfortable. We find it easy enough to accept the classical figures of nymphs thanks to their aesthetic embellishments; but we have no idea that behind these gracious figures there lurks the Dionysian mystery of antiquity, the satyr play with its tragic implications: the bloody dismemberment of the god who has become an animal. It needed a Nietzsche to expose in all its feebleness Europe's schoolboy attitude to the ancient world. But what did Dionysus mean to Nietzsche? What he says about it must be taken seriously; what

[43] Cf. "Paracelsus as a Spiritual Phenomenon," par. 214.

35. A medieval version of the "wild man."—Codex Urbanus Latinus 899
(15th cent.)

it did to him still more so. There can be no doubt that he knew,
in the preliminary stages of his fatal illness, that the dismal fate
of Zagreus was reserved for him. Dionysus is the abyss of impassioned dissolution, where all human distinctions are merged in
the animal divinity of the primordial psyche—a blissful and terrible experience. Humanity, huddling behind the walls of its
culture, believes it has escaped this experience, until it succeeds
in letting loose another orgy of bloodshed. All well-meaning
people are amazed when this happens and blame high finance,
the armaments industry, the Jews, or the Freemasons.[44]

44 I wrote this passage in spring, 1935.

119   At the last moment, friend "Pointed Beard" appears on the scene as an obliging *deus ex machina* and exorcizes the annihilation threatened by the formidable ape-man. Who knows how much Faust owed his imperturbable curiosity, as he gazed on the spooks and bogeys of the classical *Walpurgisnacht*, to the helpful presence of Mephisto and his matter-of-fact point of view! Would that more people could remember the scientific or philosophical reflections of the much-abused intellect at the right moment! Those who abuse it lay themselves open to the suspicion of never having experienced anything that might have taught them its value and shown them why mankind has forged this weapon with such unprecedented effort. One has to be singularly out of touch with life not to notice such things. The intellect may be the devil (fig. 36), but the devil is the "strange son of chaos" who can most readily be trusted to deal effectively with his mother. The Dionysian experience will give this devil plenty to do should he be looking for work, since the resultant settlement with the unconscious far outweighs the labours of Hercules. In my opinion it presents a whole world of problems which the intellect could not settle even in a hundred years—the very reason why it so often goes off for a holiday to recuperate on lighter tasks. And this is also the reason why the psyche is forgotten so often and so long, and why the intellect makes such frequent use of magical apotropaic words like "occult" and "mystic," in the hope that even intelligent people will think that these mutterings really mean something.

120   The voice finally declares, "Everything must be ruled by the light," which presumably means the light of the discerning, conscious mind, a genuine *illuminatio* honestly acquired. The dark depths of the unconscious are no longer to be denied by ignorance and sophistry—at best a poor disguise for common fear—nor are they to be explained away with pseudo-scientific rationalizations. On the contrary it must now be admitted that things exist in the psyche about which we know little or nothing at all, but which nevertheless affect our bodies in the most obstinate way, and that they possess at least as much reality as the things of the physical world which ultimately we do not understand either. No line of research which asserted that its subject was unreal or a "nothing but" has ever made any contribution to knowledge.

36. The devil as aerial spirit and ungodly intellect.—Illustration by Eugène
Delacroix (1799–1863) for *Faust*, Part I

121   With the active intervention of the intellect a new phase of the unconscious process begins: the conscious mind must now come to terms with the figures of the unknown woman ("anima"), the unknown man ("the shadow"), the wise old man ("mana personality"),[45] and the symbols of the self. The last named are dealt with in the following section.

[45] For these concepts see Jung, "The Relations between the Ego and the Unconscious."

37. The seven-petalled flower.
—Boschius, *Symbolographia* (1702)

38. Mercurius as *virgo* standing on the gold (*sol*) and silver (*luna*) fountain, with the dragon as her son.—Thomas Aquinas (pseud.), "De alchimia" (MS., 16th cent.)

39. Shri-Yantra

3. THE SYMBOLISM OF THE MANDALA

I. CONCERNING THE MANDALA

122   As I have already said, I have put together, out of a continuous series of some four hundred dreams and visions, all
those that I regard as mandala dreams. The term "mandala" was
chosen because this word denotes the ritual or magic circle used
in Lamaism and also in Tantric yoga as a *yantra* or aid to contemplation (fig. 39). The Eastern mandalas used in ceremonial

95

are figures fixed by tradition; they may be drawn or painted or, in certain special ceremonies, even represented plastically.[1]

123   In 1938, I had the opportunity, in the monastery of Bhutia Busty, near Darjeeling, of talking with a Lamaic *rimpoche*, Lingdam Gomchen by name, about the *khilkor* or mandala. He explained it as a *dmigs-pa* (pronounced "migpa"), a mental image which can be built up only by a fully instructed lama through the power of imagination. He said that no mandala is like any other, they are all individually different. Also, he said, the mandalas to be found in monasteries and temples were of no particular significance because they were external representations only. The true mandala is always an inner image, which is gradually built up through (active) imagination, at such times when psychic equilibrium is disturbed or when a thought cannot be found and must be sought for, because it is not contained in holy doctrine. The aptness of this explanation will become apparent in the course of my exposition. The alleged free and individual formation of the mandala, however, should be taken with a considerable grain of salt, since in all Lamaic mandalas there predominates not only a certain unmistakable style but also a traditional structure. For instance they are all based on a quaternary system, a *quadratura circuli*, and their contents are invariably derived from Lamaic dogma. There are texts, such as the Shri-Chakra-Sambhara Tantra,[2] which contain directions for the construction of these "mental images." The *khilkor* is strictly distinguished from the so-called *sidpe-korlo,* or World Wheel (fig. 40), which represents the course of human existence in its various forms as conceived by the Buddhists. In contrast to the *khilkor*, the World Wheel is based on a ternary system in that the three world-principles are to be found in its centre: the cock, equalling concupiscence; the serpent, hatred or envy; and the pig, ignorance or unconsciousness (*avidya*). Here we come upon the dilemma of three and four, which also crops up in Buddhism. We shall meet this problem again in the further course of our dream-series.

124   It seems to me beyond question that these Eastern symbols originated in dreams and visions, and were not invented by some Mahayana church father. On the contrary, they are among the

1 Cf. Wilhelm and Jung, *Secret of the Golden Flower,* and Zimmer, *Myths and Symbols in Indian Art and Civilization.*   2 Avalon, *The Serpent Power,* VII.

40. Tibetan World Wheel (*sidpe-korlo*)

oldest religious symbols of humanity (figs. 41–44) and may even
have existed in paleolithic times (cf. the Rhodesian rock-paint-
ings). Moreover they are distributed all over the world, a point
I need not insist on here. In this section I merely wish to show
from the material at hand how mandalas come into existence.

¹²⁵   The mandalas used in ceremonial are of great significance
because their centres usually contain one of the highest religious
figures: either Shiva himself—often in the embrace of Shakti––

97

41. The Aztec "Great Calendar Stone"

or the Buddha, Amitabha, Avalokiteshvara, or one of the great
Mahayana teachers, or simply the *dorje,* symbol of all the divine
forces together, whether creative or destructive (fig. 43). The
text of the *Golden Flower,* a product of Taoist syncretism, speci-
fies in addition certain "alchemical" properties of this centre
after the manner of the *lapis* and the *elixir vitae,* so that it is in
effect a φάρμακον ἀθανασίας.[3]

126   It is not without importance for us to appreciate the high
value set upon the mandala, for it accords very well with the
paramount significance of individual mandala symbols which
are characterized by the same qualities of a—so to speak—"metaphysical" nature.[4] Unless everything deceives us, they signify

[3] Cf. Reitzenstein, *Die hellenistischen Mysterienreligionen.*
[4] The quotation marks indicate that I am not positing anything by the term
"metaphysical": I am only using it figuratively, in the psychological sense, to
characterize the peculiar statements made by dreams.

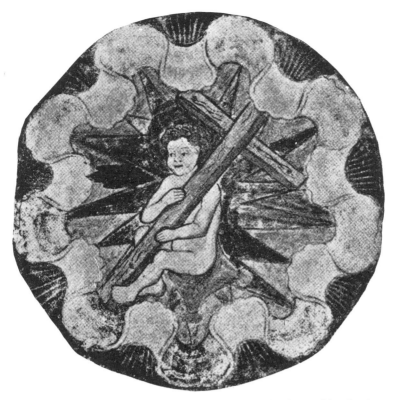

42. Mandala containing the Infant Christ carrying the Cross.—Mural painting by Albertus Pictor in the church of Harkeberga, Sweden (c. 1480)

nothing less than a psychic centre of the personality not to be identified with the ego. I have observed these processes and their products for close on thirty years on the basis of very extensive material drawn from my own experience. For fourteen years I neither wrote nor lectured about them so as not to prejudice my observations. But when, in 1929, Richard Wilhelm laid the text of the *Golden Flower* before me, I decided to publish at least a foretaste of the results. One cannot be too cautious in these matters, for what with the imitative urge and a positively morbid avidity to possess themselves of outlandish feathers and deck themselves out in this exotic plumage, far too many people are misled into snatching at such "magical" ideas and applying them externally, like an ointment. People will do anything, no matter how absurd, in order to avoid facing their

43. Lamaic Vajramandala.—Cf. Jung, "Concerning Mandala Symbolism," fig. 1

44. Mexican calendar.—Herrliberger, *Heilige Ceremonien* (1748)

own souls. They will practise Indian yoga and all its exercises, observe a strict regimen of diet, learn theosophy by heart, or mechanically repeat mystic texts from the literature of the whole world—all because they cannot get on with themselves and have not the slightest faith that anything useful could ever come out of their own souls. Thus the soul has gradually been turned into a Nazareth from which nothing good can come. Therefore let us fetch it from the four corners of the earth—the more far-fetched and bizarre it is the better! I have no wish to disturb such people at their pet pursuits, but when anybody who expects to be taken seriously is deluded enough to think that I use yoga methods and yoga doctrines or that I get my patients, whenever possible, to draw mandalas for the purpose of bringing them to the "right

101

point"—then I really must protest and tax these people with having read my writings with the most horrible inattention. The doctrine that all evil thoughts come from the heart and that the human soul is a sink of iniquity must lie deep in the marrow of their bones. Were that so, then God had made a sorry job of creation, and it were high time for us to go over to Marcion the Gnostic and depose the incompetent demiurge. Ethically, of course, it is infinitely more convenient to leave God the sole responsibility for such a Home for Idiot Children, where no one is capable of putting a spoon into his own mouth. But it is worth man's while to take pains with himself, and he has something in his soul that can grow.[5] It is rewarding to watch patiently the silent happenings in the soul, and the most and the best happens when it is not regulated from outside and from above. I readily admit that I have such a great respect for what happens in the human soul that I would be afraid of disturbing and distorting the silent operation of nature by clumsy interference. That was why I even refrained from observing this particular case myself and entrusted the task to a beginner who was not handicapped by my knowledge—anything rather than disturb the process. The results which I now lay before you are the unadulterated, conscientious, and exact self-observations of a man of unerring intellect, who had nothing suggested to him from outside and who would in any case not have been open to suggestion. Anyone at all familiar with psychic material will have no difficulty in recognizing the authentic character of the results.

[5] As Meister Eckhart says, "It is not outside, it is inside: wholly within."—Trans. Evans, p. 8.

45. Hermes as psychopomp.
—Gem in a Roman ring

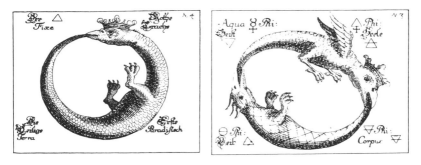

46, 47. Crowned dragon as tail-eater; two dragons forming a circle and, in the four corners, signs of the four elements.—Eleazar, *Uraltes chymisches Werk* (1760)

II. THE MANDALAS IN THE DREAMS

127   For the sake of completeness I will recapitulate the mandala symbols which occur in the initial dreams and visions already discussed:

1. The snake that described a circle round the dreamer (5).
2. The blue flower (17).
3. The man with the gold coins in his hand, and the enclosed space for a variety performance (18).
4. The red ball (19).
5. The globe (20).

128   The next mandala symbol occurs in the first dream of the new series:[6]

6. DREAM:

An unknown woman is pursuing the dreamer. He keeps running round in a circle.

129   The snake in the first mandala dream was anticipatory, as is often the case when a figure personifying a certain aspect of the unconscious does or experiences something that the subject himself will experience later. The snake anticipates a circular movement in which the subject is going to be involved; i.e., something is taking place in the unconscious which is perceived

---

6 [Inasmuch as the five mandala dreams and visions listed in par. 127 necessarily figure in this new series (though actually part of the first dream-series), the author initiated the number sequence of the new—i.e., the mandala—series with them. —EDITORS.]

as a circular movement, and this occurrence now presses into consciousness so forcefully that the subject himself is gripped by it. The unknown woman or anima representing the unconscious continues to harass the dreamer until he starts running round in circles. This clearly indicates a potential centre which is not identical with the ego and round which the ego revolves.

7. Dream:

¹³⁰   *The anima accuses the dreamer of paying too little atten-tion to her. There is a clock that says five minutes to the hour.*

¹³¹   The situation is much the same: the unconscious pesters him like an exacting woman. The situation also explains the clock, for a clock's hands go round in a circle. Five minutes to the hour implies a state of tension for anybody who lives by the clock: when the five minutes are up he must do something or other. He might even be pressed for time. (The symbol of cir-cular movement—cf. fig. 13—is always connected with a feeling of tension, as we shall see later.)

8. Dream:

¹³²   *On board ship. The dreamer is occupied with a new method of taking his bearings. Sometimes he is too far away and some-times too near: the right spot is in the middle. There is a chart on which is drawn a circle with its centre.*

¹³³   Obviously the task set here is to find the centre, the right spot, and this is the centre of a circle. While the dreamer was writing down this dream he remembered that he had dreamed shortly before of shooting at a target (fig. 48): sometimes he shot too high, sometimes too low. The right aim lay in the middle. Both dreams struck him as highly significant. The target is a circle with a centre. Bearings at sea are taken by the apparent rotation of the stars round the earth. Accordingly the dream describes an activity whose aim is to construct or locate an ob-jective centre—a centre outside the subject.

9. Dream:

¹³⁴   *A pendulum clock that goes forever without the weights running down.*

¹³⁵   This is a species of clock whose hands move unceasingly, and, since there is obviously no loss due to friction, it is a *per-*

48. The *putrefactio* without which the "goal" of the *opus* cannot be reached (hence the target-shooting).—Stolcius de Stolcenberg, *Viridarium chymicum* (1624)

petuum mobile, an everlasting movement in a circle. Here we meet with a "metaphysical" attribute. As I have already said, I use this word in a psychological sense, hence figuratively. I mean by this that eternity is a quality predicated by the unconscious, and not a hypostasis. The statement made by the dream will obviously offend the dreamer's scientific judgment, but this is just what gives the mandala its peculiar significance. Highly significant things are often rejected because they seem to contradict reason and thus set it too arduous a test. The movement without friction shows that the clock is cosmic, even transcendental; at any rate it raises the question of a quality which leaves us in some doubt whether the psychic phenomenon expressing itself in the mandala is under the laws of space and time. And this points to something so entirely different from the empirical ego that the gap between them is difficult to bridge; i.e., the other centre of personality lies on a different plane from the ego since, unlike this, it has the quality of "eternity" or relative timelessness.

10. DREAM:

136   *The dreamer is in the Peterhofstatt in Zurich with the doctor, the man with the pointed beard, and the "doll woman."
The last is an unknown woman who neither speaks nor is
spoken to. Question: To which of the three does the woman belong?*

137   The tower of St. Peter's in Zurich has a clock with a strik-
ingly large face. The Peterhofstatt is an enclosed space, a *temenos* in the truest sense of the word, a precinct of the church.
The four of them find themselves in this enclosure. The circular
dial of the clock is divided into four quarters, like the horizon.
In the dream the dreamer represents his own ego, the man with
the pointed beard the "employed" intellect (Mephisto), and the
"doll woman" the anima. Since the doll is a childish object it is
an excellent image for the non-ego nature of the anima, who is
further characterized as an object by "not being spoken to." This
negative element (also present in dreams 6 and 7 above) indicates an inadequate relationship between the conscious mind
and the unconscious, as also does the question of whom the unknown woman belongs to. The "doctor," too, belongs to the
non-ego; he probably contains a faint allusion to myself, although at that time I had no connections with the dreamer.[7]
The man with the pointed beard, on the other hand, belongs
to the ego. This whole situation is reminiscent of the relations
depicted in the diagram of functions (fig. 49). If we think of the
psychological functions[8] as arranged in a circle, then the most
differentiated function is usually the carrier of the ego and,
equally regularly, has an auxiliary function attached to it. The
"inferior" function, on the other hand, is unconscious and for
that reason is projected into a non-ego. It too has an auxiliary
function. Hence it would not be impossible for the four persons
in the dream to represent the four functions as components of
the total personality (i.e., if we include the unconscious). But
this totality is ego plus non-ego. Therefore the centre of the
circle which expresses such a totality would correspond not to
the ego but to the self as the summation of the total personality.
(The centre with a circle is a very well-known allegory of the na-

[7] As the dream at most alludes to me and does not name me, the unconscious
evidently has no intention of emphasizing my personal role.
[8] Cf. Jung, *Psychological Types,* ch. X.

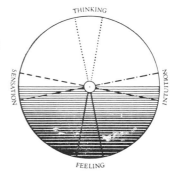

49. Diagram showing the four functions of consciousness. Thinking, the superior function in this case, occupies the centre of the light half of the circle, whereas feeling, the inferior function, occupies the dark half. The two auxiliary functions are partly in the light and partly in the dark

ture of God.) In the philosophy of the Upanishads the Self is in one aspect the *personal* atman, but at the same time it has a cosmic and metaphysical quality as the *suprapersonal* Atman.[9]

138   We meet with similar ideas in Gnosticism: I would mention the idea of the Anthropos, the Pleroma, the Monad, and the spark of light (Spinther) in a treatise of the Codex Brucianus:

> This same is he [Monogenes] who dwelleth in the Monad, which is in the Setheus, and which came from the place of which none can say where it is. . . . From Him it is the Monad came, in the manner of a ship, laden with all good things, and in the manner of a field, filled or planted with every kind of tree, and in the manner of a city, filled with all races of mankind. . . . This is the fashion of the Monad, all these being in it: there are twelve Monads as a crown upon its head. . . . And to its veil which surroundeth it in the manner of a defence [πύργος = tower] there are twelve gates. . . . This same is the Mother-City [μητρόπολις] of the Only-begotten [μονογενής].[10]

139   By way of explanation I should add that "Setheus" is a name for God, meaning "creator." The Monogenes is the Son of God. The comparison of the Monad with a field and a city corresponds to the idea of the *temenos* (fig. 50). Also, the Monad is crowned (cf. the hat which appears in dream 1 of the first series [par. 52] and dream 35 of this series [par. 254]). As "metropolis" (cf. fig. 51) the Monad is feminine, like the *padma* or lotus, the basic form of the Lamaic mandala (the Golden Flower in China and the Rose or Golden Flower in the West). The Son of

9 Deussen, *Allgemeine Geschichte der Philosophie*, I.
10 Baynes, *A Coptic Gnostic Treatise*, p. 89.

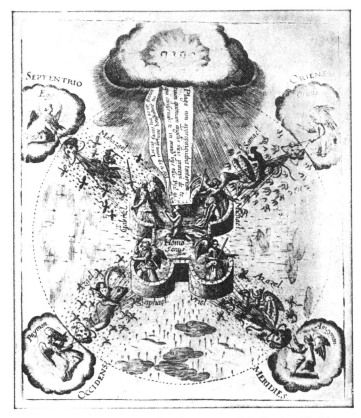

50. Baneful spirits attacking the Impregnable Castle.—Fludd,
Summum bonum (1629)

God, God made manifest, dwells in the flower.[11] In the Book of
Revelation, we find the Lamb in the centre of the Heavenly Jerusalem. And in our Coptic text we are told that Setheus dwells
in the innermost and holiest recesses of the Pleroma, a city with
four gates (equivalent to the Hindu City of Brahma on the
world-mountain Meru). In each gate there is a Monad.[12] The

11 The Buddha, Shiva, etc., in the lotus (fig. 52); Christ in the rose, in the womb
of Mary (ample material on this theme in Salzer, *Die Sinnbilder und Beiworte
Mariens*); the seeding-place of the diamond body in the golden flower. Cf. the
circumambulation of the square in dream 16, par. 164.
12 Baynes, *A Coptic Gnostic Treatise*, p. 58. Cf. the Vajramandala (fig. 43), where
the great *dorje* is found in the centre surrounded by the twelve smaller *dorjes*,

108

51. The Lapis Sanctuary, also a labyrinth, surrounded by the planetary orbits.—
Van Vreeswyck, *De Groene Leeuw* (1672)

limbs of the Anthropos born of the Autogenes (= Monogenes)
correspond to the four gates of the city. The Monad is a spark
of light (Spinther) and an image of the Father, identical with the
Monogenes. An invocation runs: "Thou art the House and the
Dweller in the House." [13] The Monogenes stands on a *tetra-peza*,[14] a table or platform with four pillars corresponding to the
quaternion of the four evangelists.[15]

140   The idea of the *lapis* has several points of contact with all
this. In the *Rosarium* the *lapis* says, quoting Hermes:[16] "I beget
the light, but the darkness too is of my nature . . . therefore

like the one Monad with the "twelve Monads as a crown upon its head." Moreover there is a *dorje* in each of the four gates.

[13] Baynes. p. 94.

[14] Ibid., p. 70. Similar to the tetramorph, the steed of the Church (fig. 53).

[15] Cf. Irenaeus, *Adversus haereses*, III, xi, and Clement of Alexandria, *Stromata*,
V, vi.

[16] *Art. aurif.*, II, pp. 239f. The Hermes quotations come from the fourth chapter of "Tractatus aureus" (*Ars chemica*, pp. 23f., or *Bibl. chem.*, I, pp. 427f.).

109

nothing better or more worthy of veneration can come to pass in the world than the conjunction of myself and my son." [17] Similarly, the Monogenes is called the "dark light," [18] a reminder of the *sol niger,* the black sun of alchemy[19] (fig. 34).

141 The following passage from chapter 4 of the "Tractatus aureus" provides an interesting parallel to the Monogenes who dwells in the bosom of the Mother-City and is identical with the crowned and veiled Monad:

> But the king reigns, as is witnessed by his brothers, [and] says: "I am crowned, and I am adorned with the diadem; I am clothed with the royal garment, and I bring joy to the heart; for, being chained to the arms and breast of my mother, and to her substance, I cause my substance to hold together and rest; and I compose the invisible from the visible, making the occult to appear; and everything that the philosophers have concealed will be generated from us. Hear then these words, and understand them; keep them, and meditate upon them, and seek for nothing more. Man is generated from the principle of Nature whose inward parts are fleshy, and from no other substance."

52. Harpokrates on the lotus.
—Gnostic gem

[17] "Ego gigno lumen, tenebrae autem naturae meae sunt . . . me igitur et filio meo conjuncto, nihil melius ac venerabilius in mundo fieri potest." The Hermes sayings as quoted by the anonymous author of the *Rosarium* contain deliberate alterations that have far more significance than mere faulty readings. They are authentic recastings, to which he lends higher authority by attributing them to Hermes. I have compared the three printed editions of the "Tractatus aureus," 1566, 1610, and 1702, and found that they all agree. The *Rosarium* quotation runs as follows in the "Tractatus aureus": "Iam Venus ait: Ego genero lumen, nec tenebrae meae naturae sunt . . . me igitur et fratri meo iunctis nihil melius ac venerabilius" (Venus says: I beget the light, and the darkness is not of my nature . . . therefore nothing is better or more worthy of veneration than the conjunction of myself and my brother).
[18] Baynes, p. 87.   [19] Cf. Mylius, *Philosophia reformata,* p. 19.

Mulier ecce fili tuu

Longinus miles

mal latro dixit me mento mei dne dum uene ris in regnu tuu.

Or ma t dm

Sub arbore ti lo suscitauit te y Rever tere sunamitis

Vere dns et loco isto

Alia nomina la cemic ca.4. Cha na.

Ecclesia

Quatuor euglist Animal et clesie

Quatu orsaci el um

Monumen ta aperta sunt multa cor pora scorum surrexerunt.

Sepulcru ade

Jeronimus refert. qd adu uarie loco ubi crucifi

53. The tetramorph, the steed of the Church.—Crucifixion in Herrad of Landsberg's *Hortus deliciarum* (12th cent.) detail

142   The "king" refers to the *lapis*. That the *lapis* is the "master" is evident from the following Hermes quotation in the *Rosarium*: [20] "Et sic Philosophus non est Magister lapidis, sed potius minister" (And thus the philosopher is not the master of the stone but rather its minister). Similarly the final production of the *lapis* in the form of the crowned hermaphrodite is called the *aenigma regis*.[21] A German verse refers to the *aenigma* as follows (fig. 54):

> Here now is born the emperor of all honour
> Than whom there cannot be born any higher,
> Neither by art nor by the work of nature
> Out of the womb of any living creature.
> Philosophers speak of him as their son
> And everything they do by him is done.[22]

143   The last two lines might easily be a direct reference to the above quotation from Hermes.

144   It looks as if the idea had dawned on the alchemists that the Son who, according to classical (and Christian) tradition, dwells eternally in the Father and reveals himself as God's gift to mankind, was something that man could produce out of his own nature—with God's help, of course (*Deo concedente*). The heresy of this idea is obvious.

145   The feminine nature of the inferior function derives from its contamination with the unconscious. Because of its feminine characteristics the unconscious is personified by the anima (that is to say, in men; in women it is masculine).[23]

146   If we assume that this dream and its predecessors really do mean something that justly arouses a feeling of significance in the dreamer, and if we further assume that this significance is more or less in keeping with the views put forward in the commentary, then we would have reached here a high point of introspective intuition whose boldness leaves nothing to be desired. But even the everlasting pendulum clock is an indigestible morsel for a consciousness unprepared for it, and likely to hamper any too lofty flight of thought.

---

[20] *Art. aurif.*, II, p. 356.   [21] Ibid., p. 359.   [22] Ibid.
[23] Cf. Jung, "The Relations between the Ego and the Unconscious," pars. 296ff.

Ænigma Regis.

**Hie ist geboren der Keyser aller ehren/
Kein höher mag vber jn geboren werden.**

54. Hermaphrodite with three serpents and one serpent.
Below, the three-headed Mercurial dragon.—*Rosarium
philosophorum*, in *Artis auriferae* (1593)

11. DREAM:

147   *The dreamer, the doctor, a pilot, and the unknown woman
are travelling by airplane. A croquet ball suddenly smashes the
mirror, an indispensable instrument of navigation, and the airplane crashes to the ground. Here again there is the same doubt:
to whom does the unknown woman belong?*

148   Doctor, pilot, and unknown woman are characterized as
belonging to the non-ego by the fact that all three of them are
strangers. Therefore the dreamer has retained possession only
of the differentiated function, which carries the ego; that is,
the unconscious has gained ground considerably. The croquet
ball is part of a game where the ball is driven under a hoop.
Vision 8 of the first series (par. 69) said that people should not
go over the rainbow (fly?), but must go *under* it. Those who go
over it fall to the ground. It looks as though the flight had been

too lofty after all. Croquet is played on the ground and not in the air. We should not rise above the earth with the aid of "spiritual" intuitions and run away from hard reality, as so often happens with people who have brilliant intuitions. We can never reach the level of our intuitions and should therefore not identify ourselves with them. Only the gods can pass over the rainbow bridge; mortal men must stick to the earth and are subject to its laws (cf. fig. 16). In the light of the possibilities revealed by intuition, man's earthliness is certainly a lamentable imperfection; but this very imperfection is part of his innate being, of his reality. He is compounded not only of his best intuitions, his highest ideals and aspirations, but also of the odious conditions of his existence, such as heredity and the indelible sequence of memories that shout after him: "You did it, and that's what you are!" Man may have lost his ancient saurian's tail, but in its stead he has a chain hanging on to his psyche which binds him to the earth—an anything-but-Homeric chain[24] of given conditions which weigh so heavy that it is better to remain bound to them, even at the risk of becoming neither a hero nor a saint. (History gives us some justification for not attaching any absolute value to these collective norms.) That we are bound to the earth does not mean that we cannot grow; on the contrary it is the *sine qua non* of growth. No noble, well-grown tree ever disowned its dark roots, for it grows not only upward but downward as well. The question of where we are going is of course extremely important; but equally important, it seems to me, is the question of *who* is going where. The "who" always implies a "whence." It takes a certain greatness to gain lasting possession of the heights, but anybody can overreach himself. The difficulty lies in striking the dead centre (cf. dream 8, par. 132). For this an awareness of the two sides of man's personality is essential, of their respective aims and origins. These two aspects must never be separated through arrogance or cowardice.

149   The "mirror" as an "indispensable instrument of navigation" doubtless refers to the intellect, which is able to think

---

[24] The Homeric chain in alchemy is the series of great wise men, beginning with Hermes Trismegistus, which links earth with heaven. At the same time it is the chain of substances and different chemical states that appear in the course of the alchemical process. Cf. *Aurea catena Homeri*.

and is constantly persuading us to identify ourselves with its insights ("reflections"). The mirror is one of Schopenhauer's favourite similes for the intellect. The term "instrument of navigation" is an apt expression for this, since it is indeed man's indispensable guide on pathless seas. But when the ground slips from under his feet and he begins to speculate in the void, seduced by the soaring flights of intuition, the situation becomes dangerous (fig. 55).

150   Here again the dreamer and the three dream figures form a quaternity. The unknown woman or anima always represents the "inferior," i.e., the undifferentiated function, which in the case of our dreamer is feeling. The croquet ball is connected with the "round" motif and is therefore a symbol of wholeness, that is, of the self, here shown to be hostile to the intellect (the mirror). Evidently the dreamer "navigates" too much by the intellect and thus upsets the process of individuation. In *De vita longa,* Paracelsus describes the "four" as *Scaiolae,* but the self as Adech (from Adam = the first man). Both, as Paracelsus emphasizes, cause so many difficulties in the "work" that one can almost speak of Adech as hostile.[25]

12. DREAM:

151   *The dreamer finds himself with his father, mother, and sister in a very dangerous situation on the platform of a tram-car.*

152   Once more the dreamer forms a quaternity with the other dream figures. He has fallen right back into childhood, a time when we are still a long way from wholeness. Wholeness is represented by the family, and its components are still projected upon the members of the family and personified by them. But this state is dangerous for the adult because regressive: it denotes a splitting of personality which primitive man experiences as the perilous "loss of soul." In the break-up the personal components that have been integrated with such pains are once more sucked into the outside world. The individual loses his guilt and exchanges it for infantile innocence; once more he can blame the wicked father for this and the unloving mother for that, and all the time he is caught in this inescapable causal nexus like a fly in a spider's web, without noticing that he has

25 Jung, "Paracelsus as a Spiritual Phenomenon," pars. 209ff.

55. Faust before the magic mirror.—Rembrandt, etching (*c.* 1652).

lost his moral freedom.[26] But no matter how much parents and grandparents may have sinned against the child, the man who is really adult will accept these sins as his own condition which has to be reckoned with. Only a fool is interested in other people's guilt, since he cannot alter it. The wise man learns only from his own guilt. He will ask himself: Who am I that all this should happen to me? To find the answer to this fateful question he will look into his own heart.

153   As in the previous dream the vehicle was an airplane, so in this it is a tram. The type of vehicle in a dream illustrates the kind of movement or the manner in which the dreamer moves forward in time—in other words, how he lives his psychic life, whether individually or collectively, whether on his own or on borrowed means, whether spontaneously or mechanically. In the airplane he is flown by an unknown pilot; i.e., he is borne along on intuitions emanating from the unconscious. (The mistake is that the "mirror" is used too much to steer by.) But in this dream he is in a collective vehicle, a tram, which anybody can ride in; i.e., he moves or behaves just like everybody else. All the same he is again one of four, which means that he is in both vehicles on account of his unconscious striving for wholeness.

13. DREAM:

154   *In the sea there lies a treasure. To reach it, he has to dive through a narrow opening. This is dangerous, but down below he will find a companion. The dreamer takes the plunge into the dark and discovers a beautiful garden in the depths, symmetrically laid out, with a fountain in the centre* (fig. 56).

155   The "treasure hard to attain" lies hidden in the ocean of the unconscious, and only the brave can reach it. I conjecture that the treasure is also the "companion," the one who goes through life at our side—in all probability a close analogy to the lonely ego who finds a mate in the self, for at first the self is the strange non-ego. This is the theme of the magical travelling companion,

---

26 Meister Eckhart says: " 'I came not upon earth to bring peace but a sword; to cut away all things, to part thee from brother, child, mother and friend, which are really thy foes.' For verily thy comforts are thy foes. Doth thine eye see all things and thine ear hear all things and thy heart remember them all, then in these things thy soul is destroyed."—Trans. Evans, I, pp. 12–13.

of whom I will give three famous examples: the disciples on the road to Emmaus, Krishna and Arjuna in the Bhagavad Gita, Moses and El-Khidr in Sura 18 of the Koran.[27] I conjecture further that the treasure in the sea, the companion, and the garden with the fountain are all one and the same thing: the self. For the garden is another *temenos*, and the fountain is the source of "living water" mentioned in John 7 : 38, which the Moses of the Koran also sought and found, and beside it El-Khidr,[28] "one of Our servants whom We had endowed with Our grace and wisdom" (Sura 18). And the legend has it that the ground round about El-Khidr blossomed with spring flowers, although it was desert. In Islam, the plan of the *temenos* with the fountain developed under the influence of early Christian architecture into the court of the mosque with the ritual wash-house in the centre (e.g., Ahmed ibn-Tulun in Cairo). We see much the same thing in our Western cloisters with the fountain in the garden. This is also the "rose garden of the philosophers," which we know from the treatises on alchemy and from many beautiful engravings. "The Dweller in the House" (cf. commentary to dream 10, par. 139) is the "companion." The centre and the circle, here represented by fountain and garden, are analogues of the *lapis*, which is among other things a living being (cf. figs. 25, 26). In the *Rosarium* the *lapis* says: "Protege me, protegam te. Largire mihi ius meum, ut te adiuvem" (Protect me and I will protect you. Give me my due that I may help you).[29] Here the *lapis* is nothing less than a good friend and helper who helps those that help him, and this points to a compensatory relationship. (I would call to mind what was said in the commentary to dream 10, pars. 138ff., more particularly the Monogenes-*lapis*-self parallel.)

156   The crash to earth thus leads into the depths of the sea, into the unconscious, and the dreamer reaches the shelter of the *temenos* as a protection against the splintering of personality caused by his regression to childhood. The situation is rather like that of dream 4 and vision 5 in the first series (pars. 58 and 62) where the magic circle warded off the lure of the unconscious and its plurality of female forms. (The dangers of temptation

27 Cf. Jung, "Concerning Rebirth," pp. 135ff.   28 Vollers, "Chidher," p. 235.
29 *Art. aurif.*, II, p. 239. This is a Hermes quotation from the "Tractatus aureus," but in the edition of 1566 (*Ars chemica*) it runs: "Largiri vis mihi meum ut adiuvem te" (You want to give me freely what is mine, that I may help you).

56. Fountain of youth.—Codex de Sphaera (Modena, 15th cent.)

approach Poliphilo in much the same way at the beginning of his *nekyia*.)

157   The source of life is, like El-Khidr, a good companion, though it is not without its dangers, as Moses of old found to his cost, according to the Koran. It is the symbol of the life force that eternally renews itself (fig. 57; cf. also figs. 25–27, 84) and of the clock that never runs down. An uncanonical saying of our Lord runs: "He who is near unto me is near unto the fire." [30] Just as this esoteric Christ is a source of fire (fig. 58)—probably not without reference to the πῦρ ἀεὶ ζῶον of Heraclitus—so the alchemical philosophers conceive their *aqua nostra* to be *ignis* (fire).[31] The source means not only the flow of life but its warmth, indeed its heat, the secret of passion, whose synonyms are always fiery.[32] The all-dissolving *aqua nostra* is an essential ingredient in the production of the *lapis*. But the source is underground and therefore the way leads underneath: only down below can we find the fiery source of life. These depths constitute the natural history of man, his causal link with the world of instinct (cf. fig. 16). Unless this link be rediscovered no *lapis* and no self can come into being.

14. DREAM:

158   *The dreamer goes into a chemist's shop with his father. Valuable things can be got there quite cheap, above all a special water. His father tells him about the country the water comes from. Afterwards he crosses the Rubicon by train.*

159   The traditional apothecary's shop, with its carboys and gallipots, its waters, its *lapis divinus* and *infernalis* and its magisteries, is the last visible remnant of the kitchen paraphernalia

---

30 A quotation from Aristotle in the *Rosarium, Art. aurif.*, II, p. 317, says: "Elige tibi pro lapide, per quem reges venerantur in Diadematibus suis . . . quia ille est propinquus igni" (Choose for your stone that through which kings are venerated in their crowns . . . because that [stone] is near to the fire).

31 Cf. the treatise of Komarios, in which Cleopatra explains the meaning of the water (Berthelot, *Collection des anciens alchimistes grecs*, IV, xx).

32 *Rosarium, Art. aurif.*, II, p. 378: "Lapis noster hic est ignis ex igne creatus et in ignem vertitur, et anima eius in igne moratur" (This our stone is fire, created of fire, and turns into fire; its soul dwells in fire). This may have been based on the following: "Item lapis noster, hoc est ignis ampulla, ex igne creatus est, et in eum vertitur" (Likewise this our stone, i.e., the flask of fire, is created out of fire and turns back into it).—"Allegoriae sapientum," *Bibl. chem. curiosa*, I, p. 468a.

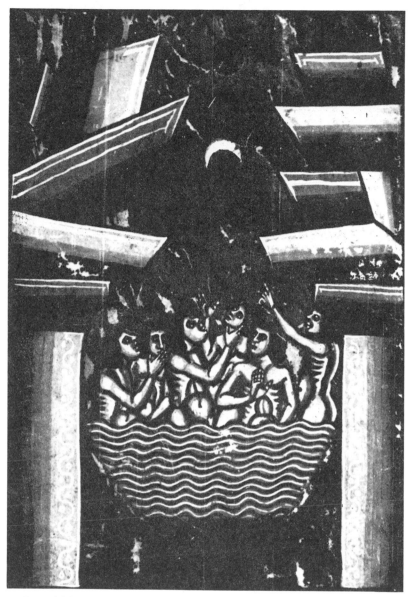

57. Imperial bath with the miraculous spring of water, beneath the influence of sun and moon.—"De balneis Puteolanis" (MS., 14th cent.)

58. Christ as the source of fire, with the "flaming" stigmata.—14th-cent. stained-glass window, church at Königsfelden, Aargau, Switzerland

of those alchemists who saw in the *donum spiritus sancti*—the precious gift—nothing beyond the chimera of goldmaking. The "special water" is literally the *aqua nostra non vulgi*.[33] It is easy

33 *Aqua nostra* is also called *aqua permanens*, corresponding to the ὕδωρ θεῖον of the Greeks: "aqua permanens, ex qua quidem aqua lapis noster pretiosissimus generatur," we read in the "Turba philosophorum," *Art. aurif.*, I, p. 14. "Lapis enim est haec ipsa permanens aqua et dum aqua est, lapis non est" (For the stone is this selfsame permanent water; and while it is water it is not the stone). —Ibid., p. 16. The commonness of the "water" is very often emphasized, as for instance in ibid., p. 30. "Quod quaerimus publice minimo pretio venditur, et si nosceretur, ne tantillum venderent mercatores" (What we are seeking is sold publicly for a very small price, and if it were recognized, the merchants would not sell it for so little).

to understand why it is his father who leads the dreamer to the source of life, since he is the natural source of the latter's life. We could say that the father represents the country or soil from which that life sprang. But figuratively speaking, he is the "informing spirit" who initiates the dreamer into the meaning of life and explains its secrets according to the teachings of old. He is a transmitter of the traditional wisdom. But nowadays the fatherly pedagogue fulfils this function only in the dreams of his son, where he appears as the archetypal father figure, the "wise old man."

160   The water of life is easily had: everybody possesses it, though without knowing its value. "Spernitur a stultis"—it is despised by the stupid, because they assume that every good thing is always outside and somewhere else, and that the source in their own souls is a "nothing but." Like the *lapis,* it is "pretio quoque vilis," of little price, and therefore, like the jewel in Spitteler's *Prometheus,* it is rejected by everyone from the high priest and the academicians down to the very peasants, and "in viam eiectus," flung out into the street, where Ahasuerus picks it up and puts it into his pocket. The treasure has sunk down again into the unconscious.

161   But the dreamer has noticed something and with vigorous determination crosses the Rubicon. He has realized that the flux and fire of life are not to be underrated and are absolutely necessary for the achievement of wholeness. But there is no recrossing the Rubicon.

15. DREAM:

162   *Four people are going down a river: the dreamer, his father, a certain friend, and the unknown woman.*

163   In so far as the "friend" is a definite person well known to the dreamer, he belongs, like the father, to the conscious world of the ego. Hence something very important has happened: in dream 11 the unconscious was three against one, but now the situation is reversed and it is the dreamer who is three against one (the latter being the unknown woman). The unconscious has been depotentiated. The reason for this is that by "taking the plunge" the dreamer has connected the upper and the lower regions—that is to say, he has decided not to live only as a bodiless abstract being but to accept the body and the world of instinct,

the reality of the problems posed by love and life, and to act accordingly.[34] This was the Rubicon that was crossed. Individuation, becoming a self, is not only a spiritual problem, it is the problem of all life.

16. DREAM:

164   *Many people are present. They are all walking to the left around a square. The dreamer is not in the centre but to one side. They say that a gibbon is to be reconstructed.*

165   Here the square appears for the first time. Presumably it arises from the circle with the help of the four people. (This will be confirmed later.) Like the *lapis*, the *tinctura rubea*, and the *aurum philosophicum*, the squaring of the circle was a problem that greatly exercised medieval minds. It is a symbol of the *opus alchymicum* (fig. 59), since it breaks down the original chaotic unity into the four elements and then combines them again in a higher unity. Unity is represented by a circle and the four elements by a square. The production of one from four is the result of a process of distillation and sublimation which takes the so-called "circular" form: the distillate is subjected to sundry distillations[35] so that the "soul" or "spirit" shall be extracted in its purest state. The product is generally called the "quintessence," though this is by no means the only name for the ever-hoped-for and never-to-be-discovered "One." It has, as the alchemists say, a "thousand names," like the *prima materia*. Heinrich Khunrath has this to say about the circular distillation: "Through Circumrotation or a Circular Philosophical revolving of the Quaternarius, it is brought back to the highest and purest Simplicity of the plusquamperfect Catholic Monad. . . . Out of the gross and impure One there cometh an exceeding pure and subtile One," and so forth.[36] Soul and spirit must be separated from the body, and this is equivalent to death: "Therefore Paul of Tarsus saith, Cupio dissolvi, et esse cum

---

[34] The alchemists give only obscure hints on this subject, e.g., the quotation from Aristotle in *Rosarium* (*Art. aurif.*, II, p. 318): "Fili, accipere debes de pinguiori carne" (Son, you must take of the fatter flesh). And in the "Tractatus aureus," ch. IV, we read: "Homo a principio naturae generatur, cuius viscera carnea sunt" (Man is generated from the principle of Nature whose inward parts are fleshy).
[35] Cf. "Paracelsus as a Spiritual Phenomenon," pars. 185ff.
[36] *Von hylealischen Chaos*, p. 204.

59. "All things do live in the three / But in the four they merry be." (Squaring the circle.)—Jamsthaler, *Viatorium spagyricum* (1625)

Christo.[37] Therefore, my dear Philosopher, must thou catch the Spirit and Soul of the Magnesia."[38] The spirit (or spirit and soul) is the *ternarius* or number three which must first be separated from its body and, after the purification of the latter, infused back into it.[39] Evidently the body is the fourth. Hence Khunrath refers to a passage from Pseudo-Aristotle,[40] where the circle re-emerges from a triangle set in a square.[41] This circular

37 ". . . having a desire to be dissolved and to be with Christ" (Phil. (D.V.) 1 : 23).
38 The "magnesia" of the alchemists has nothing to do with magnesia (MgO). In Khunrath (ibid., p. 161) it is the "materia coelestis et divina," i.e., the "materia lapidis Philosophorum," the arcane or transforming substance.
39 Ibid., p. 203.   40 Ibid., p. 207.
41 There is a figurative representation of this idea in Maier, *Scrutinium chymicum*: Emblema XXI. But Maier interprets the *ternarius* differently (cf. fig. 60). He says (p. 63): "Similiter volunt Philosophi quadrangulum in triangulum ducendum esse, hoc est, in corpus, spiritum et animam, quae tria in trinis coloribus ante rubedinem praeviis apparent, utpote corpus seu terra in Saturni nigredine, spiritus in lunari albedine, tanquam aqua, anima sive aer in solari citrinitate.

125

60. Squaring of the circle to make the two sexes one whole.—Maier, *Scrutinium chymicum* (1687)

figure, together with the Uroboros—the dragon devouring itself tail first—is the basic mandala of alchemy.

166   The Eastern and more particularly the Lamaic mandala usually contains a square ground-plan of the stupa (fig. 43). We can see from the mandalas constructed in solid form that it is really the plan of a *building*. The square also conveys the idea of a house or temple, or of an inner walled-in space[42] (cf.

Tum triangulus perfectus erit, sed hic vicissim in circulum mutari debet, hoc est in rubedinem invariabilem." (Similarly the philosophers maintain that the quadrangle is to be reduced to a triangle, that is, to body, spirit, and soul. These three appear in three colours which precede the redness: the body, or earth, in Saturnine blackness; the spirit in lunar whiteness, like water; and the soul, or air, in solar yellow. Then the triangle will be perfect, but in its turn it must change into a circle, that is into unchangeable redness.) Here the fourth is fire, and an *everlasting* fire.

[42] Cf. "city" and "castle" in commentary to dream 10, pars. 137ff. (See figs. 31,

below). According to the ritual, stupas must always be circumambulated to the right, because a leftward movement is evil. The left, the "sinister" side, is the unconscious side. Therefore a leftward movement is equivalent to a movement in the direction of the unconscious, whereas a movement to the right is "correct" and aims at consciousness. In the East these unconscious contents have gradually, through long practice, come to assume definite forms which have to be accepted as such and retained by the conscious mind. Yoga, so far as we know it as an established practice, proceeds in much the same way: it impresses fixed forms on consciousness. Its most important Western parallel is the *Exercitia spiritualia* of Ignatius Loyola, which likewise impress fixed concepts about salvation on the psyche. This procedure is "right" so long as the symbol is still a valid expression of the unconscious situation. The psychological rightness of both Eastern and Western yoga ceases only when the unconscious process—which anticipates future modifications of consciousness—has developed so far that it produces shades of meaning which are no longer adequately expressed by, or are at variance with, the traditional symbol. Then and only then can one say that the symbol has lost its "rightness." Such a process signifies a gradual shift in man's unconscious view of the world over the centuries and has nothing whatever to do with intellectual criticisms of this view. Religious symbols are phenomena of life, plain facts and not intellectual opinions. If the Church clung for so long to the idea that the sun rotates round the earth, and then abandoned this contention in the nineteenth century, she can always appeal to the psychological truth that for millions of people the sun did revolve round the earth and that it was only in the nineteenth century that any major portion of mankind became sufficiently sure of the intellectual function to grasp the proofs of the earth's planetary nature. Unfortunately there is no "truth" unless there are people to understand it.

167   Presumably the leftward circumambulation of the square indicates that the squaring of the circle is a stage on the way to the unconscious, a point of transition leading to a goal lying as yet unformulated beyond it. It is one of those paths to the centre

---

50, 51.) The alchemists similarly understand the *rotundum* arising out of the square as the *oppidum* (city). See Aegidius de Vadis, "Dialogus inter naturam et filium Philosophiae," *Theatr. chem.*, II, p. 115.

of the non-ego which were also trodden by the medieval investi-gators when producing the *lapis*. The *Rosarium* says:[43] "Out of man and woman make a round circle and extract the quadrangle from this and from the quadrangle the triangle. Make a round circle and you will have the philosophers' stone" [44] (figs. 59, 60).

168   The modern intellect naturally regards all this as poppy-cock. But this estimate fails to get rid of the fact that such con-catenations of ideas do exist and that they even played an important part for many centuries. It is up to psychology to *un-derstand* these things, leaving the layman to rant about poppy-cock and obscurantism. Many of my critics who call themselves "scientific" behave exactly like the bishop who excommunicated the cockchafers for their unseemly proliferation.

169   Just as the stupas preserve relics of the Buddha in their innermost sanctuary, so in the interior of the Lamaic quad-rangle, and again in the Chinese earth-square, there is a Holy of Holies with its magical agent, the cosmic source of energy, be

[43] A quotation attributed to Pseudo-Aristotle ("Tractatus Aristotelis," *Theatr. chem.*, V, pp. 88off.), but not traceable.

[44] In the *Tractatus aureus . . . cum Scholiis Dominici Gnosii* (1610), p. 43, there is a drawing of the "secret square of the sages." In the centre of the square is a circle surrounded by rays of light. The scholium gives the following explanation: "Divide lapidem tuum in quatuor elementa . . . et coniunge in unum et totum habebis magisterium" (Reduce your stone to the four elements . . . and unite them into one and you will have the whole magistery)—a quotation from Pseudo-Aristotle. The circle in the centre is called "mediator, pacem faciens inter inim-icos sive elementa imo hic solus efficit quadraturam circuli" (the mediator, mak-ing peace between enemies, or [the four] elements; nay rather he alone effects the squaring of the circle).—Ibid., p. 44. The circumambulation has its parallel in the "circulatio spirituum sive distillatio circularis, hoc est exterius intro, in-terius foras: item inferius et superius, simul in uno circulo conveniant, neque amplius cognoscas, quid vel exterius, vel interius, inferius vel superius fuerit: sed omnia sint unum in uno circulo sive vase. Hoc enim vas est Pelecanus verus Philosophicus, nec alius est in toto mundo quaerendus." (. . . circulation of spirits or circular distillation, that is, the outside to the inside, the inside to the

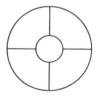

outside, likewise the lower and the upper; and when they meet together in one circle, you could no longer recognize what was outside or inside, or lower or upper; but all would be one thing in one circle or vessel. For this vessel is the true philo-sophical Pelican, and there is no other to be sought for in all the world.) This process is elucidated by the accompanying drawing. The little circle is the "inside," and the circle di-vided into four is the "outside": four rivers flowing in and out of the inner "ocean."—Ibid., pp. 262f.

61. The pearl as symbol of Ch'ien, surrounded by the four cosmic effluences (dragons).—Chinese bronze mirror of the T'ang Period (7th to 9th cent.)

it the god Shiva, the Buddha, a bodhisattva, or a great teacher. In China it is Ch'ien—heaven—with the four cosmic effluences radiating from it (fig. 61). And equally in the Western mandalas of medieval Christendom the deity is enthroned at the centre, often in the form of the triumphant Redeemer together with the four symbolical figures of the evangelists (fig. 62). The symbol in our dream presents the most violent contrast to these highly metaphysical ideas, for it is a gibbon, unquestionably an ape, that is to be reconstructed in the centre. Here we meet again the ape who first turned up in vision 22 of the first series (par. 117). In that dream he caused a panic, but he also brought about the helpful intervention of the intellect. Now he is to be "reconstructed," and this can only mean that the anthropoid—man as

62. Rectangular mandala with cross, the Lamb in the centre, surrounded by the four evangelists and the four rivers of Paradise. In the medallions, the four cardinal virtues.—Zwiefalten Abbey breviary (12th cent.)

an archaic fact—is to be put together again. Clearly the left-hand path does not lead upwards to the kingdom of the gods and eternal ideas, but down into natural history, into the bestial instinctive foundations of human existence. We are therefore dealing, to put it in classical language, with a Dionysian mystery.

170   The square corresponds to the *temenos* (fig. 31), where a drama is taking place—in this case a play of apes instead of satyrs. The inside of the "golden flower" is a "seeding-place" where the "diamond body" is produced. The synonymous term "the ancestral land" [45] may actually be a hint that this product is the result of integrating the ancestral stages.

171   The ancestral spirits play an important part in primitive rites of renewal. The aborigines of central Australia even identify themselves with their mythical ancestors of the *alcheringa* period, a sort of Homeric age. Similarly the Pueblo Indians of Taos, in preparation for their ritual dances, identify with the sun, whose sons they are. This atavistic identification with human and animal ancestors can be interpreted psychologically as an integration of the unconscious, a veritable bath of renewal in the life-source where one is once again a fish, unconscious as in sleep, intoxication, and death. Hence the sleep of incubation, the Dionysian orgy, and the ritual death in initiation. Naturally the proceedings always take place in some hallowed spot. We can easily translate these ideas into the concretism of Freudian theory: the *temenos* would then be the womb of the mother and the rite a regression to incest. But these are the neurotic misunderstandings of people who have remained partly infantile and who do not realize that such things have been practised since time immemorial by adults whose activities cannot possibly be explained as a mere regression to infantilism. Otherwise the highest and most important achievements of mankind would ultimately be nothing but the perverted wishes of children, and the word "childish" would have lost its *raison d'être*.

172   Since the philosophical side of alchemy was concerned with problems that are very closely related to those which interest the most modern psychology, it might perhaps be worth while to probe a little deeper into the dream motif of the ape that is to be reconstructed in the square. In the overwhelming majority of cases alchemy identifies its transforming substance with the

45 Wilhelm and Jung, *Secret of the Golden Flower* (1962 edn.), p. 22.

63. Hermes.—Greek vase painting (Hamilton Collection)

argentum vivum or Mercurius. Chemically this term denotes quicksilver, but philosophically it means the *spiritus vitae,* or even the world-soul (cf. fig. 91), so that Mercurius also takes on the significance of Hermes, god of revelation. (This question has been discussed in detail elsewhere.[46]) Hermes is associated with the idea of roundness and also of squareness, as can be seen particularly in Papyrus V (line 401) of the *Papyri Graecae Magicae,*[47] where he is named στρογγύλος καὶ τετράγωνος, "round and square." He is also called τετραγλώχιν, "quadrangular." He is in general connected with the number four; hence there is a Ἑρμῆς τετρακέφαλος, a "four-headed Hermes." [48] These attributes were known also in the Middle Ages, as the work of Cartari,[49] for instance, shows. He says:

Again, the square figures of Mercury [Hermes] [fig. 63], made up of nothing but a head and a virile member, signify that the Sun is the head of the world, and scatters the seed of all things; while the four sides of the square figure have the same significance as the four-stringed sistrum which was likewise attributed to Mercury, namely, the four quarters of the world or the four seasons of the year; or

46 Cf. Jung, "The Spirit Mercurius."
47 Ed. Preisendanz, *Papyri Graecae Magicae,* I, p. 195.
48 Cf. Bruchmann, *Epitheta deorum,* s.v.   49 *Les Images des dieux,* p. 403.

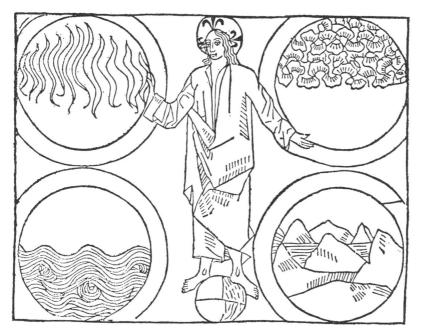

64. Christ as Anthropos, standing on the globe, flanked by the four elements.
—Glanville, *Le Propriétaire des choses* (1482)

again, that the two equinoxes and the two solstices make up between them the four parts of the whole zodiac.

173   It is easy to see why such qualities made Mercurius an eminently suitable symbol for the mysterious transforming substance of alchemy; for this is round and square, i.e., a totality consisting of four parts (four elements) Consequently the Gnostic quadripartite original man[50] (fig. 64) as well as Christ Pantokrator is an *imago lapidis* (fig. 65). Western alchemy is mainly of Egyptian origin, so let us first of all turn our attention to the Hellenistic figure of Hermes Trismegistus, who, while standing sponsor to the medieval Mercurius, derives ultimately from the ancient Egyptian Thoth (fig. 66). The attribute of Thoth was the baboon, or again he was represented outright as an ape.[51] This idea was visibly preserved all through the numberless editions of the Book of the Dead right down to the most

50 "Paracelsus as a Spiritual Phenomenon," pars. 168, 206ff.
51 Budge, *The Gods of the Egyptians,* I, pp. 21 and 404.

133

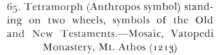

65. Tetramorph (Anthropos symbol) standing on two wheels, symbols of the Old and New Testaments.—Mosaic, Vatopedi Monastery, Mt. Athos (1213)

recent times. It is true that in the existing alchemical texts—which with few exceptions belong to the Christian era—the ancient connection between Thoth-Hermes and the ape has disappeared, but it still existed at the time of the Roman Empire. Mercurius, however, had several things in common with the devil—which we will not enter upon here—and so the ape once more crops up in the vicinity of Mercurius as the *simia Dei* (fig. 67). It is of the essence of the transforming substance to be on the one hand extremely common, even contemptible (this is expressed in the series of attributes it shares with the devil, such as serpent, dragon, raven, lion, basilisk, and eagle), but on the other hand to mean something of great value, not to say divine. For the transformation leads from the depths to the heights, from the bestially archaic and infantile to the mystical *homo maximus*.

174   The symbolism of the rites of renewal, if taken seriously, points far beyond the merely archaic and infantile to man's innate psychic disposition, which is the result and deposit of all ancestral life right down to the animal level—hence the ancestor

134

66. Ammon-Ra, the Egyptian spirit of the four elements.—Temple of Esneh,
Ptolemaic, from Champollion, *Panthéon égyptien*

67. Demon in the shape of a monkey.—"Speculum humanae salvationis"
(Cod. Lat. 511, Paris, 14th cent.)

and animal symbolism. The rites are attempts to abolish the separation between the conscious mind and the unconscious, the real source of life, and to bring about a reunion of the individual with the native soil of his inherited, instinctive make-up. Had these rites of renewal not yielded definite results they would not only have died out in prehistoric times but would never have arisen in the first place. The case before us proves that even if the conscious mind is miles away from the ancient conceptions of the rites of renewal, the unconscious still strives to bring them closer in dreams. It is true that without the qualities of autonomy and autarky there would be no consciousness at all, yet these qualities also spell the danger of isolation and stagnation since, by splitting off the unconscious, they bring about an unbearable alienation of instinct. Loss of instinct is the source of endless error and confusion.

175   Finally the fact that the dreamer is "not in the centre but to one side" is a striking indication of what will happen to his ego: it will no longer be able to claim the central place but must presumably be satisfied with the position of a satellite, or at least of a planet revolving round the sun. Clearly the important place in the centre is reserved for the gibbon about to be reconstructed. The gibbon belongs to the anthropoids and, on account of its kinship with man, is an appropriate symbol for that part of the psyche which goes down into the subhuman. Further, we have seen from the cynocephalus or dog-headed baboon associated with Thoth-Hermes (fig. 68), the highest among the apes known to the Egyptians, that its godlike affinities make it an equally appropriate symbol for that part of the unconscious which transcends the conscious level. The assumption that the human psyche possesses layers that lie *below* consciousness is not likely to arouse serious opposition. But that there could just as well be layers lying *above* consciousness seems to be a surmise which borders on a *crimen laesae majestatis humanae.* In my experience the conscious mind can claim only a relatively central position and must accept the fact that the unconscious psyche transcends and as it were surrounds it on all sides. Unconscious contents connect it *backwards* with physiological states on the one hand and archetypal data on the other. But it is extended *forwards* by intuitions which are determined partly by archetypes and partly by subliminal perceptions depending on the

relativity of time and space in the unconscious. I must leave it to the reader, after thorough consideration of this dream-series and the problems it opens up, to form his own judgment as to the possibility of such an hypothesis.

176   The following dream is given unabridged, in its original text:

17. DREAM:

All the houses have something theatrical about them, with stage scenery and decorations. The name of Bernard Shaw is mentioned. The play is supposed to take place in the distant future. There is a notice in English and German on one of the sets:

This is the universal Catholic Church.
It is the Church of the Lord.
All those who feel that they are the instruments of the Lord
may enter.

Under this is printed in smaller letters: "The Church was founded by Jesus and Paul"—like a firm advertising its long standing.
I say to my friend, "Come on, let's have a look at this." He replies, "I do not see why a lot of people have to get together when they're feeling religious." I answer, "As a Protestant you will never understand." A woman nods emphatic approval. Then I see a sort of proclamation on the wall of the church. It runs:

Soldiers!

When you feel you are under the power of the Lord, do not address him directly. The Lord cannot be reached by words. We also strongly advise you not to indulge in any discussions among yourselves concerning the attributes of the Lord. It is futile, for everything valuable and important is ineffable.

(Signed) Pope . . . (Name illegible)

Now we go in. The interior resembles a mosque, more particularly the Hagia Sophia: no seats—wonderful effect of space; no images, only framed texts decorating the walls (like the Koran texts in the Hagia Sophia). One of the texts reads "Do not flatter your benefactor." The woman who had agreed with me before bursts into tears and cries, "Then there's nothing

138

68. Thoth as cynocephalus.—From
tomb of Amen-her-khopshef, near
Der el-Medina, Luxor (XXth dy-
nasty, 12th cent. B.C.)

left!" I reply, "I find it quite right!" but she vanishes. At first I stand with a pillar in front of me and can see nothing. Then I change my position and see a crowd of people. I do not belong to them and stand alone. But they are quite distinct, so that I can see their faces. They all say in unison, "We confess that we are under the power of the Lord. The Kingdom of Heaven is within us." They repeat this three times with great solemnity. Then the organ starts to play and they sing a Bach fugue with chorale. But the original text is omitted; sometimes there is only a sort of coloratura singing, then the words are repeated: "Everything else is paper" (meaning that it does not make a living impression on me). When the chorale has faded away the gemüt-*lich part of the ceremony begins; it is almost like a students' party. The people are all cheerful and equable. We move about, converse, and greet one another, and wine (from an episcopal seminary) is served with other refreshments. The health of the Church is drunk and, as if to express everybody's pleasure at the increase in membership, a loudspeaker blares out a ragtime melody with the refrain, "Charles is also with us now." A priest explains to me: "These somewhat trivial amusements are officially approved and permitted. We must adapt a little to American methods. With a large crowd such as we have here this is inevitable. But we differ in principle from the American churches by our decidedly anti-ascetic tendency." Thereupon I awake with a feeling of great relief.*

177   Unfortunately I must refrain from commenting on this dream as a whole[52] and confine myself to our theme. The *temenos* has become a sacred building (in accordance with the hint given earlier). The proceedings are thus characterized as "religious." The grotesque-humorous side of the Dionysian mystery comes out in the so-called *gemütlich* part of the ceremony, where wine is served and a toast drunk to the health of the Church. An inscription on the floor of an Orphic-Dionysian shrine puts it very aptly: μόνον μὴ ὕδωρ (Only no water!).[53] The

---

[52] It was considered at length in my "Psychology and Religion." pp. 24ff.

[53] Orphic mosaic from Tramithia (Eisler, *Orpheus—the Fisher,* pp. 271f.). We can take this inscription as a joke without offending against the spirit of the ancient mysteries. (Cf. the frescoes in the Villa dei Misteri in Pompeii—Maiuri, *La Villa dei Misteri*—where drunkenness and ecstasy are not only closely related but actually one and the same thing.) But, since initiations have been connected

Dionysian relics in the Church, such as the fish and wine symbolism, the Damascus chalice, the seal-cylinder with the crucifix and the inscription ΟΡΦΕΟϹ ΒΑΚΚΙΚΟϹ,[54] and much else besides, can be mentioned only in passing.

178   The "anti-ascetic" tendency clearly marks the point of difference from the Christian Church, here defined as "American" (cf. commentary to dream 14 of the first series). America is the ideal home of the reasonable ideas of the practical intellect, which would like to put the world to rights by means of a "brain trust."[55] This view is in keeping with the modern formula "intellect = spirit," but it completely forgets the fact that "spirit" was never a human "activity," much less a "function." The movement to the left is thus confirmed as a withdrawal from the modern world of ideas and a regression to pre-Christian Dionysos worship, where "asceticism" in the Christian sense is unknown. At the same time the movement does not lead right out of the sacred spot but remains within it; in other words it does not lose its sacramental character. It does not simply fall into chaos and anarchy, it relates the Church directly to the Dionysian sanctuary just as the historical process did, though from the opposite direction. We could say that this regressive development faithfully retreads the path of history in order to reach the pre-Christian level. Hence it is not a relapse but a kind of systematic descent *ad inferos* (fig. 69), a psychological *nekyia*.[56]

179   I encountered something very similar in the dream of a clergyman who had a rather problematical attitude to his faith: *Coming into his church at night, he found that the whole wall of the choir had collapsed. The altar and ruins were overgrown with vines hanging full of grapes, and the moon was shining in through the gap.*

180   Again, a man who was much occupied with religious problems had the following dream: *An immense Gothic cathedral, almost completely dark. High Mass is being celebrated. Suddenly the whole wall of the aisle collapses. Blinding sunlight bursts into the interior together with a large herd of bulls and*

with healing since their earliest days, the advice may possibly be a warning against water drinking, for it is well known that the drinking water in southern regions is the mother of dysentery and typhoid fever.
54 Eisler, *Orpheus—the Fisher.*   55 This is roughly the opinion of the dreamer.
56 Cf. figs. 170, 171, 172, 174, 176, 177.

69. Dante and Virgil on their journey to the underworld.—Illumination for the
Inferno, Canto XVII, Codex Urbanus Latinus 365 (15th cent.)

cows. This setting is evidently more Mithraic, but Mithras is
associated with the early Church in much the same way Dionysos
is.

181   Interestingly enough, the church in our dream is a syn-
cretistic building, for the Hagia Sophia is a very ancient Christian church which, however, served as a mosque until quite recently. It therefore fits in very well with the purpose of the
dream: to attempt a combination of Christian and Dionysian
religious ideas. Evidently this is to come about without the one
excluding the other, without any values being destroyed. This is
extremely important, since the reconstruction of the "gibbon"
is to take place in the sacred precincts. Such a sacrilege might
easily lead to the dangerous supposition that the leftward movement is a *diabolica fraus* and the gibbon the devil—for the devil
is in fact regarded as the "ape of God." The leftward movement
would then be a perversion of divine truth for the purpose of
setting up "His Black Majesty" in place of God. But the uncon-

142

scious has no such blasphemous intentions; it is only trying to restore the lost Dionysos who is somehow lacking in modern man (*pace* Nietzsche!) to the world of religion. At the end of vision 22 (par. 117), where the ape first appears, it was said that "everything must be ruled by the light," and everything, we might add, includes the Lord of Darkness with his horns and cloven hoof—actually a Dionysian corybant who has rather unexpectedly risen to the rank of Prince.

182   The Dionysian element has to do with emotions and affects which have found no suitable religious outlets in the predominantly Apollonian cult and ethos of Christianity. The medieval carnivals and *jeux de paume* in the Church were abolished relatively early; consequently the carnival became secularized and with it divine intoxication vanished from the sacred precincts. Mourning, earnestness, severity, and well-tempered spiritual joy remained. But intoxication, that most direct and dangerous form of possession, turned away from the gods and enveloped the human world with its exuberance and pathos. The pagan religions met this danger by giving drunken ecstasy a place within their cult. Heraclitus doubtless saw what was at the back of it when he said, "But Hades is that same Dionysos in whose honour they go mad and keep the feast of the wine-vat." For this very reason orgies were granted religious license, so as to exorcise the danger that threatened from Hades. Our solution, however, has served to throw the gates of hell wide open.

18. DREAM:

183   *A square space with complicated ceremonies going on in it, the purpose of which is to transform animals into men. Two snakes, moving in opposite directions, have to be got rid of at once. Some animals are there, e.g., foxes and dogs. The people walk round the square and must let themselves be bitten in the calf by these animals at each of the four corners (cf. fig. 118). If they run away all is lost. Now the higher animals come on the scene—bulls and ibexes. Four snakes glide into the four corners. Then the congregation files out. Two sacrificial priests carry in a huge reptile and with this they touch the forehead of a shapeless animal lump or life-mass. Out of it there instantly rises a human head, transfigured. A voice proclaims: "These are attempts at being."*

70. Pagan rites of transformation in the Middle Ages, with serpents.—
Gnostic design

184   One might almost say that the dream goes on with the "explanation" of what is happening in the square space. Animals
are to be changed into men; a "shapeless life-mass" is to be
turned into a transfigured (illuminated) human head by magic
contact with a reptile. The animal lump or life-mass stands for
the mass of the inherited unconscious which is to be united with
consciousness. This is brought about by the ceremonial use of
a reptile, presumably a snake. The idea of transformation and
renewal by means of a serpent is a well-substantiated archetype
(fig. 70). It is the healing serpent, representing the god (cf. figs.
203, 204). It is reported of the mysteries of Sabazius: "Aureus
coluber in sinum demittitur consecratis et eximitur rursus ab in-
ferioribus partibus atque imis" (A golden snake is let down into
the lap of the initiated and taken away again from the lower
parts).[57] Among the Ophites, Christ was the serpent. Probably
the most significant development of serpent symbolism as regards renewal of personality is to be found in Kundalini yoga.[58]
The shepherd's experience with the snake in Nietzsche's *Zarathustra* would accordingly be a fatal omen (and not the only one
of its kind—cf. the prophecy at the death of the rope-dancer).

185   The "shapeless life-mass" immediately recalls the ideas of the
alchemical "chaos," [59] the *massa* or *materia informis* or *confusa*

57 Arnobius, *Adversus gentes*, V, 21 (Migne, *P.L.*, vol. 5, col. 1125). For similar
practices during the Middle Ages, cf. Hammer-Purgstall, *Mémoire sur deux coffrets gnostiques du moyen âge*. See fig. 70.
58 Avalon, *The Serpent Power*; Woodroffe, *Shakti and Shakta*.
59 The alchemists refer to Lactantius, *Opera*, I, p. 14, 20: "a chao, quod est
rudis inordinataeque materiae confusa congeries" (from the chaos, which is a
confused assortment of crude disordered matter).

71. Creation of Adam from the clay of the *prima materia.*—Schedel, *Das Buch der Chroniken* (1493)

which has contained the divine seeds of life ever since the Creation. According to a midrashic view, Adam was created in much the same way: in the first hour God collected the dust, in the second made a shapeless mass out of it, in the third fashioned the limbs, and so on[60] (fig. 71).

186 But if the life-mass is to be transformed a *circumambulatio* is necessary, i.e., exclusive concentration on the centre, the place of creative change. During this process one is "bitten" by animals; in other words, we have to expose ourselves to the animal impulses of the unconscious without identifying with them and without "running away"; for flight from the unconscious would defeat the purpose of the whole proceeding. We must hold our ground, which means here that the process initiated by the

[60] Dreyfuss, *Adam und Eva,* quoted by Reitzenstein, *Poimandres,* p. 258.

dreamer's self-observation must be experienced in all its ramifications and then articulated with consciousness to the best of his understanding. This often entails an almost unbearable tension because of the utter incommensurability between conscious life and the unconscious process, which can be experienced only in the innermost soul and cannot touch the visible surface of life at any point. The principle of conscious life is: "Nihil est in intellectu, quod non prius fuerit in sensu." But the principle of the unconscious is the autonomy of the psyche itself, reflecting in the play of its images not the world but *itself,* even though it utilizes the illustrative possibilities offered by the sensible world in order to make its images clear. The sensory datum, however, is not the *causa efficiens* of this; rather, it is autonomously selected and exploited by the psyche, with the result that the rationality of the cosmos is constantly being violated in the most distressing manner. But the sensible world has an equally devastating effect on the deeper psychic processes when it breaks into them as a *causa efficiens.* If reason is not to be outraged on the one hand and the creative play of images not violently suppressed on the other, a circumspect and farsighted synthetic procedure is required in order to accomplish the paradoxical union of irreconcilables (fig. 72). Hence the alchemical parallels in our dreams.

187   The focusing of attention on the centre demanded in this dream and the warning about "running away" have clear parallels in the *opus alchymicum:* the need to concentrate on the work and to meditate upon it is stressed again and again. The tendency to run away, however, is attributed not to the operator but to the transforming substance. Mercurius is evasive and is labelled *servus* (servant) or *cervus fugitivus* (fugitive stag). The vessel must be well sealed so that what is within may not escape. Eirenaeus Philalethes[61] says of this *servus:* "You must be very wary how you lead him, for if he can find an opportunity he will give you the slip, and leave you to a world of misfortune." [62] It did not occur to these philosophers that they were chasing a projection, and that the more they attributed to the substance the further away they were getting from the psychological source of

[61] Pseudonymous author ("peaceable lover of truth") who lived in England at the beginning of the 17th century.
[62] Philalethes, *Ripley Reviv'd,* p. 100.

146

72. The "union of irreconcilables": marriage of water and fire. The
two figures each have four hands to symbolize their many different
capabilities.—After an Indian painting

their expectations. From the difference between the material in
this dream and its medieval predecessors we can measure the
psychological advance: the running away is now clearly apparent
as a characteristic of the dreamer, i.e., it is no longer projected
into the unknown substance. Running away thus becomes a
moral question. This aspect was recognized by the alchemists in
so far as they emphasized the need for a special religious devotion at their work, though one cannot altogether clear them of
the suspicion of having used their prayers and pious exercises for
the purpose of forcing a miracle—there are even some who
aspired to have the Holy Ghost as their familiar! [63] But, to do

[63] [Cf. *Mysterium Coniunctionis*, p. 288, n. 116.—EDITORS.]

them justice, one should not overlook the fact that there is more than a little evidence in the literature that they realized it was a matter of their own transformation. For instance, Gerhard Dorn exclaims, "Transmutemini in vivos lapides philosophicos!" (Transform yourselves into living philosophical stones!)

188   Hardly have conscious and unconscious touched when they fly asunder on account of their mutual antagonism. Hence, right at the beginning of the dream, the snakes that are making off in opposite directions have to be removed; i.e., the conflict between conscious and unconscious is at once resolutely stopped and the conscious mind is forced to stand the tension by means of the *circumambulatio*. The magic circle thus traced will also prevent the unconscious from breaking out again, for such an eruption would be equivalent to psychosis. "Nonnulli perierunt in opere nostro": "Not a few have perished in our work," we can say with the author of the *Rosarium*. The dream shows that the difficult operation of thinking in paradoxes—a feat possible only to the superior intellect—has succeeded. The snakes no longer run away but settle themselves in the four corners, and the process of transformation or integration sets to work. The "transfiguration" and illumination, the conscious recognition of the centre, has been attained, or at least anticipated, in the dream. This potential achievement—if it can be maintained, i.e., if the conscious mind does not lose touch with the centre again[64]— means a renewal of personality. Since it is a subjective state whose reality cannot be validated by any external criterion, any further attempt to describe and explain it is doomed to failure, for only those who have had this experience are in a position to understand and attest its reality. "Happiness," for example, is such a noteworthy reality that there is nobody who does not long for it, and yet there is not a single objective criterion which would prove beyond all doubt that this condition necessarily exists. As so often with the most important things, we have to make do with a subjective judgment.

189   The arrangement of the snakes in the four corners is indicative of an order in the unconscious. It is as if we were confronted with a pre-existent ground plan, a kind of Pythagorean

64 Cf. the commentary to dream 10, second series, par. 141: "And, being chained to the arms and breast of my mother, and to her substance, I cause my substance to hold together and rest." ("Tractatus aureus," ch. IV.)

73. The deliverance of man from the power of the dragon.—Codex Palatinus
Latinus 412 (15th cent.)

tetraktys. I have very frequently observed the number four in this connection. It probably explains the universal incidence and magical significance of the cross or of the circle divided into four. In the present case the point seems to be to capture and regulate the animal instincts so as to exorcise the danger of falling into unconsciousness. This may well be the empirical basis of the cross as that which vanquishes the powers of darkness (fig. 73).

190   In this dream the unconscious has managed to stage a powerful advance by thrusting its contents dangerously near to the conscious sphere. The dreamer appears to be deeply entangled in the mysterious synthetic ceremony and will unfailingly carry a lasting memory of the dream into his conscious life. Experience shows that this results in a serious conflict for the conscious mind, because it is not always either willing or able to put forth the extraordinary intellectual and moral effort needed to take a paradox seriously. Nothing is so jealous as a truth.

191   As a glance at the history of the medieval mind will show, our whole modern mentality has been moulded by Christianity. (This has nothing to do with whether we believe the truths of Christianity or not.) Consequently the reconstruction of the ape in the sacred precincts as proposed by the dream comes as such a shock that the majority of people will seek refuge in blank incomprehension. Others will heedlessly ignore the abysmal depths of the Dionysian mystery and will welcome the rational Darwinian core of the dream as a safeguard against mystic exaltation. Only a very few will feel the collision of the two worlds and realize what it is all about. Yet the dream says plainly enough that in the place where, according to tradition, the deity dwells, the ape is to appear. This substitution is almost as bad as a Black Mass.

192   In Eastern symbolism the square—signifying the earth in China, the *padma* or lotus in India—has the character of the *yoni:* femininity. A man's unconscious is likewise feminine and is personified by the anima.[65] The anima also stands for the "in-

---

65 The idea of the anima as I define it is by no means a novelty but an archetype which we meet in the most diverse places. It was also known in alchemy, as the following scholium proves ("Tractatus aureus," in *Bibl. chem. curiosa,* I, p. 417): "Quemadmodum in sole ambulantis corpus continuo sequitur umbra . . . sic hermaphroditus noster Adamicus, quamvis in forma masculi appareat semper

74. Heaven fertilizing Earth and begetting mankind.—Thenaud, "Traité de la cabale" (MS., 16th cent.)

ferior" function[66] and for that reason frequently has a shady character; in fact she sometimes stands for evil itself. She is as a rule the *fourth* person (cf. dreams 10, 11, 15; pars. 136, 147, 162). She is the dark and dreaded maternal womb (fig. 74), which is of an essentially ambivalent nature. The Christian deity is one in three persons. The fourth person in the heavenly drama is undoubtedly the devil. In the more harmless psychological version he is merely the inferior function. On a moral

---

tamen in corpore occultatam Evam sive foeminam suam secum circumfert" (As the shadow continually follows the body of one who walks in the sun, so our hermaphroditic Adam, though he appears in the form of a male, nevertheless always carries about with him Eve, or his wife, hidden in his body).

[66] Cf. Jung, *Psychological Types*, Def. 30.

valuation he is a man's sin, a function belonging to him and presumably masculine. The feminine element in the deity is kept very dark, the interpretation of the Holy Ghost as Sophia being considered heretical. Hence the Christian metaphysical drama, the "Prologue in Heaven," has only masculine actors, a point it shares with many of the ancient mysteries. But the feminine element must obviously be somewhere—so it is presumably to be found in the dark. At any rate that is where the ancient Chinese philosophers located it: in the *yin*.[67] Although man and woman unite they nevertheless represent irreconcilable opposites which, when activated, degenerate into deadly hostility. This primordial pair of opposites symbolizes every conceivable pair of opposites that may occur: hot and cold, light and dark, north and south, dry and damp, good and bad, conscious and unconscious. In the psychology of the functions there are two conscious and therefore masculine functions, the differentiated function and its auxiliary, which are represented in dreams by, say, father and son, whereas the unconscious functions appear as mother and daughter. Since the conflict between the two auxiliary functions is not nearly as great as that between the differentiated and the inferior function, it is possible for the third function—that is, the unconscious auxiliary one—to be raised to consciousness and thus made masculine. It will, however, bring with it traces of its contamination with the inferior function, thus acting as a kind of link with the darkness of the unconscious. It was in keeping with this psychological fact that the Holy Ghost should be heretically interpreted as Sophia, for he was the mediator of birth in the flesh, who enabled the deity to shine forth in the darkness of the world. No doubt it was this association that caused the Holy Ghost to be suspected of femininity, for Mary was the dark earth of the field—"illa terra virgo nondum pluviis irrigata" (that virgin earth not yet watered by the rains), as Tertullian called her.[68]

¹⁹³   The fourth function is contaminated with the unconscious and, on being made conscious, drags the whole of the uncon-

---

67 "Tractatus aureus," *Ars chemica,* p. 12: "Verum masculus est coelum foeminae et foemina terra masculi" (The male is the heaven of the female, and the female is the earth of the male).

68 *Adversus Judaeos,* 13 (Migne, *P.L.,* vol. 2, col. 655).

scious with it. We must then come to terms with the unconscious and try to bring about a synthesis of opposites.[69] At first a violent conflict breaks out, such as any reasonable man would experience when it became evident that he had to swallow a lot of absurd superstitions. Everything in him would rise up in revolt and he would defend himself desperately against what looked to him like murderous nonsense. This situation explains the following dreams.

19. DREAM:

194 *Ferocious war between two peoples.*

195 This dream depicts the conflict. The conscious mind is defending its position and trying to suppress the unconscious. The first result of this is the expulsion of the fourth function, but, since it is contaminated with the third, there is a danger of the latter disappearing as well. Things would then return to the state that preceded the present one, when only two functions were conscious and the other two unconscious.

20. DREAM:

196 *There are two boys in a cave. A third falls in as if through a pipe.*

197 The cave represents the darkness and seclusion of the unconscious; the two boys correspond to the two unconscious functions. Theoretically the third must be the auxiliary function, which would indicate that the conscious mind had become completely absorbed in the differentiated function. The odds now stand 1 : 3, greatly in favour of the unconscious. We may therefore expect a new advance on its part and a return to its former position. The "boys" are an allusion to the dwarf motif (fig. 77), of which more later.

---

69 Alchemy regarded this synthesis as one of its chief tasks. The *Turba philosophorum* (ed. Ruska, p. 26) says: "Coniungite ergo masculinum servi rubei filium suae odoriferae uxori et iuncti artem gignunt" (Join therefore the male son of the red slave to his sweet-scented wife, and joined together they will generate the Art). This synthesis of opposites was often represented as a brother-and-sister incest, which version undoubtedly goes back to the "Visio Arislei," *Art. aurif.*, I (see fig. 167), where the cohabitation of Thabritius and Beya, the children of the *Rex marinus*, is described (see infra, pars. 434ff.).

21. DREAM:

198   *A large transparent sphere containing many little spheres.*
A green plant is growing out of the top.

199   The sphere is a whole that embraces all its contents; life
which has been brought to a standstill by useless struggle becomes possible again. In Kundalini yoga the "green womb" is
a name for Ishvara (Shiva) emerging from his latent condition.

75. Trimurti picture. The triangle symbolizes the tendency of the universe to
converge towards the point of unity. The
tortoise represents Vishnu; the lotus growing out of the skull between two flames,
Shiva. The shining sun of Brahma forms
the background. The whole picture corresponds to the alchemical *opus*, the tortoise symbolizing the *massa confusa*, the
skull the *vas* of transformation, and the
flower the "self" or wholeness.—After an
Indian painting

22. DREAM:

200   *The dreamer is in an American hotel. He goes up in the lift*
to about the third or fourth floor. He has to wait there with a lot
of other people. A friend (an actual person) is also there and
says that the dreamer should not have kept the dark unknown
woman waiting so long below, since he had put her in his (the
dreamer's) charge. The friend now gives him an unsealed note
for the dark woman, on which is written: "Salvation does not
come from refusing to take part or from running away. Nor does
it come from just drifting. Salvation comes from complete sur-
render, with one's eyes always turned to the centre." On the mar-
gin of the note there is a drawing: a wheel or wreath with eight
spokes. Then a lift-boy appears and says that the dreamer's room
is on the eighth floor. He goes on up in the lift, this time to the
seventh or eighth floor. An unknown red-haired man, standing
there, greets him in a friendly way. Then the scene changes.
There is said to be a revolution in Switzerland: the military
party is making propaganda for "completely throttling the left."
The objection that the left is weak enough anyway is met by the

answer that this is just why it ought to be throttled completely. Soldiers in old-fashioned uniforms now appear, who all resemble the red-haired man. They load their guns with ramrods, stand in a circle, and prepare to shoot at the centre. But in the end they do not shoot and seem to march away. The dreamer wakes up in terror.

201 The tendency to re-establish a state of wholeness—already indicated in the foregoing dream—once more comes up against a consciousness with a totally different orientation. It is therefore appropriate that the dream should have an American background. The lift is going up, as is right and proper when something is coming "up" from the "sub-"conscious. What is coming up is the unconscious content, namely the mandala characterized by the number four (cf. figs. 61, 62). Therefore the lift should rise to the fourth floor; but, as the fourth function is taboo, it only rises to "about the third or fourth." This happens not to the dreamer alone but to many others as well, who must all wait like him until the fourth function can be accepted. A good friend then calls his attention to the fact that he should not have kept the dark woman, i.e., the anima who stands for the tabooed function, waiting "below," i.e., in the unconscious, which was just the reason why the dreamer himself had to wait upstairs with the others. It is in fact not merely an individual but a collective problem, for the animation of the unconscious which has become so noticeable in recent times has, as Schiller foresaw, raised questions which the nineteenth century never even dreamed of. Nietzsche in his *Zarathustra* decided to reject the "snake" and the "ugliest man," thus exposing himself to an heroic cramp of consciousness which led, logically enough, to the collapse foretold in the same book.

202 The advice given in the note is as profound as it is to the point, so that there is really nothing to add. After it has been more or less accepted by the dreamer the ascent can be resumed. We must take it that the problem of the fourth function was accepted, at least broadly, for the dreamer now reaches the seventh or eighth floor, which means that the fourth function is no longer represented by a quarter but by an eighth, and is apparently reduced by a half.

203 Curiously enough, this hesitation before the last step to wholeness seems also to play a part in *Faust II,* where, in the

Cabiri scene, "resplendent mermaids" come from over the water:[70]

NEREIDS AND TRITONS:	Bear we, on the waters riding, That which brings you all glad tiding. In Chelone's giant shield Gleams a form severe revealed: These are gods that we are bringing; Hail them, you high anthems singing.
SIRENS:	Little in length, Mighty in strength! Time-honoured gods Of shipwreck and floods.
NEREIDS AND TRITONS:	Great Cabiri do we bear, That our feast be friendly fair: Where their sacred powers preside Neptune's rage is pacified.

76. The tortoise: an alchemical instrument.
—Porta, *De distillationibus* (1609)

A "form severe" is brought by "mermaids," feminine figures (cf. figs. 10, 11, 12, 157) who represent as it were the sea and the waves of the unconscious. The word "severe" reminds us of "severe" architectural or geometrical forms which illustrate a definite idea without any romantic (feeling-toned) trimmings.

[70] [Based on the translation by Philip Wayne (*Faust, Part Two*, pp. 145f.). Slight modifications have been necessary to accommodate his version to Jung's commentary.—TRANS.]

It "gleams" from the shell of a tortoise[71] (fig. 76), which, primitive and cold-blooded like the snake, symbolizes the instinctual side of the unconscious. The "image" is somehow identical with the unseen, creative dwarf-gods (fig. 77), hooded and cloaked

77. Telesphorus, one of the Cabiri, the *familiaris* of Aesculapius: (*a*) Bronze figure from Roman Gaul; (*b*) Marble statuette from Austria.

manikins who are kept hidden in the dark *cista,* but who also appear on the seashore as little figures about a foot high, where, as kinsmen of the unconscious, they protect navigation, i.e., the venture into darkness and uncertainty. In the form of the Dactyls they are also the gods of invention, small and apparently insignificant like the impulses of the unconscious but endowed with the same mighty power. (*El gabir* is "the great, the mighty one.")

NEREIDS AND   Three have followed where we led,
TRITONS: But the fourth refused to call;
                He the rightful seer, he said,
                His to think for one and all.

---

[71] The *testudo* (tortoise) is an alchemical instrument, a shallow bowl with which the cooking-vessel was covered on the fire. See Rhenanus, *Solis e puteo emergentis,* p. 40.

SIRENS:	A god may count it sport
	To set a god at naught.
	Honour the grace they bring,
	And fear their threatening.

204   It is characteristic of Goethe's feeling-toned nature that the fourth should be the thinker. If the supreme principle is "feeling is all," then thinking has to play an unfavourable role and be submerged. *Faust I* portrays this development. Since Goethe acted as his own model, thinking became the fourth (taboo) function. Because of its contamination with the unconscious it takes on the grotesque form of the Cabiri, for the Cabiri, as dwarfs, are chthonic gods and misshapen accordingly. ("I call them pot-bellied freaks of common clay.") They thus stand in grotesque contrast to the heavenly gods and poke fun at them (cf. the "ape of God"). The Nereids and Tritons sing:

Seven there should really be.

SIRENS:	Where, then, stay the other three?
NEREIDS AND TRITONS:	That we know not. You had best
	On Olympus make your quest.
	There an eighth may yet be sought
	Though none other gave him thought.
	Well inclined to us in grace,
	Not all perfect yet their race.
	Beings there beyond compare,
	Yearning, unexplainable,
	Press with hunger's pang to share
	In the unattainable.

205   We learn that there are "really" seven of them; but again there is some difficulty with the eighth as there was before with the fourth. Similarly, in contradiction to the previous emphasis placed on their lowly origin in the dark, it now appears that the Cabiri are actually to be found on Olympus; for they are eternally striving from the depths to the heights and are therefore always to be found both below *and* above. The "severe image" is obviously an unconscious content that struggles towards the light. It seeks, and itself is, what I have elsewhere called "the treasure hard to attain." [72] This hypothesis is immediately confirmed:

72 Jung, *Symbols of Transformation,* index, s.v.

SIRENS: Fame is dimmed of ancient time,
           Honour droops in men of old;
           Though they have the Fleece of Gold,
           Ye have the Cabiri.

206   The Golden Fleece is the coveted goal of the argosy, the perilous quest that is one of the numerous synonyms for attaining the unattainable. Thales makes this wise remark about it:

> That is indeed what men most seek on earth:
> 'Tis rust alone that gives the coin its worth!

207   The unconscious is always the fly in the ointment, the skeleton in the cupboard of perfection, the painful lie given to all idealistic pronouncements, the earthliness that clings to our human nature and sadly clouds the crystal clarity we long for. In the alchemical view rust, like verdigris, is the metal's sickness. But at the same time this leprosy is the *vera prima materia*, the basis for the preparation of the philosophical gold. The *Rosarium* says:

> Our gold is not the common gold. But thou hast inquired concerning the greenness [*viriditas*, presumably verdigris], deeming the bronze to be a leprous body on account of the greenness it hath upon it. Therefore I say unto thee that whatever is perfect in the bronze is that greenness only, because that greenness is straightway changed by our magistery into our most true gold.[73]

208   The paradoxical remark of Thales that the rust alone gives the coin its true value is a kind of alchemical quip, which at bottom only says that there is no light without shadow and no psychic wholeness without imperfection. To round itself out, life calls not for perfection but for completeness; and for this the "thorn in the flesh" is needed, the suffering of defects without which there is no progress and no ascent.

209   The problem of three and four, seven and eight, which Goethe has tackled here was a great puzzle to alchemy and goes back historically to the texts ascribed to Christianos.[74] In the

---

[73] *Art. aurif.*, II, p. 220: a quotation from Senior. *Viriditas* is occasionally called *azoth*, which is one of the numerous synonyms for the stone.

[74] According to Berthelot (*Origines de l'alchimie*, p. 100), the anonymous author called Christianos was a contemporary of Stephanos of Alexandria, and must therefore have lived about the beginning of the 7th century.

78. Maria Prophetissa. In the background, the union (*coniunctio*) of upper and
lower.—Maier, *Symbola aureae mensae* (1617)

treatise on the production of the "mythical water" it is said:
"Therefore the Hebrew prophetess cried without restraint, 'One
becomes two, two becomes three, and out of the third comes
the One as the fourth.' " [75] In alchemical literature this prophetess is taken to be Maria Prophetissa[76] (fig. 78), also called
the Jewess, sister of Moses, or the Copt, and it is not unlikely
that she is connected with the Maria of Gnostic tradition. Epiphanius testifies to the existence of writings by this Maria,
namely the "Interrogationes magnae" and "Interrogationes
parvae," said to describe a vision of how Christ, on a mountain,
caused a woman to come forth from his side and how he mingled himself with her.[77] It is probably no accident that the trea-

75 Berthelot, *Alchimistes grecs*, VI, v, 6. The almost bestial κραυγάζειν (shriek)
points to an ecstatic condition.
76 A treatise (of Arabic origin?) is ascribed to her under the title "Practica Mariae
Prophetissae in artem alchemicam," *Art. aurif.*, I, pp. 319ff.
77 *Panarium*, XXVI. Concerning further possible connections with Mariamne and
with the Mary Magdalene of the *Pistis Sophia*, cf. Leisegang, *Die Gnosis*, pp. 113f.,
and Schmidt, "Gnostische Schriften," pp. 596ff. [On *Panarium*, cf. *Aion*, pars.
314ff.]

tise of Maria (see n. 76) deals with the theme of the *matrimonium alchymicum* in a dialogue with the philosopher Aros,[78] from which comes the saying, often repeated later: "Marry gum with gum in true marriage." [79] Originally it was "gum arabic," and it is used here as a secret name for the transforming substance, on account of its adhesive quality. Thus Khunrath[80] declares that the "red" gum is the "resin of the wise"—a synonym for the transforming substance. This substance, as the life force (*vis animans*), is likened by another commentator to the "glue of the world" (*glutinum mundi*), which is the medium between mind and body and the union of both.[81] The old treatise "Consilium coniugii" explains that the "philosophical man" consists of the "four natures of the stone." Of these three are earthy or in the earth, but "the fourth nature is the water of the stone, namely the viscous gold which is called red gum and with which the three earthy natures are tinted." [82] We learn here that gum is the critical fourth nature: it is duplex, i.e., masculine and feminine, and at the same time the one and only *aqua mercurialis*. So the union of the two is a kind of self-fertilization, a characteristic always ascribed to the mercurial dragon.[83] From these hints it can easily be seen who the philosophical man is: he is the androgynous original man or Anthropos of Gnosticism[84] (cf. figs. 64, 82, 117, 195), whose parallel in India is *purusha*. Of him the Brihadaranyaka Upanishad says: "He was as large as a man and woman embracing. He divided his self

---

[78] Aros = Horos. Ἴσις προφῆτις τῷ υἱῷ αὐτῆς (Berthelot, *Alchimistes grecs*, I, xiii) may be an earlier version of the Maria dialogue. Isis and Maria were easy to confuse.
[79] "Matrimonifica gummi cum gummi vero matrimonio."—*Art. aurif.*, I, p. 320.
[80] *Von hylealischen Chaos*, pp. 239f.
[81] "Aphorismi Basiliani," *Theatr. chem.*, IV, p. 368.
[82] *Ars chemica*, pp. 247, 255.
[83] Arnaldus de Villanova ("Carmen," *Theatr. chem.*, IV, p. 614) has summed up the quintessence of Maria's treatise very aptly in the following verses:

> "Maria mira sonat breviter, quod talia tonat.
> Gummis cum binis fugitivum figit in imis. . . .
> Filia Plutonis consortia iungit amoris,
> Gaudet in assata sata per tria sociata."

(Maria utters brief wonders because such are the things that she thunders.
She fixes what runs to the bottom with double-strong gums. . . .
This daughter of Pluto unites love's affinities,
Delighting in everything sown, roasted, assembled by threes.)
[84] Cf. my remarks on Paracelsus' "Adech" in "Paracelsus as a Spiritual Phenomenon," pars. 168, 203ff.

[Atman] in two, and thence arose husband and wife. He united himself with her and men were born," etc.[85] The common origin of these ideas lies in the primitive notion of the bisexual original man.

210   The fourth nature—to return to the text of the "Consilium coniugii"—leads straight to the Anthropos idea that stands for man's wholeness, that is, the conception of a unitary being who existed before man and at the same time represents man's goal. The one joins the three as the fourth and thus produces the synthesis of the four in a unity[86] (fig. 196). We seem to be dealing with much the same thing in the case of seven and eight, though this motif occurs much less frequently in the literature. It is, however, to be found in Paracelsus' *Ein ander Erklärung der gantzen Astronomie,*[87] to which Goethe had access. "One is powerful, Six are subjects, the Eighth is also powerful"—and somewhat more so than the first. One is the king, the six are his servants and his son; so here we have King Sol and the six planets or metallic homunculi as depicted in the *Pretiosa margarita novella* of Petrus Bonus (Lacinius edition, 1546)[88] (fig. 79). As a matter of fact the eighth does not appear in this text; Paracelsus seems to have invented it himself. But since the eighth is even more "powerful" than the first, the crown is presumably bestowed on him. In *Faust II,* the eighth who dwells on Olympus is a direct reference to the Paracelsan text in so far as this describes the "astrology of Olympus" (that is, the structure of the *corpus astrale*).[89]

211   Returning now to our dream, we find at the critical point— the seventh or eighth floor—the red-haired man, a synonym for

[85] 1. 4. 3. (Cf. Max Müller, *The Upanishads,* II, pp. 85–86.)

[86] There is a rather different formulation in Distinction XIV of the "Allegoriae sapientum" (*Theatr. chem.,* V, p. 86): "Unum et est duo, et duo et sunt tria, et tria et sunt quatuor, et quatuor et sunt tria, et tria et sunt duo, et duo et sunt unum" (One, and it is two; and two, and it is three; and three, and it is four; and four, and it is three; and three, and it is two; and two, and it is one). This evidently represents the quartering (tetrameria) of the one and the synthesis of the four in one.

[87] In Sudhoff/Matthiessen, XII.

[88] Folio VIII[v]. The *aqua mercurialis* is characterized here as the "bright and clear fluid of Bacchus." The king and the son are united in the operation, so that at the end only the renewed king and his five servants are left. The *senarius* (sixth) plays a modest role only in later alchemy.

[89] Paracelsus, *Opera,* ed. Huser, I, p. 503.

79. King Sol with his six planet-sons.—Bonus, *Pretiosa margarita novella* (1546)

the "man with the pointed beard" and hence for the shrewd
Mephisto, who magically changes the scene because he is concerned with something that Faust himself never saw: the "severe
image," symbolizing the supreme treasure, the immortal self.[90]
He changes himself into the soldiers, representatives of uniformity, of collective opinion, which is naturally dead against
tolerating anything "unsuitable." For collective opinion the
numbers three and seven are, on the highest authority, sacred;
but four and eight are the very devil, something inferior—"common clay"—that in the stern judgment of bonzes of every hue
has no right to exist. The "left" is to be "completely throttled,"
meaning the unconscious and all the "sinister" things that come
from it. An antiquated view, no doubt, and one that uses antiquated methods; but even muzzle-loaders can hit the mark. For
reasons unknown, i.e., not stated in the dream, the destructive
attack on the "centre"—to which, according to the advice in the
note, "one's eyes must always be turned"—peters out. In the
drawing on the margin of the note this centre is portrayed as a
wheel with eight spokes (cf. fig. 80).

[90] The angels bear Faust's "immortal part" to heaven, after cheating the devil
of it. This, in the original version, is "Faust's entelechy."

80. Mercurius turning the eight-spoked wheel which symbolizes the process. In one hand he holds the *telum passionis.*—"Speculum veritatis" (MS., 17th cent.)

23. DREAM:

212   *In the square space. The dreamer is sitting opposite the unknown woman whose portrait he is supposed to be drawing. What he draws, however, is not a face but three-leaved clovers or distorted crosses in four different colours: red, yellow, green, and blue.*

213   In connection with this dream the dreamer spontaneously drew a circle with quarters tinted in the above colours. It was a wheel with eight spokes. In the middle there was a four-petalled blue flower. A great many drawings now followed at short intervals, all dealing with the curious structure of the "centre," and arising from the dreamer's need to discover a configuration that adequately expresses the nature of this centre. The drawings were based partly on visual impressions, partly on intuitive perceptions, and partly on dreams.

214   It is to be noted that the wheel is a favourite symbol in alchemy for the circulating process, the *circulatio.* By this is meant firstly the *ascensus* and *descensus,* for instance the ascending and descending birds symbolizing the precipitation of vapours,[91] and secondly the rotation of the universe as a model for the work,

91 Cf. the movements of the transforming substance in the "Tabula smaragdina" (*De alchemia,* p. 363).

164

and hence the cycling of the year in which the work takes place. The alchemist was not unaware of the connection between the *rotatio* and his drawings of circles. The contemporary moral allegories of the wheel emphasize that the *ascensus* and *descensus* are, among other things, God's descent to man and man's ascent to God. (On the authority of one of St. Bernard's sermons: "By his descent he established for us a joyful and wholesome ascent." [92]) Further, the wheel expresses virtues that are important for the work: *constantia, obedientia, moderatio, aequalitas,* and *humilitas.*[93] The mystical associations of the wheel play no small part in Jakob Böhme. Like the alchemists he too operates with the wheels of Ezekiel, saying: "Thus we see that the spiritual life stands turned in upon itself, and that the natural life stands turned out of and facing itself. We can then liken it to a round spherical wheel that goes on all its sides, as the wheel in Ezekiel shows." [94] He goes on to explain: "The wheel of nature turns in upon itself from without; for God dwells within himself and has such a figure, not that it can be painted, it being only a natural likeness, the same as when God paints himself in the figure of this world; for God is everywhere entire, and so dwells in himself. Mark: the outer wheel is the zodiac with the stars, and after it come the seven planets," etc.[95] "Albeit this figure is not fashioned sufficiently, it is nevertheless a meditation: and we could make a fine drawing of it on a great circle for the meditation of those of less understanding. Mark therefore, desire goes in upon itself to the heart, which is God," etc. But Böhme's wheel is also the "impression" (in alchemical terms, the *informatio*) of the eternal will. It is Mother Nature, or the "mind [*Gemüth*] of the mother, from whence she continually creates and works; and these are the stars with the planetary orb [after the model] of the eternal *astrum*, which is only a spirit, and the eternal mind in the wisdom of God, viz., the Eternal Nature, from whence the eternal spirits proceeded and entered into a creaturely being." [96] The "property" of the wheel is *life* in the form of "four bailiffs"

---

92 "Suo nobis descensu suavem ac salubrem dedicavit ascensum." *Sermo IV de Ascensione Domini* (Migne, *P.L.,* vol. 183, col. 312).
93 Picinelli, *Mundus symbolicus,* s.v. "rota."
94 "Vom irdischen und himmlischen Mysterium," ch. V, 1f.
95 *Von dem dreyfachen Leben,* ch. IX, 58f.
96 *De signatura rerum,* ch. XIV, 15 (trans. Bax, p. 179).

who "manage the dominion in the life-giving mother." These bailiffs are the four elements "to which the wheel of the mind, viz., the *astrum*, affords will and desire; so that this whole essence is but one thing only, like the mind of a man. Even as he is in soul and body, so also is this whole essence"; for he is created in the likeness of this "whole essence." But nature in her four elements is also a whole essence with a soul.[97] This "sulphurean wheel" is the origin of good and evil, or rather it leads into them and out of them.[98]

215   Böhme's mysticism is influenced by alchemy in the highest degree. Thus he says: "The form of the birth is as a turning wheel, which Mercurius causes in the sulphur." [99] The "birth" is the "golden child" (*filius philosophorum* = archetype of the divine child [100]) whose "master-workman" is Mercurius.[101] Mercurius himself is the "fiery wheel of the essence" in the form of a serpent. Similarly the (unenlightened) soul is just "such a fiery Mercurius." Vulcan kindles the fiery wheel of the essence in the soul when it "breaks off" from God; whence come desire and sin, which are the "wrath of God." The soul is then a "worm" like the "fiery serpent," a "larva" and a "monster." [102]

216   The interpretation of the wheel in Böhme reveals something of the mystical secret of alchemy and is thus of considerable importance in this respect as well as from the psychological point of view: the wheel appears here as a concept for wholeness which represents the essence of mandala symbolism and therefore includes the *mysterium iniquitatis*.

217   The idea of the "centre," which the unconscious has been repeatedly thrusting upon the conscious mind of the dreamer, is beginning to gain foothold there and to exercise a peculiar fascination. The next drawing is again of the blue flower (cf. fig. 85), but this time subdivided into eight; then follow pictures of four mountains round a lake in a crater, also of a red ring lying on the ground with a withered tree standing in it, round which a green snake (cf. fig. 13) creeps up with a leftward movement.

218   The layman may be rather puzzled by the serious attention devoted to this problem. But a little knowledge of yoga and of

97 Ibid., 16 (p 179).   98 Ibid.   99 Ibid., IV, 28 (Bax, p. 37).
100 Cf. Jung, "The Psychology of the Child Archetype."
101 Böhme, *De signatura rerum*, ch. IV, 27 (Bax, p. 37).
102 Böhme, *Gespräch einer erleuchteten und unerleuchteten Seele*, 11–24.

the medieval philosophy of the *lapis* would help him to understand. As we have already said, the squaring of the circle was one of the methods for producing the *lapis;* another was the use of *imaginatio,* as the following text unmistakably proves:

And take care that thy door be well and firmly closed, so that he who is within cannot escape, and—God willing—thou wilt reach the goal. Nature performeth her operations gradually; and indeed I would have thee do the same: let thy imagination be guided wholly by nature. And observe according to nature, through whom the substances regenerate themselves in the bowels of the earth. And imagine this with true and not with fantastic imagination.[103]

219   The *vas bene clausum* (well-sealed vessel) is a precautionary measure very frequently mentioned in alchemy, and is the equivalent of the magic circle. In both cases the idea is to protect what is within from the intrusion and admixture of what is without, as well as to prevent it from escaping.[104] The *imaginatio* is to be understood here as the real and literal power to create images (*Einbildungskraft* = imagination)—the classical use of the word in contrast to *phantasia,* which means a mere "conceit" in the sense of insubstantial thought. In the *Satyricon* this connotation is more pointed still: *phantasia* means something ridiculous.[105] *Imaginatio* is the active evocation of (inner) images *secundum naturam,* an authentic feat of thought or ideation, which does not spin aimless and groundless fantasies "into the blue"—does not, that is to say, just play with its objects, but tries to grasp the inner facts and portray them in images true to their nature. This activity is an *opus,* a work. And we cannot call the manner in which the dreamer handles the objects of his inner experience anything but true work, considering how conscientiously, accurately, and carefully he records and elaborates the content now pushing its way into consciousness. The resemblance to the *opus* is obvious enough to anyone familiar with alchemy. Moreover

---

103 *Rosarium, Art. aurif.,* II, p. 214.

104 Ibid., p. 213: "Nec intrat in eum [lapidem], quod non sit ortum ex eo, quoniam si aliquid extranei sibi apponatur, statim corrumpitur" (Nothing enters into it [the stone] that did not come from it; since, if anything extraneous were to be added to it, it would at once be spoilt).

105 Petronius, *Satyricon,* par. 38: "Phantasia non homo" (He's a fantasy, not a man).

81. "Sol et eius umbra." The earth is midway between light and darkness.
—Maier, *Scrutinium chymicum* (1687)

the analogy is borne out by the dreams themselves, as dream 24 will show.

220   The present dream, from which the above-mentioned drawings originated, shows no signs of the "left" having been in any way "throttled." On the contrary, the dreamer finds himself once more in the *temenos* facing the unknown woman who personifies the fourth or "inferior" function.[106] His drawing of the

---

[106] Prescription for preparation of the *lapis* (Hermes quotation in *Rosarium, Art. aurif.*, II, p. 317): "Fili, extrahe a radio suam umbram: accipe ergo quartam partem sui, hoc est, unam partem de fermento et tres partes de corpore imperfecto," etc. (Son, extract from the ray its shadow: then take a fourth part of it, i.e., one part of the ferment and three parts of the imperfect body, etc.). For *umbra,* see ibid., p. 233: "Fundamentum artis est sol et eius umbra" (The basis of the art is the sun and its shadow) (fig. 81). The above quotation gives only the sense of the "Tractatus aureus" and is not literal.

wheel with a four-petalled blue flower in the middle was anticipated by the dream: what the dream represents in personified
form the dreamer reproduces as an abstract ideogram. This
might well be a hint that the *meaning* of the personification
could also be represented in quite another form. This "other
form" (three-leaved clover, distorted cross) refers back to the ace
of clubs in dream 16 of the first series (par. 97), where we pointed
out its analogy with the irregular cross. The analogy is confirmed
here. In this dream, however, the symbol of the Christian Trinity has been overshadowed or "coloured" by the alchemical quaternity. The colours appear as a concretization of the *tetraktys*.
The *Rosarium* quotes a similar statement from the "Tractatus
aureus": "Vultur[107] . . . clamat voce magna, inquiens: Ego
sum albus niger et rubeus citrinus" [108] (The vulture . . . exclaims in a loud voice: I am the white black and the red yellow).
On the other hand it is stressed that the *lapis* unites *omnes
colores* in itself. We can thus take it that the quaternity represented by the colours is a kind of preliminary stage of the *lapis*.
This is confirmed by the *Rosarium*: "Our stone is from the four
elements." [109] (Cf. figs. 64, 82, 117.) The same applies to the
aurum philosophicum: "In the gold the four elements are contained in equal proportions." [110] The fact is that the four colours
in the dream represent the transition from trinity to quaternity
and thus to the squared circle (figs. 59, 60), which, according to
the alchemists, comes nearest to the *lapis* on account of its roundness or perfect simplicity. For this reason a recipe for the preparation of the *lapis*, attributed to Raymundus, says:

Take of the body that is most simple and round, and do not take
of the triangle or quadrangle but of the round, for the round is
nearer to simplicity than the triangle. Hence it is to be noted that

[107] Cf. dream 58, par. 304. The alchemical vulture, eagle, and crow are all essentially synonymous.
[108] This quotation from Hermes is likewise an arbitrary reading. The passage
runs literally: "Ego sum albus nigri et rubeus albi et citrinus rubei et certe
veridicus sum" (I am the white of the black, and the red of the white, and the
yellow of the red, and I speak very truth). In this way three meanings are expressed by four colours, in contrast to the formula of Hortulanus which attributes
four natures and three colours to the *lapis*.—*De alchemia*, p. 372.
[109] *Art. aurif.*, II, p. 207: "Lapis noster est ex quatuor elementis."
[110] Ibid., p. 208: "In auro sunt quatuor elementa in aequali proportione aptata."

82. The Anthropos with the four elements.—Russian MS. (18th cent.)

a simple body has no corners, for it is the first and last among the planets, like the sun among the stars.[111]

24. DREAM:

221   *Two people are talking about crystals, particularly about a diamond.*

222   Here one can hardly avoid thinking of the *lapis*. In fact this dream discloses the historical background and indicates that we really are dealing with the coveted *lapis,* the "treasure hard

111 Ibid., p. 317: "Recipe de simplicissimo et de rotundo corpore, et noli recipere de triangulo vel quadrangulo sed de rotundo: quia rotundum est propinquius simplicitati quam triangulus. Notandum est ergo, quod corpus simplex nullum habens angulum, quia ipsum est primum et posterius in planetis, sicut Sol in stellis."

170

to attain." The dreamer's *opus* amounts to an unconscious recapitulation of the efforts of Hermetic philosophy. (More about
the diamond in dreams 37, 39, 50 below.)

25. DREAM:

223   *It is a question of constructing a central point and making
the figure symmetrical by reflection at this point.*

224   The word "constructing" points to the synthetic character
of the *opus* and also to the laborious building process that
taxes the dreamer's energy. The "symmetry" is an answer to the
conflict in dream 22 ("completely throttling the left"). Each side
must perfectly balance the other as its mirror-image, and this
image is to fall at the "central point," which evidently possesses
the property of reflection—it is a *vitrum*,[112] a crystal or sheet of
water (cf. fig. 209). This power of reflection seems to be another
allusion to the underlying idea of the *lapis*, the *aurum philosophicum*, the elixir, the *aqua nostra*, etc. (cf. fig. 265).

225   Just as the "right" denotes the world of consciousness and
its principles, so by "reflection" the picture of the world is to
be turned round to the left, thus producing a corresponding
world in reverse. We could equally well say: through reflection
the right appears as the reverse of the left. Therefore the left
seems to have as much validity as the right; in other words, the
unconscious and its—for the most part unintelligible—order becomes the symmetrical counterpart of the conscious mind and
its contents, although it is still not clear which of them is reflected and which reflecting (cf. fig. 55). To carry our reasoning
a step further, we could regard the centre as the point of intersection of two worlds that correspond but are inverted by reflection.[113]

226   The idea of creating a symmetry would thus indicate some
kind of climax in the task of accepting the unconscious and in-
corporating it in a general picture of the world. The unconscious here displays a "cosmic" character.

---

112 A quotation from Ademarus (ibid., p. 353): "[Lapis] nihilominus non fundi-
tur, nec ingreditur, nec permiscetur, sed vitrificatur" (But [the stone] can neither
be melted nor penetrated nor mixed but is made as hard as glass).

113 There are very interesting parapsychological parallels to this, but I cannot
enter upon them here.

26. DREAM:

227   *It is night, with stars in the sky. A voice says, "Now it will begin." The dreamer asks, "What will begin?" Whereupon the voice answers, "The circulation can begin." Then a shooting star falls in a curious leftward curve. The scene changes, and the dreamer is in a rather squalid night club. The proprietor, who appears to be an unscrupulous crook, is there with some bedraggled-looking girls. A quarrel starts about left and right. The dreamer then leaves and drives round the perimeter of a square in a taxi. Then he is in the bar again. The proprietor says, "What they said about left and right did not satisfy my feelings. Is there really such a thing as a left and a right side of human society?" The dreamer answers, "The existence of the left does not contradict that of the right. They both exist in everyone. The left is the mirror-image of the right. Whenever I feel it like that, as a mirror-image, I am at one with myself. There is no right and no left side to human society, but there are symmetrical and lopsided people. The lopsided are those who can fulfil only one side of themselves, either left or right. They are still in the childhood state." The proprietor says meditatively, "Now that's much better," and goes about his business.*

228   I have given this dream in full because it is an excellent illustration of how the ideas hinted at in the last dream have been taken up by the dreamer. The idea of symmetrical proportion has been stripped of its cosmic character and translated into psychological terms, expressed in social symbols. "Right" and "left" are used almost like political slogans.

229   The beginning of the dream, however, is still under the cosmic aspect. The dreamer noted that the curious curve of the shooting star corresponded exactly to the line he drew when sketching the picture of the eightfold flower (cf. par. 217). The curve formed the edge of the petals. Thus the shooting star traces the outline, so to speak, of a flower that spreads over the whole starry heaven. What is now beginning is the circulation of the light.[114] This cosmic flower corresponds roughly to the rose in Dante's *Paradiso* (fig. 83).

230   The "cosmic" nature of an experience—as an aspect of some

114 See pars. 245f., 258f.; and my commentary on *The Secret of the Golden Flower*, ch. I, sec. 2.

83. Dante being led before God in the heavenly rose.—Illumination for the
Paradiso, Canto XXXI, Codex Urbanus Latinus 365 (15th cent.)

inner occurrence that can only be understood psychologically —is offensive and at once provokes a reaction "from below." Evidently the cosmic aspect was too high and is compensated "downward," so that the symmetry is no longer that of two world pictures but merely of human society, in fact of the dreamer himself. When the proprietor remarks that the latter's psychological understanding is "much better," he is making an estimate whose conclusion should run: "but still not good enough."

231   The quarrel about right and left that starts in the bar is the conflict which breaks out in the dreamer himself when he is called upon to recognize the symmetry. He cannot do this because the other side looks so suspicious that he would rather not investigate it too closely. That is the reason for the magical *circumambulatio* (driving round the square): he has to stay inside and learn to face his mirror-image without running away. He does this as best he can, though not quite as the other side would wish. Hence the somewhat chill recognition of his merits.

27. VISUAL IMPRESSION:

232   *A circle with a green tree in the middle. In the circle a fierce battle is raging between savages. They do not see the tree.*

233   Evidently the conflict between right and left has not yet ended. It continues because the savages are still in the "childhood state" and therefore, being "lopsided," only know either the left or the right but not a third that stands above the conflict.

28. VISUAL IMPRESSION:

234   *A circle: within it, steps lead up to a basin with a fountain inside.*

235   When a condition is unsatisfactory because some essential aspect of the unconscious content is lacking, the unconscious process reverts to earlier symbols, as is the case here. The symbolism goes back to dream 13 (par. 154), where we met the mandala garden of the philosophers with its fountain of *aqua nostra* (fig. 84; cf. also figs. 25, 26, 56). Circle and basin emphasize the mandala, the rose of medieval symbolism.[115] The "rose garden of the philosophers" is one of alchemy's favourite symbols.[116]

115 Valli, "Die Geheimsprache Dantes."
116 Cf. "Rosarius minor," *De alchemia*, p. 309.

84. The fountain in the walled garden, symbolizing *constantia in adversis* —a situation particularly characteristic of alchemy.—Boschius, *Symbolographia* (1702)

29. VISUAL IMPRESSION:

236 *A bunch of roses, then the sign ≣, but it should be ✳.*

237 A rose bouquet is like a fountain fanning out. The meaning of the first sign—possibly a tree—is not clear, whereas the correction represents the eightfold flower (fig. 85). Evidently a mistake is being corrected which somehow impaired the wholeness of the rose. The aim of the reconstruction is to bring the problem of the mandala—the correct valuation and interpretation of the "centre"—once more into the field of consciousness.

30. DREAM:

238 *The dreamer is sitting at a round table with the dark unknown woman.*

239 Whenever a process has reached a culmination as regards either its clarity or the wealth of inferences that can be drawn from it, a regression is likely to ensue. From the dreams that come in between the ones we have quoted here it is evident that the dreamer is finding the insistent demands of wholeness somewhat disagreeable; for their realization will have far-reaching practical consequences, whose personal nature, however, lies outside the scope of our study.

240 The round table again points to the circle of wholeness, and the anima comes in as representative of the fourth function, especially in her "dark" aspect, which always makes itself felt when something is becoming concrete, i.e., when it has to be translated, or threatens to translate itself, into reality. "Dark"

175

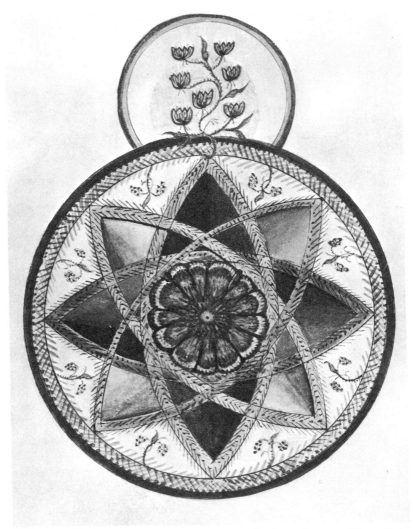

85. The eight-petalled flower as the eighth or the first of seven.—"Recueil de figures astrologiques" (MS., 18th cent.)

means chthonic, i.e., concrete and earthy. This is also the source of the fear that causes the regression.[117]

31. DREAM:

241   *The dreamer is sitting with a certain man of unpleasant aspect at a round table. On it stands a glass filled with a gelatinous mass.*

242   This dream is an advance on the last in that the dreamer has accepted the "dark" as his own darkness, to the extent of producing a real "shadow" belonging to him personally.[118] The anima is thus relieved of the moral inferiority projected upon her and can take up the living and creative function[119] which is properly her own. This is represented by the glass with its peculiar contents which we, like the dreamer, may compare with the undifferentiated "life-mass" in dream 18 (par. 183). It was then a question of the gradual transformation of primitive animality into something human. So we may expect something of the sort here, for it seems as if the spiral of inner development had come round to the same point again, though higher up.

117 "Symbola Pythagore phylosophi" in Ficino, *Auctores platonici*, Fol. X, III, says: "Ab eo, quod nigram caudam habet abstine, terrestrium enim deorum est" (Keep your hands from that which has a black tail, for it belongs to the gods of the earth).

118 Although the theme of this study does not permit a full discussion of the psychology of dreams, I must make a few explanatory remarks at this point. Sitting together at one table means relationship, being connected or "put together." The round table indicates that the figures have been brought together for the purpose of wholeness. If the anima figure (the personified unconscious) is separated from ego-consciousness and therefore unconscious, it means that there is an isolating layer of personal unconscious embedded between the ego and the anima. The existence of a personal unconscious proves that contents of a personal nature which could really be made conscious are being kept unconscious for no good reason. There is thus an inadequate or even non-existent consciousness of the shadow. The shadow corresponds to a negative ego-personality and includes all those qualities we find painful or regrettable. Shadow and anima, being unconscious, are then contaminated with each other, a state that is represented in dreams by "marriage" or the like. But if the existence of the anima (or the shadow) is accepted and understood, a separation of these figures ensues, as has happened in the case of our dreamer. The shadow is thus recognized as belonging, and the anima as not belonging, to the ego.

119 Cf. what I have said about the anima in "The Archetypes of the Collective Unconscious." pars. 53ff. In Hermes' treatise, *An die menschliche Seele*, she is called "the highest interpreter and nearest custodian (of the eternal)," which aptly characterizes her function as mediator between conscious and unconscious.

86. The alchemical apparatus for distillation, the *unum vas*, with the serpents of the (double) Mercurius.—Kelley, *Tractatus de Lapide philosophorum* (1676)

243   The glass corresponds to the *unum vas* of alchemy (fig. 86) and its contents to the living, semi-organic mixture from which the body of the *lapis,* endowed with spirit and life, will emerge —or possibly that strange Faustian figure who bursts into flame three times: the Boy Charioteer, the Homunculus who is dashed against the throne of Galatea, and Euphorion (all symbolizing a dissolution of the "centre" into its unconscious elements). We know that the *lapis* is not just a "stone" since it is expressly stated to be composed "de re animali, vegetabili et minerali," and to consist of body, soul, and spirit;[120] moreover, it grows from flesh and blood.[121] For which reason the philosopher (Hermes in the "Tabula smaragdina") says: "The wind hath carried it in his belly" (fig. 210). Therefore "wind is air, air is life, and life is soul." "The stone is that thing midway between perfect and imperfect bodies, and that which nature herself begins is brought to perfection through the art."[122] The stone "is named the stone of invisibility" (*lapis invisibilitatis*).[123]

244   The dream takes up the question of giving the centre life and reality—giving birth to it, so to speak. That this birth can issue from an amorphous mass has its parallel in the alchemical idea of the *prima materia* as a chaotic *massa informis* impregnated by the seeds of life (figs. 162, 163). As we have seen, the qualities of gum arabic and glue are attributed to it, or again it is called *viscosa* and *unctuosa.* (In Paracelsus the "Nostoc" is the arcane substance.) Although modern conceptions of nutrient soil, jelly-like growths, etc., underlie the dreamer's "gelatinous mass," the atavistic associations with far older alchemical ideas

120 *Rosarium, Art. aurif.,* II, p. 237.   121 Ibid., p. 238.
122 P. 236.   123 P. 231.

still persist, and these, although not consciously present, nevertheless exert a powerful unconscious influence on the choice of symbols.

32. DREAM:

245 *The dreamer receives a letter from an unknown woman. She writes that she has pains in the uterus. A drawing is attached to the letter, looking roughly like this:* [124]

• = Uterus

[124] The uterus is the centre, the life-giving vessel (fig. 87). The stone, like the grail, is itself the creative vessel, the *elixir vitae*. It is surrounded by the spiral, the symbol of indirect approach by means of the *circumambulatio*.

179

In the primeval forest there are swarms of monkeys. Then a panorama of white glaciers opens out.

246   The anima reports that there are painful processes going on in the life-creating centre, which in this case is no longer the "glass" containing the life-mass but a point designated as a "uterus," to be reached—so the spiral suggests—by means of a *circumambulatio*. At all events the spiral emphasizes the centre and hence the uterus, which is a synonym frequently employed for the alchemical vessel, just as it is one of the basic meanings of the Eastern mandala.[125] The serpentine line leading to the vessel is analogous to the healing serpent of Aesculapius (figs. 203, 204) and also to the Tantric symbol of *Shiva bindu*, the creative, latent god without extension in space who, in the form of a point or *lingam*, is encircled three and a half times by the Kundalini serpent.[126] With the primeval forest we meet the animal or ape motif again, which appeared before in vision 22 of the first series (par. 117) and in dreams 16 and 18 of this (pars. 164, 183). In vision 22 it led to the announcement that "everything must be ruled by the light" and, in dream 18, to the "transfigured" head. Similarly the present dream ends with a panorama of white "glaciers," reminding the dreamer of an earlier dream (not included here) in which he beheld the Milky Way and was having a conversation about immortality. Thus the glacier symbol is a bridge leading back again to the cosmic aspect that caused the regression. But, as is nearly always the case, the earlier content does not return in its first simple guise—it brings a new complication with it, which, though it might have been expected logically, is no less repugnant to the intellectual consciousness than the cosmic aspect was. The complication is the memory of the conversation about immortality. This theme was

---

[125] The centre of the mandala corresponds to the calyx of the Indian lotus, seat and birthplace of the gods. This is called the *padma,* and has a feminine significance. In alchemy the *vas* is often understood as the uterus where the "child" is gestated. In the Litany of Loreto, Mary is spoken of three times as the "vas" ("vas spirituale," "honorabile," and "insigne devotionis") and in medieval poetry she is called the "flower of the sea" which shelters the Christ (cf. dream 36). The grail (fig. 88) is closely related to the Hermetic vessel: Wolfram von Eschenbach calls the stone of the grail "lapsit exillis." Arnold of Villanova (d. ?1312) calls the *lapis* "lapis exilis," the uncomely stone (*Rosarium, Art. aurif.,* II, p. 210), which may be of importance for the interpretation of Wolfram's term.
[126] See Avalon, *The Serpent Power.*

88. Vision of the Holy Grail.—"Roman de Lancelot du lac" (MS., Paris, 15th cent.)

already hinted at in dream 9 (par. 134), with its pendulum clock, a *perpetuum mobile*. Immortality is a clock that never runs down, a mandala that revolves eternally like the heavens. Thus the cosmic aspect returns with interest and compound interest. This might easily prove too much for the dreamer, for the "scientific" stomach has very limited powers of digestion.

247   The unconscious does indeed put forth a bewildering profusion of semblances for that obscure thing we call the mandala or "self." It almost seems as if we were ready to go on dreaming in the unconscious the age-old dream of alchemy, and to continue to pile new synonyms on top of the old, only to know as much or as little about it in the end as the ancients themselves. I will not enlarge upon what the *lapis* meant to our forefathers, and what the mandala still means to the Lamaist and Tantrist, Aztec

and Pueblo Indian, the "golden pill" [127] to the Taoist, and the "golden seed" to the Hindu. We know the texts that give us a vivid idea of all this. But what does it mean when the unconscious stubbornly persists in presenting such abstruse symbolisms to a cultured European? The only point of view I can apply here is a psychological one. (There may be others with which I am not familiar.) From this point of view, as it seems to me, everything that can be grouped together under the general concept "mandala" expresses the essence of a certain kind of *attitude*. The known attitudes of the conscious mind have definable aims and purposes. But a man's attitude towards the self is the only one that has no definable aim and no visible purpose. It is easy enough to say "self," but exactly what have we said? That remains shrouded in "metaphysical" darkness. I may define "self" as the totality of the conscious and unconscious psyche, but this totality transcends our vision; it is a veritable *lapis invisibilitatis*. In so far as the unconscious exists it is not definable; its existence is a mere postulate and nothing whatever can be predicated as to its possible contents. The totality can only be experienced in its parts and then only in so far as these are contents of consciousness; but *qua* totality it necessarily transcends consciousness. Consequently the "self" is a pure borderline concept similar to Kant's *Ding an sich*. True, it is a concept that grows steadily clearer with experience—as our dreams show—without, however, losing anything of its transcendence. Since we cannot possibly know the boundaries of something unknown to us, it follows that we are not in a position to set any bounds to the self. It would be wildly arbitrary and therefore unscientific to restrict the self to the limits of the individual psyche, quite apart from the fundamental fact that we have not the least knowledge of these limits, seeing that they also lie in the unconscious. We may be able to indicate the limits of consciousness, but the unconscious is simply the unknown psyche and for that very reason illimitable because indeterminable. Such being the case, we should not be in the least surprised if the empirical manifestations of unconscious contents bear all the marks of something illimitable, something not determined by space and time. This quality is numinous and therefore alarming, above all to a cautious mind that knows the value of

[127] Synonymous with the "golden flower."

precisely delimited concepts. One is glad not to be a philosopher or theologian and so under no obligation to meet such numina professionally. It is all the worse when it becomes increasingly clear that numina are psychic *entia* that force themselves upon consciousness, since night after night our dreams practise philosophy on their own account. What is more, when we attempt to give these numina the slip and angrily reject the alchemical gold which the unconscious offers, things do in fact go badly with us, we may even develop symptoms in defiance of all reason, but the moment we face up to the stumbling-block and make it—if only hypothetically—the cornerstone, the symptoms vanish and we feel "unaccountably" well. In this dilemma we can at least comfort ourselves with the reflection that the unconscious is a necessary evil which must be reckoned with, and that it would therefore be wiser to accompany it on some of its strange symbolic wanderings, even though their meaning be exceedingly questionable. It might perhaps be conducive to good health to relearn Nietzsche's "lesson of earlier humanity."

248   The only objection I could make to such rationalistic explanations is that very often they do not stand the test of events. We can observe in these and similar cases how, over the years, the entelechy of the self becomes so insistent that consciousness has to rise to still greater feats if it is to keep pace with the unconscious.

249   All that can be ascertained at present about the symbolism of the mandala is that it portrays an autonomous psychic fact, characterized by a phenomenology which is always repeating itself and is everywhere the same. It seems to be a sort of atomic nucleus about whose innermost structure and ultimate meaning we know nothing. We can also regard it as the actual—i.e., effective—reflection of a conscious attitude that can state neither its aim nor its purpose and, because of this failure, projects its activity entirely upon the virtual centre of the mandala.[128] The compelling force necessary for this projection always lies in some situation where the individual no longer knows how to help himself in any other way. That the mandala is merely a psychological reflex is, however, contradicted firstly by the autonomous nature of this symbol, which sometimes manifests itself

128 Projection is considered here a spontaneous phenomenon, and not the deliberate extrapolation of anything. It is not a phenomenon of the will.

89. The pelican nourishing its young
with its own blood, an allegory of Christ.
—Boschius, *Symbolographia* (1702)

with overwhelming spontaneity in dreams and visions, and secondly by the autonomous nature of the unconscious as such,
which is not only the original form of everything psychic but also
the condition we pass through in early childhood and to which
we return every night. There is no evidence for the assertion that
the activity of the psyche is merely reactive or reflex. This is at
best a biological working hypothesis of limited validity. When
raised to a universal truth it is nothing but a materialistic myth,
for it overlooks the creative capacity of the psyche, which—
whether we like it or not—exists, and in face of which all so-
called "causes" become mere occasions.

33. DREAM:

250   *A battle among savages, in which bestial cruelties are per-
petrated.*

251   As was to be foreseen, the new complication ("immortality") has started a furious conflict, which makes use of the same
symbols as the analogous situation in dream 27 (par. 232).

34. DREAM:

252   *A conversation with a friend. The dreamer says, "I must
carry on with the figure of the bleeding Christ before me and
persevere in the work of self-redemption."*

253   This, like the previous dream, points to an extraordinary,
subtle kind of suffering (fig. 89) caused by the breaking through
of an alien spiritual world which we find very hard to accept—
hence the analogy with the tragedy of Christ: "My kingdom is
not of this world." But it also shows that the dreamer is now con-
tinuing his task in deadly earnest. The reference to Christ may
well have a deeper meaning than that of a mere moral re-

184

minder: we are concerned here with the process of individuation, a process which has constantly been held up to Western man in the dogmatic and religious model of the life of Christ. The accent has always fallen on the "historicity" of the Saviour's life, and because of this its symbolical nature has remained in the dark, although the Incarnation formed a very essential part of the *symbolon* (creed). The efficacy of dogma, however, by no means rests on Christ's unique historical reality but on its own symbolic nature, by virtue of which it expresses a more or less ubiquitous psychological assumption quite independent of the existence of any dogma. There is thus a "pre-Christian" as well as a "non-Christian" Christ, in so far as he is an autonomous psychological fact. At any rate the doctrine of prefiguration is founded on this idea. In the case of the modern man, who has no religious assumptions at all, it is therefore only logical that the Anthropos or Poimen figure should emerge, since it is present in his own psyche (figs. 117, 195).

35. DREAM:

²⁵⁴   *An actor smashes his hat against the wall, where it looks like this:*

²⁵⁵   As certain material not included here shows, the "actor" refers to a definite fact in the dreamer's personal life. Up to now he had maintained a certain fiction about himself which prevented him from taking himself seriously. This fiction has become incompatible with the serious attitude he has now attained. He must give up the actor, for it was the actor in him who rejected the self. The hat refers to the first dream of all, where he put on a *stranger's* hat. The actor throws the hat against the wall, and the hat proves to be a mandala. So the "strange" hat was the self, which at that time—while he was still playing a fictitious role—seemed like a stranger to him.

36. DREAM:

256   *The dreamer drives in a taxi to the Rathausplatz, but it is called the "Marienhof."*

257   I mention this dream only in passing because it shows the feminine nature of the *temenos,* just as *hortus conclusus* (enclosed garden) is often used as an image for the Virgin Mary in medieval hymns, and *rosa mystica* is one of her attributes in the Litany of Loreto (cf. fig. 26).

37. DREAM:

258   *There are curves outlined in light around a dark centre. Then the dreamer is wandering about in a dark cave, where a battle is going on between good and evil. But there is also a prince who knows everything. He gives the dreamer a ring set with a diamond and places it on the fourth finger of his left hand.*

259   The circulation of light that started in dream 26 reappears more clearly. Light always refers to consciousness, which at present runs only along the periphery. The centre is still dark. It is the dark cave, and to enter it is obviously to set the conflict going again. At the same time it is like the prince who stands aloof, who knows everything and is the possessor of the precious stone. The gift means nothing less than the dreamer's vow to the self—for as a rule the wedding ring is worn on the fourth finger of the left hand. True, the left is the unconscious, from which it is to be inferred that the situation is still largely shrouded in unconsciousness. The prince seems to be the representative of the *aenigma regis* (fig. 54; cf. commentary to dream 10, par. 142). The dark cave corresponds to the vessel containing the warring opposites. The self is made manifest in the opposites and in the conflict between them; it is a *coincidentia oppositorum.* Hence the way to the self begins with conflict.

38. DREAM:

260   *A circular table with four chairs round it. Table and chairs are empty.*

261   This dream confirms the above conjecture. The mandala is not yet "in use."

90. The bear representing the dangerous aspect of the *prima materia*.—Thomas
Aquinas (pseud.), "De alchimia" (MS., 16th cent.)

39. VISUAL IMPRESSION:

262   *The dreamer is falling into the abyss. At the bottom there
is a bear whose eyes gleam alternately in four colours: red, yellow, green, and blue. Actually it has four eyes that change into
four lights. The bear disappears and the dreamer goes through
a long dark tunnel. Light is shimmering at the far end. A treasure is there, and on top of it the ring with the diamond. It is
said that this ring will lead him on a long journey to the east.*

263   This waking dream shows that the dreamer is still preoccu-
pied with the dark centre. The bear stands for the chthonic element that might seize him. But then it becomes clear that the
animal is only leading up to the four colours (cf. dream 23,
par. 212), which in their turn lead to the *lapis*, i.e., the diamond
whose prism contains all the hues of the rainbow. The way to
the east probably points to the unconscious as an antipode. Ac-

cording to the legend the Grail-stone comes from the east and must return there again. In alchemy the bear corresponds to the *nigredo* of the *prima materia* (fig. 90), whence comes the colourful *cauda pavonis*.

40. DREAM:

264 *Under the guidance of the unknown woman the dreamer has to discover the Pole at the risk of his life.*

265 The Pole is the point round which everything turns—hence another symbol of the self. Alchemy also took up this analogy: "In the Pole is the heart of Mercurius, who is the true fire, wherein his master rests. When navigating over this great sea . . . he sets his course by the aspect of the North star." [129] Mercurius is the world-soul, and the Pole is its heart (fig. 140). The idea of the *anima mundi* (fig. 91; cf. fig. 8) coincides with that of the collective unconscious whose centre is the self. The symbol of the sea is another synonym for the unconscious.

41. VISUAL IMPRESSION:

266 *Yellow balls rolling round to the left in a circle.*

267 Rotation about a centre, recalling dream 21 (par. 198).

42. DREAM:

268 *An old master points to a spot on the ground illuminated in red.*

269 The *philosophus* shows him the "centre." The redness may mean the dawn, like the *rubedo* in alchemy, which as a rule immediately preceded the completion of the work.

43. DREAM:

270 *A yellow light like the sun looms through the fog, but it is murky. Eight rays go out from the centre. This is the point of penetration: the light ought to pierce through, but has not quite succeeded.*

271 The dreamer himself observed that the point of penetration was identical with the Pole in dream 40. So it is, as we surmised, a question of the sun's appearing, which now turns yellow. But

129 "In polo est cor Mercurii, qui verus est ignis, in quo requies est Domini sui, navigans per mare hoc magnum . . . cursum dirigat per aspectum astri septentrionalis"—Philalethes, "Introitus apertus," *Musaeum hermeticum,* p. 655.

91. *Anima Mundi.*—Thurneisser zum Thurn, *Quinta essentia* (1574)

the light is still murky, which probably means insufficient understanding. The "penetration" alludes to the need for effort in coming to a decision. In alchemy yellow (*citrinitas*) often coincides with the *rubedo*. The "gold" is yellow or reddish yellow.

44. Dream:

272　　*The dreamer is in a square enclosure where he must keep still. It is a prison for Lilliputians (or children?). A wicked woman is in charge of them. The children start moving and begin to circulate round the periphery. The dreamer would like to run away but may not do so. One of the children turns into an animal and bites him in the calf* (fig. 118).

273　　The lack of clarity demands further efforts of concentration; hence the dreamer finds himself still in the childhood state

189

(figs. 95, 96), hence "lopsided" (cf. dream 26, par. 227), and imprisoned in the *temenos* in the charge of a wicked mother-anima. The animal appears as in dream 18 (par. 183) and he is bitten, i.e., he must expose himself and pay the price. The *circumambulatio* means, as always, concentration on the centre. He finds this state of tension almost unendurable. But he wakes up with an intense and pleasant feeling of having solved something, "as if he held the diamond in his hand." The children point to the dwarf motif, which may express Cabiric elements, i.e., it may represent unconscious formative powers (see dreams 56ff., below), or it may at the same time allude to his still childish condition.

45. DREAM:

274　　*A parade ground with troops. They are not equipping themselves for war but form an eight-rayed star rotating to the left.*

275　　The essential point here is that the conflict seems to be overcome. The star is not in the sky and not a diamond, but a configuration on the earth formed by human beings.

46. DREAM:

276　　*The dreamer is imprisoned in the square enclosure. Lions and a wicked sorceress appear.*

277　　He cannot get out of the chthonic prison because he is not yet ready to do something that he should. (This is an important personal matter, a duty even, and the cause of much misgiving.) Lions, like all wild animals, indicate latent affects. The lion plays an important part in alchemy and has much the same meaning. It is a "fiery" animal, an emblem of the devil, and stands for the danger of being swallowed by the unconscious.

47. DREAM:

278　　*The wise old man shows the dreamer a place on the ground marked in a peculiar way.*

279　　This is probably the place on earth where the dreamer belongs if he is to realize the self (similar to dream 42).

48. DREAM:

280　　*An acquaintance wins a prize for digging up a potter's wheel.*

281　　The potter's wheel rotates on the ground (cf. dream 45) and

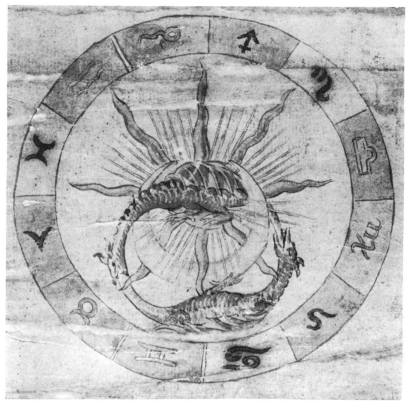

92. The alchemical process in the zodiac.—"Ripley Scrowle" (MS., 1588)

produces earthenware ("earthly") vessels which may figuratively be called "human bodies." Being round, the wheel refers to the self and the creative activity in which it is manifest. The potter's wheel also symbolizes the recurrent theme of circulation.

49. DREAM:

282   *A starry figure rotating. At the cardinal points of the circle there are pictures representing the seasons.*

283   Just as the place was defined before, so now the time. Place and time are the most general and necessary elements in any definition. The determination of time and place was stressed right at the beginning (cf. dreams 7, 8, 9; pars. 130–34). A definite location in place and time is part of a man's reality. The seasons refer to the quartering of the circle which corresponds to

the cycle of the year (fig. 92). The year is a symbol of the original man[130] (figs. 99, 100, 104). The rotation motif indicates that the symbol of the circle is to be thought of not as static but as dynamic.

50. DREAM:

284   *An unknown man gives the dreamer a precious stone. But he is attacked by a gang of apaches. He runs away (nightmare) and is able to escape. The unknown woman tells him afterwards that it will not always be so: sometime he will have to stand his ground and not run away.*

285   When a definite time is added to a definite place one is rapidly approaching reality. That is the reason for the gift of the jewel, but also for the fear of decision, which robs the dreamer of the power to make up his mind.

51. DREAM:

286   *There is a feeling of great tension. Many people are circulating round a large central oblong with four smaller oblongs on its sides. The circulation in the large oblong goes to the left and in the smaller oblongs to the right. In the middle there is the eight-rayed star. A bowl is placed in the centre of each of the smaller oblongs, containing red, yellow, green, and colourless water. The water rotates to the left. The disquieting question arises: Is there enough water?*

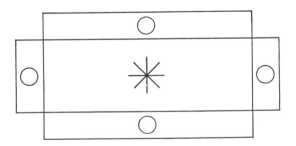

287   The colours point once more to the preliminary stage. The "disquieting" question is whether there is enough water of life —*aqua nostra*, energy, libido—to reach the central star (i.e., the

130 See "Paracelsus as a Spiritual Phenomenon," pars. 229, 237.

"core" or "kernel"; cf. next dream). The circulation in the central oblong is still going to the left, i.e., consciousness is moving towards the unconscious. The centre is therefore not yet sufficiently illuminated. The rightward circulation in the smaller oblongs, which represent the quaternity, seems to suggest that the four functions are becoming conscious. The four are generally characterized by the four colours of the rainbow. The striking fact here is that the blue is missing, and also that the square ground-plan has suddenly been abandoned. The horizontal has extended itself at the cost of the vertical. So we are dealing with a "disturbed" mandala.[131] We might add by way of criticism that the antithetical arrangement of the functions has not yet become sufficiently conscious for their characteristic polarity to be recognized.[132] The predominance of the horizontal over the vertical indicates that the ego-consciousness is uppermost, thus entailing a loss of height and depth.

52. DREAM:

288   *A rectangular dance hall. Everybody is going round the periphery to the left. Suddenly the order is heard: "To the kernels!" But the dreamer has first to go into the adjoining room to crack some nuts. Then the people climb down rope ladders to the water.*

289   The time has come to press on to the "kernel" or core of the matter, but the dreamer still has a few more "hard nuts" to crack in the little rectangle (the "adjoining room"), i.e., in one of the four functions. Meanwhile the process goes on and descends to the "water." The vertical is thus lengthened, and from the incorrect oblong we again get the square which expresses the complete symmetry of conscious and unconscious with all its psychological implications.

---

131 "Disturbed" mandalas occur from time to time. They consist of all forms that deviate from the circle, square, or regular cross, and also of those based not on the number four but on three or five. The numbers six and twelve are something of an exception. Twelve can be based on either four or three. The twelve months and the twelve signs of the zodiac are definite symbolic circles in daily use. And six is likewise a well-known symbol for the circle. Three suggests the predominance of ideation and will (trinity), and five that of the physical man (materialism).

132 Cf. the psychological functions in *Psychological Types,* ch. X.

53. DREAM:

290   *The dreamer finds himself in an empty square room which is rotating. A voice cries, "Don't let him out. He won't pay the tax!"*

291   This refers to the dreamer's inadequate self-realization in the personal matter already alluded to, which in this case was one of the essential conditions of individuation and therefore could not be circumvented. As was to be expected, after the preparatory emphasis on the vertical in the preceding dream, the square is now re-established. The cause of the disturbance was an underestimation of the demands of the unconscious (the vertical), which led to a flattening of the personality (recumbent oblong).

292   After this dream the dreamer worked out six mandalas in which he tried to determine the right length of the vertical, the form of "circulation," and the distribution of colour. At the end of this work came the following dream (given unabridged):

54. DREAM:

293   *I come to a strange, solemn house—the "House of the Gathering." Many candles are burning in the background, arranged in a peculiar pattern with four points running upward. Outside, at the door of the house, an old man is posted. People are going in. They say nothing and stand motionless in order to collect themselves inwardly. The man at the door says of the visitors to the house, "When they come out again they are cleansed." I go into the house myself and find I can concentrate perfectly. Then a voice says: "What you are doing is dangerous. Religion is not a tax to be paid so that you can rid yourself of the woman's image, for this image cannot be got rid of. Woe unto them who use religion as a substitute for another side of the soul's life; they are in error and will be accursed. Religion is no substitute; it is to be added to the other activities of the soul as the ultimate completion. Out of the fulness of life shall you bring forth your religion; only then shall you be blessed!" While the last sentence is being spoken in ringing tones I hear distant music, simple chords on an organ. Something about it reminds me of Wagner's Fire Music. As I leave the house I see a burning mountain and I feel: "The fire that is not put out is a holy fire" (Shaw, St. Joan).*

194

Within the illustration the following labels appear:

IGNIS   AERIS

AQVÆ   TERRÆ

TINCTVR.
COAGVLATION.
DISTILLATION.
PVTREFACTION.
SOLVTION.
SVBLIMATION.
CALTINATION.

93. The Mountain of the Adepts. The temple of the wise ("House of the Gathering" or of "Self-Collection"), lit by the sun and moon, stands on the seven stages,
surmounted by the phoenix. The temple is hidden in the mountain—a hint that
the philosophers' stone lies buried in the earth and must be extracted and
cleansed. The zodiac in the background symbolizes the duration of the *opus*,
while the four elements indicate wholeness. In foreground, blindfolded man and
the investigator who follows his natural instinct.—Michelspacher, *Cabala* (1654)

294   The dreamer notes that this dream was a "powerful experience." Indeed it has a numinous quality and we shall therefore not be far wrong if we assume that it represents a new climax of insight and understanding. The "voice" has as a rule an absolutely authoritative character and generally comes at decisive moments.

295   The house probably corresponds to the square, which is a "gathering place" (fig. 93). The four shining points in the background again indicate the quaternity. The remark about cleansing refers to the transformative function of the taboo area. The production of wholeness, which is prevented by the "tax evasion," naturally requires the "image of the woman," since as anima she represents the fourth, "inferior" function, feminine because contaminated with the unconscious. In what sense the "tax" is to be paid depends on the nature of the inferior function and its auxiliary, and also on the attitude type.[133] The payment can be either concrete or symbolic, but the conscious mind is not qualified to decide which form is valid.

296   The dream's view that religion may not be a substitute for "another side of the soul's life" will certainly strike many people as a radical innovation. According to it, religion is equated with wholeness; it even appears as the expression of the integration of the self in the "fulness of life."

297   The faint echo of the Fire Music—the Loki motif—is not out of key, for what does "fulness of life" mean? What does "wholeness" mean? I feel that there is every reason here for some anxiety, since man as a whole being casts a shadow. The fourth was not separated from the three and banished to the kingdom of everlasting fire for nothing. Does not an uncanonical saying of our Lord declare: "Whoso is near unto me is near unto the fire"?[134] (Cf. fig. 58.) Such dire ambiguities are not meant for grown-up children—which is why Heraclitus of old was named "the dark," because he spoke too plainly and called life itself an "ever-living fire." And that is why there are uncanonical sayings for those that have ears to hear.

---

133 *Psychological Types*, pars. 556ff.

134 "Ait autem ipse salvator: Qui iuxta me est, iuxta ignem est, qui longe est a me, longe est a regno" (The Saviour himself says: He that is near me is near the fire. He that is far from me is far from the kingdom).—Origen, *Homiliae in Jeremiam*, XX, 3; cited in James, *Apocryphal New Testament*, p. 35.

94. Etna: "gelat et ardet."—Boschius, *Symbolographia* (1702)

298   The theme of the Fire Mountain (fig. 94) is to be met with in the Book of Enoch.[135] Enoch sees the seven stars chained "like great mountains and burning with fire" at the angels' place of punishment. Originally the seven stars were the seven great Babylonian gods, but at the time of Enoch's revelation they had become the seven Archons, rulers of "this world," fallen angels condemned to punishment. In contrast to this menacing theme there is an allusion to the miracles of Jehovah on Mount Sinai, while according to other sources the number seven is by no means sinister, since it is on the seventh mountain of the western land that the tree with the life-giving fruit is to be found, i.e., the *arbor sapientiae* (cf. fig. 188).[136]

55. DREAM:

299   *A silver bowl with four cracked nuts at the cardinal points.*

300   This dream shows that some of the problems in dream 52 have been settled, though the settlement is not complete. The dreamer pictured the goal that has now been attained as a circle divided into four, with the quadrants painted in the four colours. The circulation is to the left. Though this satisfies the demands of symmetry, the polarity of the functions is still unrecognized —despite the last, very illuminating dream—because, in the painting, red and blue, green and yellow, are side by side instead of opposite one another. From this we must conclude that the "realization" is meeting with strong inner resistances, partly of a philosophical and partly of an ethical nature, the justification

[135] Book of Enoch 18 · 13 and ch. 21 (Charles, *Apocrypha and Pseudepigrapha,* II, pp. 200, 201).
[136] A more detailed commentary on this dream is to be found in Jung, "Psychology and Religion," pars. 59ff.

95. *Ludus puerorum.*—Trismosin, "Splendor solis" (MS., 1582)

96. Pygmies (helpful child-gods).—Fragments of an Egyptian mechanical toy

for which cannot lightly be set aside. That the dreamer has an inadequate understanding of the polarity is shown by the fact that the nuts have still to be cracked in reality, and also that they are all alike, i.e., not yet differentiated.

56. DREAM:

301 *Four children are carrying a large dark ring. They move in a circle. The dark unknown woman appears and says she will come again, for it is the festival of the solstice.*

302 In this dream the elements of dream 44 come together again: the children and the dark woman, who was a wicked witch before. The "solstice" indicates the turning-point. In alchemy the work is completed in the autumn (*Vindemia Hermetis*). Children (fig. 95), dwarf-gods, bring the ring—i.e., the symbol of wholeness is still under the sway of childlike creative powers. Note that children also play a part in the *opus alchymicum:* a certain portion of the work is called *ludus puerorum.* Save for the remark that the work is as easy as "child's play," I have found no explanation for this. Seeing that the work is, in the unanimous testimony of all the adepts, exceedingly difficult, it must be a euphemistic and probably also a symbolical definition. It would thus point to a co-operation on the part of "infantile" or unconscious forces represented as Cabiri and hobgoblins (homunculi: fig. 96).

97. The "Grand Peregrination" by ship. Two eagles fly round the earth in opposite directions, indicating that it is an odyssey in search of wholeness.—Maier, *Viatorium* (1651)

98. The philosophical egg, whence the double eagle is hatched, wearing the spiritual and temporal crowns.—Codex Palatinus Latinus 412 (15th cent.)

57. VISUAL IMPRESSION:

303 *The dark ring, with an egg in the middle.*

58. VISUAL IMPRESSION:

304 *A black eagle comes out of the egg and seizes in its beak the ring, now turned to gold. Then the dreamer is on a ship and the bird flies ahead.*

305 The eagle signifies height. (Previously the stress was on depth: people descending to the water.) It seizes the whole mandala and, with it, control of the dreamer, who, carried along on a ship, sails after the bird (fig. 97). Birds are thoughts and the

flight of thought. Generally it is fantasies and intuitive ideas that are represented thus (the winged Mercurius, Morpheus, genii, angels). The ship is the vehicle that bears the dreamer over the sea and the depths of the unconscious. As a man-made thing it has the significance of a system or method (or a way: cf. Hinayana and Mahayana = the Lesser and Greater Vehicle, the two schools of Buddhism). The flight of thought goes ahead and methodical elaboration follows after. Man cannot walk the rainbow bridge like a god but must go underneath with whatever reflective afterthoughts he may have. The eagle—synonymous with phoenix, vulture, raven—is a well-known alchemical symbol. Even the *lapis*, the *rebis* (compounded of two parts and therefore frequently hermaphroditic as an amalgam of Sol and Luna), is often represented with wings (figs. 22, 54, 208), denoting intuition or spiritual (winged) potentiality. In the last resort all these symbols depict the consciousness-transcending fact we call the self. This visual impression is rather like a snapshot of an evolving process as it leads on to the next stage.

306   In alchemy the egg stands for the chaos apprehended by the artifex, the *prima materia* containing the captive world-soul. Out of the egg—symbolized by the round cooking-vessel—will rise the eagle or phoenix, the liberated soul, which is ultimately identical with the Anthropos who was imprisoned in the embrace of Physis (fig. 98).

99. Time-symbol of the *lapis:* the cross and the evangelical emblems mark its
analogy with Christ.—Thomas Aquinas (pseud.), "De alchimia" (MS., 16th cent.)

III. THE VISION OF THE WORLD CLOCK

59. THE "GREAT VISION":[137]

307   There is a vertical and a horizontal circle, having a common centre. This is the world clock. It is supported by the black
bird.

   The vertical circle is a blue disc with a white border divided
into 4 × 8 = 32 partitions. A pointer rotates upon it.

   The horizontal circle consists of four colours. On it stand
four little men with pendulums, and round about it is laid the

137 This vision is treated in greater detail in Jung, "Psychology and Religion,"
pars. 112ff.

203

ring that was once dark and is now golden (formerly carried by the children).

The "clock" has three rhythms or pulses:

1. The small pulse: *the pointer on the blue vertical disc advances by 1/32.*

2. The middle pulse: *one complete revolution of the pointer. At the same time the horizontal circle advances by 1/32.*

3. The great pulse: *32 middle pulses are equal to one revolution of the golden ring.*

308   This remarkable vision made a deep and lasting impression on the dreamer, an impression of "the most sublime harmony," as he himself puts it. The world clock may well be the "severe image" which is identical with the Cabiri, i.e., the four children or four little men with the pendulums. It is a three-dimensional mandala—a mandala in bodily form signifying realization. (Unfortunately medical discretion prevents my giving the biographical details. It must suffice to say that this realization did actually take place.) Whatever a man does in reality he himself becomes.

309   Just why the vision of this curious figure should produce an impression of "the most sublime harmony" is, in one sense, very difficult to understand; but it becomes comprehensible enough as soon as we consider the comparative historical material. It is difficult to feel our way into the matter because the meaning of the image is exceedingly obscure. If the meaning is impenetrable and the form and colour take no account of aesthetic requirements, then neither our understanding nor our sense of beauty is satisfied, and we are at a loss to see why it should give rise to the impression of "the most sublime harmony." We can only venture the hypothesis that disparate and incongruous elements have combined here in the most fortunate way, simultaneously producing an image which realizes the "intentions" of the unconscious in the highest degree. We must therefore assume that the image is a singularly happy expression for an otherwise unknowable psychic fact which has so far only been able to manifest apparently disconnected aspects of itself.

310   The impression is indeed extremely abstract. One of the underlying ideas seems to be the intersection of two heterogeneous systems by the sharing of a common centre. Hence if we start as before from the assumption that the centre and its periphery

represent the totality of the psyche and consequently the self, then the figure tells us that two heterogeneous systems intersect in the self, standing to one another in a functional relationship that is governed by law and regulated by "three rhythms." The self is by definition the centre and the circumference of the conscious and unconscious systems. But the regulation of their functions by three rhythms is something that I cannot substantiate. I do not know what the three rhythms allude to. But I do not doubt for a moment that the allusion is amply justified. The only analogy I could adduce would be the three *regimina* mentioned in the Introduction (par. 31), by which the four elements are converted into one another or synthesized in the quintessence:

> 1st *regimen*: earth to water.
> 2nd   "   : water to air.
> 3rd   "   : air to fire.

311   We shall hardly be mistaken if we assume that our mandala aspires to the most complete union of opposites that is possible, including that of the masculine trinity and the feminine quaternity on the analogy of the alchemical hermaphrodite.

312   Since the figure has a cosmic aspect—world clock—we must suppose it to be a small-scale model or perhaps even a source of space-time, or at any rate an embodiment of it and therefore, mathematically speaking, four-dimensional in nature although only visible in a three-dimensional projection. I do not wish to labour this argument, for such an interpretation lies beyond my powers of proof.

313   The thirty-two pulses may conceivably derive from the multiplication of 4×8, as we know from experience that the quaternity found at the centre of a mandala often becomes 8, 16, 32, or more when extended to the periphery. The number 32 plays an important role in the Cabala. Thus we read in the *Sepher Yetsirah* (1 : 1): "Jehovah, the Lord of Hosts, the God of Israel, the living God and King of the world . . . has graven his name in thirty-two mysterious paths of wisdom." These consist of "ten self-contained numbers [*Sephiroth*] and twenty-two basic letters" (1 : 2). The meaning of the ten numbers is as follows: "1: the spirit of the Living God; 2: spirit from spirit; 3: water from spirit; 4: fire from water; 5-10: height, depth, East, West, South,

North." [138] Cornelius Agrippa mentions that "the learned Jews attribute the number 32 to Wisdom, for so many are the ways of Wisdom described by Abram." [139] Franck establishes a connection between 32 and the cabalistic trinity, Kether, Binah, and Hokhmah: "These three persons contain and unite in themselves everything that exists, and they in turn are united in the White Head, the Ancient of Days, for he is everything and everything is he. Sometimes he is represented with three heads which make but a single head, and sometimes he is likened to the brain which, without impairing its unity, divides into three parts and spreads through the whole body by means of thirty-two pairs of nerves, just as God spreads through the universe along thirty-two miraculous paths." [140] These thirty-two "canales occulti" are also mentioned by Knorr von Rosenroth,[141] who calls Hokhmah "the supreme path of all, embracing all," on the authority of Job 28 : 7 (A.V.): "There is a path which no fowl knoweth, and which the vulture's eye hath not seen." Allendy, in his very valuable account of number symbolism, writes: "32 . . . is the differentiation which appears in the organic world; not creative generation, but rather the plan and arrangement of the various forms of created things which the creator has modelled—as the product of 8×4. . . ." [142] Whether the cabalistic number 32 can be equated with the thirty-two fortunate signs (*mahavyanjana*) of the Buddha-child is doubtful.

314   As to the interpretation based on comparative historical material, we are in a more favourable position, at least as regards the general aspects of the figure. We have at our disposal, firstly, the whole mandala symbolism of three continents, and secondly, the specific time symbolism of the mandala as this developed under the influence of astrology, particularly in the West. The horoscope (fig. 100) is itself a mandala (a clock) with a dark centre, and a leftward *circumambulatio* with "houses" and planetary phases. The mandalas of ecclesiastical art, particularly those on the floor before the high altar or beneath the transept, make frequent use of the zodiacal beasts or the yearly seasons. A related idea is the identity of Christ with the Church calendar, of which

138 Bischoff, *Die Elemente der Kabbalah*, I, pp. 63ff. Further associations with "32" on pp. 175ff.   139 Agrippa, *De incertitudine*, II, ch. XV.
140 Franck, *Die Kabbala*, p. 137.
141 Knorr von Rosenroth, *Kabbala denudata*, I, p. 602.
142 Allendy, *Le Symbolisme des nombres*, p. 378.

100. Horoscope, showing the houses, zodiac, and planets.—Woodcut by Erhard
Schoen for the nativity calendar of Leonhard Reymann (1515)

101. Christ in the mandorla, surrounded by the symbols of the four evangelists. —Mural painting, church of Saint-Jacques-des-Guérets, Loir-et-Cher, France

he is the fixed pole and the life. The Son of Man is an anticipation of the idea of the self (fig. 99): hence the Gnostic adulteration of Christ with the other synonyms for the self among the Naassenes, recorded by Hippolytus. There is also a connection with the symbolism of Horus: on the one hand, Christ enthroned with the four emblems of the evangelists—three animals and an angel (fig. 101); on the other, Father Horus with his four sons, or Osiris with the four sons of Horus[143] (fig. 102). Horus is also the ἥλιος ἀνατολῆς (rising sun),[144] and Christ was still worshipped as such by the early Christians.

[143] Bas-relief at Philae (Budge, *Osiris and the Egyptian Resurrection,* I, p. 3); and *The Book of the Dead* (1899), Papyrus of Hunefer, pl. 5. Sometimes there are three with animal heads and one with a human head, as in the Papyrus of Kerasher (ibid.). In a 7th-century manuscript (Gellone) the evangelists actually wear their animal heads, as in several other Romanesque monuments.

[144] So called by Melito of Sardis, *De baptismo,* in Pitra, *Analecta sacra,* II, p. 5.

102. Osiris, with the four sons of Horus on the lotus.—*The Book of the Dead*

315   We find a remarkable parallel in the writings of Guillaume
de Digulleville, prior of the Cistercian monastery at Châlis, a
Norman poet who, independently of Dante, composed three
"pélerinages" between 1330 and 1355: *Les Pélerinages de la vie
humaine, de l'âme,* and *de Jésus Christ.*[145] The last canto of the
Pélerinage de l'âme contains a vision of Paradise, which consists
of seven large spheres each containing seven smaller spheres.[146]

145 Delacotte, *Guillaume de Digulleville.*
146 An idea which corresponds to dream 21 (par. 198), of the large sphere containing many little spheres.

All the spheres rotate, and this movement is called a *siècle* (*saeculum*). The heavenly *siècles* are the prototypes of the earthly centuries. The angel who guides the poet explains: "When holy Church ends her prayers with *in saecula saeculorum* [for ever and ever], she has in mind, not earthly time, but eternity." At the same time the *siècles* are spherical spaces in which the blessed dwell. *Siècles* and *cieux* are identical. In the highest heaven of pure gold the King sits on a round throne which shines more brightly than the sun. A *couronne* of precious stones surrounds him. Beside him, on a circular throne that is made of brown crystal, sits the Queen, who intercedes for the sinners (fig. 103).

316   "Raising his eyes to the golden heaven, the pilgrim perceived a marvellous circle which appeared to be three feet across. It came out of the golden heaven at one point and re-entered it at another, and it made the whole tour of the golden heaven." This circle is sapphire-coloured. It is a small circle, three feet in diameter, and evidently it moves over a great horizontal circle like a rolling disc. This great circle intersects the golden circle of heaven.

317   While Guillaume is absorbed in this sight, three spirits suddenly appear clad in purple, with golden crowns and girdles, and enter the golden heaven. This moment, so the angel tells him, is *une fête,* like a church festival on earth:

> Ce cercle que tu vois est le calendrier
> Qui en faisant son tour entier,
> Montre des Saints les journées
> Quand elles doivent être fêtées.
> Chacun en fait le cercle un tour,
> Chacune étoile y est pour jour,
> Chacun soleil pour l'espace
> De jours trente ou zodiaque.

> (This circle is the calendar
> Which spinning round the course entire
> Shows the feast day of each saint
> And when it should be celebrate.
> Each saint goes once round all the way,
> Each star you see stands for a day,
> And every sun denotes a spell
> Of thirty days zodiacal.)

103. *Sponsus et sponsa.*—Detail from *Polittico con l'Incoronazione,* by Stefano da Sant'Agnese (15th cent.)

104. God as Father and Logos creating the zodiac.—Peter Lombard, "De sacramentis" (MS., 14th cent.)

318   The three figures are saints whose feast day is even now being celebrated. The small circle that enters the golden heaven is *three* feet in width, and likewise there are *three* figures who make their sudden entry. They signify the moment of time in eternity, as does the circle of the calendar (fig. 104). But why this should be exactly three feet in diameter and why there are three figures remains a mystery. We naturally think of the three rhythms in our vision which are started off by the pointer moving over the blue disc, and which enter the system just as inexplicably as the calendar-circle enters the golden heaven.

319   The guide continues to instruct Guillaume on the significance of the signs of the zodiac with particular reference to sacred history, and ends with the remark that the feast of the twelve fishermen will be celebrated in the sign of Pisces, when the twelve will appear before the Trinity. Then it suddenly occurs to Guillaume that he has never really understood the nature of the Trinity, and he begs the angel for an explanation. The angel answers, "Now, there are three principal colours, namely green, red, and gold. These three colours are seen united in divers works of watered silk and in the feathers of many birds, such as the peacock. The almighty King who puts three colours in one, cannot he also make one substance to be three?" Gold, the royal colour, is attributed to God the Father; red to God the Son, because he shed his blood; and to the Holy Ghost

105. The Virgin, personifying the starry heaven.—"Speculum
humanae saluacionis" (MS., Vatican, 15th cent.)

green, "la couleur qui verdoye et qui réconforte." Thereupon
the angel warns Guillaume not to ask any more questions, and
disappears. The poet wakes up to find himself safely in his bed,
and so ends the *Pélerinage de l'âme*.

320   There is, however, one thing more to be asked: "Three there
are—but where is the fourth?" Why is blue missing? This colour
was also missing in the "disturbed" mandala of our dreamer (see
par. 287). Curiously enough, the *calendrier* that intersects the
golden circle is blue, and so is the vertical disc in the three-dimensional mandala. We would conjecture that blue, standing
for the vertical, means height and depth (the blue sky above, the
blue sea below), and that any shrinkage of the vertical reduces
the square to an oblong, thus producing something like an inflation of consciousness.[147] Hence the vertical would correspond to

147 Cf. my remarks on "inflation" in "The Relations between the Ego and the Unconscious," pars. 227ff.

213

the unconscious. But the unconscious in a man has feminine characteristics, and blue is the traditional colour of the Virgin's celestial cloak (fig. 105). Guillaume was so absorbed in the Trinity and in the threefold aspect of the *roy* that he quite forgot the *reyne*. Faust prays to her in these words: "Supreme Mistress of the world! Let me behold thy secret in the outstretched azure canopy of heaven."

321   It was inevitable that blue should be missing for Guillaume in the tetrad of rainbow colours, because of its feminine nature. But, like woman herself, the anima means the height and depth of a man. Without the blue vertical circle the golden mandala remains bodiless and two-dimensional, a mere abstraction. It is only the intervention of time and space here and now that makes reality. Wholeness is realized for a moment only—the moment that Faust was seeking all his life.

322   The poet in Guillaume must have had an inkling of the heretical truth when he gave the King a Queen sitting on a throne made of earth-brown crystal. For what is heaven without Mother Earth? And how can man reach fulfilment if the Queen does not intercede for his black soul? She understands the darkness, for she has taken her throne—the earth itself—to heaven with her, if only by the subtlest of suggestions. She adds the missing blue to the gold, red, and green, and thus completes the harmonious whole.

106. "Elixir of the moon."
—Codex Reginensis Latinus 1458
(17th cent.)

IV. THE SYMBOLS OF THE SELF

323   The vision of the "world clock" is neither the last nor the highest point in the development of the symbols of the objective psyche. But it brings to an end the first third of the material, consisting in all of some four hundred dreams and visions. This series is noteworthy because it gives an unusually complete description of a psychic fact that I had observed long before in many individual cases.[148] We have to thank not only the completeness of the objective material but the care and discernment of the dreamer for having placed us in a position to follow, step by step, the synthetic work of the unconscious. The troubled course of this synthesis would doubtless have been depicted in even greater completeness had I taken account of the 340 dreams interspersed among the 59 examined here. Unfortunately this was impossible, because the dreams touch to some extent on the intimacies of personal life and must therefore remain unpublished. So I had to confine myself to the impersonal material.

324   I hope I may have succeeded in throwing some light upon the development of the symbols of the self and in overcoming, partially at least, the serious difficulties inherent in all material drawn from actual experience. At the same time I am fully aware that the comparative material so necessary for a complete elucidation could have been greatly increased. But, so as not to burden the exposition unduly, I have exercised the greatest reserve in this respect. Consequently there is much that is only hinted at, though this should not be taken as a sign of superficiality. I believe myself to be in a position to offer ample evidence for my views, but I do not wish to give the impression that I imagine I have said anything final on this highly complicated subject. It is true that this is not the first time I have dealt with a series of spontaneous manifestations of the unconscious. I did so once before, in my book *Psychology of the Unconscious*,[149] but there it was more a problem of neurosis in puberty, whereas this is the broader problem of individuation.

148 Cf. my commentary on *The Secret of the Golden Flower*, pars. 31ff. Cf. also "Concerning Mandala Symbolism."
149 Revised edition: *Symbols of Transformation*.

107. Virgin carrying the Saviour.—"Speculum humanae saluacionis" (MS., Vatican, 15th cent.)

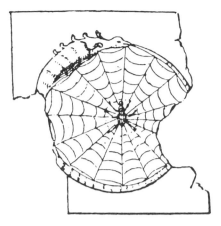

108. Maya, eternal weaver of the illusory world of the senses, encircled by the Uroboros.—Damaged vignette from a collection of Brahminic sayings

Moreover, there is a very considerable difference between the two personalities in question. The earlier case, which I never saw at first hand, ended in psychic catastrophe—a psychosis; but the present case shows a normal development such as I have often observed in highly intelligent persons.

325 What is particularly noteworthy here is the consistent development of the central symbol. We can hardly escape the feeling that the unconscious process moves spiral-wise round a centre, gradually getting closer, while the characteristics of the centre grow more and more distinct. Or perhaps we could put it the other way round and say that the centre—itself virtually unknowable—acts like a magnet on the disparate materials and processes of the unconscious and gradually captures them as in a crystal lattice. For this reason the centre is (in other cases) often pictured as a spider in its web (fig. 108), especially when the conscious attitude is still dominated by fear of unconscious processes. But if the process is allowed to take its course, as it was in our case, then the central symbol, constantly renewing itself, will steadily and consistently force its way through the apparent chaos of the personal psyche and its dramatic entanglements, just as the great Bernoulli's epitaph[150] says of the spiral: "Eadem mutata resurgo." Accordingly we often find spiral representations of the centre, as for instance the serpent coiled round the creative point, the egg.

326 Indeed, it seems as if all the personal entanglements and

150 In the cloisters of Basel Cathedral.

dramatic changes of fortune that make up the intensity of life were nothing but hesitations, timid shrinkings, almost like petty complications and meticulous excuses for not facing the finality of this strange and uncanny process of crystallization. Often one has the impression that the personal psyche is running round this central point like a shy animal, at once fascinated and frightened, always in flight, and yet steadily drawing nearer.

327   I trust I have given no cause for the misunderstanding that I know anything about the nature of the "centre"—for it is simply unknowable and can only be expressed symbolically through its own phenomenology, as is the case, incidentally, with every object of experience. Among the various characteristics of the centre the one that struck me from the beginning was the phenomenon of the quaternity (fig. 109). That it is not simply a question of, shall we say, the "four" points of the compass or something of that kind is proved by the fact that there is often a competition between four and three.[151] There is also, but more rarely, a competition between four and five, though five-rayed mandalas must be characterized as abnormal on account of their lack of symmetry.[152] It would seem, therefore, that there is normally a clear insistence on four, or as if there were a greater statistical probability of four. Now it is—as I can hardly refrain from remarking—a curious "sport of nature" that the chief chemical constituent of the physical organism is carbon, which is characterized by four valencies; also it is well known that the diamond is a carbon crystal. Carbon is black—coal, graphite—but the diamond is "purest water." To draw such an analogy would be a lamentable piece of intellectual bad taste were the phenomenon of four merely a poetic conceit on the part of the conscious mind and not a spontaneous product of the objective psyche. Even if we supposed that dreams could be influenced to any appreciable extent by auto-suggestion—in which case it would naturally be more a matter of their meaning than of their form —it would still have to be proved that the conscious mind of the dreamer had made a serious effort to impress the idea of the qua-

151 This was observed chiefly in men, but whether it was mere chance I am unable to say.
152 Observed mainly in women. But it occurs so rarely that it is impossible to draw any further conclusions.

109. The four evangelists with their symbols and the four rivers of paradise.
Centre, the wheels of Ezekiel with the *spiritus vitae* that "was in the wheels"
(Ezek. 1 : 21).—Miniature in an Evangeliary, Aschaffenburg (13th cent.)

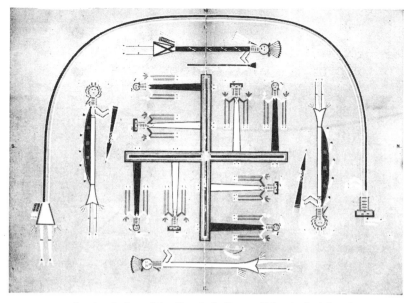

110. Sand-painting of the Navajo Indians.—Ethnological drawing

ternity on the unconscious. But in this case as in many other cases I have observed, such a possibility is absolutely out of the question, quite apart from the numerous historical and ethnological parallels[153] (fig. 110; cf. also figs. 50, 61–66, 82, 109). Surveying these facts as a whole, we come, at least in my opinion, to the inescapable conclusion that there is some psychic element present which expresses itself through the quaternity. No daring speculation or extravagant fancy is needed for this. If I have called the centre the "self," I did so after mature consideration and a careful appraisal of the empirical and historical data. A materialistic interpretation could easily maintain that the "centre" is "nothing but" the point at which the psyche ceases to be knowable because it there coalesces with the body. And a spiritualistic interpretation might retort that this "self" is nothing but "spirit," which animates both soul and body and irrupts into time and space at that creative point. I purposely refrain from all such physical and metaphysical speculations and content myself with establishing the empirical facts, and this seems to me infinitely more important for the advance of human knowledge

153 I have mentioned only a few of these parallels here.

than running after fashionable intellectual crazes or jumped-up "religious" creeds.

328   To the best of my experience we are dealing here with very important "nuclear processes" in the objective psyche—"images of the goal," as it were, which the psychic process, being goal-directed, apparently sets up of its own accord, without any external stimulus.[154] Externally, of course, there is always a certain condition of psychic need, a sort of hunger, but it seeks for familiar and favourite dishes and never imagines as its goal some outlandish food unknown to consciousness. The goal which beckons to this psychic need, the image which promises to heal, to make whole, is at first strange beyond all measure to the conscious mind, so that it can find entry only with the very greatest difficulty. Of course it is quite different for people who live in a time and environment when such images of the goal have dogmatic validity. These images are then *eo ipso* held up to consciousness, and the unconscious is thus shown its own secret reflection, in which it recognizes itself and so joins forces with the conscious mind.

329   As to the question of the origin of the mandala motif, from a superficial point of view it looks as if it had gradually come into being in the course of the dream-series. The fact is, however, that it only *appeared* more and more distinctly and in increasingly differentiated form; in reality it was always present and even occurred in the first dream—as the nymphs say later: "We were always there, only you did not notice us." It is therefore more probable that we are dealing with an *a priori* "type," an archetype which is inherent in the collective unconscious and thus beyond individual birth and death. The archetype is, so to speak, an "eternal" presence, and the only question is whether it is perceived by the conscious mind or not. I think we are forming a more probable hypothesis, and one that better explains the observed facts, if we assume that the increase in the clarity and frequency of the mandala motif is due to a more accurate perception of an already existing "type," rather

154 The image that presents itself in this material as a goal may also serve as the origin when viewed from the historical standpoint. By way of example I would cite the conception of paradise in the Old Testament, and especially the creation of Adam in the Slavonic Book of Enoch. Charles, *Apocrypha and Pseudepigrapha*, II, 425ff.; Förster, "Adams Erschaffung und Namengebung."

than that it is generated in the course of the dream-series.[155] The latter assumption is contradicted by the fact, for instance, that such fundamental ideas as the hat which epitomizes the personality, the encircling serpent, and the *perpetuum mobile* appear right at the beginning (first series: dream 1, par. 52, and vision 5, par. 62; second series: dream 9, par. 134).

330   If the motif of the mandala is an archetype it ought to be a collective phenomenon, i.e., theoretically it should appear in everyone. In practice, however, it is to be met with in distinct form in relatively few cases, though this does not prevent it from functioning as a concealed pole round which everything ultimately revolves. In the last analysis every life is the realization of a whole, that is, of a self, for which reason this realization can also be called "individuation." All life is bound to individual carriers who realize it, and it is simply inconceivable without them. But every carrier is charged with an individual destiny and destination, and the realization of these alone makes sense of life. True, the "sense" is often something that could just as well be called "nonsense," for there is a certain incommensurability between the mystery of existence and human understanding. "Sense" and "nonsense" are merely man-made labels which serve to give us a reasonably valid sense of direction.

331   As the historical parallels show, the symbolism of the mandala is not just a unique curiosity; we can well say that it is a regular occurrence. Were it not so there would be no comparative material, and it is precisely the possibility of comparing the mental products of all times from every quarter of the globe that shows us most clearly what immense importance the *consensus gentium* has always attached to the processes of the objective psyche. This is reason enough not to make light of them, and my medical experience has only confirmed this estimate. There are people, of course, who think it unscientific to take anything seriously; they do not want their intellectual play-

---

155 If we divide the four hundred dreams into eight groups of fifty each, we come to the following results:

I	....	6 mandalas	V	....	11 mandalas
II	....	4 "	VI	....	11 "
III	....	2 "	VII	....	11 "
IV	....	9 "	VIII	....	17 "

So a considerable increase in the occurrence of the mandala motif takes place in the course of the whole series.

ground disturbed by graver considerations. But the doctor who fails to take account of man's feelings for values commits a serious blunder, and if he tries to correct the mysterious and well-nigh inscrutable workings of nature with his so-called scientific attitude, he is merely putting his shallow sophistry in place of nature's healing processes. Let us take the wisdom of the old alchemists to heart: "Naturalissimum et perfectissimum opus est generare tale quale ipsum est." [156]

[156] "The most natural and perfect work is to generate its like."

111. The *cauda pavonis,* combination of all colours, symbolizing wholeness.—Boschius, *Symbolographia* (1702)

112. The principal symbols of alchemy.—Trismosin, *La Toyson d'or* (1612), title-page detail

III

RELIGIOUS IDEAS IN ALCHEMY

AN HISTORICAL SURVEY OF ALCHEMICAL IDEAS

> *Habentibus symbolum facilis est transitus* (For those who have the symbol the passage is easy).— An alchemical *verbum magistri* from Mylius, *Philosophia reformata.*

113. Moon and sun furnaces, showing the *coniunctio,* the union of opposites.
—*Mutus liber* (1702)

1. BASIC CONCEPTS OF ALCHEMY

I. INTRODUCTION

332   Slowly, in the course of the eighteenth century, alchemy perished in its own obscurity. Its method of explanation—"obscurum per obscurius, ignotum per ignotius" (the obscure by the more obscure, the unknown by the more unknown)—was incompatible with the spirit of enlightenment and particularly with the dawning science of chemistry towards the end of the century. But these two new intellectual forces only gave the *coup de grâce* to alchemy. Its inner decay had begun at least a century earlier, at the time of Jakob Böhme, when many alchemists deserted their alembics and melting-pots and devoted themselves entirely to (Hermetic) philosophy. It was then that the chemist and the Hermetic philosopher parted company. Chemistry became natural science, whereas Hermetic philosophy lost the empirical ground from under its feet and aspired to bombastic allegories and inane speculations which were kept alive only by memories of a better time.[1] This was a time

---

[1] An alarming example of this kind of "alchemy" is to be found in the illustrated work *Geheime Figuren der Rosenkreuzer,* belonging to the 16th and 17th centuries. The so-called Sachse Codex, belonging to the first half of the 18th century, also gives an excellent idea of this amazing literature. (Cf. Hall, *Codex Rosae Crucis.*)

when the mind of the alchemist was still grappling with the problems of matter, when the exploring consciousness was confronted by the dark void of the unknown, in which figures and laws were dimly perceived and attributed to matter although they really belonged to the psyche. Everything unknown and empty is filled with psychological projection; it is as if the investigator's own psychic background were mirrored in the darkness. What he sees in matter, or thinks he can see, is chiefly the data of his own unconscious which he is projecting into it. In other words, he encounters in matter, as apparently belonging to it, certain qualities and potential meanings of whose psychic nature he is entirely unconscious. This is particularly true of classical alchemy, when empirical science and mystical philosophy were more or less undifferentiated. The process of fission which separated the φυσικά from the μυστικά set in at the end of the sixteenth century and produced a quite fantastic species of literature whose authors were, at least to some extent, conscious of the psychic nature of their "alchemystical" transmutations. On this aspect of alchemy, especially as regards its psychological significance, Herbert Silberer's book *Problems of Mysticism and Its Symbolism* gives us abundant information. The fantastic symbolism bound up with it is graphically described in a paper by R. Bernoulli,[2] and a detailed account of Hermetic philosophy is to be found in a study by J. Evola.[3] But a comprehensive study of the ideas contained in the texts, and of their history, is still lacking, although we are indebted to Reitzenstein for important preparatory work in this field.

II. THE ALCHEMICAL PROCESS AND ITS STAGES

333   Alchemy, as is well known, describes a process of chemical transformation and gives numberless directions for its accomplishment. Although hardly two authors are of the same opinion regarding the exact course of the process and the sequence of its stages, the majority are agreed on the principal points at issue, and have been so from the earliest times, i.e., since the be-

2 "Spiritual Development as Reflected in Alchemy and Related Disciplines."
3 *La tradizione ermetica.*

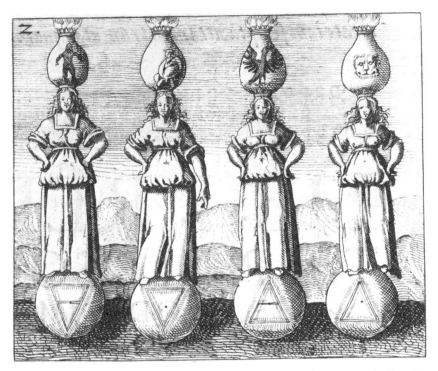

114. The four stages of the alchemical process. The four elements are indicated
on the balls.—Mylius, *Philosophia reformata* (1622)

ginning of the Christian era. Four stages are distinguished (fig.
114), characterized by the original colours mentioned in Heraclitus: *melanosis* (blackening), *leukosis* (whitening), *xanthosis*
(yellowing), and *iosis* (reddening).[4] This division of the process
into four was called the τετραμερεῖν τὴν φιλοσοφίαν, the quartering of the philosophy. Later, about the fifteenth or sixteenth
century, the colours were reduced to three, and the *xanthosis*,
otherwise called the *citrinitas,* gradually fell into disuse or was
but seldom mentioned. Instead, the *viriditas* sometimes appears
after the *melanosis* or *nigredo* in exceptional cases, though it
was never generally recognized. Whereas the original tetrameria
corresponded exactly to the quaternity of elements, it was now
frequently stressed that although there were four elements
(earth, water, fire, and air) and four qualities (hot, cold, dry, and
moist), there were only three colours: black, white, and red.

4 This word comes from ἰός (poison). But since it has about the same meaning
as the red tincture of later alchemy I have translated *iosis* as "reddening."

229

115. The *nigredo*: eclipse of *Mercurius senex*, exhaling the *spiritus* and *anima*.
The raven is a *nigredo* symbol.—Jamsthaler, *Viatorium spagyricum* (1625)

Since the process never led to the desired goal and since the individual parts of it were never carried out in any standardized manner, the change in the classification of its stages cannot be due to extraneous reasons but has more to do with the symbolical significance of the quaternity and the trinity; in other words, it is due to inner psychological reasons.[5]

334   The *nigredo* or blackness (fig. 115) is the initial state, either present from the beginning as a quality of the *prima materia*, the chaos or *massa confusa*, or else produced by the separation (*solutio, separatio, divisio, putrefactio*) of the elements. If the separated condition is assumed at the start, as sometimes hap-

[5] This is particularly evident in the writings of Dorn, who violently attacked the quaternity from the trinitarian standpoint, calling it the "quadricornutus serpens" (four-horned serpent). See Jung, "Psychology and Religion," pars. 103f.

116. Crowned hermaphrodite representing the union of king and queen, between the sun and moon trees.—"Traité d'alchimie" (MS., Paris, 17th cent.)

pens, then a union of opposites is performed under the likeness of a union of male and female (called the *coniugium, matrimonium, coniunctio, coitus*), followed by the death of the product of the union (*mortificatio, calcinatio, putrefactio*) and a corresponding *nigredo*. From this the washing (*ablutio, baptisma*) either leads direct to the whitening (*albedo*), or else the soul (*anima*) released at the "death" is reunited with the dead body and brings about its resurrection, or again the "many colours" (*omnes colores*), or "peacock's tail" (*cauda pavonis*), lead to the one white colour that contains all colours. At this point the first main goal of the process is reached, namely the *albedo, tinctura alba, terra alba foliata, lapis albus,* etc., highly prized by many alchemists as if it were the ultimate goal. It is the silver or moon condition, which still has to be raised to the sun condition. The *albedo* is, so to speak, the daybreak, but not till the *rubedo* is it sunrise. The transition to the *rubedo* is formed by the *citrinitas,* though this, as we have said, was omitted later. The *rubedo* then follows direct from the *albedo* as the result of raising the heat of the fire to its highest intensity. The red and the white are King and Queen, who may also celebrate their "chymical wedding" at this stage (fig. 116).

III. CONCEPTIONS AND SYMBOLS OF THE GOAL

335   The arrangement of the stages in individual authors depends primarily on their conception of the goal: sometimes this is the white or red tincture *(aqua permanens)*; sometimes the philosophers' stone, which, as hermaphrodite, contains both; or again it is the panacea *(aurum potabile, elixir vitae),* philosophical gold, golden glass *(vitrum aureum),* malleable glass *(vitrum malleabile).* The conceptions of the goal are as vague and various as the individual processes. The *lapis philosophorum,* for instance, is often the *prima materia,* or the means of producing the gold; or again it is an altogether mystical being that is sometimes called *Deus terrestris, Salvator,* or *filius macrocosmi,* a figure we can only compare with the Gnostic Anthropos, the divine original man[6] (fig. 117).

336   Besides the idea of the *prima materia,* that of water *(aqua permanens)* and that of fire *(ignis noster)* play an important part. Although these two elements are antagonistic and even constitute a typical pair of opposites, they are yet one and the same according to the testimony of the authors.[7] Like the *prima mate-*

---

[6] Cf. Jung, "Paracelsus as a Spiritual Phenomenon," pars. 165ff., 203ff.

[7] *Rosarium, Art. aurif.,* II, p. 264: the *aqua permanens* is the "fiery form of the true water." Ripley, *Opera omnia chemica,* p. 62: "Anima aerea est secretus ignis nostrae philosophiae, oleum nostrum, nostra aqua mystice" (The aerial soul is the secret fire of our philosophy, our oil, our mystic water). "Figurarum Aegyptiorum secretarum" (MS. in author's coll.), p. 6: "The water of the philosophers

117. Anthropos as *anima mundi*, containing the four elements and characterized by the number 10, which represents perfection $(1 + 2 + 3 + 4)$.—Albertus Magnus, *Philosophia naturalis* (1650)

ria the water has a thousand names;[8] it is even said to be the original material of the stone.[9] In spite of this we are on the other hand assured that the water is extracted from the stone or *prima materia* as its life-giving soul (*anima*).[10] This perplexity comes out very clearly in the following passage from the "VIII Exercitatio in Turbam":

Many dispute in long controversies whether the stone, under different names, consists of several substances, or of two, or only of one. But this philosopher [Scites] [11] and Bonellus[12] say that the whole work and the substance of the whole work are nothing but the water; and that the treatment [*regimen*] of the same also takes place in nothing but the water. And there is in fact one substance in which everything is contained and that is the *sulphur philosophorum*, [which] is water and soul, oil, Mercurius and Sol, the fire of nature, the eagle, the *lachryma*, the first *hyle* of the wise, the *materia prima* of the perfect body. And by whatever names the philosophers have called their stone they always mean and refer to this one substance, i.e., to the water from which everything [originates] and in which everything [is contained], which rules everything, in which errors are made and in which the error is itself corrected. I call it "philosophical" water, not ordinary [*vulgi*] water but *aqua mercurialis*, whether it be simple or composite. For both are the philo-

---

is fire." Philalethes, "Introitus apertus," *Mus. herm.*, p. 653: "Est nempe in Aqua nostra requisitus . . . Ignis" etc. (For in our water fire . . . is sought). *Aurora* I, ch. XI, parab. VI: Senior saith: "And when they desire to extract this divine water, which is fire, they warm it with their fire, which is water, which they have measured unto the end and have hidden on account of the unwisdom of fools." *Aurora* II, *Art. aurif.*, I, p. 212 (quotation from Senior): "Ignis noster est aqua." Ibid., p. 227: "Philosophus autem per aquam, vulgus vero per ignem" (The philosopher through water, ordinary people through fire).

8 Zosimos, in Berthelot, *Alch. grecs*, III, lii, 2.

9 "Turba philosophorum," *Art. aurif.*, I, p. 14: ". . . aqua permanens, ex qua quidem aqua lapis noster preciosissimus generatur" (. . . the permanent water, out of which water our most precious stone is generated). "Cons. coniug." *Ars chem.*, p. 128: "Lapidem esse aquam fontis vivi" (That stone is water of a living fountain).

10 Ibid., p. 66: "Vita uniuscuiusque rei . . . est vivum quod non moritur, quamdiu mundus est, quia est caput mundi" etc. ([Water is] the life of everything; it is alive because it does not die as long as the world exists, for it is the head [i.e., principle] of the world).

11 Scites, Frictes, Feritis = Socrates (*Turba* [ed. Ruska], p. 25).

12 Bonellus, Balinus, Belinus = Apollonius of Tyana (Steinschneider and Berthelot, cited in Ruska, ibid., p. 26).

Spiritus, Anima, Corpus.

118. Brother-sister pair in the "bath of life," being bitten in the calf by dragons while the lunar water, fertilized by the divine breath, is poured over their heads.—*Theatrum chemicum Britannicum* (1652)

sophical water, although the vulgar mercury is different from the philosophical. That [water] is simple [and] unmixed, this [water] is composed of two substances: namely of our mineral and of simple water. These composite waters form the philosophical Mercurius. from which it must be assumed that the substance, or the *prima materia* itself, consists of composite water. Some [alchemists] put three together, others, only two. For myself two species are sufficient: male and female or brother and sister [fig. 118]. But they also call the simple water poison, quicksilver [*argentum vivum*], cambar, *aqua permanens*, gum, vinegar, urine, sea-water, dragon, and serpent.[13]

337   This account makes one thing very evident: the philosophical water is the stone or the *prima materia* itself; but at the same time, it is also its solvent, as is proved by the prescription immediately following:

Grind the stone to a very fine powder and put it into the sharpest celestial [*coelestino*] vinegar, and it will at once be dissolved into the philosophical water.

[13] "In Turbam philosophorum exercitationes," *Art. aurif.*, I, p. 167.

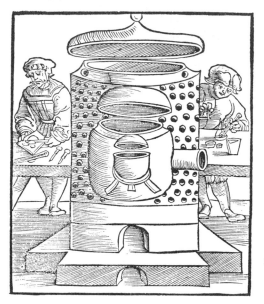

119. Alchemical furnace.—
Geber, *De alchimia* (1529)

338 It can also be shown that fire played the same role as water.
Another, no less important, idea is that of the Hermetic vessel
(*vas Hermetis*), typified by the retorts or melting-furnaces that
contained the substances to be transformed (fig. 119). Although
an instrument, it nevertheless has peculiar connections with the
prima materia as well as with the *lapis*, so it is no mere piece of
apparatus. For the alchemists the vessel is something truly marvellous: a *vas mirabile*. Maria Prophetissa (fig. 78) says that the
whole secret lies in knowing about the Hermetic vessel. "Unum
est vas" (the vessel is one) is emphasized again and again.[14] It
must be completely round,[15] in imitation of the spherical cosmos,[16] so that the influence of the stars may contribute to the

[14] For instance, "Unum in uno circulo sive vase" (One in one circle or vessel).—
Scholia to the Hermetic "Tractatus aureus," *Bibl. chem. curiosa*, I, p. 442.
[15] Therefore it is called "domus vitrea sphaeratilis sive circularis" (the spherical
or circular house of glass).—"Epistola ad Hermannum," *Theatr. chem.*, V, p. 896.
The *vas* is a "sphaera, quam cribrum vocamus" (sphere, which we call a sieve).—
"Allegoriae super librum Turbae," *Art. aurif.*, I, p. 144. This idea appears as early
as Greek alchemy, for instance in Olympiodorus (Berthelot, *Alch. grecs*, II, iv, 44, ll.
17–18). The *vas* is an ὄργανον κυκλικόν, a φιάλη σφαιροειδής (a circular instrument,
a phial of spherical shape).
[16] "Vas spagiricum ad similitudinem vasis naturalis construendum. Videmus enim
totum caelum et elementa similitudinem habere sphaerici corporis, in cuius centro viget ignis calor inferioris . . . necessarium igitur fuit nostrum ignem poni

236

120. Mercurius in the vessel.
—Barchusen, *Elementa chemiae* (1718)

success of the operation.[17] It is a kind of matrix or uterus from
which the *filius philosophorum,* the miraculous stone, is to be
born[18] (fig. 120). Hence it is required that the vessel be not only

extra nostrum vas, et sub eius rotundi fundi centro, instar solis naturalis." (The
spagyric vessel is to be constructed after the model of the natural vessel. For we
see that the whole sky and the elements resemble a spherical body, in the centre
of which lives the heat of the lower fire. . . . It was therefore necessary to put
our fire outside our vessel, beneath the centre of its rounded base, like the natural
sun.)—Dorn, "Physica Trismegisti," *Theatr. chem.,* I, p. 430. "Vas est sicut opus
Dei in vase germinis divi" (The vessel is like the work of God in the vessel of
divine germination). "Vas autem factum est rotundum ad imitationem superi[oris]
et inferi[oris]" (The vessel is made round, in imitation of the upper and the
lower).—"Liber Platonis quartorum," *Theatr. chem.,* V, pp. 148, 152. Reitzenstein
(*Poimandres,* p. 141) is therefore justified in comparing the *vas mirabile* on the
head of the angel (in the treatise "Isis to Horus" in Berthelot, *Alch. grecs,* I, xiii,
1) to the κύκλος δισκοειδής on the head of Chnuphis in Porphyry. (Cf. fig. 203.)
17 Dorn, "Congeries," *Theatr. chem.,* I, p. 574: "Vas nostrum ad hunc modum
esse debet, ut in eo materia regi valeat a caelestibus corporibus. Influentiae
namque caelestes invisibiles et astrorum impressiones apprime necessariae sunt
ad opus." (Our vessel must be such that in it matter can be influenced by the
heavenly bodies. For the invisible celestial influences and the impressions of the
stars are necessary to the work.)
18 *Vas* as *matrix:* Ripley, *Opera omnia,* p. 23; "In Turbam philosophorum excr-
citationes," *Art. aurif.,* I, p. 159; *Aurora* II, *Art. aurif.,* I, p. 203; "Consil. coniug.,"
Ars chem., p. 204.

237

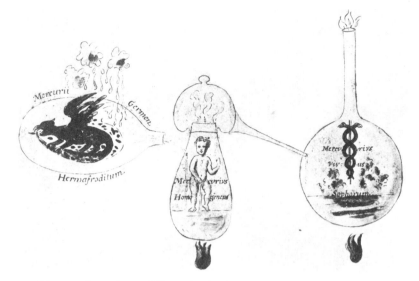

121. The transformations of Mercurius in the Hermetic vessel. The homunculus shown as a "pissing manikin" is an allusion to the *urina puerorum* (= *aqua permanens*).—"Cabala mineralis" (MS., British Museum, Add. 5245)

round but egg-shaped [19] (fig. 121; cf. fig. 22). One naturally thinks of this vessel as a sort of retort or flask; but one soon learns that this is an inadequate conception since the vessel is more a mystical idea, a true symbol like all the central ideas of alchemy. Thus we hear that the *vas* is the water or *aqua permanens,* which is none other than the Mercurius of the philosophers.[20] But not only is it the water, it is also its opposite: fire.[21]

[19] Ripley, *Opera omnia,* p. 30: "In uno vitro debent omnia fieri, quod sit forma ovi" (Everything must be done in one glass, which must be egg-shaped).

[20] Philalethes, "Fons chymicae veritatis," *Mus. herm.,* p. 803: "Quum igitur de vase nostro loquimur, intellige aquam nostram, quum de igne, itidem aquam intellige, et quum de furno disputamus, nihil ab aqua diversum aut divisum volumus" (When, therefore, we speak of "our vessel," understand "our water"; when we speak of fire, again understand water; and when we discuss the furnace, we mean nothing that is different or distinct from water). Mercurius, i.e., the *aqua permanens,* is "vas nostrum verum occultum, hortus item Philosophicus, in quo Sol noster orietur et surgit" (our true hidden vessel, and also the Philosophical Garden in which our sun rises and ascends). (Philalethes, "Metallorum metamorphosis," *Mus. herm.,* p. 770.) Other names are *mater, ovum, furnus secretus,* etc. (Ibid., p. 770; also *Aurora* II, *Art. aurif.,* I, p. 203). "The vessel of the Philosophers is their water" (Hermes quotation in Hoghelande, "De alchimiae difficultatibus," *Theatr. chem.,* I, p. 199).

339   I will not enter further into all the innumerable synonyms for the vessel. The few I have mentioned will suffice to demonstrate its undoubted symbolical significance.

340   As to the course of the process as a whole, the authors are vague and contradictory. Many content themselves with a few summary hints, others make an elaborate list of the various operations. Thus in 1576, Josephus Quercetanus, alchemist, physician, and diplomat, who in France and French Switzerland played a somewhat similar role to that of Paracelsus, established a sequence of twelve operations[22] as follows (fig. 122):

1. *Calcinatio*	7. *Cibatio*
2. *Solutio*	8. *Sublimatio*
3. *Elementorum separatio*	9. *Fermentatio*
4. *Coniunctio*	10. *Exaltatio*
5. *Putrefactio*	11. *Augmentatio*
6. *Coagulatio*	12. *Proiectio*

Every single one of these terms has more than one meaning; we need only look up the explanations in Ruland's *Lexicon* to get a more than adequate idea of this. It is therefore pointless to go further into the variations of the alchemical procedure in the present context.

341   Such is, superficially and in the roughest outline, the framework of alchemy as known to us all. From the point of view of our modern knowledge of chemistry it tells us little or nothing, and if we turn to the texts and the hundreds and hundreds of procedures and recipes left behind by the Middle Ages and antiquity, we shall find relatively few among them with any recognizable meaning for the chemist. He would probably find most of them nonsensical, and furthermore it is certain beyond all doubt that no real tincture or artificial gold was ever produced during the many centuries of earnest endeavour. What then, we may fairly ask, induced the old alchemists to go on labouring—

---

21 *Vas* = *ignis verus* (Philalethes, "Metallorum metamorphosis," *Mus. herm.*, p. 770) and *vinum ardens, ignis* (Mylius, *Philosophia reformata*, p. 245). "[Vas Hermetis] est mensura ignis tui" (The vessel of Hermes is the measure of your fire). "Practica Mariae," *Art. aurif.*, I, p. 323. In the alchemical commentary ("Recueil stéganographique") to Béroalde de Verville's *Songe de Poliphile*, fire and water are interpreted morally as "flames and tears."
22 Quercetanus, "De ortu et causis metallorum," *Theatr. chem.*, II, pp. 198ff.

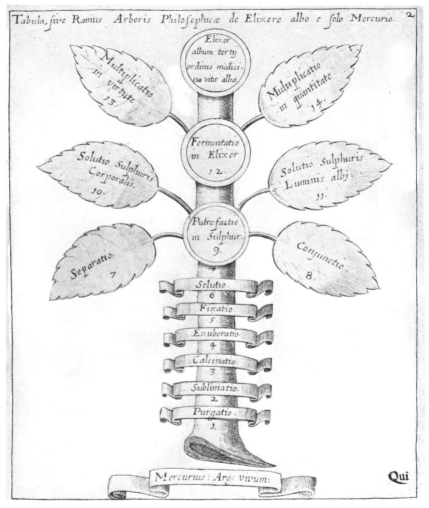

122. The twelve alchemical operations in the form of the *arbor philosophica.*
—Samuel Norton, *Mercurius redivivus* (1630)

or, as they said, "operating"—so steadfastly and to write all those treatises on the "divine" art if their whole undertaking was so portentously futile? To do them justice we must add that all knowledge of the nature of chemistry and its limitations was still completely closed to them, so that they were as much entitled to hope as those who dreamed of flying and whose successors made the dream come true after all. Nor should we underestimate the sense of satisfaction born of the enterprise, the excitement of the adventure, of the *quaerere* (seeking) and the *invenire* (finding). This always lasts as long as the methods employed seem sensible. There was nothing at that time to convince the alchemist of the senselessness of his chemical operations; what is more, he could look back on a long tradition which contained not a few testimonies of such as had achieved the marvellous result.[23] Finally the matter was not entirely without promise, since a number of useful discoveries did occasionally emerge as by-products of his labours in the laboratory. As the forerunner of chemistry alchemy had a sufficient *raison d'être*. Hence, even if alchemy had consisted in—if you like—an unending series of futile and barren chemical experiments, it would be no more astonishing than the venturesome endeavours of medieval medicine and pharmacology.

[23] Even Meyrink (in the 20th century) still believed in the possibility of the alchemical procedure. We find a remarkable report of his own experiments in his introduction to *Aquinas: Abhandlung über den Stein*, pp. xxixff.

123. Hermaphrodite.—*Hermaphroditisches Sonn- und Mondskind* (1752)

241

124. Alchemists at work.—*Mutus liber* (1702)

2. THE PSYCHIC NATURE OF THE
ALCHEMICAL WORK

I. THE PROJECTION OF PSYCHIC CONTENTS

342   The alchemical *opus* deals in the main not just with chemical experiments as such, but with something resembling psychic processes expressed in pseudochemical language.[1] The ancients knew more or less what chemical processes were; therefore they must have known that the thing they practised was, to say the least of it, no ordinary chemistry. That they realized the difference is shown even in the title of a treatise by (Pseudo-)Democritus, ascribed to the first century: τὰ φυσικὰ καὶ τὰ μυστικά. And soon afterwards a wealth of evidence accumulates to show

---

[1] Evola (*La tradizione ermetica,* pp. 28f.) says: "The spiritual constitution of man in the premodern cycles of culture was such that each physical perception had simultaneously a psychic component which 'animated' it, adding a 'significance' to the bare image, and at the same time a special and potent emotional tone. Thus ancient physics was both a theology and a transcendental psychology, by reason of the illuminating flashes from metaphysical essences which penetrated through the matter of the bodily senses. Natural science was at once a spiritual science, and the many meanings of the symbols united the various aspects of a single knowledge."

that in alchemy there are two—in our eyes—heterogeneous currents flowing side by side, which we simply cannot conceive as being compatible. Alchemy's "tam ethice quam physice" (as much ethical—i.e., psychological—as physical) is impenetrable to our logic. If the alchemist is admittedly using the chemical process only symbolically, then why does he work in a laboratory with crucibles and alembics? And if, as he constantly asserts, he is describing chemical processes, why distort them past recognition with his mythological symbolisms?

343   This puzzle has proved something of a headache to many an honest and well-meaning student of alchemy. On the one hand the alchemist declares that he is concealing the truth intentionally, so as to prevent wicked or stupid people from gaining possession of the gold and thus precipitating a catastrophe. But, on the other hand, the same author will assure us that the gold he is seeking is not—as the stupid suppose—the ordinary gold (*aurum vulgi*), it is the philosophical gold or even the marvellous stone, the *lapis invisibilitatis* (the stone of invisibility),[2] or the *lapis aethereus* (the ethereal stone),[3] or finally the unimaginable hermaphroditic *rebis* (fig. 125), and he will end up by saying that all recipes whatsoever are to be despised.[4] For psychological reasons, however, it is highly unlikely that the motive prompting the alchemist to secrecy and mystification was consideration for mankind. Whenever anything real is discovered it is usually announced with a flourish of trumpets. The fact is that the alchemists had little or nothing to divulge in the way of chemistry, least of all the secret of goldmaking.

344   Mystification can be pure bluff for the obvious purpose of exploiting the credulous. But any attempt to explain alchemy as a whole from this angle is, in my opinion, contradicted by the fact that a fair number of detailed, scholarly, and conscientious

2 *Rosarium, Art. aurif.*, II, p. 231: "Et ille dicitur lapis invisibilitatis, lapis sanctus, res benedicta" (And it is called the stone of invisibility, the sacred stone, the blessed thing).

3 Maier, *Symbola aureae mensae*, p. 386: ". . . non parvis sumptibus illam invenere artem,/Qua non ars dignior ulla est,/Tingendi lapidem Aetherium . . ." (. . . not with small expense did they find that art, than which there is no more worthy art; the art of tincturing the ethereal stone). This is a reference to Marcellus Palingenius, "poeta et sacerdos," and his group.

4 "Omnes receptae spernendae sunt in arte" (*Rosarium, Art. aurif.*, II, p. 223).

125. Mercurius as the sun-moon hermaphrodite (*rebis*), standing on the (round) chaos.—Mylius, *Philosophia reformata* (1622)

treatises were written and published anonymously, and therefore could not be of unlawful advantage to anyone. At the same time there are undoubtedly a great many fraudulent productions written by charlatans.

315   But mystification can also arise from another source. The real mystery does not behave mysteriously or secretively; it speaks a secret language, it adumbrates itself by a variety of images which all indicate its true nature. I am not speaking of a secret personally guarded by someone, with a content known to its possessor, but of a mystery, a matter or circumstance which is "secret," i.e., known only through vague hints but essentially unknown. The real nature of matter was unknown to the alchemist: he knew it only in hints. In seeking to explore it he projected the unconscious into the darkness of matter in order to illuminate it. In order to explain the mystery of matter he projected yet another mystery—his own unknown psychic background—into what was to be explained: *Obscurum per ob-*

244

scurius, ignotum per ignotius! This procedure was not, of course, intentional; it was an involuntary occurrence.

346   Strictly speaking, projection is never made; it happens, it is simply there. In the darkness of anything external to me I find, without recognizing it as such, an interior or psychic life that is my own. It would therefore be a mistake in my opinion to explain the formula "tam ethice quam physice" by the theory of correspondences, and to say that this is its "cause." On the contrary, this theory is more likely to be a rationalization of the experience of projection. The alchemist did not practise his art because he believed on theoretical grounds in correspondence; the point is that he had a theory of correspondence because he experienced the presence of pre-existing ideas in physical matter. I am therefore inclined to assume that the real root of alchemy is to be sought less in philosophical doctrines than in the projections of individual investigators. I mean by this that while working on his chemical experiments the operator had certain psychic experiences which appeared to him as the particular behaviour of the chemical process. Since it was a question of projection, he was naturally unconscious of the fact that the experience had nothing to do with matter itself (that is, with matter as we know it today). He experienced his projection as a property of matter; but what he was in reality experiencing was his own unconscious. In this way he recapitulated the whole history of man's knowledge of nature. As we all know, science began with the stars, and mankind discovered in them the dominants of the unconscious, the "gods," as well as the curious psychological qualities of the zodiac: a complete projected theory of human character. Astrology is a primordial experience similar to alchemy. Such projections repeat themselves whenever man tries to explore an empty darkness and involuntarily fills it with living form.

347   This being so, I turned my attention to the question of whether the alchemists themselves had reported any such experiences in the course of their work. I had no reason to hope for a very rich find, since they would be "unconscious" experiences which would escape record for precisely that reason. But in point of fact there are one or two unmistakable accounts in the literature. Characteristically enough, the later accounts are more detailed and specific than the earlier ones. The most recent ac-

count comes from a treatise[5] alleged to have been translated from Ethiopian into Latin and from Latin into German, of which Chapter VIII, "The Creation," reads:

Take of common rainwater a good quantity, at least ten quarts, preserve it well sealed in glass vessels for at least ten days, then it will deposit matter and faeces on the bottom. Pour off the clear liquid and place in a wooden vessel that is fashioned round like a ball, cut it through the middle and fill the vessel a third full, and set it in the sun about midday in a secret or secluded spot.

When this has been done, take a drop of the consecrated red wine and let it fall into the water, and you will instantly perceive a fog and thick darkness on top of the water, such as also was at the first creation. Then put in two drops, and you will see the light coming forth from the darkness; whereupon little by little put in every half of each quarter hour first three, then four, then five, then six drops, and then no more, and you will see with your own eyes one thing after another appearing by and by on top of the water, how God created all things in six days [fig. 126], and how it all came to pass, and such secrets as are not to be spoken aloud and I also have not the power to reveal. Fall on your knees before you undertake this operation. Let your eyes judge of it; for thus was the world created. Let all stand as it is, and in half an hour after it began it will disappear.

By this you will see clearly the secrets of God, that are at present hidden from you as from a child. You will understand what Moses has written concerning the creation; you will see what manner of body Adam and Eve had before and after the Fall, what the serpent was, what the tree, and what manner of fruits they ate: where and what Paradise is, and in what bodies the righteous shall be resurrected; not in this body that we have received from Adam, but in that which we attain through the Holy Ghost, namely in such a body as our Saviour brought from heaven.

348   In Chapter IX, "The Heavens," we read:

You shall take seven pieces of metal, of each and every metal as they are named after the planets, and shall stamp on each the character of the planet in the house of the same planet, and every piece shall be as large and thick as a rose noble.[6] But of Mercury only the

5 Jurain, *Hyle und Coahyl; aus dem Aethiopischen ins Lateinische, und aus dem Lateinischen in das Teutsche translatiret und übergesetzt durch D. Johann Elias Müller* (Hamburg, 1732). The text is by no means old, and bears all the traits of the decadent period (18th century). I am indebted to Prof. Th. Reichstein (Basel) for introducing me to this little book.

6 Rose noble = English gold coin of the 15th and 16th centuries.

126. The six days of creation, culminating in the seventh day.—St. Hildegarde of Bingen, "Scivias" (MS., 12th cent.)

fourth part of an ounce by weight and nothing stamped upon it.

Then put them after the order in which they stand in the heavens into a crucible, and make all windows fast in the chamber that it may be quite dark within, then melt them all together in the midst of the chamber and drop in seven drops of the blessed Stone, and forthwith a flame of fire will come out of the crucible [fig. 127] and spread itself over the whole chamber (fear no harm), and will light up the whole chamber more brightly than sun and moon, and over your heads you shall behold the whole firmament as it is in the starry heavens above, and the planets shall hold to their appointed courses as in the sky. Let it cease of itself, in a quarter of an hour everything will be in its own place.

127. The transformation of Mercurius in the fire.—Barchusen, *Elementa chemiae* (1718)

349   Let us take another example from a treatise by Theobald de
Hoghelande (sixteenth century):

They say also that different names are given to the stone on account of the wonderful variety of figures that appear in the course of
the work, inasmuch as colours often come forth at the same time,
just as we sometimes imagine in the clouds or in the fire strange
shapes of animals, reptiles, or trees. I found similar things in a fragment of a book ascribed to Moses: when the body is dissolved, it is
there written, then will appear sometimes two branches, sometimes
three or more, sometimes also the shapes of reptiles; on occasion it
also seems as if a man with a head and all his limbs were seated upon
a cathedra.[7]

[7] "De alchimiae difficultatibus," *Theatr. chem.*, I, p. 164. Likewise Philalethes,
"Introitus apertus," *Mus. herm.*, p. 687: "Terra enim germinandi avida aliquid
semper fabricat, interdum aves aut bestias reptiliaque in vitro conspicere imag-
inabere . . ." (The earth, being eager to germinate, always produces something;
sometimes you will imagine that you see birds or beasts or reptiles in the glass).
The man on the cathedra undoubtedly refers to a vision of Hermes such as can
be found in the old treatise *Senioris Zadith filii Hamuelis Tabula chymica*, pp.
1ff. (see fig. 128). Senior was an Arabic author of the 10th century. The figure as

248

128. Hermes Trismegistus.—Senior, *De chemia,* in Mangetus,
Bibliotheca chemica curiosa (1702)

350   Like the two preceding texts, Hoghelande's remarks prove
that during the practical work certain events of an hallucinatory
or visionary nature were perceived, which cannot be anything
but projections of unconscious contents. Hoghelande quotes
Senior as saying that the "vision" of the Hermetic vessel "is
more to be sought than the scripture." [8] The authors speak of
seeing with the eyes of the spirit, but it is not always clear
whether they mean vision in a real or a figurative sense. Thus
the "Novum lumen" says:

> To cause things hidden in the shadow to appear, and to take away
> the shadow from them, this is permitted to the intelligent philos-
> opher by God through nature. . . . All these things happen, and
> the eyes of the common men do not see them, but the eyes of the
> understanding [intellectus] and of the imagination perceive them
> [percipiunt] with true and truest vision [visu].[9]

351   Raymond Lully writes:

> You should know, dear son, that the course of nature is turned
> about, so that without invocation [e.g., of the familiaris] and with-
> out spiritual exaltation you can see certain fugitive spirits condensed
> in the air in the shape of divers monsters, beasts and men, which
> move like the clouds hither and thither [fig. 129].[10]

---

depicted in the treatise, of a wise old man holding the book of secrets on his
knees, was taken over in the frontispiece of Béroalde de Verville, Le Songe de
Poliphile (see fig. 4). The oldest vision extant of this kind is perhaps that of
Krates. The "Book of Krates" was handed down in Arabic and—in its present
form—would appear to belong to the 9th century, but the greater part of it is
of Greek origin and therefore considerably older. Berthelot gives the following
passage: "Then I saw an old man, the handsomest of men, sitting in a chair. He
was dressed in white, and was holding in his hand a board from the chair, on
which rested a book. . . . When I asked who this old man was, I was told: He is
Hermes Trismegistus, and the book he has in front of him is one of those which
contain the explanation of the secret things he has hidden from men." (La
Chimie au moyen âge, III, pp. 46ff.)
8 "De alch. diff.," Theatr. chem., I, p. 199. It is not clear whether by "scripture"
he means the traditional description of the vessel in the treatises of the masters,
or the Holy Scripture.
9 Sendivogius, "Novum lumen," Mus. herm., p. 574.
10 "Compendium," Bibl. chem. curiosa, I, p. 875.

129. Personified *spiritus* escaping from the heated *prima materia.*—Thomas
Aquinas (pseud.), "De alchimia" (MS., 16th cent.)

352   Dorn says much the same:

> Thus he will come to see with his mental eyes [*oculis mentalibus*]
> an indefinite number of sparks shining through day by day and
> more and more and growing into a great light.[11]

353   The psychologist will find nothing strange in a figure of
speech becoming concretized and turning into an hallucination.
Thus in his biographical notes (1594), Hoghelande describes
how, on the third day of the *decoctio,* he saw the surface of the
substance cover itself with colours, "chiefly green, red, grey, and
for the rest iridescent." Whenever he remembered that day a
verse of Virgil's came into his mind: "Ut vidi, ut perii, ut me
malus abstulit error" (When I saw, how utterly I perished and
evil delusion took me off). This error or optical illusion ("lu-
dibrium oculis oblatum"), he said, was the cause of much subsequent trouble and expense, for he had believed that he was on
the point of attaining the *nigredo.* But a few days later his fire
went out in the night, which led to an *irreparabile damnum;* in
other words, he never succeeded in repeating the phenomenon.[12]
Not that the iridescent skin on molten metal is necessarily an
hallucination; but the text shows a remarkable willingness on
the part of the author to suspect something of the sort.

354   The "Tractatus Aristotelis" contains a passage that is noteworthy from the point of view of the alchemist's psychology:

11 "Speculativa philosophia," *Theatr. chem.,* I, p. 275.
12 Hoghelande, "De alch. diff.," *Theatr. chem.,* I, p. 150.

The serpent is more cunning than all the beasts of the earth; under the beauty of her skin she shows a harmless face, and she forms herself in the manner of a *materia hypostatica,* through illusion, when immersed in water.[13] There she gathers together the virtues from the earth, which is her body. Because she is very thirsty she drinks immoderately and becomes drunken, and she causes the nature wherewith she is united to vanish [*decipere*].[14]

355   The serpent is Mercurius, who as the fundamental substance (*hypostatica*) forms himself in the water and swallows the nature to which he is joined (fig. 130). (Cf. sun drowning in the Fountain of Mercurius, lion devouring the sun [fig. 169], Beya dissolving Gabricus in her own body.) Matter is thus formed through illusion, which is necessarily that of the alchemist. This illusion might well be the *vera imaginatio* possessed of "informing" power.

356   The fact that visions allied themselves to the alchemical work may also explain why dreams and dream-visions are often mentioned as important intermezzi or as sources of revelation. Thus Nazari, for instance, puts his doctrine of transmutation in the form of three dreams,[15] a fairly plain analogy to *Poliphilo.* The classical "Visio Arislei" has a similar dream form.[16] Ostanes likewise communicates his doctrine dressed up as a revelation in a dream.[17] While the dreams and visions in these texts (as also in Senior and Krates) are mainly a literary convention, the dream-vision of Zosimos has a much more authentic character.[18] It is repeatedly stressed in the literature that the much-sought-after *aqua permanens* would be revealed in a dream.[19] Gen-

---

13 Text of the operative passage: ". . . quasi Materia Hypostatica fingit se in aquam demersum per illusionem. . . ." The illusion could refer to *demergere* or to *fingere.* Since the former makes no sense I have chosen the latter possibility.
14 *Theatr. chem.,* V, p. 884.
15 *Della tramutatione metallica.* A song by Josephus Avantius about Nazari runs: "Somnia credentur vix; non tamen omnia falsa, / Quae tali fuerint praemeditata viro" (The dreams will hardly be believed; they are not, however, all false that were meditated by such a man).
16 *Art. aurif.,* I, pp. 146ff.   17 Berthelot, *Chimie au moyen âge,* III, p. 119.
18 Cf. Jung, "The Visions of Zosimos."
19 Sendivogius, "Parabola," *Bibl. chem.,* II, p. 475. Khunrath (*Von hylealischen Chaos,* p. 42) says; "[The] Cabalistic *habitaculum Materiae Lapidis* was originally made known from on high through Divine Inspiration and special Revelation, both with and without instrumental help, 'awake as well as asleep or in dreams.' "

130. The Mercurial serpent devouring itself in water or fire.—Barchusen,
Elementa chemiae (1718)

erally speaking the *prima materia*, indeed the stone itself—or the secret of its production—is revealed to the operator by God. Thus Laurentius Ventura says: "But one cannot know the procedure unless it be a gift of God, or through the instruction of a most experienced Master: and the source of it all is the Divine Will." [20] Khunrath[21] is of the opinion that one could "perfectly prepare our Chaos Naturae [= *prima materia*] in the highest simplicity and perfection" from a "special Secret Divine Vision and revelation, without further probing and pondering of the causes." [22] Hoghelande explains the necessity for divine illumination by saying that the production of the stone transcends reason[23] and that only a supernatural and divine knowledge knows the exact time for the birth of the stone.[24] This means that God alone knows the *prima materia*.[25] After the time of Paracelsus the source of enlightenment was the *lumen naturae*:

This Light is the true Light of nature, which illuminates all the God-loving Philosophers who come into this World. It is in the World and the whole edifice of the World is beautifully adorned and will be naturally preserved by it until the last and great day of the Lord, but the World knows it not. Above all it is the Subject of the Catholic and Great Stone of the Philosophers, which the whole World has before its eyes yet knows not.[26]

20 "De ratione conficiendi lapidis," *Theatr. chem.*, II, p. 256.
21 *Von hylealischen Chaos*, p. 185.
22 Similar views in Hoghelande, "De alch. diff.," *Theatr. chem.*, I, p. 154; *Turba*, ed. Ruska, p. 155, 8; and Dorn, "Physica Trismegisti," *Theatr. chem.*, I, p. 413; and these tracts in *Musaeum hermeticum:* "Tractatus aureus," p. 8; Madathanus, "Aureum saeculum," p. 55; "Aquarium sapientum," p. 75; "Gloria mundi," p. 212.
23 "De alch. diff.," *Theatr. chem.*, I, p. 194. He refers there to *Turba* XXXIX (ed. Ruska, p. 147, 2): "Maius est, quam quod ratione percipiatur [nisi] divina inspiratione" (It is too great to be conceived by reason without divine inspiration).
24 "De alch. diff.," p. 205.
25 Sendivogius, "Novum lumen," *Mus. herm.*, p. 577: "Materia prima, quam solus Deus scit."
26 Khunrath, *Von hyleal. Chaos,* pp. 71f. Note the implied reference to the Logos (John 1 : 9–11).

II. THE MENTAL ATTITUDE TOWARDS THE OPUS

357   A somewhat different aspect of the psyche's relations to the chemical work is apparent in the following quotation from the text of an anonymous author:[27] "I pray you, look with the eyes of the mind at this little tree of the grain of wheat, regarding all its circumstances, that you may be able to plant the tree of the philosophers." [28] (Fig. 131; cf. also figs. 135, 188, 189, 221.) This seems to point to active imagination as the thing that sets the process really going.

358   Dorn says in his "Philosophia meditativa": "Thou wilt never make from others the One that thou seekest, except there first be made one thing of thyself." [29] Whatever he may have meant by the "One" [30] it must refer to the "artifex," whose unity is postu-

---

[27] "Instructio de arbore," *Theatr. chem.*, VI, p. 168. [Though Espagnet is held on good authority to be the author of this work and it is listed under his name in the bibliography for purposes of reference, his authorship is controversial. —Editors.]

[28] "Quaeso, oculis mentis hanc grani tritici arbusculam secundum omnes suas circumstantias aspice, ut arborem Philosophorum plantare . . . queas."

[29] *Theatr. chem.*, I, p. 472: "Ex aliis nunquam unum facies quod quaeris, nisi prius ex te ipso fiat unum."

[30] Probably a reference to the "Tabula smaragdina" (ed. Ruska, p. 2): "Et sicut omnes res fuerunt ab uno, meditatione unius: sic omnes res natae," etc. (And as all things proceed from the One, through the meditation of the One, so all things are born . . . etc.). Hence the rule that the alchemist must not have any serious physical defects, mutilated limbs, etc. See Geber, *Summa perfectionis*, Lib. I: "Si vero fuerit artificis corpus debile et aegrotum, sicut febrientium, vel leprosorum corpora, quibus membra cadunt, et in extremis vitae laborantium, et iam aetatis decrepitae senum ad artis complementum non perveniet. His igitur naturalibus corporis impotentiis impeditur artifex in intentione sua." (But if the body of the artifex is weak and sick, like bodies of people with fever or leprosy, whose limbs fall off, or like the bodies of people labouring at the end of their life, or of old men of decrepit age, he will not achieve the completion of the Art. By these natural disabilities of the body the artifex is hindered in his intention.) Another old text, the "Septem tractatus seu capitula Hermetis Trismegisti aurei," *Ars chemica*, ch. I, gives similar advice: "Ecce vobis exposui, quod celatum fuerat, quoniam opus vobiscum, et apud vos est, quod intus arripiens et permanens in terra vel in mari habere potes" (I have expounded to you what had been hidden; the work is with you and among you, and grasping it steadfastly you can have it on land or sea).

131. Adam as *prima materia*, pierced by the arrow of Mercurius. The *arbor philosophica* is growing out of him.—"Miscellanea d'alchimia" (MS., 14th cent.)

lated as the absolute condition for the completion of the work. We can hardly doubt that the *psychological* condition for the *opus* is meant, and that this is of fundamental importance.

359 The *Rosarium* says:[31]

Who therefore knows the salt and its solution knows the hidden secret of the wise men of old. Therefore turn your mind upon the salt and think not of other things; for in it alone [i.e., the mind] is the science concealed and the most excellent and most hidden secret of all the ancient philosophers.[32]

360 The Latin text has "in *ipsa sola*," referring therefore to "mens." One would have to assume a double misprint were the secret after all concealed in the *salt*. But as a matter of fact "mind" and "salt" are close cousins—*cum grano salis!*[33] Hence, according to Khunrath, the salt is not only the physical centre of the earth but at the same time the *sal sapientiae*,[34] of which he says: "Therefore direct your feelings, senses, reason and thoughts upon this salt alone." [35] The anonymous author of the *Rosarium* says in another place that the work must be performed "with the true and not with the fantastic imagination," [36] and again that the stone will be found "when the search lies heavy on the searcher." [37] This remark can only be understood as meaning that a certain psychological condition is indispensable for the discovery of the miraculous stone.

31 *Art. aurif.*, II. p. 244. Ruska (*Turba*, p. 342) dates the *Rosarium* to the middle of the 15th century.

32 "Ponc ergo mentem tuam super salem, nec cogites de aliis. Nam in *ipsa sola* occultatur scientia et arcanum praecipuum, et secretissimum omnium antiquorum Philosophorum." The *Bibliotheca chemica* version, p. 95, has "ipsa sola"; likewise the *Rosarium philosophorum* of 1550. Unfortunately I have no access to the manuscripts.

33 Cf. the *sal sapientiae* which, according to the ancient rite of baptism, was and still is given to the baptized.

34 Khunrath, *Von hyleal. Chaos*, pp. 257, 260, 262.

35 Ibid., p. 258.

36 *Art. aurif.*, II, p. 214: "Et vide secundum naturam, de qua regenerantur corpora in visceribus terrae. Et hoc imaginare per veram imaginationem et non phantasticam." (And look according to nature, by which the bodies are regenerated in the bowels of the earth. And imagine this with the true and not with the fantastic imagination.)

37 Ibid., p. 243: "Et invenitur in omni loco et in quolibet tempore et apud omnem rem, cum inquisitio aggravat inquirentem" (And it is found in every place and at any time and in every circumstance, when the search lies heavy on the searcher).

361   Both these remarks, therefore, make it seem very possible that the author was in fact of the opinion that the essential secret of the art lies hidden in the human mind—or, to put it in modern terms, in the unconscious (fig. 132).

362   If it really did dawn on the alchemists that their work was somehow connected with the human psyche and its functions, then it seems to me probable that the passage from the *Rosarium* is no mere misprint. It agrees too well with the statements of other authors. They insist throughout upon careful study and meditation of the books. Thus Richardus Anglicus[38] says in his so-called "Correctorium alchymiae":

Therefore all those who desire to attain the blessing of this art should apply themselves to study, should gather the truth from the books and not from invented fables and untruthful works. There is no way by which this art can truly be found (although men meet with many deceptions), except by completing their studies and understanding the words of the philosophers. . . .[39]

363   Bernard of Treviso tells us how he struggled in vain for many years till at last he was "directed into the straight path" through a *sermo* of Parmenides in the *Turba*.[40]

364   Hoghelande says:

He should collect the books of different authors, because otherwise it is impossible to understand them, and he should not throw aside a book which he has read once, twice, or even three times, although he has not understood it, but should read it again ten, twenty, fifty times or even more. At last he will see wherein the authors are mainly agreed: there the truth lies hidden. . . .[41]

365   Quoting Raymond Lully as his authority, the same author says that owing to their ignorance men are not able to accomplish the work until they have studied universal philosophy, which will show them things that are unknown and hidden from others. "Therefore our stone belongs not to the vulgar but to the

[38] Canon of St. Paul's, London, physician in chief to Pope Gregory XII, died *c.* 1252 (Ferguson, *Bibliotheca chemica,* II, p. 271).
[39] *Theatr. chem.,* II, p. 444.
[40] "Liber de alchemia," *Theatr. chem.,* I, p. 793: "Parmenides . . . qui me primum retraxit ab erroribus, et in rectam viam direxit" (Parmenides . . . who first pulled me back from errors, and directed me into the straight path).
[41] "De alch. diff.," *Theatr. chem.,* I, pp. 213f.

132. The "secret" contents of the work. Centre, the *soror mystica*, with the artifex, fishing for Neptune (animus); below, artifex, with *soror*, fishing for Melusina (anima).—*Mutus liber* (1702)

very heart of our philosophy." [42] Dionysius Zacharius relates that a certain "religiosus Doctor excellentissimus" advised him to refrain from useless expense in "sophisticationibus diabolicis" and to devote himself rather to the study of the books of the old philosophers, so as to acquaint himself with the *vera materia*. After a fit of despair he revived with the help of the Holy Spirit and, applying himself to a serious study of the literature, read diligently, and meditated day and night until his finances were exhausted. Then he worked in his laboratory, saw the three colours appear, and on Easter Day of the following year the wonder happened: "Vidi perfectionem"—"I saw the perfect fulfilment": the quicksilver was "conversum in purum aurum prae meis oculis." This happened, so it was said, in 1550.[43] There is an unmistakable hint here that the work and its goal depended very largely on a mental condition. Richardus Anglicus rejects all the assorted filth the alchemists worked with, such as eggshells, hair, the blood of a red-haired man, basilisks, worms, herbs, and human faeces. "Whatsoever a man soweth that also shall he reap. Therefore if he soweth filth, he shall find filth." [44] "Turn back, brethren, to the way of truth of which you are ignorant; I counsel you for your own sake to study and to labour with steadfast meditation on the words of the philosophers, whence the truth can be summoned forth." [45]

366   The importance or necessity of understanding and intelligence is insisted upon all through the literature, not only because intelligence above the ordinary is needed in the performance of so difficult a work, but because it is assumed that a species of magical power capable of transforming even brute matter dwells in the human mind. Dorn, who devoted a series of interesting treatises[46] to the problem of the relationship between the work and the man (fig. 133), says: "In truth the form, which is the intellect of man, is the beginning, middle and end of the procedure: and this form is made clear by the saffron colour, which indicates that man is the greater and principal form in the spagyric *opus*." [47] Dorn draws a complete parallel between

---

[42] Ibid., p. 206.   [43] Zacharius, "Opusculum," *Theatr. chem.*, I, pp. 813, 815f.

[44] Richardus, "Correctorium alchymiae," *Theatr. chem.*, II, p. 451.

[45] Ibid., p. 459.   [46] In *Theatr. chem.*, I.

[47] "Philosophia chemica," *Theatr. chem.*, I, p. 485: "Verum forma quae hominis est intellectus, initium est, medium, et finis in praeparationibus: et ista denotatur a croceo colore, quo quidem indicatur hominem esse maiorem formam et princi-

133. Alchemists at work: various stages of the process. Sol appears below, bringing the golden flower.—*Mutus liber* (1702)

the alchemical work and the moral-intellectual transformation of man. His thought, however, is often anticipated in the Harranite "Treatise of Platonic Tetralogies," the Latin title of which is "Liber Platonis quartorum." [48] Its author establishes four series of correspondences, each containing four "books," "for the help of the investigator": [49]

I	II [53]	III	IV
1. De opere natu-ralium (Concerning the work of natural things)	1. Elementum aquae	1. Naturae compositae (Composite natures)	1. Sensus (Senses)
2. Exaltatio divisionis naturae (Emphasis on —or exaltation of—the division of nature) [50]	2. Elementum terrae	2. Naturae discretae (Discriminated natures)	2. Discretio intellectualis (Intellectual discrimination)
3. Exaltatio animae (Emphasis on —or exaltation of—the soul) [51]	3. Elementum aëris	3. Simplicia (Simple things)	3. Ratio (Reason) [54]
4. Exaltatio intellectus (Emphasis on —or exaltation of—the intellect) [52]	4. Elementum ignis	4. Aetheris simplicioris (Things pertaining to yet simpler ether)	4. Res quam concludunt hi effectus praecedentes (The thing included in the foregoing effects) [55]

palem in opere spagirico." The forma works through informatio (also described as fermentatio). Forma is identical with idea. Gold, silver, and so on are forms of matter, therefore one can make gold if one succeeds in impressing the form of gold (impressio formae) on the informis massa or chaos, i.e., the prima materia.
48 Theatr. chem., V.   49 Ibid., p. 137.
50 This "book" explains "quid separetur et praeparetur." The separatio or solutio refers to the decomposition of the original matter into elements.
51 The text says: ". . . liber in exaltatione animae, cum sit separatio naturae, et ingenium in conversione sua a materia sua" (. . . the book [treating of] the

367   The four series show four aspects of the *opus*. The first horizontal series begins with natural things, the *prima materia* as represented by water. These things are composite, i.e., mixed. Their "correspondence" in column IV is sense perception. The second horizontal series represents a higher stage in the process: in column I, the composite natures are decomposed or changed back into their initial elements; in column II, the earth is separated from the (primal) water as in the Book of Genesis, a favourite theme in alchemy; in column III, there is a separation into categories; and column IV is concerned with the psychological act of discrimination.

368   The third horizontal series shows the upward advance still more clearly: in column I, the soul emerges from nature; in column II, there is an elevation into the realm of air; in column III, the process reaches the "simple" things which, because of their unalloyed quality, are incorruptible, eternal, and akin to Platonic ideas; and in column IV, there is the final ascent from *mens* to *ratio,* to the *anima rationalis,* i.e., the highest form of the soul. The fourth horizontal series illustrates the perfection or completion of each of the vertical columns.

369   *First vertical series:* This column has a "phenomenological" character, if such a modern term is permissible here. The psychic

---

exaltation of the soul, its separation from nature, its intrinsic spirituality and its conversion from its own materiality). The *anima* is separated from its body (*separatio*). As an *ingenium*, it is the body's essential quality or "soul," whose material nature has to be transformed into something higher.

52 "Est sicut praeparatio totius, et conversio naturae ad simplex . . . et necesse est in eo elevari ab animalitate, plus quam natura, ut assimuletur praeparation[e] ipsis intelligentiis, altissimis, veris" (It is like the preparation of the whole, and the conversion of nature to the simple . . . and it is necessary to rise above animality more than does nature, in order to be assimilated by means of this preparation to the highest, truest intelligences). So the chief work falls to the intellect, namely sublimation up to the highest stage, where nature is transformed into the *res simplex*, which, in accordance with its own nature, is akin to the spirits, angels, and eternal ideas. In the second column this highest stage is fire, "qui est super omnia elementa, et agit in eis"; in the third column it is the ethereal (highest) form of transformed nature, and in the fourth it is the goal of the whole process.

53 There is an introductory remark to this series: "Vel si vis potes illas [*scil.* exaltationes] comparare elementis" (If you wish you can compare those [exaltations] to the elements).

54 ". . . rationis vere dirigentis ad veritatem" (. . . [of] reason that truly leads to truth).

55 The *effectus* refer to the preceding stages in the process of transformation.

element emerges from the sum of natural phenomena and culminates in the *exaltatio intellectus,* the phenomenon of clear insight and understanding. We can, without doing violence to the text, take this *intellectus* as the highest lucidity of which consciousness is capable.

370   *Second vertical series:* The earth emerges from the chaotic waters of the beginning, from the *massa confusa,* in accordance with the ancient alchemical view; above it lies air, the volatile element rising from the earth. Highest of all comes fire[56] as the "finest" substance, i.e., the fiery pneuma[57] which reaches up to the seat of the gods[58] (fig. 134; cf. figs. 166, 178, 200).

371   *Third vertical series:* This column has a categorical or ideal character; hence it contains intellectual judgments. All composites are dissolved into their "discriminated" components, which in their turn are reduced to the "simple" substance. From this there finally emerge the quintessences, the simple primordial ideas. Ether is the quintessence.[59]

372   *Fourth vertical series:* This column is exclusively "psychological." The senses mediate perception, while the *discretio intellectualis* corresponds to apperception. This activity is subject to the *ratio* or *anima rationalis,* the highest faculty bestowed by God on man. Above the *anima rationalis* there is only the *res,* which is the product of all the preceding effects. The "Liber Platonis quartorum" interprets this *res* as the

invisible and immovable God [60] whose will created the intelligence; from the will and intelligence [to be understood here as *intellectus*] is produced the simple soul;[61] but the soul gives rise to the discriminated natures from which the composite natures are produced, and these show that a thing cannot be comprehended save by something superior to it. The soul is above nature and through it nature is comprehended, but the intelligence is above the soul and through it

[56] Ἀνωτάτω μὲν οὖν εἶναι τὸ πῦρ (Fire has the uppermost place).—Diogenes Laertius, *Lives of Eminent Philosophers,* VII, i (on Zeno), 137.

[57] Stoic doctrine.

[58] The soul still has a luminous or fiery nature in Lactantius.

[59] Aristotle, *De Coelo* (trans. Guthrie, I, p. 3), and *Meteorologica* (ed. Bekker), I, p. 3.

[60] Ibid., XII, p. 7: God is οὐσία τις ἀίδιος καὶ ἀκίνητος (an eternal and immovable being).

[61] Fechner (*Elemente der Psychophysik,* II, p. 526) thinks in the same way: "That which is psychically homogeneous and simple is associated with physical multiplicity, whereas physical multiplicity contracts psychically into the homogeneous, the simple, and yet simpler."

134. Saturn, or *Mercurius senex,* being cooked in the bath until the spirit
or white dove (*pneuma*) ascends.—Trismosin, "Splendor solis" (MS., 1582)

the soul is comprehended, and the intelligence is comprehended by that which is above itself, and is surrounded by the One God whose nature is not to be comprehended.[62]

373   The original text runs:

. . . scias quod scientia antiquorum quibus appraeparatae sunt scientiae et virtutes, est quod res ex qua sunt res, est Deus invisibilis et immobilis, cuius voluntate intelligentia condita est; et voluntate et intelligentia[63] est anima simplex; per animam sunt naturae discretae, ex quibus generatae sunt compositae, et indicant quod res non cognoscitur, nisi per suam superius. Anima vero est super naturam, et per eam cognoscitur natura, sed intelligentia est superior anima et per eam cognoscitur anima, et intelligentia[m][64] noscit, qui[65] superior ea est, et circundat eam Deus unus, cuius qualitas apprehendi non potest.

374   The author adds a quotation whose origin I have not been able to trace. It runs:

The philosopher said in the Book of Dialogues: I went about the three heavens, namely the heaven of composite nature, the heaven of discriminated nature, and the heaven of the soul. But when I sought to go about the heaven of intelligence, the soul said to me: That way is not for thee. Then nature attracted me, and I was attracted. This saying of the philosopher was not intended by him to specify this science, but because he wished that his words should not fail to make clear the power which liberates the creature, and that by their means the lower process in this kind of work should be made known through the higher.[66]

375   In this very ancient text—which in its Arabic form cannot be much later than the tenth century, many of its components being still older—we find a systematic classification of the correspondences between the *opus alchemicum* and the philosophical and psychological processes running parallel with it. The text makes it abundantly clear just how much the chemical processes

[62] *Theatr. chem.,* V, p. 145.   [63] Instead of "intelligentiae."
[64] Instead of "intelligentia."   [65] Instead of "et quid."
[66] "Et dixit philosophus in libro Dialogorum: Circuivi tres coelos, scilicet coelum naturae compositae, coelum naturae discretae et coelum animae. Cum autem volui circumire coelum intelligentiae, dixit mihi anima, non habes illuc iter, et attraxit me natura et attractus sum. Hoc autem dictum principale, non posuit philosophus ad significandam hanc scientiam, sed quia voluit ut sermones sui non vacarent manifestatione, virtutis liberantis creaturam, et voluit per eos in hac specie operis, ut cognoscatur praeparatio deterior, per praeparationem superiorem."—"Liber Platonis Quartorum," *Theatr. chem.,* V, p. 145.

coincided with spiritual or psychic factors for these thinkers. Indeed the connection went so far that the product to be extracted from matter was known as the *cogitatio*.[67] This strange idea is explicable only on the assumption that the old philosophers did have a faint suspicion that psychic contents were being projected into matter. Because of the intimate connection between man and the secret of matter, both Dorn and the much earlier "Liber Platonis quartorum" demand that the operator should rise to the height of his task: he must accomplish in his own self the same process that he attributes to matter, "for things are perfected by their like." Therefore the operator must himself participate in the work ("oportet operatorem interesse operi"), "for if the investigator does not remotely possess the likeness [i.e., to the work] he will not climb the height I have described, nor reach the road that leads to the goal."[68]

376   As a result of the projection there is an unconscious identity between the psyche of the alchemist and the arcane substance, i.e., the spirit imprisoned in matter. The "Liber Platonis quartorum" accordingly recommends the use of the *occiput* (fig. 75) as the vessel of transformation,[69] because it is the container of thought and intellect[70] (fig. 135). For we need the brain as the seat of the "divine part." The text continues:

Through time and exact definition things are converted into intellect, inasmuch as the parts are assimilated [to one another] in composition and in form. But on account of its proximity to the *anima rationalis* the brain had to be assimilated to the amalgam, and the *anima rationalis* is simple, as we have said.[71]

67 Ibid., p. 144: "Sedentes super flumina Eufrates sunt Caldaei . . . priores, qui adinvenerunt extrahere cogitationem" (The Chaldaeans dwelling on the river Euphrates were . . . the first to find out how to extract the cogitation).
68 Ibid., p. 137.
69 Ibid., p. 124: "Si utaris opere exteriori, non utaris nisi occipitio capitis et invenies" (If you use an exterior operation you should use only the occiput and then you will find [the goal]). The conjecture "goal" is subject to the reservation that I have not yet been able to obtain the Arabic text.
70 Ibid., p. 124: "Os capitis est mundum et est . . . minus os, quod sit in [h]omine [text: nomine], et vas mansionis cogitationis et intellectus . . . ." (The skull is pure and . . . moreover it is a comparatively small bone in [man], and it is the vessel of cogitation and intellect . . .).
71 "Res convertuntur per tempus ad intellectum per certitudinem, quantum partes assimulantur in compositione et in forma. Cerebrum vero propter vicinitatem cum anima rationali [the "et" here should be deleted] permixtioni oportuit assimulari, et anima rationalis est simplex sicut diximus."

135. The skull, symbol of the *mortificatio* of Eve, the feminine aspect of the *prima materia*. Whereas in the case of Adam the tree corresponds to the phallus (see fig. 131), here the tree grows out of Eve's head.—"Miscellanea d'alchimia" (MS., 14th cent.)

377   The assumption underlying this train of thought is the causative effect of analogy. In other words, just as in the psyche the multiplicity of sense perceptions produces the unity and simplicity of an idea, so the primal water finally produces fire, i.e., the ethereal substance—not (and this is the decisive point) as a mere analogy but as the result of the mind's working on matter. Consequently Dorn says: "Within the human body is concealed a certain metaphysical substance, known to very few, which needs no medicament, being itself an incorrupt medicament." This medicine is "of threefold nature: metaphysical, physical, and moral" ("moral" is what we would call "psychological"). "From this," Dorn goes on, "the attentive reader will conclude that one must pass from the metaphysical to the physical by a philosophic procedure." [72] This medicine is clearly the arcane substance which he defines elsewhere as *veritas:*

> There is in natural things a certain truth which cannot be seen with the outward eye, but is perceived by the mind alone [*sola mente*], and of this the Philosophers have had experience, and have ascertained that its virtue is such as to work miracles.[73]
>
> In this [truth] lies the whole art of freeing the spirit [*spiritus*] from its fetters, in the same way that, as we have said, the mind [*mens*] can be freed [i.e., morally] from the body.[74]
>
> As faith works miracles in man, so this power, the *veritas efficaciae,* brings them about in matter. This truth is the highest power and an impregnable fortress wherein the stone of the philosophers lies hid.[75]

378   By studying the philosophers man acquires the skill to attain this stone. But again, the stone is man. Thus Dorn exclaims: "Transform yourselves from dead stones into living philosophical stones!" [76] Here he is expressing in the clearest possible way the identity of something in man with something concealed in matter.

379   In his "Recueil stéganographique" [77] Béroalde de Verville says:

72 "Speculativa philosophia," *Theatr. chem.*, I. p. 265.
73 Ibid., p. 298.   74 Ibid., p. 264.   75 Ibid., p. 266.
76 Ibid., p. 267: "Transmutemini de lapidibus mortuis in vivos lapides philosophicos."
77 To *Le Tableau des riches inventions.*

If any man wish at times to change the drop of mastic, and by pressing it to cause a clear tear to issue from it, let him take care, and he will see in a fixed time, under the gentle pressure of the fire, a like substance issue from the philosophic matter; for as soon as its violet darkness is excited for the second time, it will stir up from it as it were a drop or flower or flame or pearl, or other likeness of a precious stone, which will be diversified until it runs out in very clear whiteness, which thereafter will be capable of clothing itself with the honour of beauteous rubies, or ethereal stones, which are the true fire of the soul and light of the philosophers.

380   It should now be sufficiently clear that from its earliest days alchemy had a double face: on the one hand the practical chemical work in the laboratory, on the other a psychological process, in part consciously psychic, in part unconsciously projected and seen in the various transformations of matter.

381   Not much effort is needed at the beginning of the work; it is sufficient to approach it with "a free and empty mind," as one text says.[78] But one important rule must be observed: "the mind [*mens*] must be in harmony with the work" [79] and the work must be above all else. Another text says that in order to acquire the "golden understanding" (*aurea apprehensio*) one must keep the eyes of the mind and soul well open, observing and contemplating by means of that inner light which God has lit in nature and in our hearts from the beginning.[80]

382   Since the investigator's psyche was so closely bound up with the work—not only as its necessary medium but also as its cause and point of departure—it is easy to understand why so much emphasis was laid on the psychic condition and mental attitude of the laboratory worker. Alphidius says: "Know that thou canst not have this science unless thou shalt purify thy mind before God, that is, wipe away all corruption from thy heart." [81] According to *Aurora*, the treasure-house of Hermetic wisdom rests on a

---

[78] Mehung, "Demonstratio naturae," *Mus. herm.*, p. 157: "liberi et vacui anima." (Jean de Meung, born between 1250 and 1280.)

[79] Norton, "Ordinale," *Mus. herm.*, p. 519: "nam mens eius cum opere consentiat. . . ."

[80] "Aquarium sapientum," *Mus. herm.*, p. 107.

[81] *Aurora consurgens* I, ch. X, parab. V: "Alfidius: Scito quod hanc scientiam habere non poteris, quousque mentem tuam deo purifices, hoc est in corde omnem corruptionem deleas."

firm foundation of fourteen principal virtues: health, humility, holiness, chastity, virtue,[82] victory, faith, hope, charity, goodness (*benignitas*), patience, temperance, a spiritual discipline or understanding,[83] and obedience.

383   The Pseudo-Thomas who is author of this same treatise quotes the saying "Purge the horrible darknesses of our mind,"[84] and gives as a parallel Senior's "he maketh all that is black white . . ."[85] Here the "darknesses of our mind" coincide unmistakably with the *nigredo* (figs. 34, 48, 115, 137); i.e., the author feels or experiences the initial stage of the alchemical process as identical with his own psychic condition.

384   Another old authority is Geber. The *Rosarium* says that in his *Liber perfecti magisterii* Geber requires the following psychological and characterological qualities of the artifex: He must have a most subtle mind and an adequate knowledge of metals and minerals. But he must not have a coarse or rigid mind, nor should he be greedy and avaricious, nor irresolute and vacillating. Further, he must not be hasty or vain. On the contrary, he must be firm in purpose, persevering, patient, mild, long-suffering, and good-tempered.[86]

385   The author of the *Rosarium* goes on to say that he who wishes to be initiated into this art and wisdom must not be arrogant, but devout, upright, of profound understanding, humane, of a cheerful countenance and a happy nature. He continues: "My son, above all I admonish thee to fear God, who knoweth

[82] The text has ". . . virtus, de qua dicitur: virtus ornat animam. Et Hermes: et recipit virtutem superiorum et inferiorum planetarum et sua virtute penetrat omnem rem solidam." (. . . virtue of which it is said: virtue adorneth the soul. And Hermes: and it receiveth the virtue of the upper and lower planets and by its virtue penetrateth every solid thing.) Cf. "Tabula smaragdina," ed. Ruska, p. 2: "et recipit vim superiorum et inferiorum."

[83] The text explains by quoting the Vulgate, Eph. 4 : 23, 24: "Renovamini [autem] spiritu mentis vestrae, et induite novum hominem . . ." (D.V.: "And be renewed in the spirit of your mind: and put on the new man . . .") and adds: "hoc est intellectum subtilem."

[84] *Aurora* I, ch. IV, parab. IV: ". . . horridas nostrae mentis purga tenebras."

[85] Ibid.: "Senior: et facit omne nigrum album . . ."

[86] *Art. aurif.*, II, p. 228. The text in Geber's *Summa perfectionis* is much more detailed. It occupies the whole of ch. V of Lib. I, under the title "De impedimentis ex parte animae artificis." See Darmstaedter, *Die Alchemie des Geber*, pp. 20ff.

what manner of man thou art and in whom is help for the solitary, whosoever he may be."[87]

386　　Particularly instructive is the introduction to the art given by Morienus to Kalid:[88]

This thing for which you have sought so long is not to be acquired or accomplished by force or passion. It is to be won only by patience and humility and by a determined and most perfect love. For God bestows this divine and immaculate science on his faithful servants, namely those on whom he resolved to bestow it from the original nature of things.[89] . . . [Some remarks follow concerning the handing down of the art to pupils.] Nor were they [the elect] able to hold anything back save through the strength granted to them by God, and they themselves could no longer direct their minds save towards the goal[90] appointed for them by God. For God charges those of his servants whom he has purposely chosen [fig. 136] that they seek this divine science which is hidden from men, and that they keep it to themselves. This is the science that draws its master away from the suffering of this world and leads to the knowledge of future good.

When Morienus was asked by the king why he lived in mountains and deserts rather than in hermitages, he answered: "I do not doubt that in hermitages and brotherhoods I would find greater repose, and fatiguing work in the deserts and in the mountains; but no one reaps who does not sow. . . . Exceeding narrow is the gateway to peace, and none may enter save through affliction of the soul."[91]

---

[87] *Art. aurif.*, II, p. 227: "Deum timere, in quo dispositionis tuae visus est, et adjuvatio cujuslibet sequestrati." This quotation derives from the "Tractatus aureus" in what was probably the first edition (*Ars chemica*). But there the passage (which comes at the beginning of ch. II) runs: "Fili mi, ante omnia moneo te Deum timere, in quo est nisus tuae dispositionis et adunatio cuiuslibet sequestrati" (My son, above all I admonish thee to fear God in whom is the strength of thy disposition, and companionship for the solitary, whosoever he may be). Concerning the alteration of the Hermes quotations in *Rosarium,* see par. 140, n. 17.

[88] Cf. Reitzenstein, "Alchemistische Lehrschriften." Morienus (Morienes or Marianus) is said to have been the teacher of the Omayyad prince, Kalid or Khalid ibn-Jazid ibn-Muawiyah (635–704). Cf. Lippmann, *Entstehung und Ausbreitung der Alchemie,* I, p. 357. The passage is to be found in Morienus, "De transmutatione metallorum," *Art. aurif.,* II, pp. 22f.

[89] "Quibus eam a primaeva rerum natura conferre disposuit" (ibid., p. 22).

[90] "Animos suos etiam ipsi regere non possunt diutius, nisi usque ad terminum," etc. (ibid., p. 23).

[91] ". . . nisi per animae afflictionem" (ibid., pp. 17f.).

136. God enlight-
ening the artifex.
—Barchusen, *Ele-
menta chemiae*
(1718)

387   We must not forget, in considering this last sentence, that Morienus is not speaking for the general edification but is referring to the divine art and its work. Michael Maier expresses himself in similar vein when he says:

There is in our chemistry a certain noble substance, in the beginning whereof is wretchedness with vinegar, but in its ending joy with gladness. Therefore I have supposed that the same will happen to me, namely that I shall suffer difficulty, grief, and weariness at first, but in the end shall come to glimpse pleasanter and easier things.[92]

388   The same author also affirms that "our chemistry stirs up the artifex to a meditation of the heavenly good," [93] and that whoso is initiated by God into these mysteries "casts aside all insignificant cares like food and clothing, and feels himself as it were new-born." [94]

389   The difficulty and grief to be encountered at the beginning of the work once more coincide with the *nigredo*, like the "horrible darknesses of our mind" of which *Aurora* speaks; and these in their turn are surely the same as the "affliction of soul" mentioned by Morienus. The term he uses for the attitude of the

92 Maier, *Symbola aureae mensae*, p. 568.
93 Ibid., p. 144.   94 Ibid., p. 143.

adept —*amor perfectissimus*—expresses an extraordinary devotion to the work. If this "serious meditation" is not mere bragging—and we have no reason to assume any such thing—then we must imagine the old adepts carrying out their work with an unusual concentration, indeed with religious fervour (cf. below). Such devotion would naturally serve to project values and meanings into the object of all this passionate research and to fill it with forms and figures that have their origin primarily in the unconscious of the investigator.

III. MEDITATION AND IMAGINATION

390   The point of view described above is supported by the alchemist's remarkable use of the terms *meditatio* and *imaginatio*. Ruland's *Lexicon alchemiae* defines *meditatio* as follows: "The word *meditatio* is used when a man has an inner dialogue with someone unseen. It may be with God, when He is invoked, or with himself, or with his good angel" [95] (fig. 137). The psychologist is familiar with this "inner dialogue"; it is an essential part of the technique for coming to terms with the unconscious.[96] Ruland's definition proves beyond all doubt that when the alchemists speak of *meditari* they do not mean mere cogitation, but explicitly an inner dialogue and hence a living relationship to the answering voice of the "other" in ourselves, i.e., of the unconscious. The use of the term "meditation" in the Hermetic dictum "And as all things proceed from the One through the meditation of the One" must therefore be understood in this alchemical sense as a creative dialogue, by means of which things pass from an unconscious potential state to a manifest one. Thus we read in a treatise of Philalethes:[97] "Above all it is marvellous that our stone, although already perfect and able to impart a perfect tincture, does voluntarily humble itself again and will

[95] P. 327: "Meditatio (s.v.) dicitur, quoties cum aliquo alio colloquium habetur internum, qui tamen non videtur. Ut cum Deo ipsum invocando, vel cum se ipso, vel proprio angelo bono." This description is very similar to the *colloquium* in the *Exercitia spiritualia* of Ignatius of Loyola. All the authors are unanimous in emphasizing the importance of meditation. Examples are unnecessary.
[96] Cf. Jung, "The Relations between the Ego and the Unconscious," pars. 341ff.
[97] "Introitus apertus," *Mus. herm.*, p. 693.

137. Alchemist in the initial *nigredo* state, meditating.—Jamsthaler, *Viatorium spagyricum* (1625)

meditate a new volatility, apart from all manipulation."[98] What is meant by a "meditated volatility" we discover a few lines lower down, where it says: "Of its own accord it will liquefy . . . and by God's command become endowed with spirit, which will fly up and take the stone with it."[99] Again, therefore, to "meditate" means that through a dialogue with God yet more spirit will be infused into the stone, i.e., it will become still more spiritualized, volatilized, or sublimated (cf. fig. 178). Khunrath says much the same thing:

Therefore study, meditate, sweat, work, cook . . . so will a healthful flood be opened to you which comes from the Heart of the Son of the great World, a Water which the Son of the Great World pours forth from his Body and Heart, to be for us a True and Natural Aqua Vitae. . . .[100]

[98] ". . . novam volatilitatem citra ullam manuum impositionem meditabitur."
[99] Cf. the Mohammedan legend of the rock in the mosque of Omar, at Jerusalem, which wanted to fly up with Mohammed when he ascended to heaven.
[100] *Von hyleal. Chaos*, pp. 274f.

391   Likewise the "meditation of the heavenly good," mentioned earlier, must be taken in the sense of a living dialectical relationship to certain dominants of the unconscious. We have excellent confirmation of this in a treatise by a French alchemist living in the seventeenth and eighteenth centuries.[101] He says:

How often did I see them [the *Sacerdotes Aegyptiorum*] overcome with joy at my understanding, how affectionately they kissed me, for the true grasp of the ambiguities of their paradoxical teaching came easily to my mind. How often did their pleasure in the wonderful discoveries I made concerning the abstruse doctrines of the ancients move them to reveal unto my eyes and fingers the Hermetic vessel, the salamander [fig. 138; cf. figs. 129, 130], the full moon and the rising sun.

392   This treatise, although it is not so much a personal confession as a description of the golden age of alchemy, nevertheless tells us how the alchemist imagined the psychological structure of his *opus*. Its association with the invisible forces of the psyche was the real secret of the *magisterium*. In order to express this secret the old masters readily resorted to allegory. One of the oldest records of this kind, which had a considerable influence on the later literature, is the "Visio Arislei," [102] and its whole character relates it very closely to those visions known to us from the psychology of the unconscious.

393   As I have already said, the term *imaginatio*, like *meditatio*, is of particular importance in the alchemical opus. Earlier on we came across that remarkable passage in the *Rosarium* telling us that the work must be done with the true *imaginatio*, and we saw elsewhere [par. 357] how the philosophical tree can be made to grow through contemplation (figs. 131, 135). Ruland's *Lexi-*

---

101 I take this text from a manuscript in my possession entitled "Figurarum Aegyptiorum secretarum . . ." *Incipit:* "Ab omni aevo aegyptiorum sacerdotes." Colophon: "laus jesu in saecula." (Fol. 47, parchment, 18th cent.) The pictures in this manuscript are identical with those in MS. No. 973 (18th cent.), Bibliothèque de l'Arsenal, Paris. They come from the "Pratique" of Nicolas Flamel (1330–1418). The origin of the Latin text in my manuscript is at present unknown. (See figs. 23, 148, 157, 164.) [See also *Mysterium Coniunctionis*, par. 720.]

102 *Art. aurif.*, I. Cf. Ruska's version in *Historische Studien und Skizzen* (ed. Sudhoff), pp. 22ff. A still older series of visions is that of Zosimos in περὶ ἀρετῆς (Berthelot, *Alch. grecs*, III) and also of Krates (Berthelot, *Chimie au moyen âge*, III).

138. The Mercurial spirit of the *prima materia*, in the shape of a salamander, frolicking in the fire.—Maier, *Scrutinium chymicum* (1687)

con once more helps us to understand what the alchemist meant by *imaginatio*.

394   Ruland says, "Imagination is the star in man, the celestial or supercelestial body." [103] This astounding definition throws a quite special light on the fantasy processes connected with the *opus*. We have to conceive of these processes not as the immaterial phantoms we readily take fantasy-pictures to be, but as something corporeal, a "subtle body" (fig. 139), semi-spiritual in nature. In an age when there was as yet no empirical psychology such a concretization was bound to be made, because everything unconscious, once it was activated, was projected into matter— that is to say, it approached people from outside. It was a hybrid

[103] "Astrum in homine, coeleste sive supracoeleste corpus." Since Ruland joins forces with Paracelsus here, I refer the reader to my "Paracelsus as a Spiritual Phenomenon" [especially par. 173].

139. Hermes conjuring the winged soul out
of an urn.—Attic funeral lekythos

phenomenon, as it were, half spiritual, half physical; a concretization such as we frequently encounter in the psychology of primitives. The *imaginatio*, or the act of imagining, was thus a physical activity that could be fitted into the cycle of material changes, that brought these about and was brought about by them in turn. In this way the alchemist related himself not only to the unconscious but directly to the very substance which he hoped to transform through the power of imagination. The singular expression "astrum" (star) is a Paracelsan term, which in this context means something like "quintessence." [104] Imagination is therefore a concentrated extract of the life forces, both physical and psychic. So the demand that the artifex must have a sound physical constitution is quite intelligible, since he works with and through his own quintessence and is himself the indispensable condition of his own experiment. But, just because of this intermingling of the physical and the psychic, it always remains an obscure point whether the ultimate transformations in the alchemical process are to be sought more in the material or more in the spiritual realm. Actually, however, the question is wrongly put: there was no "either-or" for that age, but there did exist an intermediate realm between mind and matter, i.e., a psychic realm of subtle bodies[105] whose characteristic it is to

[104] Ruland, *Lexicon*, s.v. "astrum": "virtus et potentia rerum, ex praeparationibus acquisita" (the virtue and power of things, that is acquired through the preparations). Hence also extract or Quinta Essentia.
[105] Figulus (*Rosarium novum olympicum*, p. 109) says: "[*Anima*] is a subtle imperceptible smoke."

manifest themselves in a mental as well as a material form. This is the only view that makes sense of alchemical ways of thought, which must otherwise appear nonsensical. Obviously, the existence of this intermediate realm comes to a sudden stop the moment we try to investigate matter in and for itself, apart from all projection; and it remains non-existent so long as we believe we know anything conclusive about matter or the psyche. But the moment when physics touches on the "untrodden, untreadable regions," and when psychology has at the same time to admit that there are other forms of psychic life besides the acquisitions of personal consciousness—in other words, when psychology too touches on an impenetrable darkness—then the intermediate realm of subtle bodies comes to life again, and the physical and the psychic are once more blended in an indissoluble unity. We have come very near to this turning-point today.

395   Such reflections are unavoidable if we want to gain any understanding of alchemy's peculiar terminology. The earlier talk of the "aberration" of alchemy sounds rather old-fashioned today when the psychological aspects of it have faced science with new tasks. There are very modern problems in alchemy, though they lie outside the province of chemistry.

396   The concept of *imaginatio* is perhaps the most important key to the understanding of the *opus*. The author of the treatise "De sulphure" [106] speaks of the "imaginative faculty" of the soul in that passage where he is trying to do just what the ancients had failed to do, that is, give a clear indication of the secret of the art. The soul, he says, is the vice-regent of God (*sui locum tenens seu vice Rex est*) and dwells in the life-spirit of the pure blood. It rules the mind (*illa gubernat mentem*) and this rules the body. The soul functions (*operatur*) in the body, but has the greater part of its function (*operatio*) outside the body (or, we might add by way of explanation, in projection). This peculiarity is divine, since divine wisdom is only partly enclosed in the body of the world: the greater part of it is *outside, and it imagines far higher things than the body of the world can conceive (concipere)*. And these things are outside nature: God's own secrets. The soul is an example of this: it too imagines many things of the utmost profundity (*profundissima*) outside

106 Sendivogius, in *Mus. herm.*, pp. 601ff.

the body, just as God does. True, what the soul imagines happens only in the mind (*non exequitur nisi in mente*), but what God imagines happens in reality. "The soul, however, has absolute and independent power [*absolutam et separatam potestatem*] to do other things [*alia facere*] than those the body can grasp. But, when it so desires, it has the greatest power over the body [*potestatem in corpus*], for otherwise our philosophy would be in vain. Thou canst conceive the greater, for we have opened the gates unto thee." [107]

IV. SOUL AND BODY

397   The passage just quoted affords us valuable insight into the alchemical way of thinking. The soul in this text is evidently an *anima corporalis* (figs. 91, 208) that dwells in the blood. It would therefore correspond to the unconscious, if this is understood as the psychic phenomenon that mediates between consciousness and the physiological functions of the body. In the Tantric *chakra* system[108] this *anima* would be located below the diaphragm. On the other hand it is God's lieutenant or viceroy, the analogue of the *Deus Creator*. There are people who can never understand the unconscious as anything but a *sub*conscious, and who therefore feel impelled to put a superconscious alongside or possibly above it. Such hypotheses do not trouble our philosophers, for according to their teaching every form of life, however elementary, contains its own inner antithesis, thus anticipating the problem of opposites in modern psychology. What our author has to say about the element of air is significant in this respect:

The air is a pure uncorrupted element, in its kind the most worthy, being uncommonly light and invisible, but inside heavy, visible, and solid. Enclosed within it [*inclusus*] is the spirit of the Highest that moved over the waters before the Creation, according to the testimony of the Holy Scripture: "And . . . he did fly upon the wings of the wind." [109] All things are integrated [*integrae*] in this element by the imagination of the fire.[110]

107 Ibid., p. 618.   108 Avalon, *The Serpent Power*.
109 "Et . . . volavit super pennas ventorum."—Vulgate, Ps. 17 : 11 (A.V., Ps. 18 : 10).   110 Sendivogius, "De sulphure," *Mus. herm.*, p. 612.

70.

atrando recopera metallum sustin
tantur pre spiritum perpetuo sm

140. The artifex with his *soror mystica*, holding the keys to the work.—Thomas
Aquinas (pseud.), "De alchimia" (16th cent.)

398   In order to understand such a statement we must obviously empty our minds of all modern ideas about the nature of gases, and take it as purely psychological. In this sense, it deals with the projection of pairs of opposites such as light-heavy, visible-invisible, and so on. Now, identity of opposites is a characteristic feature of every psychic event in the unconscious state. Thus the *anima corporalis* is at the same time *spiritualis,* and the air's heavy, solid kernel is at the same time the *spiritus creator* which moves over the waters. And just as "the images of all creatures" are contained in the creative spirit, so all things are imagined or "pictured" in air "through the power of fire"; firstly because fire surrounds the throne of God and is the source from which the angels and, descending in rank and quality, all other living beings are created or "imagined" through infusion of the fiery *anima* into the breath of life;[111] secondly because fire destroys all composite things and infuses their images back into the air in the form of smoke.

399   The soul, says our author, is only partly confined to the body, just as God is only partly enclosed in the body of the world. If we strip this statement of its metaphysics it asserts that the psyche is only partly identical with our empirical conscious being; for the rest it is projected and in this state it imagines or realizes those greater things which the body cannot grasp, i.e., cannot bring into reality. The "greater things" (*majora*) correspond to the "higher" (*altiora*), referring to the world-creating imagination of God; but because these higher things are imagined by God they at once become substantial instead of lingering in a state of potential reality, like the contents of the unconscious. That this activity of the soul "outside the body" refers to the alchemical *opus* is evident from the remark that the soul has the greatest power over the body, otherwise the royal art or philosophy would be in vain. "Thou canst conceive the greater," says our author; therefore your body can bring it into reality— with the help of the art and with God's permission (*Deo concedente*), this being a fixed formula in alchemy.

400   The *imaginatio,* as the alchemists understand it, is in truth

---

111 Ibid., p. 615. Christ is similarly "imagined" in us—"Aquarium sapientum," *Mus. herm.,* p. 113: "Deus, antequam Christus filius eius in nobis formatus imaginatusque fuit, nobis potius terribilis Deus" (Before Christ his son was formed and imagined in us, God was more terrible to us).

a key that opens the door to the secret of the *opus* (fig. 140). We now know that it was a question of representing and realizing those "greater" things which the soul, on God's behalf, imagines creatively and *extra naturam*—or, to put it in modern language, a question of actualizing those contents of the unconscious[112] which are outside nature, i.e., not a datum of our empirical world, and therefore an *a priori* of archetypal character. The place or the medium of realization is neither mind nor matter, but that intermediate realm of subtle reality which can be adequately expressed only by the symbol. The symbol is neither abstract nor concrete, neither rational nor irrational, neither real nor unreal. It is always both: it is *non vulgi*, the aristocratic preoccupation of one who is set apart (*cuiuslibet sequestrati*), chosen and predestined by God from the very beginning.

[112] All "our secrets" are formed from an "image" (*imago*), says Ripley (*Opera omnia chemica*, p. 9).

141. The artifex with book and altar. In the background, a cornfield (allegory of the *opus*) and the quickening *coniunctio* of *sol* and *luna*.—Kelley, *Tractatus de Lapide philosophorum* (1676)

142. The sequence of stages in the alchemical process.—Libavius, *Alchymia* (1606)
(For explanation, see following pages)

In an *explicatio locorum signatorum,* Libavius gives the following "explanation" of this picture (fig. 142):

A Pedestal or base = earth.

BB Two giants or Atlases kneeling on the base and supporting a sphere with their hands.

C Four-headed dragon from whose breath the sphere takes shape. The four grades of fire: the first mouth emits a kind of air, the second a subtle smoke, the third smoke and fire, and the fourth pure fire.

D Mercurius with a silver chain, to which two recumbent animals are attached.

E The green lion.

F One-headed dragon. E and F both mean the same thing: the Mercurial fluid which is the *materia prima* of the stone.

G A three-headed silver eagle, two of whose heads droop while the third spits white water or the Mercurial fluid into the sea, which is marked H.

I Picture of the wind, sending forth the breath of the spirit (*spiritus*) into the sea below.

K Picture of the red lion, with red blood flowing from his breast into the sea below, because the sea must be coloured as if it were a mixture of silver and gold or white and red. The picture is applied to body, soul, and spirit by those who have sought three [principles] from the beginning, or to the blood of the lion and the lime of the eagle. For, because they accept three, they have a double Mercurius. Those who accept two have one only, which comes from a crystal or from the unripe metal of the philosophers.

L A stream of black water, as in the chaos, representing the *putrefactio.* From it there rises a mountain, which is black at the bottom and white at the top, so that a silver stream flows down from the summit. For it is the picture of the first dissolution and coagulation and of the resultant second dissolution.

M The above-mentioned mountain.

NN The heads of black ravens that are looking out of the sea.

O Silver rain falling from the clouds on to the summit of the mountain. Sometimes this represents the nourishment and cleansing of the Lato by Azoch, sometimes the second dissolution, whereby the element of air is extracted from the earth and water. (The earth is a form of the mountain, and the water is the liquid of the sea aforementioned.)

PP The clouds from which [come] the dew or rain and the nourishing moisture.

Q A vision of heaven, where a dragon lies on his back and devours his own tail: he is an image of the second coagulation.

RR An Ethiopian man and woman, supporting two higher spheres. They sit on the big sphere and accordingly represent the *nigredo* of the second operation in the second putrefaction.

SS A sea of pure silver, which represents the Mercurial fluid whereby the tinctures are united.

T A swan swimming on the sea, spitting out a milky liquid from his beak. This swan is the white elixir, the white chalk, the arsenic of the philosophers, the thing common to both ferments. He has to support the upper sphere with his back and wings.

V Eclipse of the sun.

XX The sun diving into the sea, i.e., into the Mercurial water into which the elixir also must flow. This leads to the true eclipse of the sun and one should put a rainbow on either side to suggest the peacock's tail that then appears in the coagulation.

YY Eclipse of the moon, which likewise has a rainbow on either side and [also] in the lowest part of the sea, into which the moon must dive. This is the picture of the white fermentation. But both seas should be fairly dark.

ZZ The moon gliding into the sea.

a The king, clad in purple, with a golden crown, has a golden lion beside him. He has a red lily in his hand, whereas the queen has a white lily.

b The queen, crowned with a silver crown, strokes a white or silver eagle standing beside her.

c The phoenix on the sphere, cremating itself; many gold and silver birds fly out of the ashes. It is the sign of multiplication and increase.

143. Alchemists at work.—*Mutus liber* (1702)

3. THE WORK

I. THE METHOD

401   The basis of alchemy is the work (*opus*). Part of this work is practical, the *operatio* itself, which is to be thought of as a series of experiments with chemical substances. In my opinion it is quite hopeless to try to establish any kind of order in the infinite chaos of substances and procedures. Seldom do we get even an approximate idea of how the work was done, what materials were used, and what results were achieved. The reader usually finds himself in the most impenetrable darkness when it comes to the names of the substances—they could mean almost anything. And it is precisely the most commonly used substances, like quicksilver, salt, and sulphur, whose alchemical meaning is one of the secrets of the art. Moreover, one must not imagine for a moment that the alchemists always understood one another. They themselves complain about the obscurity of the texts, and occasionally betray their inability to understand even their own symbols and symbolic figures. For instance, the learned Michael Maier accuses the classical authority Geber of being the obscurest of all, saying that it would require an

Oedipus to solve the riddle of the "Gebrina Sphinx." [1] Bernard of Treviso, another famous alchemist, goes so far as to call Geber an obscurantist and a Proteus who promises kernels and gives husks.

402   The alchemist is quite aware that he writes obscurely. He admits that he veils his meaning on purpose, but nowhere—so far as I know—does he say that he cannot write in any other way. He makes a virtue of necessity by maintaining either that mystification is forced on him for one reason or another, or that he really wants to make the truth as plain as possible, but cannot proclaim aloud just what the *prima materia* or the *lapis* is.

403   The profound darkness that shrouds the alchemical procedure comes from the fact that although the alchemist was interested in the chemical part of the work he also used it to devise a nomenclature for the psychic transformations that really fascinated him. Every original alchemist built himself, as it were, a more or less individual edifice of ideas, consisting of the dicta of the philosophers and of miscellaneous analogies to the fundamental concepts of alchemy. Generally these analogies are taken from all over the place. Treatises were even written for the purpose of supplying the artist with analogy-making material.[2] The method of alchemy, psychologically speaking, is one of boundless amplification. The *amplificatio* is always appropriate when dealing with some obscure experience which is so vaguely adumbrated that it must be enlarged and expanded by being set in a psychological context in order to be understood at all. That is why, in analytical psychology, we resort to amplification in the interpretation of dreams, for a dream is too slender a hint to be understood until it is enriched by the stuff of association and analogy and thus amplified to the point of intelligibility. This *amplificatio* forms the second part of the *opus*, and is understood by the alchemist as *theoria*.[3] Originally the theory was

1 Maier, *Symbola aureae mensae*, p. 202: "Sunt enim plerique libri adeo obscure scripti, ut a solis auctoribus suis percipiantur" (For many of the books are written so obscurely that they are understood only by their authors). Cf. also Maier, *Scrutinium chymicum*, p. 33.

2 For instance, the second part of the *Aurora*, in *Art. aurif.*, I.

3 Philalethes ("Introitus apertus," *Mus. herm.*, p. 660): "Sunt enim in principiis nostris multae heterogenae superfluitates, quae in puritatem nunquam reduci possunt, ea propter penitus expurgare illas expedit, quod factu impossibile erit absque arcanorum nostrorum theoria, qua medium docemus, quo cum ex

144. Left, three artists in the library. Right, the artist, or his assistant, working in the laboratory.—Maier, *Tripus aureus* (1618)

the so-called "Hermetic philosophy," but quite early on it was broadened by the assimilation of ideas taken over from Christian dogma. In the oldest alchemy known to the West the Hermetic fragments were handed down mostly through Arabic originals. Direct contact with the *Corpus Hermeticum* was only established in the second half of the fifteenth century, when the Greek manuscript reached Italy from Macedonia and was translated into Latin by Marsilio Ficino.

404   The vignette (fig. 144) that is on the title-page to the *Tripus aureus* (1618) is a graphic illustration of the double face of alchemy. The picture is divided into two parts.[4] On the right is a laboratory where a man, clothed only in trunks, is busy at

---

meretricis menstruo excernatur Diadema Regale" (For there are in our initial material many superfluities of various kinds which can never be reduced to purity. Therefore it is advantageous to wash them all out thoroughly, but this cannot be done without the *theoria* of our secrets, in which we give instructions for extracting the Royal Diadem from the menstruum of a whore). The *Rosarium philosophorum*, subtitled *secunda pars alchemiae,* is such a *theoria* in the true sense of a *visio* (spectacle, watching scenes in a theatre, etc.). Cf. the *theorica* of Paracelsus, in Jung, "Paracelsus the Physician," par. 41.
[4] There is a similar illustration in Khunrath's *Amphitheatrum* (cf. fig. 145).

145. Laboratory and oratory.—Khunrath, *Amphitheatrum sapientiae* (1604)

the fire; on the left a library, where an abbot,[5] a monk,[6] and a layman[7] are conferring together. In the middle, on top of the furnace, stands the tripod with a round flask on it containing a winged dragon. The dragon symbolizes the visionary experience of the alchemist as he works in his laboratory and "theorizes."[8]

[5] John Cremer, Abbot of Westminster, who lived at the beginning of the 14th century. His "Testamentum" is printed in the *Musaeum Hermeticum*.
[6] Basilius Valentinus, a legendary or fictitious personality.
[7] Thomas Norton, putative author of the famous "Ordinall of Alchimy." On the question of his personality, cf. Nierenstein and Chapman, "Enquiry into the Authorship of the *Ordinall of Alchimy*."
[8] The vision of the father of Benvenuto Cellini—described in Cellini's autobiography, I, iv, p. 6—gives us a good idea of such visions: "When I was about five years old my father happened to be in a basement chamber of our house,

291

146. Mercurius as "uniting symbol."—Valentinus, "Duodecim claves," in *Musaeum hermeticum* (1678)

The dragon in itself is a *monstrum*—a symbol combining the chthonic principle of the serpent and the aerial principle of the bird. It is, as Ruland says,[9] a variant of Mercurius. But Mercurius is the divine winged Hermes (fig. 146) manifest in matter, the god of revelation, lord of thought and sovereign psychopomp. The liquid metal, *argentum vivum*—"living silver," quicksilver—was the wonderful substance that perfectly expressed the nature of the στίλβων: that which glistens and animates within. When the alchemist speaks of Mercurius, on

where they had been washing, and where a good fire of oak logs was still burning; he had a viol in his hand, and was playing and singing alone beside the fire. The weather was very cold. Happening to look into the fire, he spied in the middle of those most burning flames a little creature like a lizard, which was sporting in the core of the intensest coals. Becoming instantly aware of what the thing was, he had my sister and me called, and pointing it out to us children, gave me a great box on the ears, which caused me to howl and weep with all my might. Then he pacified me good-humouredly, and spoke as follows: 'My dear little boy, I am not striking you for any wrong that you have done, but only to make you remember that that lizard which you see in the fire is a salamander, a creature which has never been seen before by anyone of whom we have credible information.' So saying, he kissed me and gave me some pieces of money."
9 *Lexicon alchemiae*, s.v. "draco."

147. Uroboros.—Codex Marcianus (11th cent.)

the face of it he means quicksilver, but inwardly he means the world-creating spirit concealed or imprisoned in matter. The dragon is probably the oldest pictorial symbol in alchemy of which we have documentary evidence. It appears as the οὐροβόρος, the tail-eater, in the Codex Marcianus (fig. 147), which dates from the tenth or eleventh century,[10] together with the legend: ἕν τὸ πᾶν (the One, the All).[11] Time and again the alchemists reiterate that the *opus* proceeds from the one and leads back to the one,[12] that it is a sort of circle like a dragon biting its own tail (cf. figs. 20, 44, 46, 47). For this reason the *opus* was often called *circulare* (circular) or else *rota* (the wheel) (fig. 80). Mercurius stands at the beginning and end of the work: he is the *prima materia*, the *caput corvi*, the *nigredo;* as dragon he devours himself and as dragon he dies, to rise again as the *lapis*. He is the play of colours in the *cauda pavonis* and the division into four elements. He is the hermaphrodite that was in

[10] Cf. Taylor, "A Survey of Greek Alchemy."
[11] Reproduced in Berthelot, *Alch. grecs*, Introduction, p. 132.
[12] *Rosarium, Art. aurif.*, II, p. 206: "Unius ergo esto voluntatis in opere naturae, nec modo hoc, modo illud attentare praesumas quia in rerum multitudine ars nostra non perficitur. Quantumcunque enim diversificentur eius nomina, tamen semper una sola res est, et de eadem re. . . ." (Therefore you must be single-minded in the work of nature, and you must not try now this, now that, because our art is not perfected in a multiplicity of things. For however much its names may differ, yet it is ever one thing alone, and from the *same* thing. . . .) "Unus est lapis, una medicina, unum vas, unum regimen, unaque dispositio" (One is the stone, one the medicine, one the vessel, one the method, and one the disposition). Cf. Reitzenstein, "Alchemistische Lehrschriften," p. 71. Morienus ("De transmutatione metall.," *Art. aurif.*, II, pp. 25f.) quotes the Emperor Heraclius (610–41): "Hercules dixit: Hoc autem magisterium ex una primum radice procedit quae postmodum in plures res expanditur et iterum ad unam revertitur. . . ." (Hercules [Heraclius] said: This magistery proceeds first from one root, which afterwards expands into several things, and returns again to the one.)

293

148. Mercurius as caduceus, uniting the paired opposites.—"Figurarum Aegyptiorum secretarum" (MS., 18th cent.)

the beginning, that splits into the classical brother-sister duality and is reunited in the *coniunctio,* to appear once again at the end in the radiant form of the *lumen novum,* the stone. He is metallic yet liquid, matter yet spirit, cold yet fiery,[13] poison and yet healing draught—a symbol uniting all opposites (fig. 148).[14]

II. THE SPIRIT IN MATTER

405   All these ideas were the common property of alchemy from earliest times. Zosimos, writing in the third century A.D., quotes one of the very oldest authorities on alchemy in his treatise "Concerning the Art and Its Interpretation," [15] namely Ostanes,[16] who belongs to the dawn of history and was known even to Pliny. His connection with Democritus, another of the earliest alchemical writers, probably dates from the first century B.C.[17] This Ostanes is reported to have said:

Go to the waters of the Nile and there you will find a stone that has a spirit [πνεῦμα]. Take this, divide it, thrust in your hand and draw out its heart: for its soul [ψυχή] is in its heart[18] [fig. 149]. [An interpolator adds:] There, he says, you will find this stone that has a spirit, which refers to the expulsion of the quicksilver [ἐξυδραργύρωσις].[19]

---

13 *Rosarium, Art. aurif.,* II. p. 210: "Scitote ergo, quod argentum vivum est ignis, corpora comburens magis quam ignis" (Know therefore that the quicksilver is a fire which burns bodies more than fire [itself]).

14 Cf. the meaning of the uniting symbol in Jung, *Psychological Types,* pars. 318ff.

15 Berthelot, *Alch. grecs,* III, vi, 5.

16 A text ascribed to Ostanes, and transmitted in Arabic, is to be found in Berthelot, *Chimie au moyen âge,* III, pp. 116ff.; also a Greek text in Berthelot, *Alch. grecs,* IV, ii.

17 Lippmann, *Entstehung und Ausbreitung der Alchemie,* I, p. 334.

18 Cf. Maier, *Symbola aureae mensae,* p. 19: "[ol]eum extrahere a cordibus statuarum" (extract the oil from the hearts of statues), referring to Raymond Lully, "Codicillus" (*Bibl. chem. curiosa,* I, p. 894). Cf. also the "extraction of the cogitation" mentioned above (par. 375, n. 67).

19 Berthelot, *Alch. grecs,* III, vi, 5.

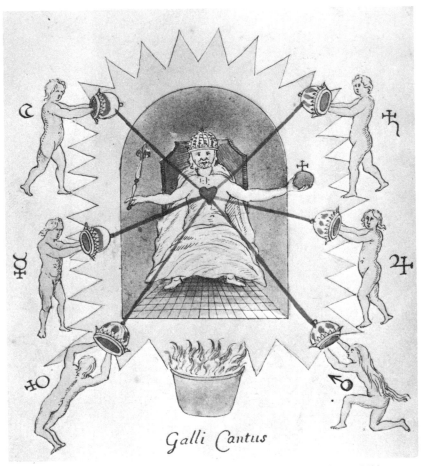

Galli Cantus

149. The sick king (*prima materia*), from whose heart the planet-children receive their crowns.—"La Sagesse des anciens" (MS., 18th cent.)

406   Nietzsche's metaphor in *Zarathustra,* "an image slumbers for me in the stone," says much the same thing, but the other way round. In antiquity the material world was filled with the projection of a psychic secret, which from then on appeared as the secret of matter and remained so until the decay of alchemy in the eighteenth century. Nietzsche, with his ecstatic intuition, tried to wrest the secret of the superman from the stone in which it had long been slumbering. It was in the likeness of this slumbering image that he wished to create the superman, whom, in the language of antiquity, we may well call the divine man. But it is the other way about with the alchemists: they were looking

296

150. The penetrating Mercurius.—"Speculum veritatis" (MS., 17th cent.)

for the marvellous stone that harboured a pneumatic essence in order to win from it the substance that penetrates all substances —since it is itself the stone-penetrating "spirit"—and transforms all base metals into noble ones by a process of coloration. This "spirit-substance" is like quicksilver, which lurks unseen in the ore and must first be expelled if it is to be recovered *in substantia*. The possessor of this penetrating Mercurius (fig. 150) can "project" it into other substances and transform them from the imperfect into the perfect state.[20] The imperfect state is like the sleeping state; substances lie in it like the "sleepers chained in Hades" (fig. 151)[21] and are awakened as from death to a new and more beautiful life by the divine tincture extracted from the inspired stone. It is quite clear that we have here a tendency not only to locate the mystery of psychic transformation in matter, but at the same time to use it as a *theoria* for effecting chemical changes.

407   Just as Nietzsche made absolutely sure that nobody could mistake the superman for a sort of spiritual or moral ideal, so it is emphasized that the tincture or divine water is far from

[20] It is indeed remarkable that the alchemists should have picked on the term *proiectio* in order to express the application of the philosophical Mercurius to base metals.
[21] Berthelot, *Alch. grecs*, IV, xx, 8.

151. Prisoners in the underworld.—Izquierdo, *Praxis exercitiorum spiritualium* (1695)

being merely curative and ennobling in its effects, but that it may also act as a deadly poison which penetrates other bodies as pervasively as the pneuma penetrates its stone.[22]

408　　Zosimos was a Gnostic who was influenced by Hermes. In his missive to Theosebeia he recommends the "krater" as a vessel of transformation: she should, he says, hasten to the Poimandres in order to be baptized in the krater.[23]

409　　This krater refers to the divine vessel of which Hermes tells Thoth in the treatise entitled ὁ κρατήρ.[24] After the creation of the world, God filled this vessel with nous (νοῦς = pneuma) and sent it down to earth as a kind of baptismal font. By so doing God gave man, who wished to free himself from his natural, imperfect, sleeping state of ἄνοια (or, as we should say, insufficient consciousness), an opportunity to dip himself in the nous and thus partake of the higher state of ἔννοια, i.e., enlightenment or higher consciousness (fig. 159). The nous is thus a kind of βαφεῖον, dyestuff or tincture, that ennobles base substances. Its function is the exact equivalent of the tincturing stone-extract, which is also a pneuma and, as Mercurius, possesses the Hermetic dual significance of redeeming psychopomp[25] and quicksilver (fig. 152).

410　　Clearly enough, then, Zosimos had a mystic or Gnostic philosophy of sorts whose basic ideas he projected into matter. When we speak of psychological projection we must, as I have already pointed out, always remember that it is an unconscious process that works only so long as it stays unconscious. Since Zosimos, like all the other alchemists, is convinced not only that his philosophy can be applied to matter but that processes also take place in it which corroborate his philosophical assumptions, it follows that he must have experienced, in matter itself, at the very least an identity between the behaviour of matter and the

22 Ibid., III, vi, 8.　　23 Ibid., III, li, 8.

24 Scott, Hermetica, I, pp. 149ff.

25 Here we probably enter the realm of Neopythagorean ideas. The penetrating quality of the soul-pneuma is mentioned in Aenesidemus (Zeller, Die Philosophie der Griechen, III, p. 26). He also speaks of aer as the original substance, corresponding to the pneuma of the Stoics (p. 23). Hermes, whose pneumatic (wind-) quality (see figs. 210, 211) is indicated by his wings, leads the souls to the Highest, according to Alexander Polyhistor (p. 75), but the impure souls are fettered in the underworld by the Erinyes with unbreakable bonds, like the imperfect ones who in the treatise of Komarios are "chained in Hades" (see fig. 151).

152. Above, Saturn eating his children and being sprinkled with Mercurial water (*lac virginis, vinum ardens*). Below, the regeneration in the bath.
—Thomas Aquinas (pseud.), "De alchimia" (MS., 16th cent.)

153. The artist lifting the homunculus, the "son of the philosophers," out of the Hermetic vessel.—Kelley, *Tractatus de Lapide philosophorum* (1676)

events in his own psyche. But, as this identity is unconscious, Zosimos is no more able than the rest of them to make any pronouncement about it. For him it is simply there, and it not only serves as a bridge, it actually *is* the bridge that unites psychic and material events in one, so that "what is within is also without." Nevertheless an unconscious event which eludes the conscious mind will portray itself somehow and somewhere, it may be in dreams, visions, or fantasies. The idea of the pneuma as the Son of God, who descends into matter[26] and then frees himself from it in order to bring healing and salvation to all souls, bears the traits of a projected unconscious content (fig. 153). Such a content is an autonomous complex divorced from consciousness, leading a life of its own in the psychic non-ego and instantly projecting itself whenever it is constellated in any way—that is, whenever attracted by something analogous to it in the outside world. The psychic autonomy of the pneuma[27] is attested by the Neopythagoreans; in their view the soul was swallowed by matter and only mind—nous—was left. But the nous is outside man: it is his daemon. One could hardly formulate its autonomy more aptly. Nous seems to be identical with the god Anthropos: he appears alongside the

[26] The cabalistic idea of God pervading the world in the form of soul-sparks (*scintillae*) and the Gnostic idea of the Spinther (spark) are similar.
[27] The concepts of nous and pneuma are used promiscuously in syncretism. The older meaning of pneuma is wind, which is an aerial phenomenon; hence the equivalence of aer and pneuma (Zeller, *Die Philosophie der Griechen*, III, p. 23). Whereas in Anaximenes the original substance is aer (ibid., I. pp. 713ff.), in Archelaus of Miletus, the pupil of Anaxagoras, God is aer and nous. In Anaxagoras the world-creator is Nous, who produces a whirlpool in chaos and thus brings about the separation of ether and air (ibid., I. pp. 687ff.). Concerning the idea of pneuma in syncretism, cf. Leisegang, *Der heilige Geist*, pp. 26ff.

154, 155. The king with the six planets or metals; the renewed king (*filius philosophorum*) worshipped by the six planets.—Kelley, *Tractatus de Lapide philosophorum* (1676)

demiurge and is the adversary of the planetary spheres. He rends the circle of the spheres and leans down to earth and water (i.e., he is about to project himself into the elements). His shadow falls upon the earth, but his image is reflected in the water. This kindles the love of the elements, and he himself is so charmed with the reflected image of divine beauty that he would fain take up his abode within it. But scarcely has he set foot upon the earth when Physis locks him in a passionate embrace. From this embrace are born the seven first hermaphroditic beings.[28] The seven are an obvious allusion to the seven planets and hence to the metals (figs. 154, 155; cf. figs. 21, 79) which in the alchemical view spring from the hermaphrodite Mercurius.

411   In such visionary images as the Anthropos glimpsing his own reflection there is expressed the whole phenomenon of the unconscious projection of autonomous contents. These myth-pictures are like dreams, telling us that a projection has taken place and also what has been projected. This, as the contemporary evidence shows, was nous, the divine daemon, the god-man, pneuma, etc. In so far as the standpoint of analytical psychology is realistic, i.e., based on the assumption that the contents of the psyche are realities, all these figures stand for an unconscious component of the personality which might well be endowed with a higher form of consciousness transcending that of the ordinary human being. Experience shows that such figures always express superior insight or qualities that are not yet

28 Schultz, *Dokumente der Gnosis*, p. 64; Reitzenstein, *Poimandres*, p. 50. In the Neopythagorean view, hermaphroditism is also an attribute of the deity. Cf. Nicomachus, in Zeller, *Philosophie der Griechen*, III, p. 107.

156. The Dyad (day and night): symbolical representation of the correspondence between zodiac and man.—"Très Riches Heures du duc de Berry" (MS., Chantilly, 15th cent.)

conscious; indeed, it is extremely doubtful whether they can be attributed to the ego at all in the proper sense of the word. This problem of attribution may appear a captious one to the layman, but in practical work it is of great importance. A wrong attribution may bring about dangerous inflations which seem unimportant to the layman only because he has no idea of the inward and outward disasters that may result.[29]

412   As a matter of fact, we are dealing here with a content that up to the present has only very rarely been attributed to any human personality. The one great exception is Christ. As υἱὸς τοῦ ἀνθρώπου, the Son of Man, and as θεοῦ υἱός, the Son of God, he embodies the God-man; and as an incarnation of the Logos by "pneumatic" impregnation, he is an avatar of the divine νοῦς.

413   Thus the Christian projection acts upon the unknown in man, or upon the unknown man, who becomes the bearer of the "terrible and unheard-of secret." [30] The pagan projection, on the other hand, goes beyond man and acts upon the unknown in the material world, the unknown substance which, like the chosen man, is somehow filled with God. And just as, in Christianity, the Godhead conceals itself in the man of low degree, so in the "philosophy" it hides in the uncomely stone. In the Christian projection the *descensus spiritus sancti* stops at the *living body* of the Chosen One, who is at once very man and very God, whereas in alchemy the descent goes right down into the darkness of inanimate matter whose nether regions, according to the Neopythagoreans, are ruled by evil.[31] Evil and matter together form the Dyad, the duality (fig. 156). This is feminine in nature, an *anima mundi*, the feminine Physis who longs for the embrace of the One, the Monad, the good and perfect.[32] The Justinian Gnosis depicts her as Edem, virgin above, serpent below [33] (fig. 157). Vengefully she strives against the pneuma

[29] The effect of inflation is that one is not only "puffed up" but too "high up." This may lead to attacks of giddiness, or to a tendency to fall downstairs, to twist one's ankle, to stumble over steps and chairs, and so on.

[30] Berthelot, *Alch. grecs*, IV, xx, 8: τὸ μυστήριον τὸ φρικτὸν καὶ παράδοξον.

[31] Zeller, *Philosophie der Griechen*, II, p. 152.

[32] Ibid., III, pp. 99, 151.

[33] Hippolytus, *Elenchos*, V, 26, 1.—Alchemy transferred the Edem-motif to Mercurius, who was likewise represented as virgin above, serpent below. This is the origin of the Melusina in Paracelsus (see "Paracelsus as a Spiritual Phenomenon," pars. 179f.).

Sie dicit philosophus

157. *Anima Mercurii.*—"Figurarum Aegyptiorum secretarum" (MS., 18th cent.)

because, in the shape of the demiurge, the second form of God, he faithlessly abandoned her. She is "the divine soul imprisoned in the elements," whom it is the task of alchemy to redeem.[34]

III. THE WORK OF REDEMPTION

414   Now, all these myth-pictures represent a drama of the human psyche on the further side of consciousness, showing *man as both the one to be redeemed and the redeemer.* The first formulation is Christian, the second alchemical. In the first case man attributes the need of redemption to himself and leaves the work of redemption, the actual ἄθλον or *opus,* to the autonomous divine figure; in the latter case man takes upon himself the duty of carrying out the redeeming *opus,* and attributes the state of suffering and consequent need of redemption to the *anima mundi* imprisoned in matter.[35]

415   In both cases redemption is a *work* (fig. 158). In Christianity it is the life and death of the God-man which, by a unique sacrifice, bring about the reconciliation of man, who craves redemption and is sunk in materiality, with God. The mystical effect of the God-man's self-sacrifice extends, broadly speaking, to all men, though it is efficacious only for those who submit through faith or are chosen by divine grace; but in the Pauline acceptance it acts as an apocatastasis and extends also to non-human creation in general, which, in its imperfect state, awaits redemption like the merely natural man. By a certain "synchronicity" of events, man, the bearer of a soul submerged in the world and the flesh, is potentially related to God at the moment when he, as Mary's Son, enters into her, the *virgo terrae* and representative of matter in its highest form; and, potentially at least, man is fully redeemed at the moment when the eternal Son of God returns again to the Father after undergoing the sacrificial death.

416   The ideology of this *mysterium* is anticipated in the myths

---

[34] Cf. the salvation and purification of the ἐν τοῖς στοιχείοις συνδεθεῖσα θεία ψυχή in the Book of Sophe (Berthelot, *Alch. grecs,* III, xlii, 1).

[35] Late Jewish (cabalistic) Gnosis developed a very similar attitude to that of alchemy. Cf. the excellent description by Gaugler, "Das Spätjudentum," pp. 279ff.

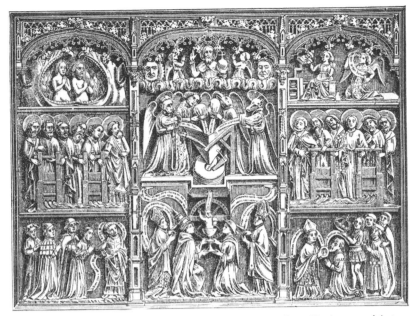

158. The "Mill of the Host." The Word, in the form of scrolls, is poured into a mill by the four evangelists, to reappear as the Infant Christ in the chalice. (Cf. John 1 : 14: "And the word was made flesh. . . .")—High altar of church at Tribsees, Pomerania (15th cent.)

of Osiris, Orpheus, Dionysus, and Hercules, and in the conception of the Messiah among the Hebrew prophets.[36] These anticipations go back to the primitive hero myths where the conquest of death is already an important factor.[37] The projections upon Attis and Mithras, more or less contemporary with the Christian one, are also worth mentioning. The Christian projection differs from all these manifestations of the mystery of redemption and

[36] The main points of resemblance are: in Osiris, his God-man nature, which guarantees human immortality, his corn characteristics, his dismemberment and resurrection; in Orpheus, the taming of the passions, the fisherman, the good shepherd, the teacher of wisdom, the dismemberment; in Dionysus, his wine characteristics, the ecstatic revelations, the fish symbolism, the dismemberment and resurrection; in Hercules, his subjection to Eurystheus and Omphale, his labours (mainly to redeem suffering humanity from various evils), the cross formed by his journeys (labours 7–10 lead South-North-East-West, while labours 11–12 lead upwards; cf. St. Paul: Eph. 3 : 18), his self-cremation and *sublimatio* culminating in divinity.

[37] Cf. for instance, the Polynesian myth of Maui (Hambruch, *Südseemärchen*, p. 289). Further material in Frobenius, *Das Zeitalter des Sonnengottes*.

transformation by reason of the historical and personal figure of Jesus. The mythical event incarnates itself in him and so enters the realm of world history as a unique historical and mystical phenomenon.

417   In the figure of the divine hero, God himself wrestles with his own imperfect, suffering, living creation; he even takes its suffering condition upon himself and, by this sacrificial act, accomplishes the *opus magnum*, the ἆθλον of salvation and victory over death. As regards the actual performance of this entirely metaphysical work, man is powerless to do anything really decisive. He looks to his Redeemer, full of faith and confidence, and does what he can in the way of "imitation"; but this never reaches the point where man himself becomes the Redeemer— or at least his own redeemer. Yet a complete imitation and re-establishment of Christ in the believer would necessarily lead to such a conclusion. But this is out of the question. Were such an approximation to occur, then Christ would have re-established himself in the believer and replaced the latter's personality. We should have to be satisfied with this statement were it not for the existence of the Church. The institution of the Church means nothing less than the everlasting continuation of the life of Christ and its sacrificial function. In the *officium divinum* or, in Benedictine parlance, the *opus divinum*, Christ's sacrifice, the redeeming act, constantly repeats itself anew while still remaining the unique sacrifice that was accomplished, and is accomplished ever again, by Christ himself inside time and outside all time. This *opus supernaturale* is represented in the sacrifice of the Mass. In the ritual act the priest as it were shows forth the mystical event, but the real agent is Christ, who sacrifices himself everywhere always. Though his sacrificial death occurred in time it is an essentially timeless occurrence. In the Thomist view the Mass is not a real *immolatio* (sacrifice) of the body of Christ but a "re-presentation" of his sacrificial death.[38] Such an interpretation would be sufficient and consistent were it not for the transubstantiation of the offered substances, the bread and wine. This offering is meant as a *sacri-*

---

38 Hauck, *Realencyklopädie*, XII, p. 689, 35: "Celebratio huius sacramenti est imago quaedam repraesentativa passionis Christi, quae est vera eius immolatio" (The celebration of this sacrament is a kind of image that represents Christ's passion, which is his true immolation).

ficium, literally a "making sacred." The etymology of the German word for sacrifice, *Opfer,* is obscure, it being a moot point whether it comes from *offerre,* "to offer," or from *operari,* "to effect, to be active." In its ancient usage *operari Deo* meant to serve the god or to sacrifice to him. But if the *Opfer* is an *opus,* then it is far more than an *oblatio,* the offering of such a modest gift as bread and wine. It must be an effectual act, giving the ritual words spoken by the priest a causal significance. The words of the consecration (*qui pridie quam pateretur,* etc.) are therefore to be taken not merely as representative, but as the *causa efficiens* of the transubstantiation. That is why the Jesuit Lessius (d. 1623) called the words of the consecration the "sword" with which the sacrificial lamb is slaughtered.[39] The so-called theory of mactation (slaughtering) occupies an important place in the literature of the Mass, though it has not been generally accepted in its more objectionable outgrowths. Perhaps the clearest of all is the Greek ritual as described by the Archbishop Nikolaus Kabasilas of Thessalonika (d. *circa* 1363).[40] In the first (preparatory) part of the Mass the bread and wine are placed not on the main altar but on the πρόθεσις, a sort of sideboard. There the priest cuts a piece off the loaf and repeats the text, "He is led as a lamb to the slaughter." Then he lays it on the table and repeats, "The lamb of God is sacrificed." The sign of the cross is then imprinted on the bread and a small lance stabbed into its side, to the text, "But one of the soldiers with a spear pierced his side and forthwith came there out blood and water." At these words water and wine are mixed in the chalice. Then comes the *oblatio* in solemn procession, with the priest carrying the offering. (Here the δῶρον, the gift, represents the giver: Christ the sacrificiant is also the sacrificed.) Thus the priest re-enacts the traditional event, and in so far as Christ, in the sacramental state, possesses a *vita corporea actualis,*[41] an actual bodily life, one could say that a physical slaying[42] (*mortificatio*) of his

---

39 This point of view finds acceptance in the Beuron edition of the Missal (p. x).

40 Kramp, *Die Opferanschauungen der römischen Messliturgie,* p. 114.

41 "Vita corporea actualis sensitiva aut a sensibus pendens" (A real bodily life, apprehended by the senses or dependent on the senses).—Cardinal Álvarez Cienfuegos, S.J. (d. 1739), in Hauck, *Realencyklopädie,* XII, p. 693, 59.

42 Cf. sacrifice of the lamb in the "Vita S. Brendani," from *La Légende latine de S. Brandaines* (based on 11th–13th century MSS.), p. 12: "Dixitque sanctus

body has taken place. This happens as a result of the consecrating words spoken by the priest, and the destruction of the offering, the *oblatio occisi ad cultum Dei* (the offering up of the slain to the service of God), brings about the transubstantiation. The latter is a transmutation of the elements, which pass from a natural, soiled, imperfect material state into a subtle body. The bread, which must be wheaten, signifies the body, and the wine, representing blood, the soul. After the transubstantiation a piece of the host is mingled with the wine, thus producing the *coniunctio* of the soul with the body (fig. 159) and establishing the living body of Christ, namely the unity of the Church.

418   St. Ambrose called the transformed bread *medicina*. It is the φάρμακον ἀθανασίας, the drug of immortality, which, in the act of communion, displays its characteristic effect in and on the

Brendanus fratribus: 'Faciamus hic *opus divinum*, et sacrificemus Deo agnum immaculatum, quia hodie cena Domini est.' Et ibi manserunt usque in Sabbatum sanctum Pasche. Invenerunt eciam ibi multos greges ovium unius coloris, id est albi, ita ut non possent terram videre pre multitudine ovium. Convocatis autem fratribus, vir sanctus dixit eis: 'Accipite que sunt necessaria at diem festum de grege.' Illi autem acceperunt unam ovem et cum illam ligassent per cornua, sequebatur quasi domestica, sequens illorum vestigia. At ille: 'Accipite, inquit, unum agnum immaculatum.' Qui cum viri Dei mandata complessent, paraverunt omnia ad opus diei crastine. . . ." (And St. Brendan said to the brothers: "Let us perform here the divine work and sacrifice to God an immaculate lamb, for today is the supper of the Lord." And they remained there until Holy Saturday. They also found there many flocks of sheep of one colour, i.e., white, so that they could not see the ground because of the great number of sheep. The holy man called the brothers together and said to them: "Take from the flock what you need for the feast day." And they took one sheep, and when they had bound it by the horns, it followed as if it were a domestic animal, following in their footsteps. And he said: "Take an immaculate lamb." And when they had done the bidding of the man of God, they prepared everything for the work of the following day.)

Ibid., p. 34: "Confestim tunc cantaverunt tres psalmos: 'Miserere mei, Deus, et Domine refugium, et Deus, deus meus.' Ad terciam vero alios tres: 'Omnes gentes, Deus in nomine, Dilexi quoniam,' cum alleluya. Deinde immolaverunt agnum immaculatum, et omnes venerunt ad communionem dicentes: 'Hoc sacrum corpus Domini, et Salvatoris nostri, sanguinem sumite vobis in vitam aeternam.'" (At once they sang three psalms: "Have mercy on me, O God," and "Lord, thou hast been our refuge," and "O God, my God"; and at terce three others: "O clap your hands, all ye nations," "Save me, O God, by thy name," and "I have loved, because," with alleluia. Then they sacrificed an immaculate lamb, and they all came to communion, saying: "This is the sacred body of the Lord our Saviour, take the blood unto you for life eternal.")

159. The *coniunctio* of soul and body: an ecclesiastical version of the alchemical marriage bath.—"Grandes heures du duc de Berry" (MS., 1413)

believer—the effect of uniting the body with the soul. This takes the form of a healing of the soul and a *reformatio* of the body. The text of the Missal shows us how this is meant:

Da nobis per huius aquae et vini mysterium, eius divinitatis esse consortes, qui humanitatis nostrae fieri dignatus est particeps, Jesus Christus . . . (Grant that through the mystery of this water and wine, we may have fellowship in the divine nature of Him who vouchsafed to become partaker of our humanity . . .).

419   Perhaps I may be allowed to introduce a personal remark here. It was a real revelation for me, as a Protestant, to read the words of the Offertory for the first time: "Deus, qui humanae substantiae dignitatem mirabiliter condidisti" (O God, who didst marvellously create the dignity of human nature) and "qui humanitatis nostrae fieri dignatus est particeps" (who vouchsafed to become partaker of our humanity). What respect for the dignity of human nature! *Deus et homo!* There is no sign of that unworthy sinful man whom Protestantism has so often slandered in the past and is only too ready to slander again. Moreover, there seems to be still something else hidden in this almost "transcendental" estimate of man. For if God "dignatus est" to become partaker of our human nature, then man may also deem himself worthy to become partaker of the divine nature. In a certain sense this is just what the priest does in the performance of the sacrificial mystery, when he offers himself as the victim in place of Christ; and the congregation does likewise when it eats the consecrated body and thus shares in the substance of Deity.

420   By pronouncing the consecrating words that bring about the transformation, the priest redeems the bread and wine from their elemental imperfection as created things. This idea is quite unchristian—it is alchemical. Whereas Catholicism emphasizes the effectual presence of Christ, alchemy is interested in the fate and manifest redemption of the substances, for in them the divine soul lies captive and awaits the redemption that is granted to it at the moment of release. The captive soul then appears in the form of the "Son of God." For the alchemist, the one primarily in need of redemption is not man, but the deity who is lost and sleeping in matter. Only as a secondary consideration does he hope that some benefit may accrue to himself from the transformed substance as the panacea, the *medicina catholica,* just as it may to the imperfect bodies, the base or "sick" metals, etc. His attention is not directed to his own salvation through God's grace, but to the liberation of God from the darkness of matter. By applying himself to this miraculous work he benefits from its salutary effect, but only incidentally. He may approach the work as one in need of salvation, but he knows that his salvation depends on the success of the work, on whether he can free the divine soul. To this end he needs meditation, fasting,

and prayer; more, he needs the help of the Holy Ghost as his πάρεδρος.[43] Since it is not man but matter that must be redeemed, the spirit that manifests itself in the transformation is not the "Son of Man" but, as Khunrath very properly puts it,[44] the *filius macrocosmi*. Therefore, what comes out of the transformation is not Christ but an ineffable material being named the "stone," which displays the most paradoxical qualities apart from possessing *corpus, anima, spiritus*, and supernatural powers (fig. 214). One might be tempted to explain the symbolism of alchemical transformation as a parody of the Mass were it not pagan in origin and much older than the latter.

421   The substance that harbours the divine secret is everywhere, including the human body.[45] It can be had for the asking and can be found anywhere, even in the most loathsome filth[46] (fig. 256). In these circumstances the *opus* is no longer a ritualistic *officium*, but the same work of redemption which God himself accomplished upon mankind through the example of Christ, and which is now recognized by the philosopher who has received the *donum spiritus sancti*, the divine art, as his own individual *opus*. The alchemists emphasize this point: "He who works through the spirit of another and by a hired hand will behold results that are far from the truth; and conversely he who gives his services to another as assistant in the laboratory will never be admitted to the Queen's mysteries."[47] One might quote the words of Kabasilas: "As kings, when they bring a gift to God, bear it themselves and do not permit it to be borne by others."

---

43 Πάρεδρος = ministering spirit. So Khunrath and others.

44 *Von hyleal. Chaos,* p. 59 *et passim.* The much earlier Morienus ("De transmutatione metall.," *Art. aurif.,* II, p. 37) says: "In hoc enim lapide quattuor continentur elementa, assimilaturque Mundo et Mundi compositioni" (For in this stone the four elements are contained, and it is made similar to the World and the composition of the World).

45 Morienus says to King Kalid (ibid., p. 37): 'Haec enim res a te extrahitur: cuius etiam minera tu existis, apud te namque illam inveniunt, et ut verius confitear, a te accipiunt: quod cum probaveris, amor eius et dilectio in te augebitur. Et scias hoc verum et indubitabile permanere." (For this thing is extracted from thee, and thou art its ore [raw material]; in thee they find it, and that I may speak more plainly, from thee they take it; and when thou hast experienced this, the love and desire for it will be increased in thee. And know that this remains true and indubitable.)

46 "In stercore invenitur."

47 Maier, *Symbola aureae mensae,* p. 336.

422   Alchemists are, in fact, decided solitaries;[48] each has his say in his own way.[49] They rarely have pupils, and of direct tradition there seems to have been very little, nor is there much evidence of any secret societies or the like.[50] Each worked in the laboratory for himself and suffered from loneliness. On the other hand, quarrels were rare. Their writings are relatively free of polemic, and the way they quote each other shows a remarkable agreement on first principles, even if one cannot understand what they are really agreeing about.[51] There is little of that disputatiousness and splitting of hairs that so often mar theology and philosophy. The reason for this is probably the fact that "true" alchemy was never a business or a career, but a genuine *opus* to be achieved by quiet, self-sacrificing work. One has the impression that each individual tried to express his own particular experiences, quoting the dicta of the masters only when they seemed to offer analogies.

423   All, from the very earliest times, are agreed that their art is sacred and divine,[52] and likewise that their work can be com-

[48] Khunrath (*Von hyleal. Chaos*, p. 410), for instance, says: "So work even in the laboratory by thyself alone, without collaborators or assistants, in order that God, the Jealous, may not withdraw the art from thee, on account of thy assistants to whom He may not wish to impart it."

[49] Geber, "Summa perfectionis," *Bibl. chem.*, I, p. 557b: "Quia nobis solis artem per nos solos investigatam tradimus et non aliis . . ." (Because we hand down the art which we alone have investigated, to ourselves alone and to no one else . . .).

[50] I am setting aside the later Rosicrucians and the early "Poimandres" community, of which Zosimos speaks [infra, par. 456]. Between these two widely separated epochs I have found only one questionable passage, in the "Practica Mariae Prophetissae" (*Art. aurif.*, I, p. 323) (see fig. 78), where the "interlocutor" Aros (Horus) asks Maria: "O domina, obedisti in societate Scoyari: O prophetissa, an invenisti in secretis Philosophorum . . ." (O lady, did you obey in the society of Scoyarus: O Prophetess, did you find the secrets of the philosophers . . . ?). The name *Scoyaris* or *Scoyarus* recalls the mysterious *Scayolus* in the writings of Paracelsus (*De vita longa*), where it means the adept. (*Scayolae* are the higher spiritual forces or principles. See "Paracelsus as a Spiritual Phenomenon," pars. 206ff.) Is there perhaps a connection here? At any rate there seems to be an allusion to a *societas*. The treatise of Maria may go back to very early times and thus to the Gnostic societies. Agrippa (*De incertitudine scientiarum*, ch. XC) mentions an alchemical initiation vow which may possibly refer to the existence of secret societies. Waite (*The Secret Tradition in Alchemy*) comes to a negative conclusion in this respect.

[51] The *Turba philosophorum* is an instructive example in this respect.

[52] Morienus, "De transmut. metall.," *Art. aurif.*, II, p. 37: "Magisterium est arca-

pleted only with the help of God. This science of theirs is given only to the few, and none understands it unless God or a master has opened his understanding.[53] The knowledge acquired may not be passed on to others unless they are worthy of it.[54] Since all the essentials are expressed in metaphors they can be communicated only to the intelligent, who possess the gift of comprehension.[55] The foolish allow themselves to be infatuated by literal interpretations and recipes, and fall into error.[56] When reading the literature, one must not be content with just *one* book but must possess many books,[57] for "one book opens another."[58] Moreover one must read carefully, paragraph by paragraph; then one will make discoveries.[59] The terminology is admitted to be quite unreliable.[60] Sometimes the nature of the coveted substance will be revealed in a dream.[61] The *materia lapidis* may be found by divine inspiration.[62] The practice of the

---

num Dei gloriosi." "Consil. coniug.," *Ars chemica*, p. 56: "Donum et secretorum secretum Dei." *Rosarium, Art. aurif.*, II, p. 280: "Divinum mysterium a Deo datum et in mundo non est res sublimior post animam rationalem" (The divine mystery was given by God and there is in the world no thing more sublime except the rational soul).

53 Ibid., pp. 212, 228.　　54 Ibid., pp. 219, 269.

55 Ibid., p. 230. Alchemy is superior to all other sciences in the opinion of Djabir or Geber (8th cent.): "Indeed, any man who is learned in any science whatever, who has not given part of his time to the study of one of the principles of the Work, in theory or in practice, his intellectual culture is utterly insufficient" (Berthelot, *Chimie au moyen âge*, III, p. 214). Djabir is said to have been a Christian or Sabaean. (See also Ruska, "Die siebzig Bücher des Gabir ibn Hajjan," p. 38.) Synesius also appeals to the intelligence (Berthelot, *Alch. grecs*, II, iii, 16). Olympiodorus even compares the art to the divine intelligence (ibid., II, iv, 45) and appeals to the intelligence of his public (ibid., II, iv, 55). Christianos too lays stress on intelligence (ibid., VI, i, 4, and iii, 2). Likewise *Aurora* II, in *Art. aurif.*, I, "Prologus": "oportet intellectum valde subtiliter et ingeniose acuere" (one must sharpen the intellect very subtly and ingeniously).

56 *Rosarium, Art. aurif.*, II, p. 210.

57 Hoghelande, "De alchem. difficultatibus," *Bibl. chem. curiosa*, I, p. 342: "Librorum magnam habeat copiam."

58 "Rhasis dixit: liber enim librum aperit." (Quoted by Bonus, "Pret. marg. nov.," *Bibl. chem.*, II, ch. VIII.)

59 *Rosarium, Art. aurif.*, II, p. 230.　　60 Ibid., pp. 211, 243, 269.

61 Sendivogius, "Parabola," *Bibl. chem. curiosa*, II, p. 475: "Aqua Philosophica tibi in somno aliquoties manifestata" (The philosophic water that was shown to you a number of times in a dream).

62 Figulus, *Rosarium novum olympicum*, ch. XI.

art is a hard road [63] and the longest road.[64] The art has no enemies except the ignorant.[65]

424   It goes without saying that there are good and bad authors
in alchemical literature as elsewhere. There are productions by
charlatans, simpletons, and swindlers. Such inferior writings are
easily recognized by their endless recipes, their careless and un-
educated composition, their studied mystification, their excruci-
ating dulness, and their shameless insistence on the making of
gold. Good books can always be recognized by the industry, care,
and visible mental struggles of the author.

[63] Figulus, "Tractatulus rhythmicus," in ibid., part I, p. 58.
[64] *Rosarium, Art. aurif.,* II, p. 230.
[65] Arnold of Villanova, in ibid., p. 210.

160. Symbol of the art as union of
water and fire.—Eleazar, *Uraltes
chymisches Werk* (1760)

161. The *prima materia* as Saturn devouring his children.—*Mutus liber* (1702)

4. THE PRIMA MATERIA

425   The basis of the *opus*, the *prima materia*, is one of the most famous secrets of alchemy. This is hardly surprising, since it represents the unknown substance that carries the projection of the autonomous psychic content. It was of course impossible to specify such a substance, because the projection emanates from the individual and is consequently different in each case. For this reason it is incorrect to maintain that the alchemists never said what the *prima materia* was; on the contrary, they gave all too many definitions and so were everlastingly contradicting themselves. For one alchemist the *prima materia* was quicksilver, for others it was ore, iron, gold, lead, salt, sulphur, vinegar, water, air, fire, earth, blood, water of life, *lapis*, poison, spirit, cloud, sky, dew, shadow, sea, mother, moon, dragon, Venus, chaos, microcosm (fig. 162). Ruland's *Lexicon* gives no less than fifty synonyms, and a great many more could be added.

426   Besides these half chemical, half mythological definitions there are also some "philosophical" ones which have a deeper

317

162. The unfettered opposites in chaos. "Chaos" is one of the names for the
prima materia.—Marolles, *Tableaux du temple des muses* (1655)

meaning. Thus in the treatise of Komarios[1] we find the definition "Hades." In Olympiodorus the black earth contains the "accursed of God" (θεοκατάρατος). The "Consilium coniugii" says that the father of gold and silver—i.e., their *prima materia* —is "the animal of earth and sea," or "man," or a "part of man," e.g., his hair, blood, etc. Dorn calls the *prima materia* "Adamica" and—basing himself on Paracelsus—*limbus microcosmicus*. The material of the stone is "no other than the fiery and perfect Mercurius" and the true hermaphroditic "Adam and Microcosm" (= man)[2] (see fig. 163). Hermes Trismegistus is said to have called the stone the "orphan." Since Dorn was a pupil of Paracelsus his views are probably connected with the Anthropos doctrine of his master. For this I must refer the reader to my essay "Paracelsus as a Spiritual Phenomenon." Further connections between man and the *prima materia* are mentioned in other authors, but I cannot quote them all here.

427   The mercurial dragon of Greek alchemy, surnamed ἓν τὸ πᾶν, gave rise to descriptions of the *prima materia* as *Unum, Unica Res,*[3] and Monad [4] and to the statement in the "Liber Platonis

---

[1] Berthelot, *Alch. grecs,* IV, xx, 8.

[2] Dorn, "Congeries Paracelsicae chemicae," *Theatr. chem.,* I, p. 578. In the same place Dorn explains: "Mercurium istum componi corpore, spiritu et anima, eumque naturam elementorum omnium et proprietatem assumpsisse. Qua prop ter ingenio et intellectu validissimis adseverarunt suum lapidem esse animalem, quem etiam vocaverunt suum Adamum, qui suam invisibilem Evam occultam in suo corpore gestaret. . . ." (This Mercurius is composed of body, spirit, and soul, and has assumed the nature and quality of all the elements. Wherefore they affirmed with most powerful genius and understanding that their stone was a living thing, which they also called their Adam, who bore his invisible Eve hidden in his body. . . .) Hoghelande ("De alch. diff.," *Theatr. chem.,* I, pp. 178f.) says: "They have compared the *prima materia* to everything, to male and female, to the hermaphroditic monster, to heaven and earth, to body and spirit, chaos, microcosm, and the confused mass [*massa confusa*]; it contains in itself all colours and potentially all metals; there is nothing more wonderful in the world, for it begets itself, conceives itself and gives birth to itself."

[3] "Tractatus aureus," *Mus. herm.,* p. 10, and many other passages.

[4] Dee, "Monas hieroglyphica," *Theatr. chem.,* II, p. 218. In Aegidius de Vadis ("Dialogus," *Theatr. chem.,* II, p. 110) the monad is the effective *forma* in matter. Khunrath (*Amphitheatrum,* p. 203) writes: "In Cabala est hominis ad monadis simplicitatem reducti, cum Deo, Unio: id in Physico-Chemia ad Lapidis nostri . . . cum Macrocosmo Fermentatio." (In the Cabala it is the Union of man, reduced to the simplicity of the monad, with God; in Physio-Chemistry it is the Fermentation [of] man reduced to [the simplicity of] our stone, with the

quartorum" that man is well qualified to complete the work because he possesses that which is *simple*, i.e., the soul.[5] Mylius describes the *prima materia* as the *elementum primordiale*. It is the "pure subject and the unity of forms," and in it any form whatsoever may be assumed (*in quo retinetur quaelibet forma cum possibilitate*).[6]

428   In the second version of the *Turba*, Eximindus says:[7]

I make known to you, ye sons of the doctrine, that the beginning of all creatures is a certain primary everlasting and infinite nature which cooks and rules everything, and whose active and passive [aspects] are known and recognized only by those on whom the knowledge of the sacred art has been bestowed.

429   In Sermo IX of the *Turba*,[8] "Eximenus" puts forward a theory of creation that corresponds to the Biblical one (creation through the "Word") but stands in flagrant contradiction to the above, according to which the beginning is a *natura perpetua et infinita*. In the *Rosarium* the *prima materia* is called *radix ipsius* (root of itself). Because it roots in itself it is autonomous and dependent on nothing.

II. THE INCREATUM

430   Being a *radix ipsius*, the *prima materia* is a true *principium*, and from this it is but a step to the Paracelsan view that it is something *increatum*, uncreated. In his "Philosophia ad Athe-

Macrocosm.) There is a similar passage in his *Von hyleal. Chaos* (pp. 33, 204), where the monad is more a symbol of the perfected *lapis*. Dorn ("De spagirico artificio Trithemii sententia," *Theatr. chem.*, I, p. 441) says: "In uno est enim unum et non est unum, est simplex et in quaternario componitur" (For in the One there is and there is not the One; it is simple and it is composed in the quaternity). In his doctrine of the *res simplex* Dorn is very much influenced by the "Liber Platonis quartorum." (On one occasion he even mentions magic.) In the same passage he also uses the term *monad* for the goal: "A ternario et quaternario fit ad monadem progressus" (The progression is from the ternary and the quaternary to the Monad). The term *lapis* is used all through the literature for the beginning and the goal.
5 *Theatr. chem.*, V, p. 130.
6 Mylius, *Philosophia reformata*, p. 174.
7 *Art. aurif.*, I, p. 66. Eximindus (Eximidius or Eximenus in the first version) is a corruption of Anaximenes or Anaximander.
8 *Turba* (ed. Ruska), p. 116.

163. Earth as *prima materia*, suckling the son of the philosophers.—Mylius,
Philosophia reformata (1622)

nienses," Paracelsus says that this unique (*unica*) *materia* is a
great secret having nothing in common with the elements. It fills
the entire *regio aetherea,* and is the mother of the elements and
of all created things (fig. 163). Nothing can express this mystery,
nor has it been created (*nec etiam creatum fuit*). This uncreated
mystery was prepared (*praeparatum*) by God in such a way that
nothing will ever be like it in the future nor will it ever return
to what it was.[9] For it was so corrupted as to be beyond repara-
tion (which presumably refers to the Fall). Dorn's rendering
gives the sense of the original text.[10]

[9] Sudhoff/Matthiessen edn., XIII, p. 390: "Thus the supreme artist has prepared
a great uncreated mystery and no mystery will ever be the same nor will it ever
return, for, just as cheese will never again become milk, so generation will never
return to its first state." Dorn ("Physica genesis," *Theatr. chem.,* I, p. 380) translates: "Increatum igitur mysterium hoc fuit ab altissimo opifice Deo praeparatum,
ut ei simile nunquam futurum sit, nec ipsum unquam rediturum, ut fuit."
[10] Paracelsus continues (XIII, pp. 390f.): "This *mysterium magnum* was a mother
to all the elements, and in them likewise a grandmother to all stars, trees, and

431   The autonomy and everlastingness of the *prima materia* in
Paracelsus suggest a principle equal to the Deity, corresponding
to a *dea mater*. Just how Paracelsus managed to reconcile such
a view with his professions of Christianity is his own private
concern; nor is it by any means an isolated instance. The interpretations contained in "Aquarium sapientum" [11]—interesting
on account of their truly preposterous character and hardly to
be outdone even by *Aurora*—carry Paracelsan speculation still
further, though without mentioning the author. The following
texts, for example, are applied to the *prima materia*: "and his
going forth is from the beginning, from the days of eternity"
(Micah 5 : 2, D.V.), and "before Abraham was made, I am"
(John 8 : 58, D.V.). This is supposed to show that the stone is
without beginning and has its *primum Ens* from all eternity,
and that it too is without end and will exist in all eternity. To
understand this properly, one must open wide the eyes of the
soul and the spirit and observe and discern accurately by means
of the inner light. God has lit this light in nature and in our
hearts from the beginning.[12] And in the same way, continues
the author, that the stone together with its material has a thousand names and is therefore called "miraculous," all these names
can in eminent degree be predicated of God,[13] and the author
thereupon proceeds to this application. A Christian can hardly
believe his ears, but this conclusion only repeats what has already
been said quite plainly in the "Liber Platonis quartorum": "Res

creatures of the flesh; for all sentient and insentient creatures, and all others
of a like form, are born from the *mysterium magnum,* just as children are born
from a mother. And it is a *mysterium magnum,* one unique mother of all mortal
things, and they have all originated in her" and so on. "Now, whereas all other
mortal beings grew out of and originated in the *mysterium increatum,* it is to be
understood that no creature was created earlier, later, or in particular, but all
were created together. For the highest arcanum and great treasure of the creator
has fashioned all things in the *increatum,* not in form, not in essence, not in
quality, but they were in the *increatum,* as an image is in the wood, although
this same is not to be seen until the other wood is cut away: thus is the image
recognized. Nor is the *mysterium increatum* to be understood in any other manner, save that through its separation the corporeal and the insentient severally
took on the form and shape that are their own."

11 *Mus. herm.,* pp. 73ff. Here I must correct a mistake which crept into my
Paracelsica. Not only the author referred to there (pp. 173f.) but the "Aquarium"
as well is concerned with heresies, and in an equally negative way. [See "Paracelsus
as a Spiritual Phenomenon," par. 231.—EDITORS.]
12 Ibid., pp. 106f.   13 Ibid., p. 111.

ex qua sunt res, est Deus invisibilis et immobilis" [14] (That from which things arise is the invisible and immovable God). The first "res" is the subject matter of the divine art. It is true that very few of the philosophers pressed forward to this conclusion *expressis verbis,* but it is an aspect that makes their hints and veiled allusions decidedly more transparent. Moreover such a conclusion was inevitable psychologically, because the unconscious, being unknown, is bound to coincide with itself everywhere: lacking all recognizable qualities, no unconscious content can be distinguished from any other. This is not a logical sophistry but a very real phenomenon of great practical importance, for it affects the problems of identity and identification in social life, which are based on the collective (and indiscriminable) nature of unconscious contents. These, once they have taken possession of certain individuals, irresistibly draw them together by mutual attraction and knit them into smaller or larger groups which may easily swell into an avalanche.

432   The above quotations clearly show that the alchemists came to project even the highest value—God—into matter. With the highest value thus safely embedded in matter, a starting-point was given for the development of genuine chemistry on the one hand and of the more recent philosophical materialism on the other, with all the psychological consequences that necessarily ensue when the picture of the world is shifted 180 degrees. However remote alchemy may seem to us today, we should not underestimate its cultural importance for the Middle Ages. Today is the child of the Middle Ages and it cannot disown its parents.

III. UBIQUITY AND PERFECTION

433   The *prima materia* has the quality of ubiquity: it can be found always and everywhere, which is to say that projection can take place always and everywhere. The English alchemist Sir George Ripley (*c.* 1415–90) writes: "The philosophers tell the inquirer that birds and fishes bring us the *lapis,*[15] every man has

---

[14] *Theatr. chem.,* V, p. 145.
[15] Cf. Grenfell et al., *New Sayings of Jesus,* pp. 15f.: "Jesus saith, (Ye ask? who are those) that draw us (to the kingdom, if) the kingdom is in Heaven? . . . the

hunc diuide istum lapidem philosophorum, unam partem serua in album ferment.

164. Mercurius, standing on the round chaos, holding the scales which signify the *pondus et mensura*. The *rotundum* is a prefiguration of the gold.—"Figurarum Aegyptiorum secretarum" (MS., 18th cent.)

it, it is in every place, in you, in me, in everything, in time and space." [16] "It offers itself in lowly form [*vili figura*]. From it there springs our eternal water [*aqua permanens*]." [17] According to Ripley the *prima materia* is water; it is the material principle of all bodies,[18] including mercury.[19] It is the *hyle* which the divine

---

fowls of the air, and all beasts that are under the earth or upon the earth, and the fishes of the sea. . . ." [16] Ripley, *Opera omnia chemica*, p. 10. [17] Ibid., p. 130. [18] Ibid., p. 369. [19] Ibid., p. 427.

act of creation brought forth from the chaos as a dark sphere[20] (*sphaericum opus:* cf. fig. 34).[21] The chaos is a *massa confusa* that gives birth to the stone (figs. 125, 164). The hylical water contains a hidden elemental fire.[22] In the treatise "De sulphure" hell-fire (*ignis gehennalis*) is attributed to the element earth as its inner opposite.[23] According to Hortulanus, the stone arises from a *massa confusa* containing in itself all the elements[24] (fig. 162). Just as the world came forth from a *chaos confusum*,[25] so does the stone.[26] The idea of the rotating aquasphere reminds us of the Neopythagoreans: in Archytas the world-soul is a circle or sphere;[27] in Philolaos it draws the world round with it in its rotation.[28] The original idea is to be found in Anaxagoras, where the nous gives rise to a whirlpool in chaos.[29] The cosmogony of Empedokles is also relevant: here the σφαῖρος (spherical being) springs from the union of dissimilars, owing to the influence of φιλία. The definition of this spherical being as εὐδαιμονέστατος Θεός, "the most serene God," sheds a special light on the perfect, "round" nature of the *lapis*,[30] which arises from, and constitutes, the primal sphere; hence the *prima materia* is often called *lapis* (figs. 164, 165). The initial state is the hidden state, but by the

---

[20] Ibid., p. 9.

[21] In the "Ripley Scrowle" (British Museum, MS. Add. 5025), the sphere of water is represented with dragon's wings (cf. fig. 228). In the "Verses belonging to an emblematicall scrowle" (*Theatr. chem. Brit.*, p. 376) the "spiritus Mercurii" says:

> "Of my blood and water I wis, Who it findeth he hath grace:
> Plenty in all the world there is. In the world it runneth over all,
> It runneth in every place;   And goeth round as a ball."

[22] Ripley, *Opera omnia chemica*, p. 197.

[23] *Mus. herm.*, p. 606.

[24] "Hortulani commentarius" in *De alchemia*, p. 366.

[25] Cf. Aegidius de Vadis ("Dialogus," *Theatr. chem.*, II, p. 101): "The chaos is the *materia confusa*. This *materia prima* is necessary to the art. Four elements are mixed in a state of disorder in the *materia prima*, because earth and water, which are heavier than the other elements, reached the sphere of the moon, while fire and air, which are lighter than the others, descended as far as the centre of the earth; for which reason such a *materia* is rightly called disordered. Only a part of this disordered material remained in the world, and this is known to everyone and is sold publicly."

[26] Hortulanus, "Commentarius," *De alchemia*, p. 371.

[27] Zeller, *Die Philosophie der Griechen*, III, p. 120.

[28] Ibid., p. 102; also p. 154.   [29] Ibid., p. 687.

[30] Also defined as "the round fish in the sea" ("Allegoriae super librum Turbae," *Art. aurif.*, I, p. 141).

165. "L'occasione": Mercurius standing on the globe (the *rotundum*). The caduceus and horns of plenty nearby symbolize the richness of his gifts.—Cartari,
Le imagini de i dei (1581)

art and the grace of God it can be transmuted into the second, manifest state. That is why the *prima materia* sometimes coincides with the idea of the initial stage of the process, the *nigredo*. It is then the black earth in which the gold or the *lapis* is sown like the grain of wheat (cf. fig. 48). It is the black, magically fecund earth that Adam took with him from Paradise, also called antimony and described as a "black blacker than black" (*nigrum nigrius nigro*).[31]

IV. THE KING AND THE KING'S SON

434   As the grain of fire lies concealed in the *hyle,* so the King's Son lies in the dark depths of the sea as though dead, but yet lives and calls from the deep[32] (fig. 166): "Whosoever will free me from the waters and lead me to dry land, him will I prosper with everlasting riches."[33]

435   The connection with the *Rex marinus* of the "Visio Arislei"[34] is obvious. Arisleus[35] tells of his adventure with the *Rex marinus,* in whose kingdom nothing prospers and nothing is begotten. Moreover there are no philosophers there. Only like mates with like,[36] consequently there is no procreation. The

31 Maier, *Symbola aureae mensae,* pp. 379f.   32 Ibid., p. 380.

33 Cf. the beginning of Parable VII in *Aurora* I, ch. XII: "Be turned to me with all your heart and do not cast me aside because I am black and swarthy, because the sun hath changed my colour [Cant. 1 : 5f.] and the waters have covered my face [Jonas 2 : 6] and the earth hath been polluted and defiled [Psalm 105 : 38] in my works, for there was darkness over it [Luc. 23 : 44] because I stick fast in the mire of the deep [Psalm 68 : 3] and my substance is not disclosed. Wherefore out of the depths have I cried [Psalm 129 : 1] and from the abyss of the earth with my voice to all you that pass by the way. Attend and see me, if any shall find one like unto me [Lam. 1 : 12], I will give into his hand the morning star [Apoc. 2 : 28]."

34 *Art. aurif.,* I, pp. 146ff.

35 Cf. Ruska, *Turba,* p. 23. Arisleus is a corruption of Archelaos, owing to Arabic transcription. This Archelaos may be a Byzantine alchemist of the 8th or 9th century. He has left us a poem on the sacred art. But since the *Turba,* which is ascribed to Arisleus, goes back to Arabic tradition—as Ruska points out—we must assume that Archelaos lived much earlier. Ruska, therefore, identifies him with the pupil of Anaxagoras (ibid., p. 23). The alchemists would have been particularly interested in his idea that the νοῦς is mixed with air: ἀέρα καὶ νοῦν τὸν θεόν (Stobaeus, *Eclogarum,* I, p. 56).

36 The pairing of like with like is to be found as early as Heraclitus (Diels, *Fragmente der Vorsokratiker,* I, p. 79[10]).

166. Background, the *Rex marinus* calling for help; foreground, his renewed form with the *rotundum* and the *columba spiritus sancti.*—Trismosin, "Splendor solis" (MS., 1582)

King must seek the counsel of the philosophers and mate Thabritius with Beya,[37] his two children whom he has hatched in his brain[38] (fig. 167).

436   When we are told that the King is *exanimis*, inanimate, or that his land is unfruitful, it is equivalent to saying that the hidden state is one of latency and potentiality. The darkness and depths of the sea symbolize the unconscious state of an invisible content that is projected. Inasmuch as such a content belongs to the total personality[39] and is only apparently severed from its context by projection, there is always an attraction between conscious mind and projected content. Generally it takes the form of a fascination. This, in the alchemical allegory, is expressed by the King's cry for help from the depths of his unconscious, dissociated state. The conscious mind should respond to this call: one should *operari regi,* render service to the King, for this would be not only wisdom but salvation as well.[40] Yet this brings with it the necessity of a descent into the dark world of the unconscious, the ritual κατάβασις εἰς ἄντρον, the perilous adventure of the night sea journey (figs. 69, 170, 171), whose end and aim is the restoration of life, resurrection, and the triumph over death (figs. 172, 174, 177). Arisleus and his companions brave the quest, which ends in catastrophe, the death of Thabritius. His death is a punishment for the incestuous *coniunctio oppositorum* (figs. 223, 226). The brother-sister pair stands allegorically for the whole conception of opposites. These have a wide range

[37] Also Gabricus, Cabricus, Cabritis, Kybric: Arabic *kibrit* = sulphur. Beja, Beya, Beua: Arabic *al-baida* = the white one. (Ruska, *Turba,* p. 324.)

[38] "Ego tamen filium et filiam meo in cerebro gestavi" ("Visio Arislei," *Art. aurif.,* I, p. 147). In Maier, *Symbola aureae mensae,* pp. 343f. (see n. 42 infra), it is a question of mother-incest, for there Gabritius is married to his mother Isis because they were the only pair of this kind. Evidently a chthonic pair of gods (symbolizing the opposites latent in the *prima materia*) is celebrating the *hierosgamos.*

[39] The "whole" or "self" comprises both conscious and unconscious contents.

[40] There is ample evidence in the literature to show that *divitiae* and *salus* are spiritual *bona futura,* and refer as much to the salvation of the soul as to the well-being of the body. We must not forget that the alchemist is not in the least concerned to torment himself with moral scruples, on the assumption that man is a sinful nonentity who complies with God's work of redemption by his irreproachable ethical behaviour. The alchemist finds himself in the role of a "redeemer" whose *opus divinum* is more a continuation of the divine work of redemption than a precautionary measure calculated to guard against possible damnation at the Last Judgment.

CONIVNCTIO SIVE
Coitus.

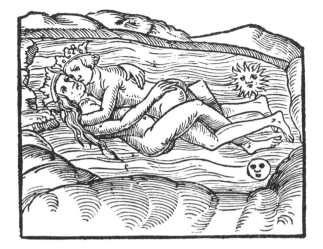

O Luna durch meyn vmbgeben/vnd ſuſſe mynne/
Wirſtu ſchön/ſtarck/vnd gewaltig als ich byn.
O Sol/ du biſt vber alle liecht zu erkennen/
So bedarffſtu doch mein als der han der hennen.

167. Allegory of the psychic union of opposites. [Verses:
"O Luna, folded by my embrace, / Be you as strong as I,
as fair of face. / O Sol, brightest of all lights known to
men, / And yet you need me, as the cock the hen."]—
Rosarium philosophorum (1550)

of variation: dry-moist, hot-cold, male-female, sun-moon, gold-
silver, mercury-sulphur, round-square, water-fire, volatile-solid,
physical-spiritual, and so on.[41] The *regius filius* is a rejuvenated

41 The antithetical nature of the *ens primum* is an almost universal idea. In
China the opposites are *yang* and *yin*, odd and even numbers, heaven and earth,
etc.; there is also a union of them in the hermaphrodite. (Cf. Hastings, *Encyclopaedia*, IV, p. 140.) Empedokles: νεῖκος and φιλία of the elements (Zeus-fire, Hera-
air). The second period of creation saw the birth of hybrids, similar to the
northern Ymir and Buri (Herrmann, *Nordische Mythologie*, p. 574). Neopythagoreans: Monad = masculine, Dyad = feminine (Zeller, *Die Philosophie der
Griechen*, III, p. 98). In Nicomachus, the Deity is the odd and even number,
therefore male-female (ibid., p. 107). Hermes Trismegistus: The Nous is hermaphroditic. Bardesanes (A.D. 154–223?): Crucified hermaphrodite (Schultz, *Dokumente der Gnosis*, p. lv). Valentinus: The creator of the world is the mother-

168. The king as *prima materia,* devouring his son.—Lambspringk, "Figurae et emblemata," in *Musaeum hermeticum* (1678)

form of the Father-King. The youth is frequently shown with a sword and represents the spirit, while the father represents the body. In the *Rosarium* version of the "Visio" the death of the son is the result of his complete disappearance into the body of Beya during coitus. In another version he is eaten by his father (fig. 168), or the Sun is drowned in Mercurius or swallowed by the lion (fig. 169). Thabritius is the masculine, spiritual principle of light and Logos which, like the Gnostic Nous, sinks into the embrace of physical nature (Physis). Death therefore represents the completion of the spirit's descent into matter. The alchemists depicted the sinful nature of this occurrence in various ways but,

father, and in Marcion the Gnostic, the Primordial Father is hermaphroditic. Among the Ophites, the Pneuma is male-female (ibid., p. 171).

169. The "green lion" devouring the sun.—*Rosarium philosophorum* (1550)

because they do not appear to have quite understood it, they rationalize or minimize the incest, in itself so repellent.[42]

[42] Maier, *Symbola aureae mensae,* p. 344: "Delphinas, anonymus philosophus in Secreti Maximi tractatu De Matre cum filio ex necessitate naturae conjungenda clarissime loquitur; si enim unus sit masculus et una foemina, eius mater, in mundo, annon hi duo conjungendi sint, ut genus humanum inde multiplicetur? . . . eodem modo cum saltem in arte Chymica sint duo subjecta, quorum unus alterius mater est, haec copulanda. . . ." (Delphinas, an anonymous philosopher in the treatise "The Greatest Secret," speaks very clearly about the Mother who must by natural necessity be united with the son. For, if there were in the world only one male and only one female, and she his mother, would they not have to be united, in order that mankind might be multiplied? In the same way, at any rate in the Chemical Art, since there are two subjects of which one is the mother of the other, they must be united. . . .)

On p. 515 of the same book there is an "Epithalamium honori nuptiarum Matris Beiae et filii Gabrici," which begins as follows:

"Ipsa maritali dum nato foedere mater
Jungitur, incestum ne videatur opus.
Sic etenim Natura iubet, sic alma requirit
Lex Fati, nec ea est res male grata Deo."

332

170. The night sea journey. Joseph in the cistern, Christ in the sepulchre, Jonah
swallowed by the whale.—*Biblia pauperum* (1471)

V. THE MYTH OF THE HERO

437   Resulting as it did from the advice of the philosophers, the
death of the King's Son is naturally a delicate and dangerous
matter. By descending into the unconscious, the conscious mind
puts itself in a perilous position, for it is apparently extinguish-
ing itself. It is in the situation of the primitive hero who is de-
voured by the dragon. Since all this means a diminution or ex-
tinction of consciousness, an *abaissement du niveau mental*
equivalent to that "peril of the soul" which is primitive man's
greatest dread (i.e., the fear of ghosts[43]), the deliberate and indeed wanton provocation of this state is a sacrilege or breach of
taboo attended by the severest punishments. Accordingly the
King imprisons Arisleus and his companions in a triple glass
house together with the corpse of the King's Son. The heroes
are held captive in the underworld at the bottom of the sea,
where, exposed to every kind of terror, they languish for eighty
days in an intense heat. At the request of Arisleus, Beya is imprisoned with them. (The *Rosarium* version of the "Visio" inter-

---

(When the mother is joined with the son in the covenant of marriage, count it
not as incest. For so doth nature ordain, so doth the holy law of fate require,
and the thing is not unpleasing to God.)

43 The fear of ghosts means, psychologically speaking, the overpowering of consciousness by the autonomous contents of the unconscious. This is equivalent to
mental derangement.

171. Hercules on the night sea journey in the vessel of the sun.—Base of an
Attic vase (5th cent. B.C.)

prets the prison as Beya's womb.[44]) Clearly, they have been overpowered by the unconscious and are helplessly abandoned, which
means that they have volunteered to die in order to beget a new
and fruitful life in that region of the psyche which has hitherto
lain fallow in darkest unconsciousness, and under the shadow of
death (fig. 171).

438   Although the possibility of life is hinted at by the brother-
sister pair, these unconscious opposites must be activated by the
intervention of the conscious mind, otherwise they will merely
remain dormant. But this is a dangerous undertaking. We can
understand the anxious plea in *Aurora consurgens:* "Horridas

44 *Art. aurif.,* II, pp. 246ff.

172. Jonah emerging from the belly of the whale. The goal of the night sea journey is equivalent to the *lapis angularis* or cornerstone.—"Speculum humanae salvationis" (Cod. Lat. 512, Paris, 15th cent.)

nostrae mentis purga tenebras, accende lumen sensibus!" [45] We can also understand why Michael Maier found few that were willing to plunge into the sea.[46] Arisleus is in danger of succumbing to the fate of Theseus and Peirithous, who descended into Hades and grew fast to the rocks of the underworld, which is to say that the conscious mind, advancing into the unknown regions of the psyche, is overpowered by the archaic forces of the unconscious: a repetition of the cosmic embrace of Nous and Physis. The purpose of the descent as universally exemplified in the myth of the hero is to show that only in the region of danger (watery abyss, cavern, forest, island, castle, etc.) can one find the "treasure hard to attain" (jewel, virgin, life-potion, victory over death) (fig. 172).

[45] I, ch. IX, par. IV. [Originally from a sequence of Notker Balbulus (*c.* 840–912).—EDITORS.] The passage is apparently derived from the first *oratio* of the third Sunday in Advent: "et mentis nostrae tenebras gratia tuae visitationis illustra."
[46] "Nonnulli perierunt in opere nostro" (Not a few have perished in our work), the *Rosarium* says. The element of torture is also emphasized in "Allegoriae super librum Turbae," *Art. aurif.,* I, pp. 139ff.: "Accipe hominem, tonde eum, et trahe super lapidem . . . donec corpus eius moriatur . . ." (Take a man, shave him, and drag him over a stone . . . until his body dies . . .).

335

173. The slaying of the king (*mortificatio*).—Stolcius de Stolcenberg, *Viridarium chymicum* (1624)

439   The dread and resistance which every natural human being experiences when it comes to delving too deeply into himself is, at bottom, the fear of the journey to Hades. If it were only resistance that he felt, it would not be so bad. In actual fact, however, the psychic substratum, that dark realm of the unknown,[47] exercises a fascinating attraction that threatens to become the more overpowering the further he penetrates into it.[48] The psycho-

[47] For the quadratic enclosure as the domain of the psyche, cf. the motif of the square in Part II, supra. According to Pythagoras the soul is a square (Zeller, *Die Philosophie der Griechen*, III, p. 120).
[48] Symbolized by a sorceress or by wanton girls, as in *Poliphilo*. Cf. fig. 33, and Béroalde de Verville, *Le Songe de Poliphile*. Similar themes in Part II of this volume.

171. Jonah in the whale.—Early Christian
earthenware lamp

logical danger that arises here is the disintegration of personality into its functional components, i.e., the separate functions of consciousness, the complexes, hereditary units, etc. Disintegration—which may be functional or occasionally a real schizophrenia—is the fate which overtakes Gabricus (in the *Rosarium* version): he is dissolved into atoms in the body of Beya,[49] this being equivalent to a form of *mortificatio* (fig. 173).

49 *Art. aurif.*, II, p. 246: "Nam Beya ascendit super Gabricum, et includit eum in suo utero. quod nil penitus videri potest de eo. Tantoque amore amplexata est Gabricum, quod ipsum totum in sui naturam concepit, et in partes indivisibiles divisit. Unde Merculinus ait: . . .

"Per se solvuntur, per se quoque conficiuntur,
Ut duo qui fuerant, unum quasi corpore fiant."

(Then Beya mounted upon Gabricus and enclosed him in her womb, so that nothing at all could be seen of him any more. And she embraced Gabricus with so much love that she absorbed him completely into her own nature, and divided him into indivisible parts. Wherefore Merculinus says: Through themselves they are dissolved, through themselves they are put together, so that they who were two are made one, as though of one body.) (NOTE: "Merculinus" is a correction of the text's "Masculinus.") The King, like the King's Son, is killed in a variety of ways. He may be struck down, or else he drinks so much water that he sickens and dissolves in it (Merlinus, "Allegoria de arcano lapidis," *Art. aurif.*, I, pp. 392ff.).

337

175. The wolf as *prima materia,* devouring the dead king. In the background, sublimation of the *prima materia* and rebirth of the king.—Maier, *Scrutinium chymicum* (1687)

440   Here again we have a repetition of the *coniunctio* of Nous and Physis.[50] But the latter is a cosmogonic event, whereas this is a catastrophe brought about by the intervention of the philosophers. So long as consciousness refrains from acting, the opposites will remain dormant in the unconscious. Once they have been activated, the *regius filius*—spirit, Logos, Nous—is swallowed up by Physis; that is to say, the body and the psychic representatives of the organs gain mastery over the conscious mind. In the hero myth[51] this state is known as being swallowed up in the belly of the whale or dragon[52] (fig. 174). The heat

---

50 Valentinus, "Practica," *Mus. herm.,* p. 394. In another version of the incorporation motif, Mars feeds the body of the King to the famished wolf (*fame acerrima occupatus*), the son of Saturn (lead). The wolf symbolizes the *prima materia's* appetite for the King, who often takes the place of the Son (fig. 175; cf. also figs. 166, 168, 169).

51 Cf. *Symbols of Transformation,* passim.

52 Espagnet, "Arcanum hermeticae philosophiae," *Bibl. chem. curiosa,* II, p. 655, §LXVIII: "This first digestion takes place as if in a belly."

there is usually so intense that the hero loses his hair,[53] i.e., he is reborn bald as a babe (fig. 176). This heat is the *ignis gehennalis*, the hell into which Christ descended in order to conquer death as part of his *opus*.

441 The philosopher makes the journey to hell as a "redeemer." The "hidden fire" forms the inner antithesis to the cold wetness of the sea.[54] In the "Visio" this heat is undoubtedly the warmth of incubation,[55] equivalent to the self-incubating or "brooding" state of meditation. In Indian yoga we find the kindred idea of *tapas*, self-incubation.[56] The aim of *tapas* is the same as in the "Visio": transformation and resurrection (cf. fig. 177).

[53] Frobenius, *Das Zeitalter des Sonnengottes.*
[54] *Turba philosophorum* (Sermo LXVIII): "Our work . . . results from a generation in the sea."
[55] Cf. the king's sweat-bath, fig. XIV of the Lambspringk "Figurae," *Mus. herm.*, p. 369, among others. We find exactly the same idea in the hatching of the egg in goldmaking, as described by Nikephorus Blemmides: περὶ τῆς ᾠοχρυσοποιίας (Berthelot, *Alch. grecs*, VI. xx).
[56] Cf. Jung, *Symbols of Transformation*, p. 380.

176. Jonah in the belly of the whale.
—Khludov Psalter (Byzantine, 9th cent.)

177. The Resurrection: Samson with the city gates of the Philistines, Christ rising from the grave, Jonah being spewed forth by the whale.—*Biblia pauperum* (1471)

VI. THE HIDDEN TREASURE

442   The "treasure hard to attain," whose presence was suspected in the dark *prima materia,* is symbolized by the alchemists in various ways. Christopher of Paris, for instance, says that the chaos (as *prima materia*) is the work of all-wise nature. Our understanding (*intellectus*), aided by the "celestial and glowing spirit," must transform this natural work of art—chaos—into the celestial nature of the quintessence, and into the life-giving (*vegetabilis*) essence of heaven. The precious substance is potentially contained in this chaos as a *massa confusa* of all the elements rolled into one, and man must diligently apply his mind to it so that "our heaven" may come into reality (*ad actum*).[57]

443   Johannes Grasseus quotes the view that the *prima materia* is the lead (*plumbum*) of the philosophers, also called the "lead of the air"[58] (an allusion to the inner opposite). This lead contains the radiant white dove (fig. 178), called the "salt of the metals." The dove is the "chaste, wise, and rich Queen of Sheba,

[57] Christopher, "Elucidarius," *Theatr. chem.,* VI, p. 228. Cf. Mithras' birth from a stone "solo aestu libidinis" (through the sole heat of libido).
[58] Cf. Sendivogius, "De sulphure," *Mus. herm.,* p. 612: "extra leve et invisible, intus vero grave, visibile et fixum" (outside it [the element air] is light and invisible, but inside heavy, visible, and solid).

Ignis

Aër

Aqua

Terra

178. The dove (*avis Hermetis*) rising from the four elements as symbol of the spirit freed from the embrace of Physis.—"De summa et universalis medicinae sapientiae veterum philosophorum" (MS., 18th cent.)

179. The alchemical trinity: the king and his son with Hermes between them (Hermes = *Spiritus Mercurii*).—Lambspringk, "Figurae et emblemata," in *Musaeum hermeticum* (1678)

veiled in white, who was willing to give herself to none but King Solomon." [59]

444   According to Basilius Valentinus, the earth (as *prima materia*) is not a dead body, but is inhabited by a spirit that is its life and soul. All created things, minerals included, draw their strength from the earth-spirit. This spirit is life, it is nourished by the stars, and it gives nourishment to all the living things it shelters in its womb. Through the spirit received from on high, the earth hatches the minerals in her womb (cf. fig. 163) as the mother her unborn child. This invisible spirit is like the reflec-

[59] Grasseus, "Arca arcani," *Theatr. chem.*, VI, p. 314. He mentions the Augustinian monk Degenhardus as the author of this image, which, as in *Aurora* (ch. V), is an obvious allusion to Sapientia.

180. The Christian Trinity with the Holy Ghost as a winged man.—Engraving
(15th cent.) by the Master of the Berlin Passion

tion in a mirror, intangible, yet it is at the same time the root of
all the substances necessary to the alchemical process or arising
therefrom (*radix nostrorum corporum*).[60]

445   A similar idea is to be found in Michael Maier:[61] The sun,
by its many millions of revolutions, spins the gold into the earth.
Little by little the sun has imprinted its image on the earth, and
that image is the gold. The sun is the image of God, the heart[62]
is the sun's image in man, just as gold is the sun's image in the
earth (also called *Deus terrenus*), and God is known in the gold.

60 "Practica," *Mus. herm.*, pp. 403f.
61 *De circulo physico quadrato*. There is a parallel idea in Emerson, *Essays*, I,
pp. 301ff. [In Jung's copy, "Circles"; but cf. also "Intellect."—EDITORS.]
62 Heart and blood as seat of the soul.

343

This golden image of God is the *anima aurea*, which, when breathed into common quicksilver, changes it into gold.

446 Ripley is of the opinion that the fire must be extracted from the chaos and made visible.[63] This fire is the Holy Ghost, who unites father and son.[64] He is often represented as a winged old man,[65] i.e., Mercurius in the form of the god of revelation, who is identical with Hermes Trismegistus[66] and, together with the King and the King's Son, forms the alchemical trinity (figs. 179, 180). God wrought this fire in the bowels of the earth, just as he wrought the purging flames of hell, and in this fire[67] God himself glows with divine love.[68]

[63] *Opera omnia*, p. 146.
[64] For instance, in Lambspringk's "Figurae et emblemata," *Mus. herm.*, p. 371. See fig. 179.
[65] A similar idea is to be found in the Indian *hamsa* (swan).
[66] Scott, *Hermetica*, I and II. [67] Also defined as *calx viva* (quicklime).
[68] "Gloria mundi," *Mus. herm.*, pp. 246f.

181. Sun as symbol of God.
—Boschius, *Symbolographia* (1702)

182. Christ as the Saviour of souls.—Mural painting (12th cent.) church of the Braunweiler monastery, Rhineland

5. THE LAPIS-CHRIST PARALLEL

I. THE RENEWAL OF LIFE

447   The examples given in the last chapter show that there is a spirit hidden in the *prima materia,* just as there was in the Nile stone of Ostanes. This spirit was eventually interpreted as the Holy Ghost in accordance with the ancient tradition of the Nous swallowed up by the darkness while in the embrace of Physis— with this difference, however, that it is not the supreme feminine principle, earth, who is the devourer, but Nous in the form of Mercurius or the tail-eating Uroboros (fig. 147). In other words, the devourer is a sort of material earth-spirit, an hermaphrodite possessing a masculine-spiritual and feminine-corporeal aspect (fig. 183; cf. figs. 54, 125). The original Gnostic myth has undergone a strange transformation: Nous and Physis are indistinguishably one in the *prima materia* and have become a *natura abscondita*.

448   The psychological equivalent of this theme is the projection of a highly fascinating unconscious content which, like all such contents, exhibits a numinous—"divine" or "sacred"—quality.

183. Androgynous deity standing between male serpent with sun and female serpent with moon.—Late Babylonian gem

Alchemy set itself the task of acquiring this "treasure hard to attain" and of producing it in visible form, as the physical gold or the panacea or the transforming tincture—in so far as the art still busied itself in the laboratory. But since the practical, chemical work was never quite free from the unconscious contents of the operator which found expression in it, it was at the same time a psychic activity which can best be compared with what we call active imagination.[1] This method enables us to get a grasp of contents that also find expression in dream life. The process is in both cases an irrigation of the conscious mind by the unconscious, and it is related so closely to the world of alchemical ideas that we are probably justified in assuming that alchemy deals with the same, or very similar, processes as those involved in active imagination and in dreams, i.e., ultimately with the process of individuation.

149   Earlier on, we left Arisleus and his companions, together with Beya and the dead Thabritius, in the triple glass house where they had been imprisoned by the *Rex marinus*. They suffer from the intense heat, like the three whom Nebuchadnezzar cast into the fiery furnace (fig. 184). King Nebuchadnezzar had a vision of a fourth, "like the Son of God," as we are told in Daniel 3 : 25. This vision is not without bearing on alchemy, since there are numerous passages in the literature stating that the stone is *trinus et unus* (fig. 185; cf. fig. 1). It consists of the four elements, with fire representing the spirit concealed in matter. This is the fourth, absent and yet present, who always ap-

[1] For a discussion of this method see Jung, "The Transcendent Function," and *Mysterium Coniunctionis*, pp. 494ff., 528ff.—EDITORS.]

184. The three youths in the fiery furnace.—Early Christian ornament on sarcophagus from Villa Carpegna, Rome

pears in the fiery agony of the furnace and symbolizes the divine presence—succour and the completion of the work. And, in their hour of need, Arisleus and his companions see their master Pythagoras in a dream and beg him for help. He sends them his disciple Harforetus, the "author of nourishment." [2] So the work is completed and Thabritius comes to life again.[3] We may suppose that Harforetus brought them the miraculous food, though

---

[2] Harforetus = Horfoltus of the Codex Berolinensis (Ruska, *Turba*, p. 324). In Ruska's opinion, he is identical with the Emperor Heraclius (610–641), but the mystical role he plays in the "Visio" points rather to some connection with Harpokrates.

[3] The "Visio Arislei" (*Art. aurif.*, I, p. 149) has: "ad Regem dicentes: quod filius tuus vivit, qui morti fuerat deputatus" (they said to the king: your son is alive, who was accounted dead). The Codex Berolinensis (in Ruska, *Turba*) has: "et misimus ad regem, quod filius tuus commotus est" (and we sent [word] to the king: Your son has been moved). (NOTE: "Commotus" is evidently intended to mean that he "moves" again or is "quick," alive.)

347

185. Below, the triad as unity; above, the quaternity standing on the binarius. —Valentinus, "Duodecim claves," in *Mus. herm.* (1678)

this only becomes clear through a discovery of Ruska's, who gave us access to the text of the Codex Berolinensis. There, in an introduction that is missing from the printed versions of the "Visio,"[4] we read: "Pythagoras says, 'Ye write and have written down for posterity how this most precious tree is planted, and how he that eats of its fruits shall hunger no more.' "[5] Since the "Visio" was written for the express purpose of leaving an example of the alchemical process to posterity, it naturally deals with the planting of trees, and the end of the legend is designed to show the miraculous regenerating effects of the fruit. While Arisleus was in such dire straits, and Thabritius lay in the sleep of death, the tree[6] was evidently growing and bearing fruit. The part played by Arisleus in the glass house is entirely passive. The decisive action comes from the master, who sends his messenger with the food of life.

450   We are told that a man can receive the secret knowledge only through divine inspiration or from the lips of a master, and also that no one can complete the work except with the help of God.[7]

[4] I use the edition of 1593 in *Artis auriferae,* I, pp. 146ff.

[5] Ruska, *Turba,* p. 324. In the *Art. aurif.,* I, this passage is changed to "how to gather the fruits of that immortal tree."

[6] The tree is often a *coralium* or *corallius,* coral, therefore, a "sea-tree" (fig. 186) ("the living coral growing in the sea"—"Allegoriae super librum Turbae," *Art. aurif.,* I, p. 141). Cf. the tree of paradise in the sea in Paracelsus, *Das Buch Azoth,* p. 529.

[7] Hence the recurrent formulae, "Deo adiuvante," "Deo concedente," etc.

186. The tree of coral in the sea.—Dioscorides, "De materia medica"
(MS., Vienna, 16th cent.)

187. The dragon spewing forth Jason, after drinking the potion prepared by
Athene.—Attic vase (5th cent. B.C.)

In the "Visio" it is the legendary master, the divine Pythagoras,[8]
who takes the place of God[9] and completes the work of regeneration (fig. 187). This divine intervention, as we may venture
to call it, occurs in a dream, when Arisleus sees the master and
implores his help. If the union of the opposites—mind and body
—portrayed by Thabritius and Beya, the putting to death, and
the cremation in the furnace are, according to one alchemist,[10]
the equivalent of the offertory in the Mass, we find an analogy

[8] The Neopythagoreans regarded Pythagoras as God incarnate. Cf. Zeller, *Die
Philosophie der Griechen*, III, p. 130.
[9] As Hermes takes the place of Poimandres. Cf. Scott, *Hermetica*, I and II.
[10] Melchior Cibinensis. (See pars. 48off.)

188. The tree of the philosophers, surrounded by symbols of the *opus*.—Mylius,
Philosophia reformata (1622)

to the petition for help in the *memento vivorum*—the inter-
cession for the living—and in the commemoration of martyrs,
both of which precede the transubstantiation in the *ordo missae*.
The invocation is made "pro redemptione animarum suarum,
pro spe salutis et incolumnitatis suae" (for the redemption of
their souls, for the hope of their health and welfare), and the
saints are remembered in order that God, for the sake of their
merits and prayers, may grant "that we be defended in all things
with the help of Thy protection." The petition ends with the
epiclesis, which ushers in the transubstantiation: "ut nobis
corpus et sanguis fiat" (that it may become for us the Body and

351

189. Dragon with tree of the Hesperides.
—Boschius, *Symbolographia* (1702)

the Blood), i.e., the miraculous food,[11] the φάρμακον ζωῆς. In the "Visio" it is the fruit of the immortal tree that brings salvation (figs. 188–90). But when the Church speaks of the "fructus sacrificii missae"—the fruits of the sacrifice of the Mass—it is not quite the same thing, since moral and other effects are meant, not the consecrated substances themselves which are likewise produced *ex opere operato* ("from the performed work").

451   Here we come to a parting of the ways. The Christian receives the fruits of the Mass for himself personally and for the circumstances of his own life in the widest sense. The alchemist, on the other hand, receives the *fructus arboris immortalis* not merely for himself but first and foremost for the King or the King's Son, for the perfecting of the coveted substance. He may play a part in the *perfectio*, which brings him health, riches, illumination, and salvation; but since he is the redeemer of God and not the one to be redeemed, he is more concerned to perfect the substance than himself. Moral qualities he takes for granted and considers them only in so far as they help or hinder the *opus*. We could say that he lays the whole emphasis on the effect *ex opere operantis* ("of the work of the operator"), naturally to a much

11 Cf. the quotation from Alphidius in Maier, *Symbola aureae mensae*, p. 65, and also in *Aurora consurgens* I, ch. I: "Qui hanc scientiam invenerit, cibus eius legitimus erit et sempiternus" (He who hath found this science, it shall be his rightful food for ever). Parable VII of *Aurora* says: "Ex his enim grani huius fructibus cibus vitae conficitur, qui de coelo descendit. Si quis ex eo manducaverit, vivet sine fame. De illo namque pane edent pauperes et saturabuntur et laudabunt Dominum, qui requirunt eum, et vivent corda eorum in saeculum." (For from the fruits of this grain is made the food of life which cometh down from heaven. If any man shall eat of it, he shall live without hunger. For of that bread the poor shall eat and shall be filled, and they shall praise the Lord that seek him, and their hearts shall live for ever.)

190. Mayan ritual tree with serpent.—Dresden Codex

higher degree than the Church, since he takes the place of the Christ who sacrifices himself in the Mass. One should not for a moment suppose that he presumes to the role of redeemer from religious megalomania. He does so even less than the officiating priest who figuratively sacrifices Christ. The alchemist always stresses his humility and begins his treatises with invocations to God. He does not dream of identifying himself with Christ; on the contrary, it is the coveted substance, the *lapis*, that he likens to Christ. It is not really a question of identification at all, but of the hermeneutic *sicut*—"as" or "like"—which characterizes the analogy. For medieval man, however, analogy was not so much a logical figure as a secret identity, a remnant of primitive thinking which is still very much alive. An instructive example of this is the rite of hallowing the fire on the Saturday before Easter (fig. 191).[12] The fire is "like unto" Christ, an *imago Christi*. The stone from which the spark is struck is the "cornerstone"—another *imago;* and the spark that leaps from the stone is yet again an *imago Christi*. The analogy with the extraction of the pneuma from the stone in the saying of Ostanes forces

[12] The rite of blessing the New Fire seems to have originated in France; at any rate it was already known there in the 8th century, although it was not yet practised in Rome, as is proved by a letter from Pope Zacharias to St. Boniface. It appears to have reached Rome only in the 9th century. (See "Feuerweihe" in Braun, *Liturgisches Handlexikon*.)

191. Descent of the Holy Ghost in the form of cloven tongues.—Munich
Lectionary or *Perikopenbuch* (12th cent.)

itself upon us. We are already familiar with the idea of pneuma
as fire, and with Christ as fire, and fire as the earth's inner
counter-element; but the "firestone" from which the spark is
struck is also analogous to the rocky sepulchre, or the stone before it. Here Christ lay as one asleep or in the fetters of death
during the three days of his descent into hell, when he went
down to the *ignis gehennalis,* from which he rises again as the
New Fire (fig. 234).

452   Without knowing it, the alchemist carries the idea of the
imitatio a stage further and reaches the conclusion we mentioned earlier, that complete assimilation to the Redeemer would
enable him, the assimilated, to continue the work of redemption
in the depths of his own psyche. This conclusion is unconscious,

354

and consequently the alchemist never feels impelled to assume that Christ is doing the work in him. It is by virtue of the wisdom and art which he himself has acquired, or which God has bestowed upon him, that he can liberate the world-creating Nous or Logos, lost in the world's materiality, for the benefit of mankind. The artifex himself bears no correspondence to Christ; rather he sees this correspondence to the Redeemer in his wonderful stone. From this point of view, alchemy seems like a continuation of Christian mysticism carried on in the subterranean darkness of the unconscious—indeed some mystics pressed the materialization of the Christ figure even to the appearance of the stigmata. But this unconscious continuation never reached the surface, where the conscious mind could have dealt with it. All that appeared in consciousness were the symbolic symptoms of the unconscious process. Had the alchemist succeeded in forming any concrete idea of his unconscious contents, he would have been obliged to recognize that he had taken the place of Christ— or, to be more exact, that he, regarded not as ego but as self,[13] had taken over the work of redeeming not man but God. He would then have had to recognize not only himself as the equivalent of Christ, but Christ as a symbol of the self. This tremendous conclusion failed to dawn on the medieval mind. What seems like a monstrous presumption to the Christian European would have been self-evident to the spirit of the Upanishads. Modern man must therefore consider himself fortunate not to have come up against Eastern ideas until his own spiritual impoverishment was so far gone that he did not even notice what he was coming up against. He can now deal with the East on the quite inadequate and therefore innocuous level of the intellect, or else leave the whole matter to Sanskrit specialists.

13 Although I take every available opportunity to point out that the concept of the self, as I have defined it, is not identical with the conscious, empirical personality, I am always meeting with the misunderstanding which equates the self with the ego. Owing to the fundamentally indefinable nature of human personality, the self must remain a borderline concept, expressing a reality to which no limits can be set.

355

192. The quaternity of the cross in the zodiac, surrounded by the six
planets. Mercurius corresponds to the cross between sun and moon: a
paraphrase of ☿.—Böhme, *Signatura rerum* (1682)

II. EVIDENCE FOR THE RELIGIOUS INTERPRETATION
OF THE LAPIS

a. Raymond Lully

453   It is not surprising that the *lapis*-Christ parallel came to the fore among the medieval Latin authors at a comparatively early date, since alchemical symbolism is steeped in ecclesiastical allegory. Although there is no doubt that the allegories of the Church Fathers enriched the language of alchemy, it remains in my opinion exceedingly doubtful just how far the *opus alchemicum*, in its various forms, can be regarded as a transmogrification of ecclesiastical rites (baptism, Mass) and dogmas (Christ's conception, birth, passion, death, and resurrection). Undeniably, borrowings were made over and over again from the Church, but when we come to the original basic ideas of alchemy we find elements that derive from pagan, and more particularly from Gnostic, sources. The roots of Gnosticism do not lie in Christianity at all—it is far truer to say that Christianity was assimilated through Gnosticism.[14] Apart from this we have a Chinese text,[15] dating from the middle of the second century, which displays fundamental similarities with Western alchemy. Whatever the connection between China and the West may have been, there is absolutely no doubt that parallel ideas exist outside the sphere of Christianity, in places where Christian influence is simply out of the question. A. E. Waite[16] has expressed the opinion that the first author to identify the stone with Christ was the Paracelsist, Heinrich Khunrath (1560–1605), whose *Amphitheatrum* appeared in 1598. In the writings of the somewhat later Jakob Böhme, who frequently uses alchemical terms, the stone has already become a metaphor for Christ (fig. 192). Waite's assumption is undoubtedly erroneous, for we have much earlier testimonies to the connection between Christ and the *lapis*, the oldest that I have so far been able to discover being contained

14 Cf. for example Simon Magus, who belonged to the apostolic era and already possessed a richly developed system.
15 Wei Po-yang, "An Ancient Chinese Treatise on Alchemy."
16 *The Secret Tradition in Alchemy.*

in the *Codicillus* (Ch. IX) of Raymond Lully (1235–1315). Even if many of the treatises ascribed to him were written by his Spanish and Provençal disciples, that does not alter the approximate date of his main works, to which the *Codicillus* belongs. At any rate I know of no authoritative opinion that puts this treatise later than the fourteenth century. There it is said:

And as Jesus Christ, of the house of David, took on human nature for the deliverance and redemption of mankind, who were in the bonds of sin on account of Adam's disobedience, so likewise in our art that which has been wrongfully defiled by one thing is absolved by its opposite; cleansed, and delivered from that stain.[17]

b. *Tractatus aureus*

454   A still older source would assuredly be the "Tractatus aureus" —ascribed to Hermes and regarded as of Arabic origin even in the Middle Ages—were Christ mentioned directly by name. The reason why I nevertheless quote it is that it describes things which bear a remarkable resemblance to the mysterious happenings at Eastertide, and yet are clothed in quite another language. The passage runs as follows:

Our precious stone, that was cast upon the dung-heap, is altogether vile. . . . But when we marry the crowned king with the red daughter, she will conceive a son in the gentle fire, and shall nourish him through our fire. . . . Then is he transformed, and his tincture remains red as flesh. Our son of royal birth takes his tincture from the fire, and death, darkness, and the waters flee away. The dragon shuns the light of the sun, and our dead son shall live. The king shall come forth from the fire and rejoice in the marriage. The hidden things shall be disclosed, and the virgin's milk be whitened. The son is become a warrior fire and surpasses the tincture, for he himself is the treasure and himself is attired in the philosophic matter. Come hither, ye sons of wisdom, and rejoice, for the dominion of death is

[17] "Et ut Jesus Christus de stirpe Davidica pro liberatione et dissolutione generis humani, peccato captivati, ex transgressione Adae, naturam assumpsit humanam, sic etiam in arte nostra quod per unum nequiter maculatur, per aliud suum contrarium a turpitudine illa absolvitur, lavatur et resolvitur."—*Bibl. chem.*, I, p. 884, 2.

193. The white and the red rose as end-product of the transformation of king and queen.—"Trésor des trésors" (MS., 17th cent.)

over, and the son reigns; he wears the red garment [fig. 193],[18] and the purple is put on.[19]

455   We can take this text as a variant of the mythical God-man and his triumph over death, and thus as an analogy of the Christian drama. Since the age and origin of this Hermetic text are still unknown, we cannot decide with any certainty whether Christian influence is at work here. Probably not. There is no reason to suspect Christian influence in the very early texts, such as that of Komarios.[20] (The Christian prefaces, etc., to these manuscripts are interpolations by Byzantine monastic copyists.) And yet it is just the Komarios text that has all the characteristics of a regeneration mystery, although here the resurrection of the

[18] Cf. the *lectio* for Wednesday in Holy Week (Isa. 62 : 11; 63 : 1–7). "Wherefore art thou red in thine apparel, and thy garments like him that treadeth in the wine-fat?" and . . . "their blood shall be sprinkled upon my garments . . ." (A.V., Isa. 63 : 2, 3). Cf. the *pallium sanguineum* of other authors.
[19] *Ars chemica* (1566), pp. 21f.
[20] Berthelot, *Alch. grecs,* IV, xx. The text probably belongs to the 1st century.

194. Sulphur as sun and Mercurius as moon bridging the river of "eternal water." — Barchusen, *Elementa chemiae* (1718)

dead is effected not by a redeemer but by the ὕδωρ θεῖον (the *aqua permanens* of the Latinists; cf. fig. 194), to which the Christian water symbolism (*aqua = spiritus veritatis*, baptism, and Eucharist) forms an unmistakable parallel.

c. *Zosimos and the Doctrine of the Anthropos*

456   In the later texts, however, which are ascribed to Zosimos, we find the Son of God in unmistakable association with the priestly art (ἱερατικῇ τέχνῃ). I give the relevant passages in a literal translation:[21]

4: . . . If you have meditated and have dwelt in human community, you will see that the Son of God has become all things for the sake of devout souls: in order to draw the soul forth from the domin-

[21] From the Greek text in Berthelot. *Alch. grecs*, III, xlix, 4–12, translated there into French by Ruelle. Ruska ("Tabula smaragdina," pp. 24–31) also gives a translation of pars. 2–19. Scott (*Hermetica*, IV, pp. 104ff.) gives this part of the text in Greek with a commentary. Cf. further Bousset, *Hauptprobleme der Gnosis*, pp. 190ff. The translation given here [i.e., the German version—TRANS.] was made by myself with the help of Dr. Marie-Louise von Franz and differs in several points from the Ruelle and Ruska versions.

ion of Heimarmene[22] into the [realm of the] incorporeal, behold how he has become all—God, angel, and man capable of suffering.[23] For having power in all, he can become all as he wills; and he obeys the Father inasmuch as he penetrates[24] all bodies and illuminates the mind of each soul,[25] spurring[26] it on to follow him up to the blessed region where it[27] was before the beginning of corporeal things,[28] yearning and led by him into the light.[29]

5: And consider the tablet which Bitos[30] also wrote, and the thrice-great Plato[31] and the infinitely great Hermes, saying that[32] the first

22 Heimarmene = fate, natural necessity.

23 The passage beginning with "behold" is omitted by Reitzenstein as a Christian interpolation. Cf. Reitzenstein, *Poimandres*, p. 103; also Ruska, "Tab. smarag.," p. 25.

24 Ibid., p. 25: "dwelling in every body." διήκειν has more the meaning of "penetrate." Cf. Bousset, *Hauptprobleme der Gnosis*, p. 191.

25 ἑκάστης Codd. The conjecture ἑκάστου is superfluous.

26 ἀνορμάω can only be meant transitively. Ruelle and Ruska translate: "So he (i.e., the son of God) has ascended. . . ." But this interpretation takes all sense from the following accusatives which refer to the object νοῦν.

27 The νοῦς. Cf. Reitzenstein, *Poimandres*, p. 103, note 11.

28 Ruska: "before it put on the flesh." But τὸ σωματικόν as predicate to γενέσθαι could not have an article. The sense is rather "before the creation." Cf. par. 9, where the men of light rescue their spiritual part by taking it ὅπου καὶ πρὸ τοῦ κόσμου ἦσαν.

29 ἀκολουθοῦντα, ὀρεγόμενον and ὁδηγούμενον refer to νοῦν which is also the object of ἀνώρμησεν. Scott (*Hermetica*, IV, p. 119) transfers this whole paragraph to the end of par. 8, because, in his opinion, it is not suitable to a Hermetic doctrine. But it constitutes the proof of the preceding idea that man should not struggle outwardly against his destiny, but should only strive inwardly for self-knowledge, the outward submission of the Son of God to suffering being an example of this.

30 Cf. Reitzenstein, *Poimandres*, pp. 107–8. Iamblichus (*De mysteriis Aegyptiorum*, VIII, 4) mentions a prophet Bitys as an interpreter of Hermes at the court of King Ammon. He is said to have found the writings of Hermes at Saïs. Cf. ibid., X, 7: αὐτὸ δὲ τὸ ἀγαθὸν τὸ μὲν θεῖον ἡγοῦνται τὸν προεννοούμενον θεόν. τὸ δὲ ἀνθρώπινον τὴν πρὸς αὐτὸν ἕνωσιν. ὅπερ Βίτυς ἐκ τῶν Ἑρμαϊκῶν βίβλων μεθηρμήνευσεν. According to Dieterich ("Papyrus magica musei Lugdunensis Batavi," p. 753) he is identical with the Thessalonian Pitys of the Magic Papyri (Wessely, "Griechische Zauberpapyrus," pp. 95, 92, 98: Πίτυος ἀγωγή—βασιλεῖ Ὀστάνη Πίτυς χαίρειν—ἀγωγὴ Πίτυος βασιλέως —Πίτυος Θεσσαλοῦ). He may also be identical, again, according to Dieterich, with Bithus of Dyrrhachium mentioned by Pliny (Book XXVIII). Scott (*Hermetica*, IV, pp. 129–30) suggests inserting "Nikotheos" or "which I wrote," and has a drawing in mind.

31 Cf. *Philebus* (18b), *Phaedrus* (274c).

32 Scott's splitting up of this sentence is inadmissible. In *Philebus* (18), Thoth is not represented as the "first man" but actually as the "divine man" and the giver of names to all things.

man is designated with the first hieratic word Thoyth,[33] who is the interpreter of all things that are and the giver of names to all corporeal things. The Chaldeans, Parthians, Medes, and Hebrews call him Adam, which is, being interpreted, virgin earth, blood-red [or bloody] earth, fiery[34] or carnal earth. This is to be found in the libraries of the Ptolemies. They put it[35] in every sanctuary, and especially in the Serapeum, at the time when Asenas[36] went to

33 Ruska: "what Thoythos interprets is in the holy language." But Thoythos must be gen. explicat. to φωνή, for in other places the nominative is "Thoyth." Cf. Bousset, *Hauptprobleme der Gnosis*, p. 191.

34 πυρὰ Codd.: probably πυρρά = "fire-coloured." Cf. Scott, *Hermetica*, IV, p. 121: "The interpretation of Adam as γῆ παρθένος is clearly a combination of the derivation from the Hebrew 'adamah' = γῆ (Philo, i. 62) and from the Greek ἀδμής = παρθένος. Hesychius gives ἀδάμα παρθενικὴ γῆ. The sense is doubtless Josephus, *Ant.*, I, i. 2: σημαίνει δὲ τοῦτο (Ἄδαμος) πυρρὸς ἐπειδήπερ ἀπὸ τῆς πυρρᾶς γῆς ἐγεγόνει, τοιαύτη γάρ ἐστιν ἡ παρθένος γῆ. Compare Olympiodorus (Berthelot, p. 89 [*Alch. grecs*, II, iv, 32]): οὗτος (Ἀδάμ) γὰρ πάντων ἀνθρώπων πρῶτος ἐγένετο ἐκ τῶν τεσσάρων στοιχείων. καλεῖται δὲ καὶ παρθένος γῆ. καὶ πυρ[ρ]ὰ γῆ. καὶ σαρκίνη γῆ. καί γῆ αἱματώδης. Cf. Eusebius, *Evangelica praeparatio*, 11, 6, 10, sq. . . ."

35 ὃν Codd.; Reitzenstein and Ruska: ὧν. It is also possible that ὃν refers to the first man: namely that they exhibited him as Osiris in every sanctuary. We find evidence for this in Lydus, *De mensibus*, IV, 53: "For there are many conflicting opinions among the theologians regarding the God who is worshipped by the Hebrews. For the Egyptians, and above all Hermes, maintain that he is Osiris, the one who exists, of whom Plato in the *Timaeus* says: 'which is the being that has no origin.' " Cf. Reitzenstein, *Poimandres*, p. 185, concerning the alleged transmission of the Jewish ideas to Egypt.

36 παρεκάλεσεν Ἀ . . . Codd.; Reitzenstein and Ruska: παρεκάλεσαν Ἀσενᾶν: "When they [the Ptolemies] sent for Asenas" (masc. or fem.). Ruelle, on the other hand, takes Asenas as subject of παρεκάλεσεν. Nothing is known concerning a high priest named Asenas. It is very probable—as Scott (*Hermetica*, IV, p. 122) remarks—that Asenath, the beautiful daughter of the Egyptian priest Potipherah of On (Heliopolis), is meant. She bore Joseph two sons during his Egyptian imprisonment, according to Gen. 41 : 50. In a midrash which has undergone a Christian revision, we find a legend of this Asenath falling in love with Joseph when he appeared as Pharaoh's steward; he rejected her, however, on account of her being an unbeliever. She then became a convert and did penance, whereupon a male messenger from heaven (in the recension: Michael)—whom she received as a δαίμων πάρεδρος, *spiritus familiaris,* in truly pagan fashion—gave her a honeycomb of paradise to eat and thus endowed her with immortality. He announces that Joseph will come to court her, and that from now on she will be called the "place of refuge."—Cf. also Batiffol, "Le Livre de la Prière d'Asenath," and Reitzenstein. *Die hellenistischen Mysterienreligionen*, pp. 248f.; further, Oppenheim, *Fabula Josephi et Asenathae*; Wilken, *Urkunden der Ptolemäerzeit*; and Kerényi, *Die griechisch-orientalische Romanliteratur in religionsgeschichtlicher Beleuchtung*, pp. 104f. It is possible that the messenger from heaven was originally Hermes. Hence our text might read as follows: "At the time when Asenath went to the High Priest of Jerusalem for help, who sent Hermes, who translated. . . ." W.

the High Priest of Jerusalem,[37] who sent Hermes, who translated the whole of the Hebrew into Greek and Egyptian.

6: So the first man is called by us Thoyth and by them Adam, which is a name in the language of the angels; but with reference to his body[38] they named him symbolically after the four elements[39] of the whole heavenly sphere [fig. 195]. For his letter A stands for ascent [$ἀνατολή$: the East] or the air; D for descent [$δύσις$: the West] . . .[40] because it [the earth] is heavy; A for arctic [$ἄρκτος$: the North]; and M for meridian [$μεσημβρία$: the South], the midmost of these bodies, the fire that burns in the midst of the fourth region.[41] Thus the fleshly Adam according to his outward and visible form is called Thoyth, but the spiritual man in him has a proper name as well as the name by which he is called. His proper name as yet[42] I know not: for Nikotheus alone knows this, and he is not to be found. But his common name is Man [$φώς$], which is Light [$φῶς$]; wherefore it came that men are called $φῶτας$.

7: Now when the Man of Light[43] abode in Paradise, pervaded[44] by the breath of Heimarmene, they [the elements][45] persuaded him,

---

Scott suggests replacing Asenath by "Eleazar," who, according to the Aristeas Letter, put the translation of the LXX (Septuagint) in hand; in this case one would also have to change the messenger Hermes into $ἑρμηνέα$, "interpreter." But it is more likely that we are dealing with an altogether different legend.

37 $τῶν$ $ἀρχιεροσολύμων$ Codd. Conjecture $τὸν$ $ἀρχιερέα$ $Ἱεροσολύμων$. Cf. Reitzenstein, Ruska, and Scott.

38 $Κατὰ$ $τὸ$ $σῶμα$ might also be understood as "in the corporeal language" in contrast to the "angel language" mentioned before. Elsewhere Zosimos contrasts the spiritual language with an $ἔνσωμος$ $φρέσις$.　　39 Also letters ($στοιχεῖα$).

40 Here we can probably assume a lacuna containing the element earth, or possibly the elements earth and water. Anyhow the text is corrupt here. Ruska suggests putting $τὸ$ $δεύτερον$ α $τὸν$ $ἄρκτον$ instead of $τὸν$ $ἀέρα$, to indicate the North. Scott is probably right to leave $τὸν$ $ἀέρα$ (the air), for the object was to combine the points of the compass with the elements; Scott therefore adds $γῆ$ (earth) after the word $δύσις$ (descent). As justification for inserting $ἄρκτος$, Scott quotes the Sibylline Oracles, III, 24: $αὐτὸς$ $δὴ$ $θεός$, $ἔσθ'$ $ὁ$ $πλάσας$ $τετραγράμματον$ $Ἀδὰμ$ $τὸν$ $πρῶτον$ $πλασθέντα$ $καὶ$ $οὔνομα$ $πληρώσαντα$ $ἀνατολίην$ $τε$ $δύσιν$ $τε$ $μεσημβρίην$ $τε$ $καὶ$ $ἄρκτον$, and the Slavonic Book of Enoch, ch. 30.

41 Ruska: "The midmost of these bodies is the ripening fire which points to the midst of the fourth region." Reitzenstein omits all this part.

42 $ἀγνοῶν$ Codd.; Reitzenstein conjectures $ἀγνοῶ$. $διὰ$ $τὸ$ $τέως$ Codd., literally "with regard to the foregoing."

43 This is a pun on $τὸ$ $φῶς$ (light) and the Homeric $ὁ$ $φώς$ (man). See Ruska.

44 Reitzenstein: $διαπνεομένῳ$, referring to Paradise: "in Paradise where blew the breath of Fate."

45 Reitzenstein adds "the archons" in explanation. But it is more likely to be the elements ($στοιχεῖα$) mentioned above. Cf. Gal. 4:9, for instance.

195. Creator, macrocosm, and microcosm in human form, the microcosm surrounded by the elements.—St. Hildegarde of Bingen, "Liber divinorum operum" (MS., 12th cent.)

who was without evil and free from their activity, to put on the Adam that was with him,[46] namely the Adam wrought of the four elements of Heimarmene[47] [cf. figs. 82, 117]. And he in his innocence did not turn aside; but they boasted that he was their slave. [Wherefore] Hesiod[48] called the outer man the bond with which[49] Zeus bound Prometheus. But after this fetter Zeus sent him yet another: Pandora, whom the Hebrews call Eve. For, in the allegorical language, Prometheus and Epimetheus are but one man, namely soul and body. And sometimes he[50] bears the likeness of the soul, sometimes that of the spirit, and sometimes the likeness of the flesh [fig. 196], because of the disobedience of Epimetheus, who heeded not the counsel of Prometheus, his own mind.[51] For our mind[52] says: "The Son of God, having power in all things and becoming all things when[53] he wills, appears[54] as he wills to each. Jesus Christ made himself one with Adam and bore him up to that place where the Men of Light dwelt before."[55]

8: But he appeared to the very feeble as a man capable of suffering and like one scourged. And after he had privily stolen away the Men of Light that were his own,[56] he made known that in truth he did not suffer, and that death was trampled down and cast out. And to this day and to the end of the world[57] he is present in many places,[58] both secretly and openly consorting with his own,[59] coun-

---

46 παρ' αὐτοῦ Codd.; Reitzenstein, Scott, and Ruska παρ' αὐτῶν: "the Adam that was with them."

47 Cf. in particular Bousset, *Hauptprobleme*, p. 193.

48 *Theogony*, 614.   49 ὃν Codd. Reitzenstein conjectures ᾧ.

50 "Prometheus" Codd. is omitted by Reitzenstein, because it probably refers to the whole man.

51 Reitzenstein conj.: νοῦ.

52 Personified in Reitzenstein: Nous (as Poimandres).

53 ὅτε Codd.; Reitzenstein has ὅτι (whatever he wills).

54 φαίνει Codd.; Ruska and Scott have φαίνεται (appears). Possibly the next sentence sets forth the essential meaning of the Son of Man?

55 Reitzenstein deletes this whole sentence as a Christian interpolation. According to Photius (*Bibliotheca*, 170; ed. Bekker, I, p. 11) Zosimos was later interpreted in a Christian sense. Scott deletes the words "Jesus Christ" and simply takes "the Son of God" as the subject.

56 συλλήσας Codd.; Reitzenstein and Scott have συλήσας. Ruska translates: "laying aside his own humanity." Concerning the stealing, cf. Hegemonius, *Acta Archelai*, XII, where it is said of God: "Hac de causa . . . furatur eis [the "principes"] animam suam" (For this reason . . . he steals from them [i.e., the princes] their soul [or "his soul"]).

57 Reitzenstein, too, relates this to what follows.

58 τόποισι Codd.; Reitzenstein has ἔπεισι ("he goes to . . .").

59 Conj.: συνῶν; Reitzenstein, Bousset, and Scott have συλῶν Codd.: συλλαλῶν: "he converses" (Ruelle).

selling them secretly, yea through their own minds,[60] to suffer confusion[61] with the Adam who was with them, that he might be beaten away from them[62] and slain, this blind chatterer who is envious of the spiritual Man of Light. [Thus] they kill their Adam.

9: And these things are so until the coming of the daemon Antimimos, the jealous one,[63] who seeks to lead them astray as before,[64] declaring that he is the Son of God, although he is formless in both body and soul. But they, having become wiser since the true Son of God has taken possession of them, deliver up to him their own Adam to be put to death, and bring their shining spirits safely back to the place where they were before the beginning of the world. Yet before Antimimos, the jealous one, does this,[65] he sends his forerunner from Persia, who circulates false fables and leads men astray through the power of Heimarmene. The letters of his name are nine, if you keep the diphthong,[66] corresponding to Heimarmene. Later, at the end of about seven periods,[67] he will appear in his own[68] shape.

10: And only the Hebrews and the sacred books of Hermes [tell of] these things concerning the Man of Light and his guide the Son of God, and concerning the earthly Adam and his guide Antimimos, who blasphemously calls himself the Son of God to lead men astray. But the Greeks call the earthly Adam Epimetheus, who was counselled by his own mind, his brother, not to accept the gifts of Zeus. Yet, inasmuch as he erred and afterwards repented, seeking the abode of bliss, he[69] makes everything plain and fully advises them

---

60 Ruelle: "He counselled his own to exchange secretly their spirit with that of Adam which they had within them. . . ." But this makes διά superfluous. Cf. also the passage φησὶ γὰρ ὁ νοῦς ἡμῶν . . . and the beginning of our text, where the Redeemer leads the soul back by enlightening the Nous of each soul.
61 ἔχειν can mean "to have to suffer." The adversaries evidently mean to injure the Men of Light.
62 Reitzenstein eliminates the second παρ' αὐτῶν. But παρά can also mean "away from someone's side."
63 δι' οὗ ζηλούμενος Codd.; Reitzenstein has διαζηλούμενος.
64 Omitted by Reitzenstein. But the meaning is "before the coming of the Redeemer."
65 πρὶν ἤ can be construed with accusative and infinitive, and then Antimimos is subject of τολμῆσαι and not object of ἀποστέλλει. Ruska inserts υἱὸς Θεοῦ as subject of τολμῆσαι. But he has not been spoken of for a long time, because he has already appeared. It is more likely that Antimimos himself has a forerunner.
66 Reitzenstein and Scott suggest Μανιχαῖος (Manichaeus).
67 περίοδον Codd.; Reitzenstein has περιόδους.
68 ἑαυτῷ Codd.; Reitzenstein has ἑαυτοῦ.
69 Reitzenstein and Ruska conjecture a lacuna after "seeking the abode of bliss," and connect "he" with Prometheus. This is unnecessary, since Epimetheus through his own fate "interprets"—ἑρμηνεύει—to those of spiritual understanding what is to be done.

196. The three manifestations of the Anthropos during his transformation: body, soul, spirit. Below, dragon and toad as preliminary forms.—"Ripley Scrowle" (MS., 1588)

that have spiritual hearing. But those that have only bodily hearing are slaves of Heimarmene, for they neither understand nor admit anything else.

11: And all who meet with success in the matter of colourings at the propitious moment, consider nothing but the great book about furnaces, for they do not esteem the art; nor do they understand the poet when he says: "But the gods have not given to men equally." [70] Neither do they observe and see the manner of men's lives: how, even in the same art, men may reach the goal in different ways and practise the same art in different ways, according to their different characters and the constellations of the stars in the exercise of the same art; how one worker is inactive,[71] another alone,[72] one blasphemously desiring too much, another too timid and therefore without progress—this is so in all the arts—and how those who practise the same art use different implements and procedures, having also different attitudes to the spiritual conception of it and its practical realization.

12: And this is more to be considered in the sacred art than in all the other arts. . . .

457   To all appearances, Zosimos' Son of God is a Gnostic Christ who has more affinity with the Iranian conception of Gayomart than with the Jesus of the Gospels. The author's connections with Christianity are by no means clear, since he undoubtedly belonged to the Hermetic Poimandres sect, as is evident from the passage about the Krater.[73] As in later Christian alchemy, the Son of God is a sort of paradigm of sublimation, i.e., of the freeing of the soul from the grip of Heimarmene. In both cases he is identical with Adam, who is a quaternity compounded of four different earths. He is the Anthropos, the first man, symbolized by the four elements, just like the *lapis* which has the same structure. He is also symbolized by the cross, whose ends correspond to the four cardinal points (fig. 197; cf. figs. 82, 192). This motif is often replaced by corresponding journeys, such as those of

---

[70] As Scott remarks, this is probably an inexact quotation of the Odyssey, VIII, 167—οὕτως οὐ πάντεσσι θεοὶ χαρίεντα δίδουσι ἄνδρασιν—from a context showing how different individuals are differently gifted by the gods. Zosimos goes on to explain how in all arts men have an individual method of working.

[71] ἄγων Codd.; Ruska conjectures ἀργὸν, Scott ἄκρον.

[72] Ruska has φιλόπονος instead of μόνος. but it is drawbacks that are enumerated here.

[73] Berthelot, *Alch. grecs*, III, li, 8.

197. Christ in the midst of the four rivers of paradise, evangelists, Fathers of the Church, virtues, etc.—Peregrinus, "Speculum virginum" (MS., 13th cent.)

Osiris,[74] the labours of Herakles,[75] the travels of Enoch,[76] and the symbolic *peregrinatio* to the four quarters in Michael Maier[77]

[74] Diodorus, *Bibliotheca*, I, p. 27.
[75] The Cretan bull led him to the south; the man-eating mares of Diomedes to the north (Thrace); Hippolytus to the east (Scythia); and the oxen of Geryon to the west (Spain). The Garden of the Hesperides (the western land of the dead) leads on to the twelfth labour, the journey to Hades (Cerberus).
[76] Book of Enoch 17–36 (Charles, *Apocrypha and Pseudepigrapha*, II, pp. 199ff.). The journeys lead to the four quarters of the earth. In the west he finds a fourfold underworld of which three parts are dark and one is light.
[77] The journey begins in Europe and leads to America, to Asia, and finally to Africa in search of Mercurius and the phoenix (*Symbola aureae mensae*, pp. 572ff.).

198. *Anser* or *cygnus Hermetis.—Hermaphroditisches Sonn- und Mondskind* (1752)

(1568–1622) (cf. fig. 97). Journeys are also related of Hermes Trismegistus,[78] and this may have inspired Maier's *peregrinatio,* although it is more probable that Maier imagined the *opus* as a wandering or odyssey, rather like the voyage of the Argonauts in quest of the *aureum vellus* (Golden Fleece), so beloved of the alchemists, a theme that figures in the title of more than one treatise. Alexander's campaign is mentioned in a treatise ascribed to Albertus Magnus, the journey ending in the discovery of Hermes' grave, where a stork is perched on the tree instead of a phoenix.[79]

458   Adam corresponds to Thoth (Θωΰϩ), the Egyptian Hermes (fig. 68). Adam's inner, spiritual man is named φῶς (light). Nikotheos, who knows the Man of Light's secret name, occurs

[78] In Marius Victorinus (Halm, *Rhetores Latini minores,* p. 223; quoted by Reitzenstein, *Poimandres,* p. 265³).

[79] "Super arborem Aristotelis," *Theatr. chem.,* II, p. 527: "Alexander invenit sepulcrum Hermetis et quandam arborem sitam ab extra intus tenentem viriditatem gloriosam: super eam ciconia ibi sedebat, quasi se appellans circulum Lunarem: et ibi ipse aedificavit sedes aureas et posuit terminum itineribus suis idoneum." (Alexander found the tomb of Hermes and outside it a certain tree with a glorious greenness inside. And on it there sat a stork, as it were calling itself the circle of the Moon. And there he built golden seats and put a fitting end to his travels.) The stork is an *avis Hermetis,* like the goose (fig. 198) and pelican.

twice in Zosimos as a mysterious personage,[80] and he is also mentioned in a Coptic Gnostic text as one who has beheld the Monogenes (*unigenitus*). Porphyry, in his life of Plotinus, speaks of him as the author of an Apocalypse.[81] The Manichees reckon him among the prophets, along with Shēm, Sēm, Enōš, and Enoch.[82]

459   Prometheus and Epimetheus represent the inner and outer man, like Christ and Adam. The ability to "become all," attributed to the Son of God, is an attribute not only of the pneuma but of the alchemical Mercurius, whose boundless powers of transformation are praised[83] in accordance with the versatility of the astrological Mercury (fig. 24). He is the *materia lapidis*, the transforming substance par excellence, and is said to penetrate all bodies[84] like a poison[85] (fig. 150).

460   Antimimos, the imitator and evil principle, appears as the antagonist of the Son of God: he too considers himself to be God's son. Here the opposites inherent in the deity are clearly divided. We meet this daemon in many other places as the ἀντίμιμον πνεῦμα: he is the spirit of darkness in a man's body, compelling his soul to fulfil all his sinful tendencies.[86] The alchemical parallel to this polarity is the double nature of Mercurius, which shows itself most clearly in the Uroboros, the

---

80 In the same treatise: Berthelot, *Alch. grecs*, III, xlix, 1.

81 Baynes, *A Coptic Gnostic Treatise*, pp. 84ff. Cf. also Bousset, *Hauptprobleme der Gnosis*, p. 189; Schmidt, "Gnostische Schriften," pp. 135ff.; also Turfan Frag., sig. M 299a, in Henning, "Ein Manichäisches Henochbuch," pp. 27f.

82 Puëch, "The Concept of Redemption in Manichaeism," p. 257.

83 Philalethes, "Metallorum metamorphosis," p. 771: "Se pro libitu suo transformat, ut varias larvas induat" (He transforms himself as he pleases, assuming various shapes [masks]). Aegidius de Vadis, "Dialogus," *Theatr. chem.*, II, p. 118: "Dicitur enim Mercurius propter suam mirabilem convertibilitatis adhaerentiam" (For he is called Mercurius because of his wonderful ability to transform himself).

84 "Tab. smarag.": "Omnem rem solidam penetrabit" (He will penetrate every solid thing). *Rosarium, Art. aurif.*, II, p. 259: "Est oleum mundissimum penetrativum in corporibus" (He is a most pure oil penetrating the bodies). "Rosinus ad Sarratantam," *Art. aurif.*, I, p. 302: ". . . spiritus vivus, et in mundo talis non est, qualis ipse est: et ipse penetrat omne corpus . . ." (A living spirit such as there is none other in the world, as he is; and he penetrates all bodies).

85 Geber, "Livre de la misericorde," in Berthelot, *Chimie au moyen âge*, p. 181. "Then he spreads his poison" (Lambspringk, "Figurae," *Mus. herm.*, p. 352); "Venenosus vapor" (Flamel, "Summarium philosophicum," *Mus. herm.*, p. 173); "Spiritus venenum" (Ripley, *Opera omnia*, p. 24); "Mercurius lethalis est" ("Gloria mundi," *Mus. herm.*, p. 250).

86 *Pistis Sophia*: trans. Schmidt, pp. 46, 207.

199. Hermaphrodite on the winged globe of chaos, with the seven planets and the
dragon.—Jamsthaler, *Viatorium spagyricum* (1625)

dragon that devours, fertilizes, begets, slays, and brings itself to
life again. Being hermaphroditic, it is compounded of opposites
and is at the same time their uniting symbol (fig. 148): at once
deadly poison, basilisk, scorpion, panacea, and saviour (fig. 199).
461   Zosimos discloses practically the whole of the recondite and
highly peculiar theology of alchemy, by drawing a parallel between the esoteric meaning of the *opus* and the Gnostic mystery
of redemption. This is only one indication that the *lapis*-Christ
parallel of the scholastic alchemists had a pagan Gnostic pre-
cursor and was by no means a mere speculation of the Middle
Ages.

Sublimatio.

200. Eagle and swan as symbols of the sublimated *spiritus*. In the foreground,
Saturn.—Mylius, *Philosophia reformata* (1622)

d. *Petrus Bonus*

462 The oldest source to treat specifically of the stone's connection with Christ would appear to be a text, *Pretiosa margarita
novella*, written by Petrus Bonus of Ferrara between 1330 and
1339,[87] from which I give the following extract:[88]

[87] Printed in *Bibliotheca chemica curiosa*, II. Gessner mentions Bonus as a contemporary of Raymond Lully (1235–1315), but Mazzuchelli (1762) maintains that
Pietro Antonio Boni lived about 1494. Ferguson (*Bibliotheca chemica*, I, p. 115)
leaves the question undecided. Hence the above dates are given with reserve. The
first edition of the *Pret. marg. nov.* is that of Lacinius (1546), fol. i ff.: "Quia con-
suevit non solum. . . ." The introduction in *Bibliotheca chemica curiosa* is missing here. All the authors quoted in the text lived before the 14th century. Nor
does the material supply any reasons for dating the text later than the first half
of the 14th century.
[88] *Bibl. chem.*, II, ch. VI, pp. 29ff.

This art is partly natural and partly divine or supernatural. At the end of the sublimation [fig. 200] there germinates, through the mediation of the spirit, a shining white soul [*anima candida*] which flies up to heaven with the spirit [cf. fig. 134]. This is clearly and manifestly the stone. So far the procedure is indeed somewhat marvellous, yet still within the framework of nature. But as regards the fixation and permanence of the soul and spirit at the end of the sublimation, this takes place when the secret stone is added, which cannot be grasped by the senses, but only by the intellect, through inspiration or divine revelation, or through the teaching of an initiate. Alexander says that there are two categories: seeing through the eye and understanding through the heart.[89] This secret stone is a gift of God. There could be no alchemy without this stone. It is the heart and tincture of the gold, regarding which Hermes says: "It is needful that at the end of the world heaven and earth be united: which is the philosophic Word." [90] Pythagoras also said in the *Turba:* "God concealed this from Apollo, so that the world should not be destroyed." Thus alchemy stands above nature and is divine. The whole difficulty of the art lies in this stone. The intellect cannot comprehend it, so must believe it, like the divine miracles and the foundation of the Christian creed. Therefore God alone is the operator, while nature remains passive. It was through their knowledge of the art that the old philosophers knew of the coming of the end of the world and the resurrection of the dead. Then the soul will be united with its original body for ever and ever. The body will become wholly transfigured [*glorificatum*], incorruptible, and almost unbelievably subtilized,[91] and it will penetrate all solids. Its nature will be as much spiritual as corporeal. When the stone decomposes to a powder like a man in his grave, God restores to it soul and spirit, and takes away all imperfection; then is that substance [*illa res*] strengthened and improved, as after the resurrection a man becomes stronger and younger than he was before. The old philosophers discerned the Last Judgment in this

[89] The psychological equivalents of these two categories are conscious cognition based on sense-perception, and the projection of unconscious contents. For these latter *cor* is an apt designation, since the heart region (fig. 149) represents a more primitive localization of consciousness, and, even at a higher level, still harbours emotive thoughts, i.e., contents that are very much under the influence of the unconscious.

[90] "Quod verbum est philosophicum." I feel impelled to translate this phrase as above, because of the later alchemical distinction between Christ as the "verbum scriptum" and the *lapis* as "verbum dictum et factum" ("Orthelii Epilogus," *Bibl. chem.*, II, p. 526).

[91] "subtilitatem fere incredibilem."

374

art, namely in the germination and birth of this stone, for in it the soul to be beatified [*beatificandae*] unites with its original body, to eternal glory. So also the ancients knew that a virgin must conceive and bring forth, for in their art the stone begets, conceives, and brings itself forth.[92] Such a thing can happen only by the grace of God. Therefore Alphidius[93] says of the stone that its mother was a virgin and that its father had never known woman. They knew besides that God would become man on the Last Day of this art[94] [*in novissima die huius artis*], when the work is perfected; and that begetter and begotten, old man and boy, father and son, all become one. Now, since no creature except man can unite with God, on account of their dissimilarity, God must needs become one with man. And this came to pass in Christ Jesus and his virgin mother.[95] Therefore Balgus says in the *Turba:* "O what miracles of nature, that have changed the soul of the old man into a youthful body, and the father has become the son" [cf. figs. 166, 167]. In like manner Plato, writing of alchemical matters, wrote a gospel which was completed long after by John the Evangelist. Plato wrote the opening verses from "In the beginning was the Word" to "There was a man sent from God."[96] God has shown the philosopher this wonderful example that he might perform supernatural works. Morienus says that God has entrusted this *magisterium* to his philosophers or prophets, for whose souls he has prepared a dwelling in his paradise.[97]

463   This text, which is at least a century older than Khunrath, shows beyond all doubt that the connection between the mystery of Christ and the mystery of the *lapis* was even then so obvious that the philosophical *opus* seemed like a parallel and imitation —perhaps even a continuation—of the divine work of redemption.

[92] As an analogy of God.

[93] Reputed to be an Arab philosopher of the 12th century.

[94] Presumably in the alchemical work, whose procedure resembles the creation and end of the world.

[95] Cf. the detailed later account in "Liber de arte chimica," *Art. aurif.*, I, pp. 581, 613.

[96] Bonus is referring to an older Pseudo-Platonic text which I have not yet been able to trace. Evidently it contained a *lapis*-Christ parallel. Possibly—as in the case of the "Tractatus aureus"—the original source was Arabic (Sabaean?).

[97] These are the *electi*. Manichean influences are not inconceivable in Morienus.

e. "Aurora consurgens" and the
Doctrine of Sapientia

464   The next source is *Aurora consurgens*,[98] of which a manuscript copy of the fifteenth century, the Codex Rhenoviensis,
from the monastery at Rheinau, is to be found in Zurich. Unfortunately the manuscript is mutilated and begins only at the
fourth parable. I was made aware of it through the fact that the
printer of *Artis auriferae* (1593) published only Part II of *Aurora*.
He prefixed to it a short notice to the reader in which he says
that he has purposely omitted the entire treatise consisting of
parables or allegories because the author, in the ancient manner
of obscurantists (*antiquo more tenebrionum*), treated almost the
whole Bible—particularly Proverbs, Psalms, but above all the
Song of Songs—in such a way as to suggest that the Holy Scriptures had been written solely in honour of alchemy. The author,
he says, has even profaned the most holy mystery of the incarnation and death of Christ by turning it into the mystery of the
lapis—not, of course, with any evil intent, as he, the typographer
Conrad Waldkirch, readily admits, but as was only to be expected in that benighted epoch (*seculum illud tenebrarum*). By
this Waldkirch meant the pre-Reformation epoch, whose conception of man and the world, and experience of the divine
presence in the mystery of matter, had entirely vanished from
the purview of the Protestants of his own day.

465   The treatise is preserved entire in the Codex Parisinus Latinus 14006. There is also a printing of it in the compilation
edited by Johannes Rhenanus, *Harmoniae inperscrutabilis
chymico-philosophicae Decades duae* (Frankfort, 1625).[99] The
age of the text, which is attributed to St. Thomas Aquinas (d.
1274), may be gauged more or less from the fact that the most
recent author quoted in it is Albertus Magnus (1193–1280). The

98 Part I of the text has been translated and edited, with a commentary, by
Marie-Louise von Franz. [Published in English under the title *Aurora Consurgens: A Document Attributed to Thomas Aquinas on the Problem of Opposites in Alchemy*.] *Aurora consurgens* is an extremely characteristic example of
the mystical side of alchemy, affording deep insight into this extraordinary state
of mind, which is sufficient justification for a separate publication of the whole
of Part I.

99 Decas II, pp. 175ff. Cf. Kopp, *Die Alchemie*, II, p. 343.

other authors who are everywhere quoted in the fifteenth century—Arnold of Villanova (d. 1313) and Raymond Lully (d. 1315)—are not mentioned. Since Thomas was canonized in 1323 and was thus at the height of his fame, it was worth while ascribing texts to him from that time on. We shall probably not be far out if we put the date in the first half of the fourteenth century. The author is evidently a cleric who knows his Vulgate by heart. His whole idiom is steeped in Biblical quotation, just as his mind is full of alchemical philosophy. Alchemy is for him absolutely identical with the *Sapientia Dei*. He begins his treatise with words taken from the Wisdom of Solomon (7 : 11) and Proverbs (1 : 20–21):

Venerunt mihi omni bona pariter cum illa[100] sapientia austri, quae foris praedicat, in plateis dat vocem suam, in capite turbarum clamitat, in foribus portarum urbis profert verba sua dicens:[101] Accedite ad me et illuminamini et operationes vestrae non confundentur;[102] omnes qui concupiscitis me[103] divitiis meis adimplemini. Venite ergo filii, audite me, scientiam Dei docebo vos. Quis sapiens et intelligit hanc, quam Alphidius dicit homines et pueros in viis et plateis praeterire et cottidie a iumentis et pecoribus in sterquilinio conculcari. . . .

(All good things come to me together with her,[100] that Wisdom of the south, who preacheth abroad, who uttereth her voice in the streets,[101] crieth out at the head of the multitudes, and in the entrance of the gates of the city uttereth her words, saying: "Come ye to me and be enlightened, and your operations shall not be confounded;[102] all ye that desire me shall be filled with my riches.[103] Come, children, hearken to me, I will teach you the science of God.

[100] Vulgate, Sap. 7 : 11: "Venerunt autem mihi omnia bona pariter cum illa [sapientia], et innumerabilis honestas per manus illius" (D.V.: "Now all good things came to me together with her, and innumerable riches through her hands").

[101] Vulgate, Prov. 1 : 20–21 verbatim (D.V.: "Wisdom preacheth abroad: she uttereth her voice in the streets, at the head of the multitudes she crieth out, in the entrance of the gates of the city she uttereth her words, saying . . .").

[102] Vulgate, Ps. 33 : 6: "Accedite ad eum [Dominum], et illuminamini: et facies vestrae non confundentur" (D.V.: "Come ye to him and be enlightened: and your faces shall not be confounded"). Also Vulgate, Ecclus. 24 : 30: "Qui audit me non confundetur, et qui operantur in me non peccabunt" (D.V.: "He that hearkeneth to me shall not be confounded: and they that work by me shall not sin").

[103] Vulgate, Ecclus. 24 : 26: "Transite ad me, omnes qui concupiscitis me, et a generationibus meis implemini" (D.V.: "Come over to me, all ye that desire me: and be filled with my fruits").

201. Sapientia as mother of the wise.—Thomas Aquinas (pseud.), "De alchimia" (MS., 16th cent.)

Who is wise, and understandeth this, of which Alphidius saith, that men and children pass her by daily in the streets and public places, and she is trodden into the mire by beasts of burden and by cattle . . .")

466   The *sapientia austri* is, in patristic usage,[104] the wisdom of the Holy Ghost. For our author Sapientia is the "regina Austri, quae ab oriente dicitur venisse, ut aurora consurgens"—Queen of the South,[105] who is said to have come from the east, like unto the morning rising[106] (fig. 201).

104 Eucherius, *Formularium spiritalis intelligentiae,* and Rabanus, *Allegoriae,* among others. Cf. Vulgate, Hab. 3 : 3: "Deus ab austro veniet, et Sanctus de monte Pharan" (D.V.: "God will come from the south: and the holy one from Mount Pharan").

105 Vulgate, Matt. 12 : 42 (Luke 11 : 31 is almost identical): "Regina austri surget in iudicio cum generatione ista, et condemnabit eam: quia venit a finibus terrae audire sapientiam Salomonis, et ecce plus quam Salomon hic" (D.V.: "The queen of the south shall rise in judgment with this generation and shall condemn it: because she came from the ends of the earth to hear the wisdom of Solomon. And behold a greater than Solomon here").

106 Ch. V. Cf. Vulgate, Cant. 6 : 9: "Quae est ista quae progreditur quasi aurora consurgens, pulchra ut luna, electa ut sol . . ." (D.V.: "Who is she that cometh forth as the morning rising, fair as the moon, bright as the sun . . .").

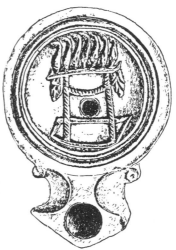

202. Communion table with seven fish.
—Christian earthenware lamp, Carthage

467   Without mentioning our text, the *Rosarium* quotes it as follows:[107]

This [Sapientia] is my daughter, for whose sake men say that the Queen of the South came out of the east, like the rising dawn, in order to hear, understand, and behold the wisdom of Solomon; power, honour, strength, and dominion are given into her hand; she wears the royal crown of seven glittering stars, like a bride adorned for her husband, and on her robe is written in golden lettering, in Greek, Arabic, and Latin: I am the only daughter of the wise, utterly unknown to the foolish.

468   This is without doubt a citation from *Aurora.* The original text has twelve instead of seven stars, the latter evidently referring to the seven stars in the hand of the apocalyptic "one like unto the Son of Man" (Rev. 1 : 13; 2 : 1). These represent the seven angels of the seven Churches and the seven spirits of God (fig. 202). The historical *sous-entendu* of the seven is the antique company of seven gods who later took up their abode in the seven metals of alchemy (figs. 21, 79, 154). They were deposed by science only during the last one hundred and fifty years. For Paracelsus the gods were still enthroned as archons in the *mysterium magnum* of the *prima materia,* "to their own undoing and ours."[108]

469   The twelve stars of the original text refer to the twelve disciples and the twelve signs of the zodiac (figs. 92, 100). The Agathodaimon serpent on Gnostic gems also has seven or twelve

107 *Art. aurif.,* II, p. 294.   108 Sudhoff, XIII, p. 403.

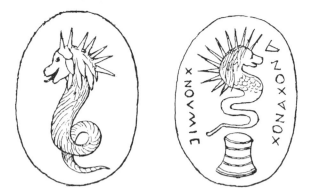

203, 204. The Chnuphis serpent with seven-rayed crown; the lion-headed, twelve-rayed **ΧΝΟΥΜΙC**-serpent, over an altar-stone.
—Gnostic gem and amulet

rays about its head (figs 203–5). In Clement's second homily it is observed that the number of apostles corresponds to the twelve months.[109] In the Manichean system the saviour constructs a cosmic wheel with twelve buckets—the zodiac—for the raising of souls.[110] This wheel has a significant connection[111] with the *rota*

109 Cumont, *Textes et monuments*, I. p. 356.
110 Hegemonius, *Acta Archelai*, pp. 12f.: "Cum autem vidisset pater vivens adfligi animam in corpore, quia est miserator et misericors, misit filium suum dilectum ad salutem animae; haec enim causa et propter Homoforum misit eum. Et veniens filius transformavit se in speciem hominis; et adparebat quidem hominibus ut homo, cum non esset homo, et homines putabant eum natum esse. Cum ergo venisset, machinam quandam concinnatam ad salutem animarum, id est rotam, statuit, habentem duodecim urceos; quae per hanc spheram vertitur, hauriens animas morientium quasque luminare maius, id est sol, radiis suis adimens purgat et lunae tradit, et ita adimpletur lunae discus, qui a nobis ita appellatur."
(But when the living father saw that the soul was tormented in the body, he sent—because he is charitable and compassionate—his beloved son for the salvation of the soul. For this cause he sent him, and on account of Homoforus. And the son came and changed into human form, and showed himself to men as a man, although he was no man, and the people thought that he had been born. And when he came he made a device for the redemption of souls, and set up a wheel with twelve buckets, which is turned by the rotation of the sphere and raises the souls of the dying; these are caught by the rays of the greater light, which is the sun, and purified and passed on to the moon, and thus is the disc of the moon filled, as we say.) The same passage is to be found in the *Panarium* of Epiphanius, Haer. LXVI.
111 There are secret connections, or at least striking parallels, between alchemy and Manicheism which still need investigating.

205. Goddess of fate as serpent with seven heads.—Seal of St. Servatius, from Maastricht Cathedral

or *opus circulatorium* of alchemy,[112] which serves the same purpose of sublimation. As Dorn says: "The wheel of creation takes its rise from the *prima materia*, whence it passes to the simple elements."[113] Enlarging on the idea of the *rota philosophica* (cf. figs. 80, 104), Ripley says that the wheel must be turned by the four seasons and the four quarters, thus connecting this symbol with the *peregrinatio* and the quaternity. The wheel turns into the wheel of the sun rolling round the heavens, and so becomes identical with the sun-god or -hero who submits to arduous labours and to the passion of self-cremation, like Herakles, or to captivity and dismemberment at the hands of the evil principle, like Osiris. A well-known parallel to the chariot of the sun is the fiery chariot in which Elijah ascended to heaven (figs. 206, 207)[114] Accordingly Pseudo-Aristotle says:[115] "Take the serpent, and place it on the chariot with four wheels, and let it be turned about on the earth until it is immersed in the depths of the sea, and nothing more is visible but the blackest dead sea." The image used here is surely that of the sun sinking into the sea, save that the sun has been replaced by the mercurial serpent,

[112] Ripley (d. 1490) describing the transformation of earth into water, water into air, and air into fire, says (*Opera omnia*, p. 23): "sic rotam elementorum circumrotasti" (Thus did you revolve the wheel of the elements).
[113] "Philosophia chemica," *Theatr. chem.*, I, p. 492: "A materia prima generationis rota sumit exordium, ad elementa simplicia transiens." Cf. also Mylius, *Phil. ref.*, p. 104: "Toties ergo reiterandum est coelum super terram, donec terra fiat coelestis et spiritualis, et coelum fiat terrestre, et iungetur cum terra, tunc completum est opus" (So many times must the heaven above the earth be reproduced, until the earth becomes heavenly and spiritual, and heaven becomes earthly, and is joined to the earth; then the work will be finished).
[114] Cumont, *Textes et monuments*, I, p. 178.
[115] "Tractatus Aristotelis," *Theatr. chem.*, V, p. 885.

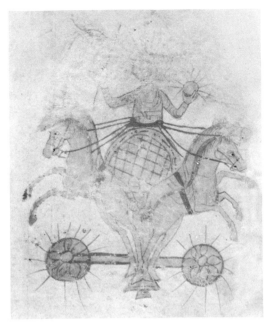

206. Helios riding a chariot with four horses.—
Theodore Psalter (1066)

i.e., the substance to be transformed. Michael Maier actually takes the *opus circulatorium* as an image of the sun's course:

For while the hero, like a joyful giant,[116] rises in the east and hastens to his sinking in the west, that he may forever return out of the east, he sets in motion these circulations, depositing in the shining substance of the quicksilver, as in a mirror, forms [wherein] by human diligence the gold may be sought, cleansed from impurities, tested by fire and water, and put to a use pleasing to God the Creator.[117]

470   The circle described by the sun is the "line that runs back on itself, like the snake that with its head bites its own tail, wherein God may be discerned." Maier calls it the "shining clay moulded by the wheel [*rota*] and hand of the Most High and Almighty Potter" into that earthly substance wherein the

[116] Reference to the Vulgate. Ps. 18 : 6–7 (D.V.): "He hath set his tabernacle in the sun: and he, as a bridegroom coming out of his bride chamber, hath rejoiced as a giant to run the way. His going out is from the end of heaven."

[117] "Dum Heroes ille, tanquam gigas exultans, ab ortu exurgit, et in occasum properans demergitur, ut iterum ab ortu redeat continue, has circulationes causatur, inque materia splendida argenti vivi, velut in speculo, ideas relinquit, ut humana industria aurum inquiratur, ab adhaerentibus segregetur, igne, aqua examinetur, et in usum Deo Creatori placentem transferatur." (*De circulo quadrato,* p. 15.)

382

207. The ascension of Elijah.
—Early Christian mural
painting, crypt of Lucina,
Rome

sun's rays are collected and caught. This substance is the
gold.[118] In "Introitus apertus," [119] Philalethes elaborates Maier's
views: there is in "our" mercury, he says, a fiery sulphur or sulphureous fire. This fire is the "spiritual seed" which our Virgin[120] has gathered in herself, because unspotted virginity can
admit of "spiritual love," according to the author of the Hermetic mystery and as experience itself shows. It is to be noted
that this virgin, who being "unspotted" (*intemerata*) is obviously
analogous to the Virgin Mary, is made pregnant by a seed deriv-
ing not from any Holy Ghost but from a "sulphureous fire,"
i.e., an *ignis gehennalis*.[121] The virgin is Mercurius[122] (fig. 208),
who, owing to the presence of sulphur, the active masculine
principle, is hermaphroditic.[123] Sulphur is the *aurum volatile*
(fig. 209), a "spiritual" gold, the *aurum non vulgi* of the *Rosarium* and at the same time the "primum movens, quod rotam

118 Maier, ibid., pp. 15f.   119 *Mus. herm.*, p. 661.
120 "Nihilominus intemerata remanens" (nevertheless remaining undefiled). Cf.
"mater amata, intemerata" (beloved mother, undefiled) of Latin hymnology; also
the "virgo pulchra, ornata, ad persuadendum valde apta" (virgin beautiful,
adorned, well suited for persuading), who appears sometimes as male and sometimes as female in the Manichean *Acta Archelai*.
121 Such parallels show, in spite of all assurances to the contrary, how much the
alchemical work is a *mysterium iniquitatis* from the Christian point of view. On
an objective view, however, it is simply a chthonic mystery which, as Part II
of this volume shows, has its roots in the transformative processes of the unconscious.
122 The feminine nature of Mercurius is connected with the moon.
123 The "male virgin" is also a Manichean idea in the writings of Theodoret.

208. Mercurius as *anima mundi*.—"Turba philosophorum" (MS., Paris, 16th cent.)

209. The winged sphere (*aurum aurae*) as the end-product of the *opus,* and its reflection in the fountain of life. Symbolic representation of the *opus* with attributes (trees, planetary mountains, etc.).—Balduinus, *Aurum hermeticum* (1675)

vertit axemque vertit in gyrum" (prime mover that turns wheel and axle in a circle).

Laurentius Ventura[124] cannot resist connecting the wheel with the vision of Ezekiel. Thus, speaking of the *lapis,* he says that Ezekiel saw "in its shape the wheel within the wheel and the spirit of the living creature that was in the midst of the wheels"[125] (figs. 109, 207). "Wherefore," he says, "this *mysterium* has been called by some the *Deus terrestris*."[126] It appears that

124 His work *De ratione conficiendi lapidis philosophici* was printed at Basel in 1571.
125 Ezech. 1 : 15 (D.V.): "Now as I beheld the living creatures, there appeared upon the earth by the living creatures one wheel with four faces. And the appearance of the wheels and the work of them was like the appearance of the sea: and the four had all one likeness. And their appearance and their work was as it were a wheel in the midst of a wheel . . . for the spirit of life was in the wheels."
126 *Theatr. chem.,* II, p. 259.

this last thought is not a conceit of Ventura's but, as he says, a quotation from "Lilium," a source I have been unable to trace, though it must go back to the fourteenth century or even earlier.[127]

172   The idea of the circulatory *opus*, or rotating arcane substance, finds expression as early as Komarios, who speaks of the "mystery of the whirlwind in the manner of a wheel" (μυστήριον τῆς λαίλαπος τροχοῦ δίκην).[128] Compare Zach. 9 : 14 (D.V.): ". . . and the Lord God will sound the trumpet and go in the whirlwind of the south." The mystic logion of Zosimos probably has some bearing here:[129] "And what meaneth this: 'the nature that conquers the natures,' and 'it is perfected and becometh like a whirl'?" [καὶ γίνεται ἱλιγγιῶσα]. The transforming substance is an analogy of the revolving universe, of the macrocosm, or a reflection of it imprinted in the heart of matter. Psychologically, it is a question of the revolving heavens being reflected in the unconscious, an *imago mundi* that was projected by the alchemist into his own *prima materia*. But such an interpretation is somewhat one-sided, since the idea of the arcane substance is itself an archetype, expressed most simply in the idea of the soul-spark (*scintilla*, *Spinther*) and the Monad.

473   The personification of Sapientia in the Wisdom of Solomon evidently caused the author of *Aurora* to identify her with the "Queen of the South." In alchemy she always appears as *Sapientia Dei*, and in the writings of the Church Fathers the south wind is an allegory of the Holy Ghost, presumably because it is hot and dry. For the same reason the process of sublimation is known in

---

127 As a matter of fact, there are two treatises known to me that are entitled "Lilium": the "Lilium inter spinas" of Grasseus (*Bibl. chem.*, II), which belongs to the 17th century, and the "Lilium de spinis evulsum" of Guilhelmus Tecenensis (*Theatr. chem.*, IV), who lived at the end of the 16th and beginning of the 17th century. The date puts the former "Lilium" out of court; but the latter might be considered because it is highly probable that the treatise is wrongly ascribed to Guilhelmus. To judge by its contents and the authors quoted (there are numerous quotations from the *Turba*, "Tractatus Micreris" [*Theatr. chem.*, V], Geber, and so on, but Albertus, Lully, and Arnaldus are missing), it appears to be an old text which might perhaps belong to the time of the "Cons. coniug." But the above passage is not to be found. "Lilium" or "Lilius" is also quoted in the *Rosarium*.
128 Berthelot, *Alch. grecs*, IV, xx, 17.
129 Ibid., III, i.

210. "The wind hath carried it in his belly" ("Tabula smaragdina"). The *foetus spagyricus* is the renewed Mercurius.—Maier, *Scrutinium chymicum* (1687)

Arabic alchemy as the "great south wind," referring to the heating of the retort.[130] The Holy Ghost, too, is fiery and causes an exaltation. His equivalent, so to speak, is the hidden fire, the *spiritus igneus* dwelling in Mercurius, whose opposite poles are an *agens* (i.e., fire) and a *patiens* (i.e., quicksilver). When therefore Abu'l Qāsim speaks of the fire as the "great south wind," he is in agreement with the ancient Greek view that Hermes was a wind-god [131] (figs. 210, 211).

130 Holmyard, *Kitāb al-'ilm al-muktasab*, p. 43. ". . . but what of the speech of *Hermes* in which he says: 'The great South wind when it acts makes the clouds to rise and raises the cloud of the sea'? He said, If the powdering is not successful the compound will not ascend into the top of the retort, and even if it does ascend it will not pour into the receiver. It is necessary to mix with it the first and second waters before it will ascend to the top of the retort. 'That,' he said, 'is the Great South Wind?' He said: 'Yea, O King' " etc.
131 Roscher, *Hermes der Windgott*.

211. The god Aër as procreator of all harmony. In the inner circle, Arion, Pythagoras, Orpheus; in the outer, the nine muses; in the corners, the four winds.
—"Recueil des fausses décrétales" (MS., 13th cent.)

212. The Trinity as *tricephalus.*—*Speculum humanae salvationis* (Augsburg, 1480)

I have dwelt at some length on the opening passages of *Aurora* because they are an excellent illustration of the composition as a whole as regards both language and subject matter. Here I will mention only a few of the *lapis*-Christ parallels. In ch. II the author calls "the science" (i.e., alchemy) a gift and a sacrament of God, a divine matter that the wise have veiled in images. From this it appears that the *opus alchemicum* is deemed the equal of the *opus divinum* or Mass.[132] In ch. VI the stone is described in the words of the Song of Songs 5 : 16, "Such is my beloved," and Ps. 44 : 3 (D.V.), "Behold ye him, beautiful above the sons of men, at whose beauty the sun and moon wonder." [133] The *filius philosophorum* is here identified with the "bridegroom" who, as we know, is interpreted as Christ. In the second parable, "Of the Flood of Waters and of Death," we read: "Then the fulness of the time shall come, when God shall send his son,[134] as he hath said, whom he hath appointed heir of all things, by whom also he made the world,[135] to whom he said of old time: "Thou art my Son, today have I begotten thee,[136] to whom the Wise Men from the East brought three precious gifts

132 See next section.

133 Psalm 44 (in A.V., Psalm 45) is defined as an *Epithalamium Christianum*—a Christian bridal song.

134 Gal. (D.V.) 4 : 4.   135 Heb. (D.V.) 1 : 2.   136 Heb. (D.V.) 1 : 5; 5 : 5.

389

. . ." Here again Christ is a parallel of the *lapis*. In the fourth parable, "Of the Philosophic Faith," a parallel is drawn with the Holy Trinity (cf. figs. 179, 180): ". . . like as the Father is, so is the Son, and so also is the Holy Spirit, and these three are One: body, spirit, and soul; for all perfection consisteth in the number three, that is, in measure, number, and weight."

475   The sixth parable, "Of Heaven and Earth and the Arrangement of the Elements," says:

In the *Turba philosophorum* it is written: The earth, since it is heavy, beareth all things,[137] for it is the foundation of the whole heaven, because it appeared dry[138] at the separation of the elements.[139] Therefore in the Red Sea there was a way without hindrance, since this great and wide sea[140] smote the rock[141] and the

[137] Ruska, *Turba*, p. 178.

[138] Espagnet, "Arcanum," *Bibl. chem.*, II, p. 656, §LXXIII: "Lapidis generatio fit ad exemplum generationis mundi, suum enim chaos et materiam suam primam habeat necesse est, in qua confusa fluctuant elementa donec spiritu igneo separentur. . . . Congregantur aquae in unum, et apparet Arida." (The generation of the stone takes place on the model of the creation of the world. For it is necessary that it have its own chaos and its own prima materia, in which the elements are to float about in confusion until they are separated by the fiery spirit. The waters are gathered into one [place] and the dry land [Arida] appears.)

[139] Ibid.: "[in nigredine] denique separatur lapis in quatuor elementa confusa, quod contingit per retrogradationem luminarium" (Lastly [in the blackness] the stone is separated into the four elements mingled together, which is brought about by the retrograde movement of the stars). This refers to the *coniunctio* of Sol and Luna, who *post coitum* are overcome by death (see fig. 223). Cf. the illustrations in the *Rosarium*, reproduced in my "Psychology of the Transference." Espagnet (*Bibl. chem.*, II, p. 655, §LXIVf.): "Nigro colori succedit albus" (on the black follows the white). This white sulphur is the *lapis*.

[140] The "Sea" of the philosophers. "Mare sapientiae" was one of the titles of Hermes (Senior, *Tabula chymica*, p. 31)—evidently an allusion to Moses.

[141] The healing water also flows from the stone whence the pneumatic spark is struck. In later alchemical literature this stone is often likened to Christ (as also in Church hermeneutics), from whom the miraculous water flows. Thus Justin Martyr says ("Dialogus cum Tryphone Judaeo," Migne, *P.G.*, vol. 6, col. 639): "As a spring of living water from God, in the land of the heathen barren of all knowledge of God, has this Christ gushed forth [see fig. 213], who appeared also to your people, and healed them that from their birth and in the flesh were blind, dumb, and lame. . . . Also he awoke the dead. . . . This he did in order to convince those who are ready to believe in him that, even if a man be afflicted with any bodily infirmity and yet keeps the commandments given by Christ, he shall be awakened at the second coming with an uncrippled body, after Christ has made him immortal and incorruptible and without sorrow."

213. Moses striking water from the rock.—Bible Moralisée (MS., 13th cent.)

metallic waters[142] flowed forth [fig. 213]. Then the rivers[143] disappeared in dry land, which make the city of God joyful;[144] when this mortal shall put on immortality, and the corruption of the living shall put on incorruption, then indeed shall that word come to pass which is written, Death is swallowed up in victory. O death, where is thy victory?[145] Where thy sin abounded, there now grace doth more abound. For as in Adam all die, so also in Christ all shall be made alive. For by a man indeed came death, and by himself the

---

[142] A frequent image: Mercurial water (*rivuli aurei*), etc.
[143] Like the "pluviae et imbres" that drench and fertilize the thirsty earth. The king in alchemy is thirsty and drinks water until he dissolves. Cf. Merlinus, "Allegoria," *Art. aurif.*, I, p. 392.
[144] Ps. 45 : 5 (D.V.): "The stream of the river maketh the city of God joyful."
[145] I Cor. (D.V.) 15 : 53f.: "For this corruptible must put on incorruption: and this mortal must put on immortality. And when this mortal hath put on immortality, then shall come to pass the saying that is written: *Death is swallowed up in victory. O death, where is thy victory? O death, where is thy sting?*"

391

resurrection of the dead. For the first Adam and his sons took their beginning from the corruptible elements, and therefore it was needful that the composed should be corrupted, but the second Adam, who is called the philosophic man, from pure elements entered into eternity. Therefore what is composed of simple and pure essence, remaineth for ever.[146] As Senior saith: There is One thing, that never dieth,[147] for it continueth by perpetual increase, when the body shall be glorified in the final resurrection of the dead, wherefore the Creed beareth witness to the resurrection of the flesh and eternal life after death. Then saith the second Adam to the first and to his sons:[148] Come, ye blessed of my Father, possess you the eternal kingdom prepared for you from the beginning of the Work,[149] and eat my bread and drink the wine which I have mingled for you, for all things are made ready for you. He that hath ears to hear, let him hear what the spirit of the doctrine saith to the sons of the discipline concerning the earthly and the heavenly Adam, which the philosophers treat of in these words: When thou hast water from earth, air from water, fire from air, earth from fire,[150] then shalt thou fully and perfectly possess our art.

476   What is particularly interesting in this passage is the parallel between the *lapis* or the *aqua sapientum* and the second Adam, which connects Christ—through the quotation in Senior (n. 147) —with the alchemical doctrine of the Anthropos: Christ is identified with the *homo philosophicus*, the Microcosm (fig. 214), the "One that dieth not, and bringeth alive anything dead." The *homo philosophicus* appears to have two meanings: he is the "One," i.e., the tincture or elixir of life, but he is also the everlasting inner man, identical or at least connected with the Anthropos (cf. figs. 117, 195). (This doctrine is elaborated by Paracelsus.[151])

146 Cf. Ruska, *Turba*, pp. 182f., 115f.

147 A Hermes quotation in Senior, *De chemia*, p. 71 (see also *Bibl. chem.*, II, p. 227a): "Est mundus minor. Item est unum quod non moritur, quamdiu fuerit mundus, et vivificat quodlibet mortuum" etc. (It is the smaller world [i.e., the Microcosm = Man]. One thing there is that dieth not, so long as the world shall endure, and it bringeth alive anything dead.) The passage refers to the *aqua philosophica*. Senior is the Latin name for Mohammed ibn Umail (10th cent.), whose work was published by Stapleton in *Three Arabic Treatises on Alchemy*.

148 The philosophers.

149 Matt. 25 : 34, with "beginning of the Work" substituted for "foundation of the world."

150 A quotation from Pseudo-Aristotle; cf. *Rosarium*, *Art. aurif.*, II, p. 286.

151 Jung, "Paracelsus as a Spiritual Phenomenon," pars. 165ff., 203ff.

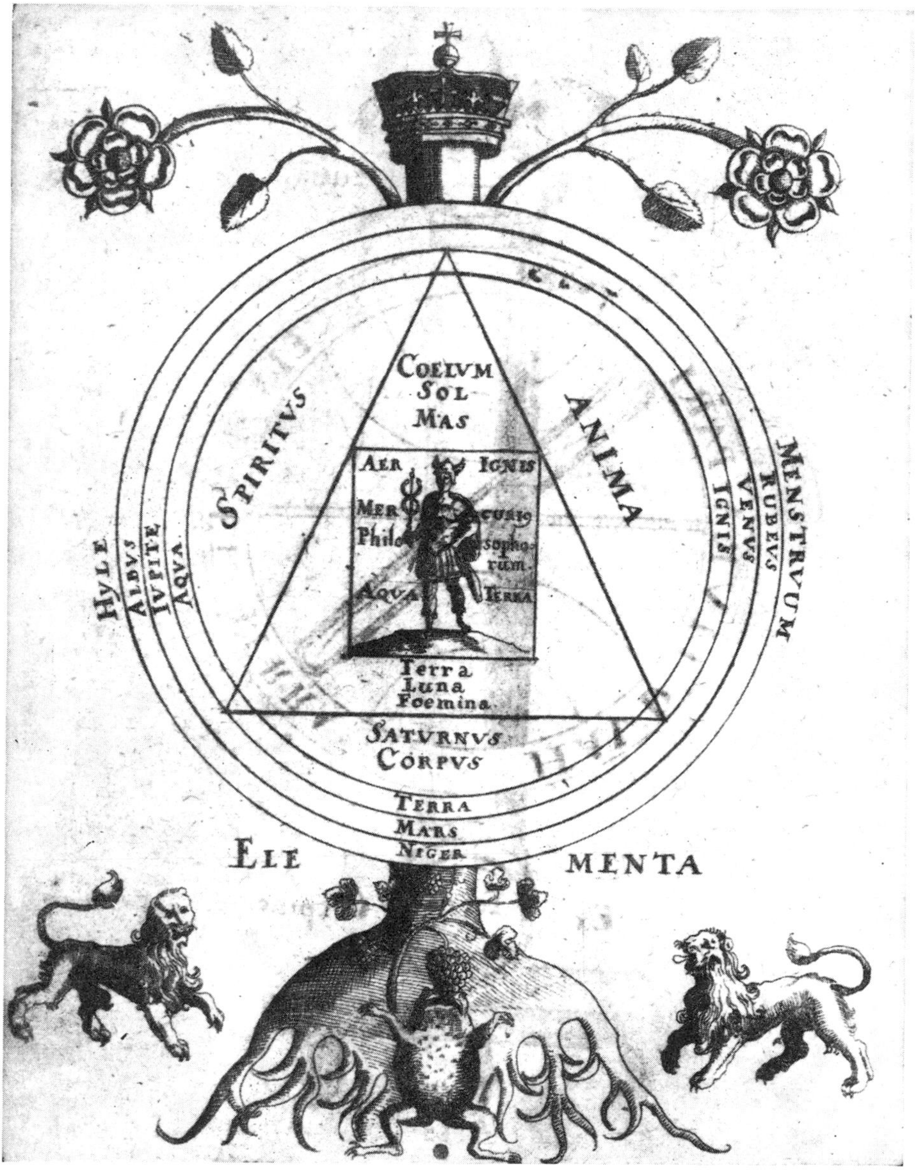
COELVM
SOL
MAS
SPIRITVS
ANIMA
AER
IGNIS
MER
CURIO
Philo
sophorum
AQVA
TERRA
Terra
Luna
Foemina
SATVRNVS
CORPVS
HYLE
ALBVS
IVPITE
AQVA
MENSTRVVM
RUBEVS
VENVS
IGNIS
TERRA
MARS
NIGER
ELE
MENTA

214. Symbol of Hermetic transformation: the *homo philosophicus* Mercurius.
—Samuel Norton, *Mercurius redivivus* (1630)

477   *Aurora* continues in the same vein and gives us in the seventh and last parable a "Confabulation of the Lover with the Beloved" (which Luther's Bible interprets as "the mutual love of Christ and his Church"), closing with the words: "Behold, how good and pleasant it is for two to dwell together in unity. Let us make therefore three tabernacles, one for thee, a second for me, and a third for our sons, for a threefold cord is not easily broken." These three tabernacles the author connects with the "Liber trium verborum" of Kalid.[152] The Three Words "wherein is hidden all the science" are to be "given to the pious, that is to the poor,[153] from the first man even unto the last." The Three Words are: "For three months water preserveth the foetus in the womb; air nourisheth it for the second three; fire guardeth it for the third three." "And this word," adds Kalid, "and this teaching and the dark goal, stand open so that all may see the truth."

478   Although the three tabernacles, according to the preceding text, are intended for the *sponsus Christus* and, we may suppose, for Sapientia as the *sponsa,* yet in the end Sapientia herself speaks and offers two of the tabernacles to the adept and the philosophers, the sons of wisdom. The "threefold cord" (fig. 215) refers primarily to the bond between Sapientia and her adepts, but, as the reference to Kalid's Three Words shows, it also means the threefold process which holds the body, soul, and spirit of the transforming substance together in imperishable union[154] (cf. figs. 185, 196). The chemical compound thus produced is the end-result of the *opus,* i.e., the *filius philosophorum* or *lapis* in a sense comparable with the "mystical body" of the Church (fig. 234): Christ the vine, the whole; the disciples the branches, the parts. One does indeed have the impression that the anonymous author of this treatise has hitched the Holy Scriptures to the triumphal car of alchemy, as was not unjustly alleged against

152 *Art. aurif.,* I, pp. 352ff. Kalid refers to the Omayyad prince Khalid ibn-Yazid (end of the 7th century), though there is good reason for believing that this treatise was not written by him at all. (Cf. Lippmann, *Entstehung und Ausbreitung der Alchemie,* II, p. 122, for the literature on this question.)

153 Another name for the alchemists. Cf. "Les poures hommes évangélisans" in Rupescissa, *La Vertu et la propriété de la quinte essence,* p. 31.

154 Here the process has three parts, in contrast to the four parts in Greek alchemy. But this may be due only to the analogy with the nine months of pregnancy. Cf. Kalid, *Art. aurif.,* I, pp. 358ff.

215. The completion of the process. Inscription: "oculatus abis" (provided with eyes, thou goest thy way). Hermes as Anthropos, united with the artifex and *soror* through the threefold cord. Below, Hercules, a favourite symbol because of his *opera*. Background, the ladder which is no longer needed.—*Mutus liber* (1702)

him. It is astonishing to see how, with a perfectly clear conscience, he launches forth into the most hair-raising interpretations without the least awareness of what he is doing. As I have shown in "Paracelsus as a Spiritual Phenomenon," we find a similar attitude in Paracelsus some two hundred years later, and also in the author of "Aquarium sapientum." Our author betrays such a ready acquaintance with the Vulgate that we might suspect him of being in holy orders. Moreover we have the testimony of the humanist Patrizi that Hermetic philosophy was not felt to be in any way inimical to the Christianity of the Church. On the contrary, people regarded it as a mainstay of the Christian faith. For which reason Patrizi addressed a plea to Pope Gregory XIV requesting him to let Hermes take the place of Aristotle.[155]

479   The text of *Aurora* is of historical importance in that it must be more than two hundred years older than Khunrath (1598) and Böhme (1610). Curiously enough, Böhme's first work bears the title "Aurora, oder die Morgenröte im Aufgang" (Aurora, or the Rising Dawn). Can it be that Böhme knew *Aurora consurgens*, at least by name?

f. Melchior Cibinensis and the Alchemical Paraphrase of the Mass

480   The next source for the *lapis*-Christ identity is an interesting document from the beginning of the sixteenth century, addressed, as its title shows,[156] to Ladislaus, King of Hungary and Bohemia. The author's name was Nicholas Melchior of Hermannstadt.[157] He expounded the alchemical process in the form of a Mass (fig. 216), which he arranged as follows:

155 Patrizi, *Nova de universis philosophia*.

156 "Addam et processum sub forma missae, a Nicolao Cibinensi, Transilvano, ad Ladislaum Ungariae et Bohemiae regem olim missum," *Theatr. chem.*, III, pp. 853ff.

157 Not identical with Melchior, Cardinal Bishop of Brixen, to whom the treatise "Von dem gelben und rotten Mann," in *Aureum vellus*, is attributed. Our author was the chaplain Nicolaus Melchior Szebeni, at the king's court as astrologer from 1490. He remained there after the death of Ladislaus II in 1516, under Louis II (1506–26). Following the defeat of Mohács (1526) and the death of Louis II, Melchior fled to the court of Ferdinand I in Vienna. He was executed by the latter in 1531. Our document must therefore have been written before 1516. Ladislaus II became King of Bohemia in 1471 and of Hungary in 1490. We find

216. The artifex as priest. Left, Earth suckling the Mercurius-child: "matrix eius terra est" ("Tabula smaragdina").—Melchior Cibinensis, *Symbolum,* from Maier, *Symbola aureae mensae* (1617)

INTROITUS MISSAE: Fundamentum vero artis est corporum solutio. (The basis of the Art is the dissolution of the bodies.)

KYRIE, FONS BONITATIS, inspirator sacrae artis, a quo bona cuncta tuis fidelibus procedunt, Eleison. (Our Lord, fount of goodness, inspirer of the sacred art, from whom all good things come to your faithful, have mercy.)

CHRISTE, Hagie, lapis benedicte artis scientiae qui pro mundi salute inspirasti lumen scientiae, ad exstirpandum Turcam, Eleison. (Christ, Holy one, blessed stone of the art of the science who for the salvation of the world hast inspired the light of the science, for the extirpation of the Turk, have mercy.)

KYRIE, IGNIS DIVINE, pectora nostra juva, ut pro tua laude pariter sacramenta artis expandere possimus, Eleison. (Our Lord, divine fire, help our hearts, that we may be able, to your praise, to expand the sacraments of the art, have mercy.)

---

the remark "ad exstirpandum Turcam" in the text. It is true that Buda was conquered by the Turks only in 1541, but the land had long suffered from Turkish invasions. [Hermannstadt is the German name of the Romanian (formerly Hungarian) city of Sibiu or Cibiu (whence "Cibinensis").—EDITORS.]

GLORIA IN EXCELSIS [merely an invocation].

COLLECTA [Prayer before the epistle is read. The main idea is that "thy servant N.N." may practise the "sacred art of alchemy" to the glory of God and the propagation of the Christian faith].

EPISTOLA [merely an invocation].

GRADUALE [usually a chorale consisting of verses from the Psalms; in the old days it was sung on the steps, *gradus*, of the ambo]: Surge aquilo et veni auster:[158] perfla hortum meum et fluant aromata illius. (Arise, O north wind, and come, O south wind; blow through my garden, and let the aromatical spices thereof flow).

VERSUS: Descendit sicut pluvia in vellus, et sicut stillicidia, stillantia super terram. Alleluja. O felix conditor terrae, nive albior, suavitate dulcior, f[r]agrans in fundo vasis instar balsami. O salutaris medicina hominum, quae curas . . . omnem corporis languorem. . . . O fons sublimis ex quo vere scaturit vera aqua vitae, in praedium tuorum fidelium. (He descends like rain upon the fleece, and as showers falling gently upon the earth. Alleluja. O blest creator of the earth, whiter than snow, sweeter than sweetness, fragrant at the bottom of the vessel like balsam. O salutary medicine for men, that curest every weakness of the body: O sublime fount whence gushes forth truly the true water of life into the garden of thy faithful.)

An Ave Praeclara follows the Gospel.

481   Here I will stress only a few of the most important points. After the reading of Gospel and Creed, Melchior introduces an Ave—not an Ave Maria, but an "Ave Praeclara," [159]—of which he mentions only these two words, without the continuation. "Ave Praeclara" is the opening of a hymn to the Virgin Mary, which has been attributed to various authors, including Albertus Magnus, whose putative authorship must have been particularly interesting to an alchemist. Rémy de Gourmont, in his *Le Latin mystique*,[160] quotes the following legend taken from the so-called Osnabrück Register of Santa Maria: A virgin in royal raiment appeared to Albertus in a dream and reproached him for not

---

[158] *Aquilo* (north wind) is an allegory of the devil, *auster* an allegory of the Holy Ghost. Cf. Migne, *P.L.*, vol. 219: "Index de allegoriis." Among the authorities quoted we meet Alain of Lille (Alanus de Insulis), who was well known to the alchemists (Maier, *Symbola aureae mensae*, p. 259).

[159] Perhaps he is enlarging on the "water of life" that has just been mentioned, or more probably the "salutary medicine" a little earlier, which is really the main theme.   [160] Pp. 129f.

having shown himself sufficiently grateful to the Virgin Mary for the blessing she had bestowed. It was on account of this dream that Albertus composed the Ave Praeclara. An alchemist would find it full of alluring allusions:

Ave praeclara maris stella, in lucem gentium Maria divinitus orta. . .
Virgo, decus mundi, regina coeli, praeelecta ut sol, pulchra lunaris ut fulgor. . .
Fac fontem dulcem, quem in deserto petra demonstravit,
    degustare cum sincera fide, renesque constringi lotos
    in mari, anguem aeneum in cruce speculari [fig. 217].
Fac igni sancto patrisque verbo, quod, rubus ut
    flamma, tu portasti, virgo mater facta, pecuali
    pelle distinctos,[161] pede, mundis labiis, cordeque propinquare.

Hail, clear-shining star of the sea, Mary, divinely born for the enlightenment of the nations. . .
Virgin, ornament of the world, queen of heaven, elect above all like the sun, lovely as the light of the moon. . .
Let us drink in steadfast faith of the sweet stream that flowed from the rock in the desert, and, girding our loins that the sea has bathed, gaze on the crucified brazen serpent [fig. 217].
O Virgin, who hast been made mother by the sacred fire and the Father's word, which thou didst bear like the Burning Bush, let us, as cattle ringstraked, speckled and spotted,[161] draw near with our feet, with pure lips and heart.

482   While Melchior's text leaves it an open question whether "praeclara" means the *aqua vitae,* he leaves us in no doubt that it refers not only to the Virgin but to a hymn in her praise, for he goes on to say: "The Ave Praeclara must be sung; it shall be called the 'testament of the art,' since the whole chemical art is figuratively concealed therein,[162] and blessed is he that understands this sequence."

483   By "this sequence" he means a hymn to Mary, in all probability the one we have quoted above, as is clear from Melchior's next words. In any case the Virgin is identified with the arcanum

---

161 See Gen. 30 : 32ff.
162 "Sequentia sancti evangelii, sub tono, Ave praeclara, cantetur; quam testamentum artis volo nuncupari, quoniam tota ars chemica, tropicis in ea verbis occultatur, et beatus," etc.

217. The crucified *serpens mercurialis,* the brazen serpent of Moses.—Abraham
le Juif, "Livre des figures hiéroglifiques" (MS., 18th cent.)

of the art, possibly on the authority—then at its height—of Raymond Lully.[163] We come across a similar idea in the treatise of Komarios: "Ostanes and his companions said to Cleopatra: 'The whole awful and marvellous secret is hidden in thee.' "[164]

484   Melchior now gives his alchemical paraphrase of the hymn to Mary:

Hail beautiful lamp of heaven, shining light [165] of the world! Here art thou united with the moon, here is made the band of Mars[166] [copula martialis] and the conjunction of Mercury.[167] From these three is born through the magistery of the art, in the river bed, the strong giant[168] whom a thousand times a thousand seek, when these three shall have dissolved, not into rain water . . . but into mercurial water, into this our blessed gum[169] which dissolves of itself and is named the Sperm of the Philosophers. Now he[170] makes haste to bind and betroth himself to the virgin bride, and to get her with child in the bath over a moderate fire [fig. 218]. But the virgin will not become pregnant at once unless she be kissed in repeated embraces. Then she conceives in her body, and thus is begotten the child of good omen, in accordance with the order of nature. Then will appear in the bottom of the vessel the mighty Ethiopian, burned, calcined, discoloured, altogether dead and lifeless[171] [fig. 219].

163 Cf. his "Codicillus," *Bibl. chem.*, I, pp. 88off.

164 "Εἰ σοι κέκρυπται ὅλον τὸ μυστήριον τὸ φρικτὸν καὶ παράδοξον (Berthelot, *Alch. grecs*, IV, xx, 8).

165 Sun.

166 Reference to Venus and Mars, caught in the net of Vulcan.

167 *Coniunctio* of Mercurius, but with whom? Or it is a *coniunctio* of two Mercurii, one male and one female? It seems to be a union of Sol with Luna, Mars, and Mercury.

168 Ruska, "Tab. smarag.," p. 2: "Hic est totius fortitudinis fortitudo fortis" (He is the strong strength of all strength).

169 This is the substance which was the special concern of Maria, the "Prophetissa" and "sister of Moses." *Art. aurif.*, I, p. 320: "Recipe alumen de Hispania, gummi album et gummi rubeum, quod est kibric Philosophorum . . . et matrimonifica gummi cum gummi vero matrimonio" (Take alum from Spain, white gum and red gum, which is the kibric of the philosophers . . . and join in true marriage gum with gum).

170 Presumably Sol, perhaps in the form of "gum." The coitus of Sol and Luna in the bath is a central mythologem in alchemy, and is celebrated in numerous illustrations (cf. figs. 159, 167, 218).

171 Namely the *caput mortuum*, the head of Osiris in the *nigredo* state. The Ethiopian comes from a treatise attributed to Albertus: "Super arborem Aristotelis," *Theatr. chem.*, II. The passage runs (p. 526): ". . . quousque caput nigrum aethiopis portans similitudinem, fuerit bene lavatum et inceperit albescere. . . ." (. . . until the black head bearing the resemblance of the Ethiopian is well

218. The "bath of the philosophers."—Mylius, *Philosophia reformata* (1622)

He asks to be buried, to be sprinkled with his own moisture and slowly calcined [172] till he shall arise in glowing form from the fierce fire. . . . Behold a wondrous restoration and renewal of the Ethiopian! Because of the bath of rebirth he takes a new name, which the philosophers call the natural sulphur and their son, this being the stone of the philosophers. And behold it is *one* thing, *one* root, *one* essence with nothing extraneous added and from which much that was superfluous is taken away by the magistery of the art. . . . It is the treasure of treasures, the supreme philosophical potion, the

washed and begins to turn white. . . .). In Rosencreutz's *Chymical Wedding* the presumptive queen of the drama is the temporary concubine of a Moor. Cf. also *Aurora consurgens,* ch. VI, parable 1.

172 The calcination probably corresponds to incineration, while the incandescent ash tends towards vitrification. This operation may likewise come from Maria Prophetissa: "Vitrifica super illud Kibrich et Zuboch [alias Zibeic] et ipsa sunt duo fumi complectentes duo lumina" (Vitrify over it Kibrich and Zuboch [alias Zibeic] and they are two vapours enveloping two lights). "Practica," *Art. aurif.,* I, p. 321. "Zaibac, Zeida, Zaibar, Zibatum . . . id est argentum vivum." Zaibar = Mercurius. Ruland's *Lexicon: zibag* (Arabic) = quicksilver. Lippmann, *Entstehung,* p. 409. Kibric = *kibrit* (Arabic) = sulphur. Cf. also Ruska, *Turba,* p. 348: "Arabisches Register."

219. The "Ethiopian" as the *nigredo*.—Trismosin, "Splendor solis" (MS., 1582)

divine secret of the ancients. Blessed is he that finds such a thing. One that has seen this thing writes and speaks openly, and I know that his testimony is true. Praise be to God for evermore!

485   The liturgy proper ends here. What now follows is a sort of recapitulation of the main parts. Melchior associates the Offertory with the stone that the builders rejected and that became the head of the corner. "This is the Lord's doing, and it is marvellous in our eyes." Then comes the Secret, leading over to the alchemical oblation. The offering is the *opus*, i.e., "our work of the blessed art of alchemy," which "shall ever be dedicated to the glorious name of God and to the saving reformation of the Church, through our Lord Jesus Christ, Amen."

486   The regeneration of the Ethiopian is actually the equivalent of the transubstantiation, but the Consecration is missing. Melchior takes the Ave Praeclara sequence to include the transubstantiation as a mystery *in gremio virginis*. This view is supported by tradition, as is shown by the following passage from Senior: "The full moon is the philosophical water and the root of the science, for she is the mistress of moisture, the perfect round stone and the sea, wherefore I know that the moon is the root of this hidden science." [173]

487   Being the mistress of moisture, the moon, like Isis, is the *prima materia* in the form of water and thus the mother of the "Hydrolith," the water-stone—another name for the *lapis* and hence for Christ. Since the terms *scientia* and *prima materia* are often used as though they were identical, *scientia* or *sapientia* is here identical with the moon, the feminine principle (fig. 220); hence the Gnostic doctrine of Sophia as the mother or bride of Christ.

488   Last of all comes the "Post-communion": "Glory be to our King who comes out of the fire,[174] who is illumined and crowned with the diadem, for ever and ever, Amen." In conclusion there is a form of compline for the strengthening of the Christian faith and the extermination of the Turk.

---

[173] *De chemia,* pp. 35f.

[174] Quotation from the "Tractatus aureus," *Ars chemica,* p. 22. It should be mentioned that Melchior recommends reading the 10th chapter of Luke before the Creed. This chapter would appear to have no connection with his theme except for the fact that it ends with the significant words: "But *one thing* is necessary. *Mary* hath chosen the best part, which shall not be taken away from her" (D.V.).

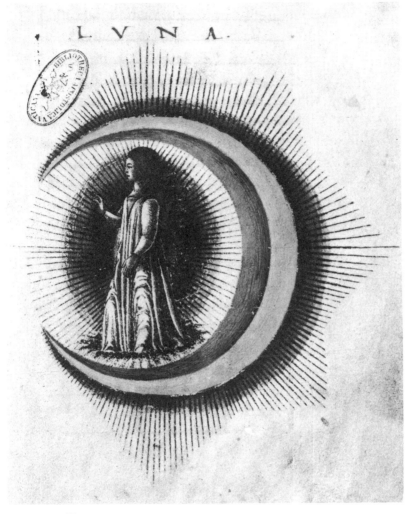

220. Figure of the moon.—Codex Urbanus Latinus 899 (15th cent.)

489   Apart from its bad taste the text is highly illuminating for our theme. Melchior obviously recognized the analogy between the two *opera* and naïvely substituted the individual *opus*, in all its poverty, for the time-honoured words of the Mass. He lived at the time of the Reformation, and not so long afterwards the Mass was replaced, over a wide area of Europe, by the far from sacrosanct words of various preachers all declaring the word of God in their own way. Melchior was doing something of this kind. If we grant him the right to a subjective credo he becomes more acceptable. It is clear enough from the text that he felt the alchemical process to be the equivalent of the transubstantiation in the Mass, and that he had the need to express his experience[175] in precisely that form. It is to be noted, however, that he puts the alchemical transmutation not in the place of the transubstantiation but somewhere in the vicinity of the Credo, so that the action breaks off before the Consecration. In the second version of the recapitulation the climax of the rite is again missing, and the sequence jumps straight from the Secret at the Offertory to the Post-communion. This peculiarity may be explained by the holy awe of the most solemn and moving part of the Mass, namely the Consecration. One could therefore take it as at least an indirect sign of a conflict of conscience—a conscience torn between the experience of a rite acting from without and an individual experience acting from within. Although Christ is nowhere mentioned as the *lapis* or *medicina,* their identity is overpoweringly evident from the whole drift of the text.

g. *Sir George Ripley*

490   Additional evidence, which ought to have been known to Waite, is furnished (cf. figs. 30, 92, 196, 228, 251, 257) by his countryman Sir George Ripley (1415–90), canon of Bridlington, whose main work, "Liber duodecim portarum," [176] is prefaced by a table of philosophical correspondences, compiled by B. à Portu,

---

175 The subjective character of the experience comes out in the incidental remark of the author: "et *scio* quod verum est testimonium eius" (and I *know* that his testimony is true).
176 *Bibl. chem. curiosa,* II, pp. 275ff., and *Theatr. chem.,* II, pp. 123ff.

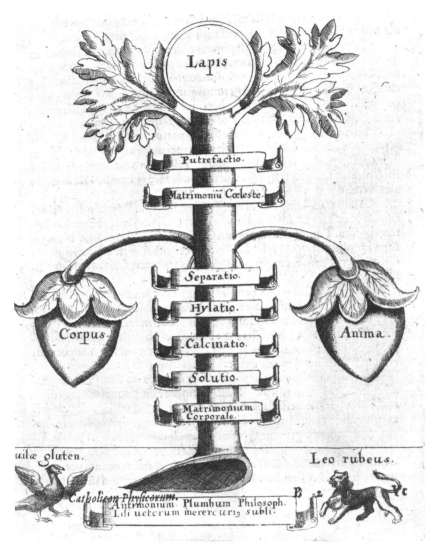

221. *Arbor philosophica:* the tree as symbol of the stages in the transformation
process.—Samuel Norton, *Catholicon physicorum* (1630)

Aquitanus. The table sets forth the correspondences between the seven metals and chemical substances and what are called "types," by which are meant the alchemical symbols, e.g., tinctures, the ages of man, signs of the zodiac, and so forth. These correspondences include seven mysteries, the *Mysterium Altaris* (i.e., the Mass) being attributed to gold, whereas the alchemical equivalent is the *transmutatio* (fig. 221). The kind of grain that belongs to this mystery is *triticum* (wheat). B. à Portu is probably to be identified with Bernhardus Georgius Penotus, the Paracelsist, who was born between 1520 and 1530 at Port-Ste-Marie in Guienne (part of the old Aquitaine) and who died in 1620 in the poorhouse at Yverdon (Vaud, Switzerland), hoary with age and disillusioned with the Paracelsan optimism that had fired his student days in Basel. He shared the inevitable fate of those who lacked sufficient humour to understand the testy old master and who found that the secret teaching about the *aurum non vulgi* remained all too secret. But his table shows that the analogy between the *opus* and the Mass was also valid in Paracelsist circles. Paracelsus was a contemporary of Melchior's, but may well have reached similar conclusions independently, for such ideas were then in the air. Michael Maier was sufficiently impressed by Melchior's analogy to use it as Symbol XI (fig. 216) in his *Symbola aureae mensae* (1617), with the motto: "Lapis, ut infans, lacte nutriendus est virginali" (The stone, like to an infant, is to be fed with virgin's milk) [cf. fig. 222].

491   We find the following legend in the "Cantilena Riplaei":[177]

There was once a noble king [the *caput corporum*] who had no descendants. He lamented his sterility and concluded that a *defectus originalis* must have arisen in him, although he was "nurtured under the wings of the sun" without any natural bodily defects. He says, in his own words: "Alas, I fear and know for a certainty that unless I can obtain the help of the species at once, I shall never beget a child. But I have heard with astonishment, by the mouth

[177] Ripley, *Opera omnia chemica*, pp. 421ff. [Professor Jung gives the "Cantilena" in prose paraphrase. For a complete translation in verse form, with commentary, see Jung, *Mysterium Coniunctionis*, pars. 370ff. In lines 7–8 of the paraphrase, the present reading replaces a reference to the "tree of Christ," as the consequence of an emendation authorized by Professor Jung; cf. ibid., par. 380, n. 88. Accordingly, a representation of "Christ on the tree of life" in fig. 222 has been replaced by another subject.—EDITORS.]

222. The sea of renewal arising from virgin's milk. Symbolic representation of the life-giving power of the unconscious (= whale).—Stolcius de Stolcenberg, *Viridarium chymicum* (1624)

of Christ above, that I shall be born anew." He then wished to return to his mother's womb and to dissolve himself in the *prima materia*. His mother encouraged him in this venture, and forthwith concealed him under her robe, until she had incarnated him again in herself. She then became pregnant. During her pregnancy she ate peacock's flesh and drank the blood of the green lion. At length she brought forth the child, who resembled the moon and then changed into the splendour of the sun. The son once more became king. The text says: "God gave thee the glorious, glittering armoury of the four elements, and the Crowned Maid [*Virgo redimita*] was in their midst." A wonderful balsam flowed from her [cf. fig. 222] and she shone with a radiant face, adorned with the precious stone. But in her lap lay the green lion,[178] with blood flowing from his side [cf. fig. 242]. She was crowned with a diadem and was set as a star in the highest heaven. The king became a supreme victor triumphant, a great healer of the sick and a redeemer [*reformator*] of all sins.

[178] The green lion is also a synonym for the unicorn. See fig. 242.

223. *Mortificatio*, or *nigredo* and *putrefactio:* Sol and Luna overcome by death after the *coniunctio.*—Mylius, *Philosophia reformata* (1622)

492   So far the "Cantilena." Elsewhere Ripley writes:[179]

Christ said: "I, if I be lifted up, will draw all men unto me." [180] From that time forward, when both parts, having been crucified and exanimated, are betrothed to one another, man and wife shall be buried together [fig. 223] and afterward quickened again by the spirit of life. Then must they be raised to heaven, so that body and soul may be there transfigured and enthroned on the clouds; then they will draw all bodies to their own high estate [fig. 224].

493   If we realize that the author was no layman but a learned canon, we can hardly suppose him to have been unaware of the parallels with certain fundamental ideas of Christian dogma. It is never said outright that the stone is Christ, but the sacred figures can easily be recognized in the guise of the King and the Virgin-Mother. Ripley must have made a deliberate choice of these parallels without being conscious of any blasphemy. The Basel typographer, Conrad Waldkirch, would have rained fire

179 *Opera omnia*, p. 81.   180 John 12 : 32.

224. Transfiguration of the body portrayed as the coronation of the Virgin Mary.
—Codex Germanicus 598 (1420)

and brimstone on his head. Ripley belonged to an age when God and his mysteries still dwelt in nature, when the mystery of redemption was at work on every level of existence, because unconscious happenings still lived in untroubled, paradisal participation with matter and could be experienced there.

494   I came across a last outcropping of this medieval view of the world in my youth, in the form of the following tale. We had at that time a cook from the Swabian part of the Black Forest, on whom fell the duty of executing the victims from the poultry yard destined for the kitchen. We kept bantams, and bantam cocks are renowned for their singular quarrelsomeness and malice. One of these exceeded all others in savagery, and my mother commissioned the cook to dispatch the malefactor for the Sunday roast. I happened to come in just as she was bringing back the decapitated cock and saying to my mother: "He died like a Christian, although he was so wicked. He cried out, 'Forgive me, forgive me!' before I cut off his head, so now he'll go to heaven." My mother answered indignantly: "What nonsense! Only human beings go to heaven." The cook retorted in astonishment: "But of course there's a chicken heaven for chickens just as there's a human heaven for humans." "But only people have an immortal soul and a religion," said my mother, equally astonished. "No, that's not so," replied the cook. "Animals have souls too, and they all have their special heaven, dogs, cats, and horses, because when the Saviour of men came down to earth, the chicken saviour also came to the chickens, and that's why they must repent of their sins before they die if they want to go to heaven."

495   The theology of our cook is a remnant of that folklore mentality which saw the drama of redemption going on at all levels and could therefore discover it even in the mysterious and incomprehensible transformations of matter.

496   As to the details of the "Cantilena," the sick king who was nevertheless born perfect is the man who suffers from spiritual sterility. In the vision of Arisleus the land is unfruitful because only like mates with like, instead of the opposites being united. The philosophers advise the king to join his son and daughter together and make the land fruitful again by means of a brother-sister incest (fig. 225). With Ripley it is a mother-son incest. Both forms are familiar to alchemy and constitute the

225. The love-potion being handed to the brother-sister pair.—Maier, *Scrutinium chymicum* (1687)

prototype of the royal marriage (fig. 32). This endogamous mating is simply a variant of the Uroboros, which, because it is by nature hermaphroditic, completes the circle in itself. The king in Arisleus remarks that he is king because he has a son and a daughter, while his subjects have none on account of their sterility. The "gestation in the brain" [181] points to a psychic content, or more accurately to a psychic pair of opposites that can become creative of their own accord (fig. 226). But evidently the king has so far not allowed his children to propagate, by repressing or ignoring the manifestations of their vitality. It looks as though he had been unconscious of their existence and had only become aware of their significance on the advice of the philosophers. The blame for his sterility is to be sought in the projection of unconscious contents, which can neither develop nor find "redemption" until they are integrated with conscious-

181 "Meo in cerebro gestavi": "Visio Arislei," *Art. aurif.*, I, p. 147.

413

226. *Coniunctio* of opposites in the Hermetic vessel or in water
(= unconscious).—"Trésor des trésors" (MS., 17th cent.)

227. *Coniunctio* as a fantastic monstrosity.—
Brant, *Hexastichon* (1503)

ness. The brother-sister pair stands for the unconscious or for
some essential content (fig. 227). A modern psychologist would
therefore have advised the king to remember the existence of his
unconscious and so put an end to his stagnation. As generally
happens in such cases, an opposition, a painful conflict, thereupon comes to the surface, and it is easy to understand why the
king preferred to remain unconscious of it. Since the conflict is
never lacking in moral complications, it is, from this point of
view, appropriately expressed in the morally obnoxious form of
incest. In Ripley the mother-incest is disguised under the classical rite of adoption, but the mother becomes pregnant all the
same. The vanishing of the king under his mother's robes corresponds to the total dissolution of Gabricus in the body of
Beya in the second version of the "Visio Arislei." [182] The king

182 *Art. aurif.*, II, p. 246: "Et includit eum in suo utero, quod nil penitus videri
potest de eo. Tantoque amore amplexata est Gabricum, quod ipsum totum in

415

228. The plumed king who plucks out his feathers for food.
—"Ripley Scrowle" (MS., 1588)

229. Eagle as symbol of the spirit ascending from the *prima materia*.—*Hermaphroditisches Sonn- und Mondskind* (1752)

represents the domineering conscious mind which, in the course of coming to terms with the unconscious, is swallowed up by it. This brings about the *nigredo* (cf. figs. 34, 137, 219), a state of darkness that eventually leads to the renewal and rebirth of the king.

497 The strange idea of the king "nurtured under the wings of the sun" (fig. 228) may refer to the passage in Malachi (D.V., 4 : 2) which helped to put the early worship of Christ as Helios or Sol on a rational basis—a tendency that St. Augustine still had to combat: "But unto you that fear my name the Sun of justice shall arise, and health in his wings; and you shall go forth and shall leap like calves of the herd." The passage has always been understood as a Messianic prophecy, and was obviously known to Ripley. The "wings of the sun" [183] is a very ancient image, and one which must have touched the Hebrew Malachi very closely: for it is the Egyptian sun-symbol. He who is nourished by this sun is the son of God, i.e., the king.[184]

---

sui naturam concepit et in partes indivisibiles divisit." (And she enclosed him in her womb so that nothing at all could be seen of him any more. And she embraced Gabricus with so much love that she absorbed him completely in her own nature, and divided him into indivisible parts.)

[183] The feathers of the phoenix, and of other birds, play a great role in alchemy, particularly in the writings of Ripley. Cf. "Scrowle," *Theatr. chem. Brit.* (See also figs. 229, 266, 270.)

[184] "Gloria mundi," *Mus. herm.*, p. 221: "Lapis . . . per Solem et Lunam generatus . . . primum . . . suum partum in terra accepit et tamen frangitur, destruitur, et mortificatur . . . per vaporem generatur, et denuo nascitur, cum vento in mare venit . . . atque cum vento ex mari in terram venit . . . et cito iterum evanescit. . . . Et quamvis cottidie denuo nascatur, nihilominus tamen ab initio

230. The peacock rising from the retort.—18th-cent. MS.

231. Mercurius as virgin (Pandora) and *arbor philosophica.*
—Reusner, *Pandora* (1588)

498   Just as in the vision of Arisleus the king's dead son is brought back to life by the fruit of the philosophical tree, so in Ripley the sick king is to be healed by the "species"—obviously a φάρμακον ζωῆς or *elixir vitae.* The mother's food during her pregnancy is blood and peacock's flesh. The peacock is an early Christian symbol for the Redeemer, though it is doubtful whether Ripley knew this. But the peacock (figs. 111, 230) is second cousin to the phoenix,[185] a Christ symbol he must surely

mundi ille fuit. . . ." (The stone . . . begotten by the sun and the moon . . . was first born . . . on the earth, and yet it is broken, destroyed and mortified. . . . It is generated through vapour, and is born anew, with the wind it comes to the sea . . . and with the wind it comes from the sea to the earth, . . . and quickly evaporates again. . . . And though it is daily born anew, yet nevertheless it existed from the beginning of the world. . . .) (Cf. John 1 : 1 and 14.)

185 Cf. Caussin, *De symbolica Aegyptiorum sapientia,* p. 71: s.v. "phoenix."

have known (see the figures in the "Ripley Scrowle"). The blood comes from the green lion that lies in the lap of the virgin, bleeding from a wound in his side;[186] these are clearly communion and Pietà symbols. The green lion is also one of the forms of Mercurius.[187]

499   As the giver of new birth, the mother is identical with the tree. In the 1588 edition of *Pandora* the tree is shown as a naked virgin[188] wearing a crown (fig. 231). The *arbor philosophica* is a favourite symbol for the alchemical process, and when Ripley speaks of the "Crowned Maid" (*virgo redimita*) we at once recognize the *anima mundi*, the feminine half of Mercurius (fig. 208).

500   The "Cantilena" ends with the apotheosis of the virgin-mother. This the above-mentioned *Pandora* depicts as a glorification of Mary, the *assumptio Beatae Mariae Virginis* (fig. 232). After her death, by a divine miracle her body was again united with her soul and both together were taken up to heaven. This has long been the view of the Church, although it has only recently been promulgated as a dogma. In fig. 232 she is marked with the words "terra" and "corpus Lyb" (body) and "die wonn der jung-frowenn wardt" (who became the joy of virgins); the dove descends upon her, and God the Father touches her with his right hand in benison. She is crowned. The figure of God holding the orb is inscribed "Anima Seel" and "Jesse pater, filius et mater." "Mater" refers to the Queen of Heaven enthroned beside him, the King; for in her the earth substance, becoming transfigured in her resurrected body, is absorbed into the Godhead.[189] On the left is a bearded figure equal in rank to God the Father, inscribed "Sapientia Wyssheit." In the shield below there is a picture of the rebis being freed from the *prima materia*. The whole has the form of a mandala, framed by the emblems of the evangelists. The inscription at the bottom of the picture reads: "Figura speculi Sanctae Trinitatis. Gstalt des

---

186 The wounding of the lion refers to his sacrifice and mortification during the process. He is sometimes shown maimed, with his paws cut off. Cf. for instance Reusner, *Pandora*, p. 227. Note the wounded unicorn lying in the lap of the virgin. (Cf. fig. 242.)

187 Ruland, *Lexicon:* "Leo viridis, quorundam opinione aurum" (The green lion; according to some people's opinion, gold).   188 P. 225.

189 Cf. the vision of Guillaume de Digulleville (pars. 315ff.).

232. Glorification of the body portrayed as coronation of the Virgin Mary. Sapientia (*Hermes senex*) takes the place of the Son, and the Holy Ghost has a quite separate entity. Together they form a quaternity. Below, extraction of the spirit of Mercurius from the *prima materia.—Speculum Trinitatis* from Reusner, *Pandora* (1588)

233. Christian quaternity: the Three and the One (Trinity and Mary).—French
School (1457), detail

Spiegels der Heiligen Dryheit" (Figure of the Mirror of the
Holy Trinity).[190]

501   Ripley portrays his king as victor, healer of the sick, and redeemer from sin. At the end of the *Rosarium* there is a picture
of the Risen Christ with the inscription (fig. 234):

> After my many sufferings and great martyry
> I rise again transfigured, of all blemish free.

[190] This picture goes back to the Codex Germanicus (see fig. 224; cf. also figs.
233, 235).

234. The Risen Christ as symbol of the *filius philoso-phorum.*—*Rosarium philosophorum* (1550)

h. *The Epigoni*

502   By "Epigoni" I mean the authors of the seventeenth century, an age which saw the full flowering of alchemy but which also inaugurated its downfall by separating the *mystica* more and more clearly from the *physica*. The mystical and philosophical trend became ever more pronounced, while on the other hand chemistry proper began to mark itself off more distinctly. The age of science and technology was dawning, and the introspective attitude of the Middle Ages was fast approaching its decline. Religious and metaphysical values became less and less able to give adequate expression to the psychic experiences

423

brought to light by the *opus alchymicum*. Only after the lapse of several centuries did it fall to empirical psychology to throw new light on the obscure psychic content of Hermetic experiences.

503   In the literature written at the close of the sixteenth and the beginning of the seventeenth centuries, mystical speculation, no doubt encouraged by humanism and the schism of the Church, began to emerge from behind the veil of the earlier esotericism, in so far as it was possible for the authors to express the inexpressible at all in words and images. But the pictorial symbolism they produced, much of it quite grotesque, not only made no contribution towards elucidating the arcanum but was largely responsible for devaluing it in the eyes of the profane, thus accelerating the decay of Hermetic wisdom. How much was lost to the spiritual heritage of Europe in this way we, with our sharpened psychological understanding, are just beginning to realize, as we contemplate the unparalleled disorganization of our continent. Happily the loss is not irreparable: *natura tamen usque recurret*.

504   In what follows I should like to mention a few more *lapis*-Christ parallels drawn from this literature.

505   In the treatise entitled "Liber de arte chymica," [191] by an anonymous author,[192] there is a Mercurius-*lapis* parallel which I cannot pass over without mention, since it is an *aequiparatio* of Mercurius with the Virgin Mary:

191 In *Art. aurif.*, I, pp. 575ff.

192 The author is supposed to be no less a person than Marsilio Ficino (1433–99). Manget (*Bibl. chem. curiosa*, II, p. 172) is of this opinion. The treatise is said (Schmieder, *Geschichte der Alchemie*, p. 235) to be contained in the collected edition (Basel, 1561 and 1576) of Ficino's works. (See also Ferguson, *Bibliotheca chemica*, I, p. 268, and Kopp, *Die Alchemie*, I, p. 212.) But it happens that the treatise (*Art. aurif.*, I, p. 596) mentions the murder of Pico della Mirandola—"Quis non intempestivam Pici Mirandulani necem lachrymis non madefaceret?" (Who would not shed tears over the untimely killing of Pico della Mirandola?)—which can only refer to the nephew of the great Pico, Gianfrancesco Pico della Mirandola, who was murdered in 1533. This *terminus a quo* occurred 34 years after the death of Ficino. The reference (*Art. aurif.*, I, p. 625) to the Minorite Father, Ulmannus, and his illustrated treatise makes it more probable that the author was a German writing in the middle of the 16th century. It is possible that the treatise of Ulmannus is connected with the *Dreifaltigkeitsbuch*. Schmieder's statement is anyway incorrect, for I have ascertained that the treatise is *not* contained in the Basel edition.

Give ear[193] to this profound parable: The ethereal heaven was closed to all men, so that they descended into hell and remained imprisoned there forever. But Christ Jesus unlocked the gate of the ethereal Olympus, and threw open the realm of Pluto, that the souls might be freed, when the Virgin Mary, with the cooperation of the Holy Ghost in an unutterable mystery and most profound sacrament, conceived in her virginal womb that which was most sublime in heaven and on earth, and finally bore for us the Saviour of the whole world, who by his overflowing goodness shall save all those who are lost in their sins, if only the sinner will often turn to him. But the Virgin remained incorrupt and inviolate; wherefore it is not without good reason that Mercurius is made equal [*non immerito . . . aequiparatur*] to the most glorious and worshipful Virgin Mary. For Mercurius is virginal, because he has never increased any kind of metallic body in the bowels of the earth, and yet has generated the stone for us by means of the solution of "heaven"; that is to say, he opens the gold and leads out the soul, which you must understand as a divinity [*divinitatem*]; and for a little while he carries it in his belly and in his own time he changes it into a purified body, whence there shall come to us the boy [*puer*], the *lapis,* by whose blood the lower bodies are tinctured [*tincta*], and taken back whole to the golden heaven.[194]

506   As the *anima mundi*, Mercurius can in fact be compared with the Gnostic παρθένος τοῦ φωτός (virgin of light) and with the Christian Virgin Mary (figs. 8, 105, 107, 164, 165, 208)—or even, as the text asserts, made her "equal," though note that I am only giving the opinion of our anonymous author. The "puer" would then be the *filius macrocosmi* (figs. 64, 192, 214, 234) and as such an analogy of Christ. The author too draws this conclusion, for he compares the corporeal nature of Christ with the effects of the stone:

In Christ's body, because he committed no sin, and on account also of the miraculous union of the divine essence, there was such a great affinity [*affinitas*] of the elements and such an alliance thereof [*colligatio*] that he would never have died, had he not sought death of his own free will, in order to redeem mankind for whose sake he was born.[195]

193 The text has a misprint: "auri" instead of "audi." Cf. *Art. aurif.,* I, p. 608: "audi similitudinem arduam."
194 Ibid., p. 582.   195 Ibid., p. 686.

507   In the stone, as we know, the chaotic antagonism of the elements is replaced by the most intense mutual alliance, which is what makes the stone incorruptible, this being the reason why, in our author's opinion, it has the same effect as the blood of the Saviour: "sanitas atque vita diuturna in foelicitate, propter quam praecipue lapis noster est petendus" (health and long life in felicity, on account of which our stone is chiefly to be sought).[196]

508   To the doubtful authors also belongs the much-quoted Basilius Valentinus, a pseudonymous writer who is supposed to have lived at the beginning of the fifteenth century.[197] Johann Thölde (c. 1600), of Frankenhausen in Thuringia, is sometimes considered as the possible author of the so-called Valentinus texts, which began to appear in 1602. One of the earliest references to them is to be found in Michael Maier's *Symbola aureae mensae* (1617). Maier is exceedingly uncertain as to the authorship of these writings: "Obscurus omnibus manere quam innotescere maluit" (Rather than become notorious he preferred to remain unknown to everyone). Stylistically, the writings undoubtedly belong to the end of the sixteenth century at the earliest. The author is strongly influenced by Paracelsus and has taken over his idea of the Archaeus as well as his doctrines about astral and elemental spirits.[198] In the complete edition of 1700, now lying before me, there is an "Allegoria sanctissimae trinitatis et lapidis philosophici," from which I extract the following:

> Therefore *Mercurius philosophorum* is to be considered a spiritual body, as the philosophers call him. From God the Father was born his own Son Jesus Christ, who is God and man, and is without sin, and who also had no need to die. But he died of his own free will, and rose again for the sake of his brothers and sisters, that they

196 Ibid., p. 627.

197 According to Schmieder (*Geschichte der Alchemie*), the Emperor Maximilian ordered a search of the Benedictine monasteries in 1515 to find out whether a monk of this name was mentioned in their registers, but no such name was found. There does not seem to be any truth in this report. Nor do there seem to be any manuscripts that could be dated before the 17th century. (See Kopp, *Die Alchemie*, I, p. 31.)

198 He also mentions the *lues Gallica*, which it appears was first described as the *morbus Gallicus* (French sickness) by the Italian physician, Fracastoro, in a didactic poem published in 1530.

might live with him without sin for ever. So, too, is the gold without flaw, and is fixed, potent to withstand all examinations, and glorious; yet, for the sake of its imperfect and sick brothers and sisters, it dies and rises again, glorious and redeemed, and tinctures them to eternal life, making them perfect like to pure gold.

The third person of the Trinity is God the Holy Ghost, a comforter sent by our Lord Jesus Christ to his faithful Christians to strengthen and console them in the faith until eternal life. Therefor the *Spiritus Solis* is likewise *materialis* or *Mercurius corporis*. When they come together, he is called *Mercurius duplicatus;* that is, the two spirits, God the Father and God the Holy Ghost: but God the Son is the *homo glorificatus,* like our glorified and fixed gold, the *lapis philosophorum;* wherefore this *lapis* is also called *trinus:* namely *ex duabus aquis vel spiritibus, minerali & vegetabili,* and from the animal *sulphure Solis.*[199]

509   In the year 1619, there appeared an alchemical book of devotions entitled *Wasserstein der Weysen.* On page 67, the anonymous author says that he will now set forth how the rejected cornerstone (*lapis angularis* = Christ) "accords and is in exceeding subtle and artful agreement with the terrestrial and corporeal Philosophical Stone," from which it will be seen "how that the terrestrial Philosophical Stone is a veritable Harmonia, Contrafactur, and Prototype of the true spiritual and heavenly Stone Jesu Christ." The demonstration occupies close on fifty pages. The book made a great stir, and even Jakob Böhme is to be counted among its admirers. Kopp, who mentions the book,[200] is scandalized by the blasphemous mixture of alchemical ideas—which make use of highly obnoxious symbols—and religion. We should not, however, judge medieval naïveté too severely, but must try to understand what such an unwieldy language was intended to convey.

510   The *lapis*-Christ parallel plays an important role in Jakob Böhme (1575–1624), but I do not want to go into this here. A characteristic passage is to be found in *De signatura rerum.*[201]

511   It is clear enough from this material what the ultimate aim of alchemy really was: it was trying to produce a *corpus subtile,* a transfigured and resurrected body, i.e., a body that was at the

---

[199] Valentinus, *Chymische Schriften,* p. 364.
[200] *Die Alchemie,* I, p. 254.
[201] X, 76f., and XII, 10 (Bax, pp. 126f., 154).

same time spirit.[202] In this it finds common ground with Chinese alchemy, as we have learned from *The Secret of the Golden Flower*. There the main concern is the "diamond body," in other words, the attainment of immortality through the transformation of the body. The diamond is an excellent symbol because it is hard, fiery, and translucent. Orthelius[203] tells us that the philosophers have never found a better medicament than that which they called the noble and blessed stone of the philosophers, on account of its hardness, transparency, and rubeous hue.

512   This same Orthelius also wrote at length on the "theology" of the *lapis*. Since he is later than Böhme I mention him here only because of his preoccupation with the spirit embedded in matter:

> There are said to be two treasures: one is the written word and the other is the word become fact [*verbum factum*]. In the *verbum scriptum* Christ is still in swaddling clothes in his cradle [*in cunis suis involutus*]; but in the *verbum dictum et factum* the word is incarnate in God's creatures, and there, in a manner of speaking, we may touch it with our hands. From them we must raise up our treasure, for the word is nothing other than the fire, the life, and the spirit which the Holy Trinity did scatter abroad from the beginning of creation, and which brooded [*incubavit*] on the face of the waters, and which was breathed into [*inspiratus*] all things by the word of God, and embodied in them, as it is written: "The spirit of God filled the whole world." Some have expressed the opinion that this

---

[202] *Aurora consurgens* II, *Art. aurif.*, I, pp. 228f.: ". . . Et notandum quod duplex est sublimatio: una corporalis, alia spiritualis: corporalis quantum ad terreitatem, spiritualis quantum ad igneitatem. . . . Facite corpus spirituale et fixum volatile. . . . Senior dicit: Egrediatur spiritus a corpore qui est ignis. . . . Unde dicitur, quod tinctura fit a natura volantium: Et illud quod firmat et fixat ipsum spiritum, est fixum et perpetuum et incremabile et nominatur sulphur Philosophorum." (. . . And it is to be noted that the sublimation is twofold: one corporeal, the other spiritual; corporeal as regards earthliness, spiritual as regards fieriness. . . . Make the body spiritual, and the fixed volatile. . . . Senior says: Let the spirit which is fire go out of the body. . . . Whence it is said that the tincture arises from the nature of flying things. And that which makes the spirit itself firm and fixed, is fixed and eternal and cannot be burned and is called the sulphur of the Philosophers.)
[203] "Epilogus et recapitulatio Orthelii," *Bibl. chem. curiosa*, II, p. 527. We know of Orthelius only as a commentator on Michael Sendivogius, who lived in the second half of the 16th century.

235. Alchemical quaternity: the Three and the One (body and female
principle).—*Rosarium philosophorum* (1550)

world spirit [*spiritus mundi*] was the third person of the Godhead;
but they have not considered the word "Elohim," which, being
plural, extends to *all* persons of the Trinity. They say this spirit
proceeded from thence and was by it created, that it became corporeal and is the chief constituent of the Saviour [*salvatoris*] or
Philosophical Stone, and is the true medium whereby body and soul
are held united during our life [fig. 235].

The *spiritus mundi*, that lay upon the waters of old, impregnated them and hatched a seed within them, like a hen upon the egg. It is the virtue that dwells in the inward parts of the earth, and especially in the metals; and it is the task of the art to separate the Archaeus,[204] the *spiritus mundi*, from matter, and to produce a quintessence whose action may be compared with that of Christ upon mankind.

513   Once more the Gnostic vision of Nous entangled in the embrace of Physis flashes forth in the work of this latecomer to alchemy. But the philosopher who once descended like a Hercules into the darkness of Acheron to fulfil a divine *opus* has become a laboratory worker with a taste for speculation; having lost sight of the lofty goal of Hermetic mysticism, he now labours to discover a tonic potion that will "keep body and soul together," as our grandfathers used to say of a good wine. This change of direction in alchemy was due to the all-powerful influence of Paracelsus, the father of modern medicine. Orthelius is already tending towards natural science, leaving mystical experience to the Church.

514   Paracelsus and Böhme between them split alchemy into natural science and Protestant mysticism. The stone returned to its former condition: *vilis vilissimus*, the vilest of the vile, *in via eiectus*, thrown out into the street, like Spitteler's jewel. Morienus[205] could say again today: "Take that which is trodden underfoot in the dunghill, for if thou dost not, thou wilt fall on thine head when thou wouldst climb without steps"—meaning that if a man refuses to accept what he has spurned, it will recoil upon him the moment he wants to go higher.

515   The *lapis*-Christ parallel recurs all through the last days of alchemy in the seventeenth century, but only in epigonic form. This was the age that saw the rise of the secret societies,

---

204 "Archaeus est summus, exaltatus et invisibilis spiritus, qui separatur a corporibus, occulta naturae virtus" (The Archaeus is the highest exalted and invisible spirit, which is separated from the bodies, the hidden virtue [or quality] of nature). Cf. Ruland's *Lexicon alchemiae*, which is strongly influenced by Paracelsus.

205 Cf. Maier, *Symbola aureae mensae*, p. 141. The words quoted do not come in this form from Morienus himself, but Maier uses them as a characteristic motto for Morienus in that section of his book dealing with this author. The original passage is to be found in Morienus, "De transmut. metall.," *Art. aurif.*, II, pp. 35f.

above all the Rosicrucians—the best proof that the secret of alchemy had worn itself out. For the whole *raison d'être* of a secret
society is to guard a secret that has lost its vitality and can only
be kept alive as an outward form. Michael Maier allows us a
glimpse into this tragedy: at the end of his chef-d'œuvre he con-
fesses that in the course of his grand *peregrinatio* he found neither Mercurius nor the phoenix, but only a feather—his pen!
This is a delicate hint at his realization that the great adventure had led to nothing beyond his copious literary achievements, whose merits would no doubt have gone unremembered
had it depended solely on the spirit of the next three centuries.
But, although the growing materialism of the age dismissed alchemy as a huge disappointment and an absurd aberration, there
is yet "quaedam substantia in Mercurio quae nunquam moritur"—a fascination that never entirely disappeared, even when
wrapped in the fool's garb of goldmaking.

236. Contents of the *vas Hermetis*.
—Kelley, *Tractatus de Lapide philosophorum* (1676)

431

237. The artifex at work with his *soror mystica.—Mutus liber* (1702)

6. ALCHEMICAL SYMBOLISM IN THE HISTORY OF RELIGION

I. THE UNCONSCIOUS AS THE MATRIX OF SYMBOLS

516   After chemistry in the real sense had broken away from the groping experiments and speculations of the royal art, only the symbolism was left as a sort of phantasmal mist, seemingly devoid of all substance. Yet it never lost a certain fascinating quality, and there was always somebody who felt its enchantment in greater or lesser degree. A symbolism as rich as that of alchemy invariably owes its existence to some adequate cause, never to mere whim or play of fancy. At the very least it is the expression of an essential part of the psyche. This psyche, however, was unknown, for it is rightly called the unconscious. Although there is, materialistically speaking, no *prima materia* at the root of everything that exists, yet nothing that exists could be discerned were there no discerning psyche. Only by virtue of psychic existence do we have any "being" at all. Consciousness grasps only a fraction of its own nature, because it is the product of a preconscious psychic life which made the development of consciousness possible in the first place. Consciousness al-

432

ways succumbs to the delusion that it developed out of itself, but scientific knowledge is well aware that all consciousness rests on unconscious premises, in other words on a sort of unknown *prima materia;* and of this the alchemists said everything that we could possibly say about the unconscious. For instance, the *prima materia* comes from the mountain in which there are no differences,[1] or as Abu'l Qāsim says, it is "derived from one thing, and not from separate things, nor from things distinguishing or distinguished." [2] And in the *mysterium magnum* of Paracelsus, which is the same as the *prima materia,* "there is no kind of gender." [3] Or the *prima materia* is found in the mountain where, as Abu'l Qāsim also says, everything is upside down: "And the top of this rock is confused with its base, and its nearest part reaches to its farthest, and its head is in the place of its back, and vice versa." [4]

517   Such statements are intuitions about the paradoxical nature of the unconscious, and the only place where intuitions of this kind could be lodged was in the unknown aspect of things, be it of matter or of man. There was a feeling, often expressed in the literature, that the secret was to be found either in some strange creature or in man's brain.[5] The *prima materia*

---

[1] Abu'l Qāsim, in Holmyard, *Kitāb al-'ilm,* p. 24: "And this prime matter is found in a mountain containing an immense collection of created things. In this mountain is every sort of knowledge that is found in the world. There does not exist knowledge or understanding or dream or thought or sagacity or opinion or deliberation or wisdom or philosophy or geometry or government or power or courage or excellence or contentment or patience or discipline or beauty or ingenuity or journeying or orthodoxy or guidance or precision or growth or command or dominion or kingdom or vizierate or rule of a councillor or commerce that is not present there. And there does not exist hatred or malevolence or fraud or villainy or deceit or tyranny or oppression or perverseness or ignorance or stupidity or baseness or violence or cheerfulness or song or sport or flute or lyre or marriage or jesting or weapons or wars or blood or killing that is not present there."

[2] Ibid., p. 22.   [3] Sudhoff, XIII, p. 402.   [4] *Kitāb al-'ilm,* p. 23.

[5] "Cum igitur spiritus ille aquarum supracoelestium in cerebro sedem et locum acquisierit," etc. (When therefore that spirit of the supra-celestial waters has taken up his abode and seat in the brain . . . etc.) (Steeb, *Coelum sephiroticum,* p. 117). The "stone that is no stone" is the λίθος ἐγκέφαλος, 'brain-stone' (Berthelot, *Alch. grecs,* I, iii, 1) and the ἀλαβάστρινος ἐγκέφαλος, 'alabaster brain' (ibid., I, iv, 1); Zosimos defines the despised, and at the same time precious, material as ἀδώρητον καὶ θεοδώρητον: "not given and given by God" (ibid., III, ii, 1). "Accipe cerebrum eius": Hermes in the *Rosarium, Art. aurif.,* II, p.

433

was thought of as an ever-changing substance, or else as the essence or soul of that substance. It was designated with the name "Mercurius," and was conceived as a paradoxical double being called *monstrum, hermaphroditus,* or *rebis* (cf. figs. 125, 199). The *lapis*-Christ parallel establishes an analogy between the transforming substance and Christ (fig. 192), in the Middle Ages doubtless under the influence of the doctrine of transubstantiation, though in earlier times the Gnostic tradition of older pagan ideas was the dominant factor. Mercurius is likened to the serpent hung on the cross (John 3 : 14) (figs. 217, 238), to mention only one of the numerous parallels.

264. The "os occiput" is used in the work because "cerebrum est mansio partis divinae" (the brain is the seat of the divine part) ("Liber Platonis quartorum," *Theatr. chem.,* V, p. 124). The "occiput" is the "vas cerebri" (ibid., p. 148) (cf. figs. 75, 135). The brain is ". . . sedes animae rationalis. Nam est triangulus compositione et est propinquius omnibus membris corporis ad similitudinem simplicis . . ." (. . . the seat of the rational soul. For it is triangular in composition [shape] and is nearer to simplicity than all other parts of the body . . .) (ibid., p. 127). It is the organ which is nearest to the simplicity of the soul, and is therefore the bridge to spiritual transformation (ibid., p. 187).

238. The brazen serpent of Moses on the cross:
serpens mercurialis (cf. fig. 217).
—Eleazar, *Uraltes chymisches Werk* (1760)

Vom Einhorn.

Einhorn ist das Thier genannt/
Vnsern Landen vnbekandt.
Arlunnus schreibt daß dieses Thier/
Zu den Jungfrauwen hab begier.
In Weibskleider man leget an
Ein Jüngling hübsch/der pflegt denn an
Demselben orth/mit Geruch gehen
Da diß Thier ist/wenns thut verstehen/
Vnd also ein schön Jungfrauw findt
In jhre Schoß/legt es sich gschwindt/
Entschlefft allda/der Jäger gut
Das Horn vom Kopff segen thut.   Bn

Von einem andern Einhorn.

Hie aber sichst stehn ein Einhorn/
Gar grimmig in die Erden born.
Schwerlich das Thier zu zähmen ist/
Weils so voller Betrug vnd List.
Erst hast gehört durch groß verlangen/
Von einer Jungfraw wirdts gfangen.
Der gdültig Job auch solches klagt/
Im dreyssigst sibenden Capitel sagt:
Das Einhorn wirst nimmer binden/
Mit Riemen hart / noch vberwinden.
Es wirdt auch nicht ein einig Mann/
Diß Thier der Krippen legen an.   G   Vom

239. Unicorn, the horn a narwhal horn.—Amman, *Ein neuw Thierbuch* (1569)[5a]

II. THE PARADIGM OF THE UNICORN

a. The Unicorn in Alchemy

518   I have chosen the example of the unicorn in order to show how the symbolism of Mercurius is intermingled with the traditions of pagan Gnosticism and of the Church. The unicorn is

[5a] [The following translation, in verse 2, line 8, cites Job 39 : 9, where the passage actually is. The German versifier may have had in mind the references in Chapter 37 to the devastating power of God, signified allegorically by the unicorn.—EDITORS.

This is the Unicorn you see/
He is not found in our country.
Arlunnus says these animals
Lust greatly after pretty girls.
This way to catch him is the best/
A youth in women's clothes is dressed
And then with mincing steps he flaunts
About the Unicorn's bright haunts.
For when this creature spies a maid
Straight in her lap he lays his head.
The huntsman/ doffing his disguise/
Saws off the horn and wins the prize.

Here is another Unicorn/
Churning the ground up with his horn.
No one can tame this animal/
He is so fierce/ so full of guile.
You have just heard how he is caught
Through his desire with maids to sport.
Even the patient Job observes/
In Chapter Thirty-Nine/ ninth verse:
That man hath never yet been born
Who'll bind and break the Unicorn/
Or fix the harness to his rib/
And make him bide beside the crib.]

240. Stag and unicorn, symbolizing soul and spirit.—Lambspringk, "Figurae et emblemata," in *Musaeum hermeticum* (1625 edn.)

not a single, clearly defined entity but a fabulous being with a great many variations: there are, for instance, one-horned horses, asses, fish, dragons, scarabs, etc. Therefore, strictly speaking, we are more concerned with the theme of the single horn (the alicorn). In the *Chymical Wedding* of Rosencreutz, a snow-white unicorn appears and makes his obeisance before the lion. Lion and unicorn are both symbols of Mercurius. A little further on in the book the unicorn gives place to a white dove,[6]

6 Rosencreutz, *Chymical Wedding*, p. 73. Concerning the dove, cf. *Aurora* I, Ch. VI: "Nive dealbabuntur in Selmon, et pennae columbae deargenteatae et posteriora dorsi eius in pallore auri: talis erit mihi filius dilectus. . . ." (They shall be whited with snow in Selmon, and shall be as the wings of a dove covered with silver, and the hinder parts of her back with the paleness of gold. Such shall be to me a beloved son.) Grasseus, "Arca arcani," *Theatr. chem.*, VI,

another symbol of Mercurius, who, in his volatile form of *spiritus,* is a parallel of the Holy Ghost. At least ten out of the fifteen figures in Lambspringk's symbols[7] are representations of the dual nature of Mercurius. Figure III shows the unicorn facing a stag (fig. 240). The latter, as *cervus fugitivus,* is also a symbol of Mercurius.[8] Mylius[9] illustrates the *opus* by a series of seven symbols, of which the sixth is the unicorn couched under a tree, symbolizing the spirit of life that leads the way to resurrection (cf. fig. 188). Penotus[10] gives a table of symbols where the unicorn, together with the lion, the eagle, and the dragon, is the co-ordinate of gold. The *aurum non vulgi,* like the lion,[11] eagle, and dragon,[12] is a synonym for Mercurius. The poem entitled "Von der Materi und Prattick des Steins"[13] says:

> I am the right true Unicorn.
> What man can cleave me hoof from horn
> And join my body up again
> So that it no more falls in twain?

519   Here I must refer once again to Ripley, where we meet the "green lion lying in the queen's lap with blood flowing from his

---

p. 314: "Plumbum philosophorum . . . in quo splendida columba alba inest, quae sal metallorum vocatur, in quo magisterium operis consistit. Haec est casta sapiens et dives illa regina ex Saba velo albo induta. . . ." (The lead of the philosophers in which is the shining white dove, which is called the salt of metals, in which consists the magistery of the work. This is that chaste, wise, and rich queen of Sheba clothed n a white veil.) *Aurora* I, Ch. XII: "Et dabit mihi pennas sicut columbae [Vulg., Ps. 54 : 7] et volabo cum ea in coelo et dicam tunc: Vivo ego in aeternum [Deut. 32 : 40]. . . ." ([And she will] give me wings like a dove, and I will fly with her to heaven, and then say: I live for ever.)

7 *Mus. herm.,* pp. 338ff.; originally in Barnaud, *Triga chemica.*

8 The fourth illustration in *Musaeum Hermeticum,* placed before the first treatise.   9 *Philosophia reformata,* p. 316.   10 *Theatr. chem.,* II, p. 123.

11 Medieval tradition associates the unicorn with the lion "because this animal is as strong, wild, and cruel as the lions." "This," says Andreas Baccius, "is the reason why they called this animal *lycornu* in France and Italy." Here *lycornu* is evidently derived from "lion." Cf. Catelanus, *Ein schöner newer historischer Discurs, von der Natur, Tugenden, Eigenschafften, und Gebrauch dess Einhorns,* p. 22.

12 Much the same is said of the unicorn as of the dragon, which as a denizen of the underworld lives in gorges and caverns. Thus unicorns "hide themselves and dwell in barren places on the high mountains, in the deepest, darkest, and most out-of-the-way caves and dens of wild beasts, amid toads and other noxious, loathly reptiles." Ibid., p. 23.   13 *Theatr. chem.,* IV, p. 286.

241. Virgin taming a unicorn.—Thomas Aquinas (pseud.), "De alchimia" (MS., 16th cent.)

side." This image is an allusion on the one hand to the Pietà, on the other to the unicorn wounded by the hunter and caught in the lap of a virgin (figs. 241, 242), a frequent theme in medieval pictures. True, the green lion has replaced the unicorn here, but that did not present any difficulty to the alchemist since the lion is likewise a symbol of Mercurius. The virgin represents his passive, feminine aspect, while the unicorn or the lion illustrates the wild, rampant, masculine, penetrating force of the *spiritus mercurialis*. Since the symbol of the unicorn as an allegory of Christ and of the Holy Ghost was current all through the Middle Ages, the connection between them was certainly known to the alchemists, so that there can be no question that Ripley had in his mind, when he used this symbol, the affinity, indeed the identity, of Mercurius with Christ.

242. Slaying the unicorn in the Virgin's lap. (Note the significance of
the "wound in his side.")—Initial from MS. Harley 4751, London

b. The Unicorn in Ecclesiastical Allegory

520   The language of the Church borrows its unicorn allegories
from the Psalms, where the unicorn stands in the first place for
the might of the Lord, as in Psalm 29 : 6: "He maketh them also
to skip like a calf; Lebanon and Sirion like a young unicorn" [14];
and in the second place for the vitality of man (figs. 243, 244), as
in Psalm 92 : 10: "But my horn shalt thou exalt like the horn of
an unicorn. . . ." [15] The power of evil is also compared to the

[14] Vulgate: ". . . et comminuet eas tamquam vitulum Libani: et dilectus quemadmodum filius unicornium." (D.V., Ps. 28 : 6: "And [he] shall reduce them to
pieces; as a calf of Libanus, and as the beloved son of unicorns.")
[15] Vulgate: "Et exaltabitur sicut unicornis cornu meum. . . ." (D.V., Ps. 91 : 11:
"But my horn shall be exalted like that of the unicorn. . . .")

439

243. Unicorn crest of the von Gachnang family (Thurgau, Switzerland).—From the Zurich Roll of Arms (1340)

strength of the unicorn, as in Psalm 22 : 21: "Save me from the lion's mouth: for thou hast heard me from the horns of the unicorns." [16] On these metaphors is based Tertullian's allusion to Christ: "His glory is that of a bull, his horn is that of a unicorn." [17] This refers to the blessing of Moses (Deut. 33 : 13, 14, 17):

> . . . Blessed of the Lord be his land, for the precious things of heaven, for the dew, and for the deep that coucheth beneath,
> And for the precious fruits brought forth by the sun, and for the precious things put forth by the moon, . . .
> His glory is like the firstling of his bullock, and his horns are like the horns of unicorns: with them he shall push the people together to the ends of the earth. . . .

521   From this it is clear that the horn of the unicorn signifies the health, strength, and happiness of the blessed. "Thus," says Tertullian, "Christ was named the bull on account of two qualities: the one hard [*ferus*, 'wild, untamed'] as a judge, the other gentle [*mansuetus*, 'tame'] as a saviour. His horns are the ends of the cross. . . ." Justin Martyr[18] interprets the same passage

[16] Vulgate: "Salva me ex ore leonis, et a cornibus unicornium humilitatem meam." (D.V., Ps. 21 : 22: "Save me from the lion's mouth; and my lowness from the horns of the unicorns.")
[17] "Tauri decor eius, cornua unicornis, cornua eius." (Tertullian, *Adversus Judaeos*, Ch. X; Migne, *P.L.*, vol. 2, col. 626.)
[18] "Dialogus cum Tryphone Judaeo," ch. 91 (Migne, *P.G.*, vol. 6, col. 691).

244. The glorification of Ariosto. (The horse's forelock is twisted into a stiff plait to make it look like the horn of the unicorn.)—Drawing by Giovanni Battista Benvenuti, called Ortolano (1488–?1525)

245. The Virgin Mary with the loving unicorn in the "enclosed garden."—
Swiss tapestry (1480)

in a similar way: *"Cornua unicornis cornu eius.* For no one can say or prove that the horns of the unicorn could be found in any other object or in any other shape than in that represented by the cross." For the might of God is manifest in Christ. Accordingly Priscillian calls God one-horned: "One-horned is God, Christ a rock to us, Jesus a cornerstone, Christ the man of men." [19] Just as the unicorn symbolizes the uniqueness of the Unigenitus, so St. Nilus uses it to express the fearless independence of the καλόγηρος, the monk: Μονόκερώς ἐστιν οὗτος, ζῷον αὐτόνομον (he is a unicorn, a creature on his own).[20]

522   St. Basil takes the *filius unicornium* to be Christ. The origin of the unicorn is a mystery, says St. Ambrose, like Christ's procreation. Nicolas Caussin, from whom I have culled these extracts, observes that the unicorn is a fitting symbol for the God of the Old Testament, because in his wrath he reduced the world to confusion like an angry rhinoceros (unicorn) until, made captive by love, he was soothed in the lap of a virgin.[21]

19 "Unicornis est Deus, nobis petra Christus, nobis lapis angularis Jesus, nobis hominum homo Christus." Priscillian, *Opera,* p. 24.
20 *Vita,* Migne, *P.G.,* vol. 120, col. 69, ch. XCI. The hermit-nature of the unicorn is mentioned in Aelian, *De natura animalium,* xvi, 20.
21 *De symbolica Aegyptiorum sapientia,* p. 401. Cf. also p. 348: "[Dei] fortitudo similis est Rhinoceroti, Exod. 15. Unicornis non admittit in antro cohabitatorem:

246. Mandala with four ornamental medallions containing a stag, lion, griffin, and unicorn. —Pavement from St. Urban's Monastery, Lucerne

This ecclesiastical train of thought has its parallel in the alchemical taming of the lion and the dragon (fig. 246). Concerning the conversion of the Old Testament Jehovah into the God of Love in the New Testament, Picinelli says: "Of a truth God, terrible beyond measure, appeared before the world peaceful and wholly tamed after dwelling in the womb of the most blessed Virgin. St. Bonaventure said: Christ was tamed and pacified by the most kindly Mary, so that he should not punish the sinner with eternal death." [22]

filius Dei aedificavit in saecula, hoc est in utero B[eatae] V[irginis]." (The strength of God is similar to [that of] the Rhinoceros, Exod. 15. The Unicorn does not admit of a fellow-dweller in his cave. The son of God has built for the centuries, i.e., in the womb of the Blessed Virgin.) Cf. Ps. 77 : 69: "Et aedificavit sicut unicornium sanctificium suum, in terra quam fundavit in saecula" (D.V.: "And he built his sanctuary as of unicorns, in the land which he founded for ever"; A.V., Ps. 78 : 69: "And he built his sanctuary like high palaces, like the earth which he hath established for ever"). Pp. 348f.: "The horn of the unicorn acts as an alexipharmic, because it expels the poison from the water, and this refers allegorically to the baptism of Christ [i.e., the consecration of the baptismal water]: rightly is it applied to Christ baptized, who, like the chosen son of unicorns, sanctified the streams of water to wash away the filth of all our sins, as Bede says." The wildness of the unicorn is emphasized in Job (A.V.) 39 : 9–10: "Will the unicorn be willing to serve thee, or abide by thy crib? Canst thou bind the unicorn with his band in the furrow? or will he harrow the valleys after thee?"

22 *Mundus symbolicus*, I, 419, b: "S. Bonaventura: Christus, inquit, per mansuetissimam Mariam mansuescit et placatur, ne se de peccatore per mortem aeternam ulciscatur." The myth of the virgin and the unicorn is handed down by Isidore of Seville (*Etymologiarum*, xii, 62). The source book is the *Physiologus Graecus:*

247. Virgin with unicorn.—Khludov Psalter
(Byzantine, 9th cent.)

523   In his *Speculum de mysteriis ecclesiae,* Honorius of Autun says:

The very fierce animal with only one horn is called unicorn. In order to catch it, a virgin is put in a field; the animal then comes to her and is caught, because it lies down in her lap. Christ is represented by this animal, and his insuperable strength[23] by its horn. He, who lay down in the womb of the Virgin, has been caught by the hunters; that is to say, he was found in human shape by those who loved him[24] [fig. 247].

Πῶς δὲ ἀγρεύεται; παρθένον ἁγνὴν ῥίπτουσιν ἔμπροσθεν αὐτοῦ. Καὶ ἄλλεται εἰς τὸν κόλπον τῆς παρθένου καὶ ἡ παρθένος θάλπει τὸ ζῷον καὶ αἴρει εἰς τὸ παλάτιον τῶν βασιλέων. (How is it hunted? They cast a sacred virgin before it. And it leaps into the lap of the virgin, and the virgin warms the animal with love and bears it to the palace of the kings.)—Pitra, *Spicilegium solesmense,* III, p. 355 ("Veterum Gnosticorum in Physiologum allegoricae interpretationes"). The *Physiologus* may go back to Didymus of Alexandria, a Christian hermeneutic of the 4th cent.

23 "Insuperabilis fortitudo," cf. "Tab. smarag.," "Totius fortitudinis fortitudo fortis" (Strong strength of all strength). Honorius, *Speculum,* Migne, *P.L.,* vol. 172, col. 847: "[Christus] . . . cuius virtus ut unicornis fuit, quia omnia obstantia cornu supprimit, quia Christus principatus et potestates mundi cornibus crucis perdomuit" ([Christ] . . . whose strength [virtue] was like that of the unicorn, because he crushed all that was in his way with his horn, for Christ subjugated the principalities and powers of the world with the horns of the cross).

24 "Qui in uterum Virginis se reclinans captus est a venatoribus id est in humana forma inventus est a suis amatoribus."

444

248. The creation of Eve, prefiguring the story of salvation: hence the presence of the unicorn.—"Trésor de sapience" (MS., 15th cent.)

⁵²⁴ St. Rupert[25] compares Christ to the rhinoceros, and Bruno of Würzburg[26] simply calls him *cornu* (horn). Caussin writes that Albertus Magnus, in his "Hypotyposes," mentions the Virgin in connection with the monoceros. Albertus was an expert on alchemy and drew his quotations from the Hermetic treatises. In the "Tabula smaragdina" there is a "son" of immense strength who comes down to earth and penetrates everything

[25] *De Trinitate* (Migne, *P.L.*, vol. 167, col. 1739).
[26] *Expositio psalmorum* (Migne, *P.L.*, vol. 142, col. 182): "In te inimicos nostros ventilabimus cornu. Et in nomine tuo spernemus insurgentes in nobis . . . cornu vero nostrum Christus est, idem et nomen Patris in quo adversarii nostri vel ventilantur vel spernuntur." (In thee we shall crush our enemies with the horn. In thy name we shall scorn those that rise up against us . . . but our horn is Christ, and also the name of the Father through whom our adversaries are crushed or scorned.)

249. Wild unicorn.—From Bock,
Kräuterbuch (1595)

solid. It is not only in astrology that Virgo is an earth-sign: in Tertullian and Augustine the Virgin actually signifies earth (fig. 248). Isidore of Seville emphasizes the "perforating" effects of the unicorn.[27] In the "Tabula" the mother-son incest is very thinly disguised,[28] a fact of which the alchemist Albertus was possibly aware.

525   As I said before, the unicorn has more than one meaning. It can also mean evil. The *Physiologus Graecus*,[29] for instance, says

[27] *Etymologiarum* (Migne, *P.L.*, vol. 82), xii, 62: ". . . aut ventilet aut perforet."
[28] It is true that the son's mother is the moon, but "nutrix eius terra est" (the earth is his nurse) (cf. fig. 163). "Ascendit a terra in coelum": therefore he is of earthly origin, ascends to heaven and returns again to permeate the earth.
[29] Sbordone, *Physiologus*, p. 263, 1–8.

of the unicorn that "it is a swift-running animal, having one horn, and evilly disposed towards man" (μνησίκακον δὲ ὑπάρχει ἐν ἀνθρώποις). And St. Basil says: "And take heed unto thyself, O man, and beware of the unicorn, who is the Demon [fig. 249]. For he plotteth evil against man, and he is cunning in evil-doing."

526 These examples should suffice to show how close is the connection between alchemical symbolism and the language of the Church. It is to be noted in the ecclesiastical quotations that the unicorn also contains the element of evil (fig. 250). Originally a monstrous and fabulous beast, it harbours in itself an inner contradiction, a *complexio oppositorum,* which makes it a singularly appropriate symbol for the *monstrum hermaphroditum* of alchemy.[30]

30 The monstrous nature of the unicorn is described by Pliny (*Hist. nat.,* Lib. VIII, ch. 21): A horse's body, an elephant's feet, and the tail of a wild boar. There is a fantastic description, which might have been especially interesting to alchemists, in the Ἰνδικά of Ctesias (*c.* 400 B.C.): "From what I hear, the wild ass in India is not much smaller than the horse. The head is of a purplish hue but the rest of the body is white, and the colour of the eyes is dark blue. There is a horn on the forehead, nearly one and a half cubits in length; the lower part of the horn is white, the upper part purple, but the middle is pitch black. I hear that the Indians drink out of these brightly coloured horns, but only the most aristocratic Indians. Moreover the horns are bound at intervals with gold rings for this purpose, as the beautiful arm of a statue is decorated with bracelets. They say that anyone who drinks from this horn is immune to incurable diseases, for he is not seized by spasms or killed by poisons and, if he has drunk anything harmful, he vomits and is cured." (*Ancient India,* trans. McCrindle, p. 363.) Also Aelian, *De natura animalium,* IV, 52, III, 41, and XVI, 20. In the last passage, Aelian says that in India the animal is called the "Kartazonon": "The strength of its horn is invincible. It is fond of lonely pastures and wanders about alone. . . . It seeks solitude." Philostratus, in his *Vita Apollonii* (Book III, ch. 2), relates that when anyone drinks from a cup made of a unicorn's horn, he is immune throughout the day to illness and pain, he can also walk through fire, and the strongest poison does him no harm. In the Χριστιανικὴ Τοπογραφία of Kosmas (beginning of the 6th century), it is related that the unicorn, in order to escape from its hunters, will plunge into an abyss and land on its horn, which is so strong that it breaks the fall (trans. McCrindle, p. 361). The complete patristic literature is to be found in Salzer, *Die Sinnbilder,* pp. 44ff.

447

250. Wild man riding the unicorn.—Engraving from the sequence of the *Grösseres Kartenspiel,* by the monogrammist E.S. (*c.* 1463)

c. The Unicorn in Gnosticism

527   There is also a connection between the language of the Church and pagan Gnostic symbolism. Hippolytus, giving an account of the doctrine of the Naassenes, says that the serpent dwells in all things and creatures, and that all temples were named after her (ναοὺς ἀπὸ τοῦ νάας: a play on the words νάας = serpent, ναός = temple). Every shrine, he says, every initiation (τελετή), and every mystery is dedicated to the serpent. This immediately recalls the passage in the "Tabula smaragdina": "Pater omnis telesmi totius mundi est hic" (This is the father of the perfection of the whole world). Τέλος, τελετή, and τελεσμός all mean the same: perfection and maturation of the *corpora imperfecta*, and of the alchemist himself.[31]

> These [Naassenes] say that the serpent is the moist element, as Thales of Miletus also said,[32] and that nothing which exists, whether immortal or mortal, animate or inanimate, could exist without it.

528   This definition of the serpent agrees with the alchemical Mercurius, who is likewise a kind of water: the "divine water" (ὕδωρ θεῖον), the wet, the *humidum radicale* (radical moisture), and the spirit of life, not only indwelling in all living things, but immanent in everything that exists, as the world-soul. Hippolytus continues:

> They say, too, that all things are subject to her [the serpent], that she is good and has something of everything in herself as in the horn of the one-horned bull [ἐν κέρατι ταύρου μονοκέρωτος]. She imparts beauty and ripeness to all things. . . .

529   Like the alicorn, therefore, the serpent is an alexipharmic and the principle that brings all things to maturity and perfection. We are already familiar with the unicorn as a symbol of Mercurius, the transforming substance par excellence which also ripens and perfects unripe or imperfect bodies and is consequently acclaimed in alchemy as the *salvator* and *servator*. "The serpent," says Hippolytus, "penetrates everything, as if coming

31 See Jung, "Paracelsus the Physician," pars. 27f., and "Paracelsus as a Spiritual Phenomenon," par. 158.
32 Thales taught that water was the first principle.

251. The seven stages of the alchemical process shown as a unity.—"Ripley Scrowle" (MS., 1588)

forth from Edem and dividing herself into the four first principles."[33] That everything proceeds from the One is a fundamental tenet of alchemy (fig. 251): "As all things proceed from the One . . . so all things are born of this one thing," says the "Tabula smaragdina"; and also that the One divides into the four elements (fig. 252) and then recombines into unity. The *prima materia* is called among other things the "paradisal earth" which Adam took with him on his expulsion from Paradise. *Mercurius philosophorum* consists of the four elements (cf. fig. 214). In one of the Mystery hymns quoted by Hippolytus, Osiris is named the "heavenly horn of the moon" (ἐπουράνιον μηνὸς κέρας), and the same primal being is also called Sophia and

[33] The passages quoted above are to be found in Hippolytus, *Elenchos*, V, 9, 12 to 15.

252. Chastity.—"Les Triomphes du Pétrarche" (MS., 16th cent.)

253. Harpokrates encircled by the Uroboros.—
Gnostic gem

Adam.[34] These analogies we already know in their alchemical aspect. Another one mentioned by Hippolytus is the "many-formed Attis." The changeability and multiformity of Mercurius is a key idea in alchemy. It is hardly necessary to enter into the ideas which this pagan system took over from Christianity; comparison with the Christian quotations should suffice.

d. The One-Horned Scarabaeus

530   An important source of information concerning the unicorn symbolism of Mercurius is the *Hieroglyphica* of Horapollo (ch. 10). This author says that the third genus of the scarab is unicorned (μονόκερως) and, on account of this peculiarity, sacred to Mercurius, like the ibis. Moreover the scarab is a μονογενής (only-begotten, *unigena*) in so far as it is an αὐτογενὲς ζῷον (a creature born of itself). In Paracelsus the *prima materia* is an *increatum,* and throughout alchemy, as Mercurius, *serpens,* or *draco,* it is bisexual, capable of self-fertilization and self-parturition (fig. 253). The *unicus filius* is the *filius philosophorum,* i.e., the stone. The scarab undergoes the same dismemberment as the dragon, the "separation of the elements," in a papyrus text: "The sun-beetle, the winged ruler standing at heaven's meridian, was beheaded and dismembered." [35] I would also mention the "sixth parable" in "Splendor solis," [36] where the *separatio* is portrayed as a dismembered corpse, accompanied by the text: "Rosinus[37] says that he would like to make plain a vision

34 Ibid., V, 9, 8.
35 From a Greek magic papyrus in Preisendanz, *Papyri Graecae Magicae,* II, p. 60, lines 44f.   36 *Aureum vellus.*   37 "Rosinus" is a corruption of Zosimos.

that he has seen of a man who was dead, whose body was yet all white like a salt, and whose limbs were divided, and his head was of fine gold but separated from the body. . . ."[38] The golden head referred originally to the head of Osiris who is described in a Greek papyrus as "headless."[39] The Greek alchemists styled themselves "Children of the Golden Head."[40]

531   The scarab is seldom mentioned in alchemical literature, but among the old texts it can be found in the "Consilium coniugii": "Nulla aqua fit quelles, nisi illa que fit de scarabaeis aquae nostrae"[41] (No water will become the elixir save that which comes from the scarabs of our water). The *aqua nostra* is nothing other than the *aqua divina*, i.e., Mercurius.

e. The Unicorn in the Vedas

532   The track of the unicorn in pre-Christian days leads us to the East.[42] We meet it as early as the hymns of the Atharva-Veda (III, 7) in a "charm against *kshetriya,* hereditary disease":[43]

1. Upon the head of the nimble antelope a remedy grows! He has driven the *kshetriya* in all directions by means of the horn.
2. The antelope has gone after thee with his four feet. O horn, loosen the *kshetriya* that is knitted into his heart!
3. (The horn) that glistens yonder like a roof with four wings (sides), with that do we drive out every *kshetriya* from thy limbs.

[38] This recalls the mysterious saying "Aufer caput, corpus ne tangito" (Carry away the head, but don't touch the body).—Béroalde de Verville, *Le Songe de Poliphile,* Folio c, III.

[39] From a Greek magic papyrus in Preisendanz, *Papyri Graecae Magicae,* I, p. 185, line 99.

[40] Χρυσέας κεφαλῆς παῖδες (Berthelot, III, x, 1).

[41] *Ars chem.,* p. 119.

[42] I had better not enter into the question of whether the unicorn existed in Assyrian and Babylonian culture. Schrader ("Die Vorstellung vom Μονόκερως," pp. 573ff.) tries to derive the whole idea of the unicorn from the representations of what appear to be one-horned animals, such as those of Persepolis, thus, in my opinion, falsely interpreting these monuments. He does not, however, take the Indian sources into account.

[43] Bloomfield, *Hymns of the Atharva-Veda,* p. 15.

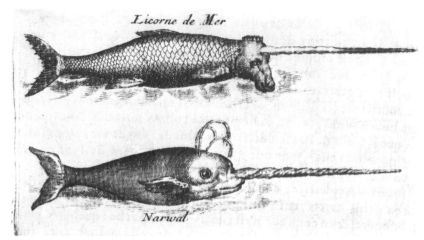

254. The so-called sea-unicorn (*monodon, monoceros*). Its tusk was used as a model in old pictures of the unicorn.—Pommet, *Histoire générale des drogues* (1694)

533   The fish of Manu (cf. fig. 254) seems to have been unicorned, although this is not specifically stated: but always its horn is mentioned, never its horns. According to the legend recounted in the Shatapatha-Brahmana,[44] Manu hooked a fish which grew larger and larger and eventually towed him over the flood to dry land. Manu tied his ship to its horn.[45] The fish is an incarnation of Vishnu (fig. 255), and Manu means "man."[46] In many respects he corresponds to the Greek Anthropos: he is the father of humanity and is descended direct from God, here called Svayambhu, the "Self-So," i.e., Brahma. He is a God-man, identified with Prajapati, Lord of created things, and even with Brahman itself, the highest soul. In the Rig-Veda he is named Father Manu, and is said to have begotten mankind on his daughter. He is the founder of the social and moral order,[47] the first sacrificiant and priest.[48] He transmitted the Upanishadic

44 Eggeling, *Shatapatha-Brahmana*, pp. 216ff.
45 "The fish then swam up to him, and to its horn he tied the rope of the ship and by that means he passed swiftly up to yonder northern mountain [Himalaya]" (ibid., p. 217, 5).
46 Bühler, *Laws of Manu*, Introduction, p. xiv. Manu "is the *heros eponymos* of the human race, and by his nature belongs both to gods and to men" (ibid., p. lvii).   47 Ibid., pp. lvii f.
48 *Vedic Hymns*, Part II, p. 96: "As thou didst perform sacrifice to the gods with the sacrificial food of the wise Manu, a sage together with sages, thus, O highly truthful Hotri," etc.

255. Vishnu in his fish incarnation.—18th-cent. Indian miniature

doctrine to mankind.[49] It is of particular interest that he is also derived from the androgynous Viraj. The Shatapatha-Brahmana associates him with a bull who was entrusted with the task of annihilating the Asuras and Rakshas (demons hostile to the gods).[50] Lastly, Manu is the father of medicine,[51] and, in Buddhist tradition, Lord of the Golden Age.[52] The horn, then, is connected with a figure which, in both name and character, has close affinities with the Anthropos.

534   The virgin and unicorn motif is to be found in the Ramayana and in the Mahabharata (III, 110–113). A hermit by name of Rishyashringa (gazelle's horn), son of Vibhandaka or Ekasringa (one-horn), is fetched out of his solitary retreat by the king's daughter Shanta, who marries him; or, in another version, he is seduced by a courtesan. Only by this means can the terrible drought that is scourging the land be broken.[53]

f. The Unicorn in Persia

535   There is an impressive account of the unicorn in the Bundahish (Ch. XIX):

Regarding the three-legged ass, they say that it stands amid the wide-formed ocean, and its feet are three, eyes six, mouths nine, ears two, and horn one, body white, food spiritual, and it is righteous. And two of its six eyes are in the position of eyes, two on the top of the head, and two in the position of the hump; with the sharpness of those six eyes it overcomes and destroys. Of the nine mouths three are in the head, three in the hump, and three in the inner part of the flanks; and each mouth is about the size of a cottage, and it is itself as large as Mount Alvand. Each one of the three feet, when it is placed on the ground, is as much as a flock of a thousand sheep comes under when they repose together; and each pastern is so great

49 Chhandogya Upanishad, Part I, p. 44, 4.
50 Eggeling, *Shatapatha-Brahmana*, p. 29, 14.
51 *Vedic Hymns*, Part I, p. 427, 13: "O Maruts, those pure medicines of yours, the most beneficent and delightful, O heroes, those which Manu, our father, chose, those I crave from Rudra, as health and wealth."
52 Cf. my remarks on the Adech of Paracelsus ("Paracelsus as a Spiritual Phenomenon," pars. 168, 203ff.).
53 Holtzmann, *Indische Sagen*, pp. 131ff.; and Lüders, *Nachrichten*. The story is also to be found in the Buddhist Jataka 526 (trans. Cowell, V, pp. 100–106).

256. Fabulous monster
containing the *massa confusa*, from which rises the
pelican (symbol of Christ
and the *lapis*).—*Herma-
phroditisches Sonn- und
Mondskind* (1752)

in its circuit that a thousand men with a thousand horses may pass
inside. As for the two ears, it is Mazendaran which they will en-
compass. The one horn is as it were of gold and hollow, and a
thousand branch horns have grown upon it, some befitting a camel,
some befitting a horse, some befitting an ox, some befitting an ass,
both great and small. With that horn it will vanquish and dissipate
all the vile corruption due to the efforts of noxious creatures.

When that ass shall hold its neck in the ocean its ears will terrify,
and all the water of the wide-formed ocean will shake with agita-
tion, and the side of Ganavad will tremble. When it utters a cry all
the female water-creatures, of the creatures of Auharmazd, will become pregnant; and all pregnant noxious water-creatures, when they
hear that cry, will cast their young. When it stales in the ocean all
the sea-water will become purified, which is in the seven regions of
the earth—it is even on that account when all asses which come
into water stale in the water—as it says thus: "If, O three-legged
ass! you were not created for the water, all the water in the sea

457

would have perished from the contamination which the poison of the evil spirit has brought into its water, through the death of the creatures of Auharmazd."

Tîstar seizes the water more completely from the ocean with the assistance of the three-legged ass. Of ambergris also (ambar-ik) it is declared, that it is the dung of the three-legged ass; for if it has much spirit food, then also the moisture of the liquid nourishment goes through the veins pertaining to the body into the urine, and the dung is cast away.[54]

536   The monster is evidently based on the number three. Its ass aspect is reminiscent of the Indian wild onager in Ctesias, but, as a cosmological being, it recalls the monstrous personifications of the *prima materia* (fig. 256) in Arabic alchemy. In the "Book of Ostanes," for instance, one such monster (with the wings of a vulture, the head of an elephant, and the tail of a dragon) gives the adept the key to the treasure-house.[55] The ass stands in the ocean, like the tree Gokard that grows from the deep mud of the sea.[56] The Bundahish says of this tree:

. . . it is necessary as a producer of the renovation of the universe, for they prepare its immortality therefrom. . . . Some say it is the proper-curing, some the energetic-curing, some the all-curing.[57]

537   The ass and the tree[58] are evidently related, because they both represent the power of life, procreation, and healing. This is a truly primitive equation: both are or have mana. The Arabic

54 West, *Pahlavi Texts*, pp. 67ff.
55 Berthelot, *Chimie au moyen âge*, III, p. 120.
56 West, *Pahlavi Texts*, p. 65 (XVIII, 1).
57 Ibid., pp. 65–66 (XVIII, 1, 9).
58 In this connection we may note the curious fact that a lizard is concealed in the tree: "The evil spirit has formed therein, among those which enter as opponents, a lizard as an opponent in that deep water, so that it may injure the Hôm" (Bundahish, XVIII, 2 in West, *Pahlavi Texts*, p. 65). Hôm = Haoma, the plant of immortality. In alchemy, the *spiritus mercurii* that lives in the tree is represented as serpent, salamander, or Melusina. We find the last-mentioned in the "Ripley Scrowle," where the lizard is half a woman and is celebrating the *coniunctio* (marriage) with the *filius philosophorum* (see fig. 257). The "Verses belonging to an Emblematicall Scrowle" (*Theatr. chem. Brit.*, p. 375) run as follows:

"And Azot is truly my Sister,
And Kibrick forsooth is my Brother:
The Serpent of Arabia is my name,
The which is leader of all this game."

257. The transformations of Mercurius. The Melusina (Lilith) on the
tree is Sapientia.—"Ripley Scrowle" (MS., 1588)

alchemists likewise obtain their *prima materia* from the tree in the western land. We read in the book of Abu'l Qāsim:[59]

> This prime matter which is proper for the form of the Elixir is taken from a single tree which grows in the lands of the West. . . . And this tree grows on the surface of the ocean as plants grow on the surface of the earth. This is the tree of which whosoever eats, man and jinn obey him; it is also the tree of which Adam (peace be upon him!) was forbidden to eat, and when he ate thereof he was transformed from his angelic form to human form. And this tree may be changed into every animal shape.

538   The monster and the tree both stand for the φάρμακον ἀθα-vασίας, the elixir, the alexipharmic, and the panacea. The tree's peculiar power to change into any animal shape is also attributed to *Mercurius versipellis* (fig. 257).

539   The ass is a *daemon triunus*, a chthonic trinity, which is portrayed in Latin alchemy as a three-headed monster and identified with Mercurius, salt, and sulphur.[60] The classical rumour about the worship of an ass in the Temple of Jerusalem, and the graffito on the Palatine showing a mock crucifixion,[61] I will mention only in passing; likewise the saturnine aspect of Jehovah and Ialdabaoth as demiurges, which brings these figures into conjunction with the equally saturnine *prima materia*.

g. *The Unicorn in Jewish Tradition*

540   The Talmud[62] tells the story of how the unicorn (*re'em*) escaped the flood: it was tied to the outside of the ark because, owing to its gigantic size, it could not go inside. Og, the King of Bashan, survived the flood in the same way. The passage runs:

> The preservation of the unicorn is easily explained by those who say that the flood did not descend on the Land of Israel; but how was it preserved in the opinion of those who say that the flood did descend? R. Jannai answered: They took young unicorns into the ark.—But Rabba b. Bar Hana reported that he had seen a young

59 Holmyard, *Kitāb al-'ilm,* p. 23.
60 Cf. fig. 54 and "Paracelsus as a Spiritual Phenomenon," frontispiece.
61 [Reproduced in *Symbols of Transformation,* pl. XLIII.]
62 Goldschmidt, *Der babylonische Talmud,* X, p. 359 ("Tractate Zebahim," Fol. 113b). Cf. the *Talmud,* ed. Epstein, "Tract. Zebahim," pp. 559f.

unicorn as large as Mount Tabor, which measures forty parasangs, and that the girth of its neck was three parasangs, and its head one and a half parasangs, and that the Jordan was choked with the dirt it voided.[63] R. Johanan answered: They took [only] its head into the ark.—But the master said that its head measured one and a half parasangs.—Peradventure they took the tip of its nose into the ark.— . . . But when the ark rose on the water?—Reš Laqiš answered: They tied its horns to the ark.—But R. Hisda said that they had sinned with heat and were punished with hot water.[64]— How was the ark preserved [65] in your opinion? And moreover where was Og, the King of Bashan? [66]—Peradventure a miracle happened to them and [the water] remained cold at the sides of the ark.

541   There is a corresponding version of this story in the midrash collection entitled *Pirkê R. Eliezer*, according to which Og "sat down on a piece of wood under the gutter of the ark." [67]

542   The "Targum Pseudo-Jonathan," commenting on Genesis 14 : 13, says that Og stayed on the roof of the ark.[68]

543   According to one Talmud legend,[69] Og was descended from one of the fallen angels mentioned in Genesis 6 who "came in unto" the daughters of men: "Take note, Sihon and Og were brothers, for the master said: 'Sihon and Og were the sons of Ahijah the son of Samhazai.'" [70] The commentary of Rashi says that Sihon and Og were the sons of Ahijah "who was descended from Shemhazai and Azael, the two angels who came down to earth in the days of Enoch."

---

63 Cf. the parallel passage in Goldschmidt, *Der babylonische Talmud*, VIII, p. 203 ("Tractate Baba Bathra," Fol. 73b; *Talmud*, ed. Epstein, pp. 290f.).

64 The water was hot, so that even if the unicorn had been able to breathe, it would still have been scalded to death. (See Goldschmidt's comments.)

65 This refers to Gen. 6 : 14, where the ark was smeared with pitch within and without. The pitch would have been melted by the hot water. (See Goldschmidt's comments.)

66 The Talmud saga according to which Og survived the flood is to be found in *Der babylonische Talmud*, XII, p. 552 ("Tractate Nidda," Fol. 61a; *Talmud*, ed. Epstein, p. 433): "For it is said [Gen. 14 : 13]: 'and there came one that had escaped, and told Abram the Hebrew,' and R. Johanan said: 'That was Og who escaped the flood.'"

67 Trans. Friedlander, p. 167. Zunz (*Die gottesdienstlichen Vorträge*, p. 277) dates this collection to the 8th cent. at earliest.

68 Retold in Joseph bin Gorion, *Sagen der Juden*, I, p. 208.

69 *Der babylonische Talmud*, XII, p. 552 ("Tractate Nidda," Fol. 61a; *Talmud*, ed. Epstein, p. 433).

70 The most important of the giants mentioned in Gen. 6 : 4. (See Goldschmidt's comments.)

544   Og's gigantic size is described in several passages of the Talmud—probably at its most gigantic in "Tractate Nidda":[71]

Abba Saul, according to others R. Johanan, said: "I was a digger of graves. One day I was chasing a deer, and I found myself inside the thigh-bone of a dead man; I chased the deer for three parasangs, yet I did not catch up with him, nor had the thigh-bone come to an end. When I turned back they told me: 'It belonged to Og, the King of Bashan.' "

545   It is conceivable that there is an inner connection between Og and the unicorn: both escaped the flood by being somehow attached to the outside of the ark, and both are gigantic. Moreover we saw that the unicorn was compared to Mount Tabor, and Og also is connected with a mountain: he uprooted a mountain and hurled it on the camp of the Israelites.[72] The parallel is carried still further in one midrash:[73] the unicorn is a mountain and is threatened by a lion, and, in the continuation of the story, Og is killed by Moses, "the servant of Jahweh," who is so often compared to a lion in the Old Testament. The midrash runs:

R. Huna bar Idi said: At the time when David was still tending the sheep, he went and found the unicorn [re'em] asleep in the desert, and thinking it was a mountain he climbed to the top and pastured his flock there. Then the unicorn shook himself and stood up. And David rode on his back and reached up to heaven. And in that hour David spoke to God: If thou wilt take me down from this unicorn I will build thee a temple, one hundred cubits in size, like the horn of this unicorn. . . . What did the Holy One, blessed be He, do for him? He ordained that a lion should come, and when the unicorn saw the lion, he was afraid and crouched down before him, because the lion is his king, and David descended on to the earth. But when David saw the lion, he was afraid. Therefore it is said: "Save me from the lion's mouth, for thou hast heard [freed] me from the horns of the unicorns."

546   Another midrash[74] shows the unicorn fighting with the lion.

[71] Fol. 24b (*Talmud,* ed. Epstein, p. 168).
[72] Goldschmidt, *Der babylonische Talmud,* I, p. 237 ("Tractate Berachoth," Fol. 54b; *Talmud,* ed. Epstein, p. 330), and "Targum Pseudo-Jonathan" on Num. 21 : 35.
[73] Midrash Tehillim (ed. Buber), on Ps. 22 : 21: "Save me from the lion's mouth: for thou hast heard me from the horns of the unicorns."
[74] "The Ten Tribes" in Eisenstein, *Ozar Midrashim,* p. 468b.

258. Unicorn and lion.—From the tapestry *La Dame à la Licorne* (16th cent.)

Here it is explicitly called the unicorn (*ha-unicorius*) and not *re'em*. The passage runs:

And in our land there is also the unicorn [*ha-unicorius*], which has a great horn on his forehead. And there are also many lions. And when the unicorn sees a lion, he drives him against a tree, and the unicorn wants to slay the lion. But the lion moves from his place and the unicorn butts his horn against the tree, and the horn pierces so deep into the tree that he cannot pull it out again, and then the lion comes and kills the unicorn, but sometimes the matter is reversed.

547   In the *Chymical Wedding*, as in the royal arms of England, lion and unicorn are combined (fig. 258); both are symbols of Mercurius in alchemy, just as they are allegories of Christ in the

259. The ch'i-lin announcing the birth of Confucius. "Before K'ung-tse was born, a ch'i-lin came to the governor's house in Tsou and spat out a jade tablet, bearing the inscription: 'The son of the mountain crystal [lit. water-essence] will perpetuate the fallen kingdom of Chou and be a king without a crown.' His mother was astonished and tied an embroidered bow to the unicorn's horn. The beast stayed for two nights and then departed."—From a Chinese illustrated work (c. 18th cent.), *Shêng Chi-t'u*

Church. Lion and unicorn stand for the inner tension of opposites in Mercurius. The lion, being a dangerous animal, is akin to the dragon; the dragon must be slain and the lion at least have his paws cut off. The unicorn too must be tamed; as a monster he has a higher symbolical significance and is of a more spiritual nature than the lion, but as Ripley shows, the lion can sometimes take the place of the unicorn. The two gigantic beings, Og and the unicorn, are reminiscent of Behemoth and Leviathan, the two manifestations of Jehovah. All four of them, as also the unicorned ass of the Bundahish, are personifications of the daemonic forces of nature. The power of God reveals itself not only in the realm of the spirit, but in the fierce animality of nature both within man and outside him. God is ambivalent so long as man remains bound to nature. The uncompromising Christian interpretation of God as the *summum bonum* obviously goes against nature; hence the secret paganism of alchemy comes out in the ambivalent figure of Mercurius. By contrast, the androgyny of Christ is conceived as exclusively spiritual and symbolic, and therefore outside the natural con-

464

text. On the other hand the very existence of an adversary, "the prince of this world," betrays the polarity of God as shown in the androgynous nature of the Son in whom he is manifest.

h. The Unicorn in China

548   The unicorn also appears in China. According to the *Li Chi,* or *Book of Rites,* there are four beneficent or spiritual animals: the unicorn (*ch'i-lin*), the phoenix, the tortoise, and the dragon. The *ch'i-lin* is chief among four-footed beasts. "It resembles the stag, but is larger, with the tail of an ox and the hoofs of a horse: it has a single horn of flesh, there are five colours in the hair of its back, and the hair of its belly is yellow (or brown), it does not tread any living grass underfoot nor eat any living creature; it shows itself when perfect rulers [*chen-jen*]

465

appear and the *Tao* of the king is accomplished." If it is wounded, this is an evil omen. Its first appearance was in the garden of the Yellow Emperor (2697 B.C.). Later two unicorns sojourned in P'ing-yang, Emperor Yao's capital. A unicorn appeared to the mother of Confucius when she was pregnant (fig. 259), and, as an omen before the death of the sage, it chanced that a charioteer wounded a unicorn (fig. 260).[75] It is worth noting that the male unicorn is called *ch'i* and the female *lin,* so that the generic term is formed by the union of both characters *(ch'i-lin).*[76] The unicorn is thus endowed with an androgynous quality. Its connection with the phoenix and the dragon also occurs in alchemy, where the dragon stands for the lowest form of Mercurius and the phoenix for the highest.

549   As mentioned before, the horn of the rhinoceros is an alexipharmic and for this reason is, even today, a favourite article of commerce between the African east coast and China, where it is made into poison-proof drinking cups. The *Physiologus Graecus* tells us that when a snake has poisoned their drinking water, the animals, noticing the poison, will wait for the unicorn to come down to the water; "for his horn is a symbol of the cross" (σταυρὸν ἐκτυπώσας τῷ κέρατι αὐτοῦ), and by drinking he dissipates the virulence of the poison.[77]

i. The Unicorn Cup

550   The healing cup is not unconnected with the "cup of salvation," the Eucharistic Chalice, and with the vessel used in divination. Migne[78] says that Cardinal Torquemada always kept a unicorn cup at table: "La corne de licorne préserve des sortilèges" (fig. 261). Hippolytus, in his summing up of the teachings of the Naassenes, says that the Greeks called "Geryon of the threefold body" the "heavenly horn of the moon." But Geryon

---

[75] From the *Tz'u-yuan,* s.v. "Ch'i-lin." The text of the captions for figs. 259 and 260 was specially translated from the Chinese for the Swiss edn. of the present volume by Dr. E. H. von Tscharner. For further reference to this Confucius legend, cf. Wilhelm, *Kung-Tse, Leben und Werk,* pp. 189 and 60.

[76] Ferguson, *Chinese [Mythology],* p. 98.

[77] Sbordone, *Physiologus,* p. 321, 10–17.

[78] Migne, *Dictionnaire des sciences occultes,* s.v. "Licorne."

261. Pope with the unicorn as the symbol of the Holy Ghost.—From Scaliger, *Explanatio imaginum* (1570); antithesis to Paracelsus, *Auslegung der Figuren* (1569)

was the "Jordan," [79] the "masculo-feminine Man in all things, by whom all things were made." In this connection Hippolytus mentions the cup of Joseph and Anacreon:

The words "without him was not any thing made" [80] refer to the world of forms, because this was created without his help through the third and fourth [members of the quaternity]. For this is . . . the cup from which the king, when he drinks, draws his omens. [81] The Greeks likewise alluded to this secret in the Anacreontic verses:

> My tankard tells me
> Speaking in mute silence
> What I must become.

This alone sufficed for it to be known among men, namely the cup of Anacreon which mutely declares the ineffable secret. For they say Anacreon's cup is dumb; yet Anacreon affirms that it tells him in mute language what he must become, that is, spiritual and not carnal, if he will hear the secret hidden in silence. And this secret is the water which Jesus, at that fair marriage, changed into wine. That was the great and true beginning of the miracles which Jesus wrought in Cana in Galilee, and thus he showed forth the kingdom of heaven. This [beginning] is the kingdom of heaven that lies

[79] Analogy to Ῑῆ-ρύων.   [80] John 1 : 3f.
[81] Allusion to the cup of Joseph in Gen. 44 : 4–5: ". . . Wherefore have ye rewarded evil for good? Is not this it in which my lord drinketh, and whereby indeed he divineth?" (A.V.)

262. The lunar unicorn.—Reverse of a medal (1447) by Antonio Pisano

within us as a treasure, like the "leaven hidden in three measures of meal." [82]

551   We have seen that the "heavenly horn of the moon" is closely connected with the unicorn. Here it means not only "Geryon of the threefold body" [83] and the Jordan, but the hermaphroditic Man as well, who is identical with the Johannine Logos. The "third and fourth" are water and earth; these two elements are thought of as forming the lower half of the world in the alchemical retort, and Hippolytus likens them to a cup (κόνδυ). This is the divining-vessel of Joseph and Anacreon: the water stands for the content and the earth for the container, i.e., the cup itself. The content is the water that Jesus changed into wine, and the water is also represented by the Jordan, which signifies the Logos, thus bringing out the analogy with the Chalice. Its content gives life and healing, like the cup in IV Ezra (14 : 39–40):

[82] Hippolytus, *Elenchos*, V, 8, 4–7. It should be pointed out that, immediately after the symbols mentioned above, the *Elenchos* goes on to the ithyphallic figures of the Samothracian Mysteries and to Hermes Kyllenios, as further analogies of the arcanum of the Naassenes.

[83] Hippolytus states that the three parts of Geryon are rational, psychic, and earthly.

263. The Campion Pendant (front view), made from the horn of a narwhal set in enamelled gold. On the back, bits of the horn have been scraped off for medicinal purposes (16th cent.?)

Then I opened my mouth, and lo! there was reached unto me a full cup, which was full as it were with water, but the colour of it was like fire.[84]

> And I took it and drank; and when I had drunk,
> My heart poured forth understanding,
> wisdom grew in my breast,
> and my spirit retained its memory.[85]

552   The secret of the cup is also the secret of the horn, which in its turn contains the essence of the unicorn as bestower of strength, health, and life (fig. 263). The alchemists attribute the same qualities to their stone, calling it the "carbuncle."[86] According to legend, this stone may be found under the horn of the unicorn, as Wolfram von Eschenbach says:

[84] Cf. the alchemical equivalence of water and fire.
[85] Charles, *Apocrypha and Pseudepigrapha*, II, p. 623.
[86] Cf. a quotation from Lilius in *Rosarium, Art. aurif.*, II, p. 329: "In fine exibit tibi Rex suo diademate coronatus, fulgens ut Sol, clarus ut carbunculus . . . perseverans in igne" (At the end the King will come forth to you crowned with his diadem, resplendent as the Sun, lambent as the carbuncle . . . abiding in the fire). The *lapis* is "shimmering carbuncle light" or "the carbuncle stone shining in the firelight" (Khunrath, *Von hyleal. Chaos*, pp. 227, 242; also *Amphitheatrum*, p. 202).

264. Mandala of the unicorn and the tree of life.—Verteuil tapestry (15th cent),
"The Hunt of the Unicorn"

> We caught the beast called Unicorn
> That knows and loves a maiden best
> And falls asleep upon her breast;
> We took from underneath his horn
> The splendid male carbuncle stone
> Sparkling against the white skull-bone.[87]

553   The horn as an emblem of vigour and strength has a masculine character, but at the same time it is a cup, which, as a receptacle, is feminine.[88] So we are dealing here with a "uniting symbol"[89] that expresses the bipolarity of the archetype (fig. 264).

554   These assorted unicorn symbolisms aim at giving no more than a sample of the extremely intricate and tangled connections between pagan and natural philosophy, Gnosticism, alchemy, and ecclesiastical tradition, which, in its turn, had a deep and lasting influence on the world of medieval alchemy. I hope that these examples have made clear to the reader just how far alchemy was a religious-philosophical or "mystical" movement. It may well have reached its peak in Goethe's religious *Weltanschauung*, as this is presented to us in *Faust*.

[87] *Parzival*, Book IX, lines 1494 1501 (in Wolfram von Eschenbach, *Parzival und Titurel*, II; translation from Shepard, *The Lore of the Unicorn*, p. 82).
[88] Scheftelowitz, "Das Hörnermotiv in den Religionen."
[89] Cf. *Psychological Types*, pars. 318ff. and Def. 51.

265. The unicorn and his reflection, depicting the motto "De moy je m'épouvante."—Boschius, *Symbolographia* (1702)

266. Double-headed eagle with crowns of Pope and Emperor, symbolizing the kingdoms of both worlds. The eagle is covered with eyes (enlightenment!).— Codex Palatinus Latinus 412 (15th cent.)

EPILOGUE

267. The *prima materia* as the dragon, being fertilized by the Holy Ghost (the *avis Hermetis*).—"Hermes Bird," *Theatrum chemicum Britannicum* (1652)

555   What the old philosophers meant by the *lapis* has never become quite clear. This question can be answered satisfactorily only when we know exactly what the unconscious content was that they were projecting. The psychology of the unconscious alone is in a position to solve this riddle. It teaches us that so long as a content remains in the projected state it is inaccessible, which is the reason why the labours of those authors have revealed so little to us of the alchemical secret. But the yield in symbolic material is all the greater, and this material is closely related to the process of individuation.

556   In dealing with alchemy we must always consider what an important part this philosophy played in the Middle Ages, what a vast literature it left behind, and what a far-reaching effect it had on the spiritual life of the time. How far the claims of alchemy itself went in this direction is best shown by the *lapis*-Christ parallel, a fact which may explain, or excuse, my excursions into fields that seem to have nothing to do with alchemy. For the moment we embark upon the psychology of alchemical thought we must take account of connections that seem, on the face of it, very remote from the historical material. But if we try to understand the phenomenon from inside, i.e., from the

475

standpoint of the psyche, we can start from a central position where many lines converge, however far apart they may be in the external world. We are then confronted with the underlying human psyche which, unlike consciousness, hardly changes at all in the course of many centuries. Here, a truth that is two thousand years old is still the truth today—in other words, it is still alive and active. Here too we find those fundamental psychic facts that remain unchanged for thousands of years and will still be unchanged thousands of years hence. From this point of view, the recent past and the present seem like episodes in a drama that began in the grey mists of antiquity and continues through the centuries into a remote future. This drama is an "Aurora consurgens"—the dawning of consciousness in mankind.

557   The alchemy of the classical epoch (from antiquity to about the middle of the seventeenth century) was, in essence, chemical research work into which there entered, by way of projection, an admixture of unconscious psychic material. For this reason the psychological conditions necessary for the work are frequently stressed in the texts. The contents under consideration were those that lent themselves to projection upon the unknown chemical substance. Owing to the impersonal, purely objective nature of matter, it was the impersonal, collective archetypes that were projected: first and foremost, as a parallel to the collective spiritual life of the times, the image of the spirit imprisoned in the darkness of the world. In other words, the state of relative unconsciousness in which man found himself, and which he felt to be painful and in need of redemption, was reflected in matter and accordingly dealt with in matter. Since the psychological condition of any unconscious content is one of potential reality, characterized by the polar opposites "being" and "not-being," it follows that the union of opposites must play a decisive role in the alchemical process. The result is something in the nature of a "uniting symbol," and this usually has a numinous character.[1] The projection of the redeemer-image, i.e., the correspondence between Christ and the *lapis*, is therefore almost a psychological necessity, as is the parallelism between the redeeming *opus* or *officium divinum* and the magistery—with the essential difference that the Christian *opus* is an *operari* in honour of God the Redeemer undertaken by man

[1] Cf. Jung, *Psychological Types*, pars. 318ff.

who stands in need of redemption, while the alchemical *opus* is the labour of Man the Redeemer in the cause of the divine world-soul slumbering and awaiting redemption in matter. The Christian earns the fruits of grace *ex opere operato,* but the alchemist creates for himself—*ex opere operantis* in the most literal sense—a "panacea of life" which he regards either as a substitute for the Church's means of grace or as the complement and parallel of the divine work of redemption that is continued in man. The two opposed points of view meet in the ecclesiastical formula of the *opus operatum* and the *opus operantis*[2]—but in the last analysis they are irreconcilable. Fundamentally it is a question of polar opposites: the collective or the individual, society or personality. This is a modern problem in so far as it needed the hypertrophy of collective life and the herding together of incredible masses of people in our own day to make the individual aware that he was being suffocated in the toils of the organized mob. The collectivism of the medieval Church seldom or never exerted sufficient pressure on the individual to turn his relations with society into a general problem. So this question, too, remained on the level of projection, and it was reserved for our own day to tackle it with at least an embryonic degree of consciousness under the mask of neurotic individualism.

558   Some time previous to this latest development, however, alchemy had reached its final summit, and with it the historical turning-point, in Goethe's *Faust,* which is steeped in alchemical forms of thought from beginning to end. The essential Faustian drama is expressed most graphically in the scene between Paris and Helen. To the medieval alchemist this episode would have represented the mysterious *coniunctio* of Sol and Luna in the retort (fig. 268); but modern man, disguised in the figure of Faust, recognizes the projection and, putting himself in the place of Paris or Sol, takes possession of Helen or Luna, his own inner, feminine counterpart. The objective process of the union thus becomes the subjective experience of the artifex: instead of watching the drama, he has become one of the actors. Faust's personal intervention has the disadvantage that the real

[2] [These Latin phrases may be translated: *ex opere operato,* 'by the performed work'; *ex opere operantis,* 'by the work of the operator'; *opus operatum,* 'the performed work'; *opus operantis,* 'the work of the operator.'—EDITORS.]

PHILOSOPHORVM.
FERMENTATIO.

Hye wird Sol aber verschlossen
Vnd mit Mercurio philosophorum vbergossen.

268. *Fermentatio*, symbolic representation of the *con-iunctio spirituum*. [Verses: "But here King Sol is tight shut in / And *Mercurius philosophorum* pours over him."]
—*Rosarium philosophorum* (1550)

goal of the entire process—the production of the incorruptible substance—is missed. Instead Euphorion, who is supposed to be the *filius philosophorum*, imperishable and "incombustible," goes up in flames and disappears—a calamity for the alchemist and an occasion for the psychologist to criticize Faust, although the phenomenon is by no means uncommon. For every archetype, at its first appearance and so long as it remains unconscious, takes possession of the whole man and impels him to play a corresponding role. Consequently Faust cannot resist supplanting Paris in Helen's affections, and the other "births" and rejuvenations, such as the Boy Charioteer and the Homunculus,

478

are destroyed by the same greed. This is probably the deeper reason why Faust's final rejuvenation takes place only in the post-mortal state, i.e., is projected into the future. Is it a mere coincidence that the perfected figure of Faust bears the name (which we have already met) of one of the most famous of the early alchemists: "Marianus" or, in its more usual spelling, Morienus?

559   By identifying with Paris, Faust brings the *coniunctio* back from its projected state into the sphere of personal psychological experience and thus into consciousness. This crucial step means nothing less than the solution of the alchemical riddle, and at the same time the redemption of a previously unconscious part of the personality. But every increase in consciousness harbours the danger of inflation, as is shown very clearly in Faust's super-human powers. His death, although necessary in his day and generation, is hardly a satisfactory answer. The rebirth and transformation that follow the *coniunctio* take place in the here-after, i.e., in the unconscious—which leaves the problem hang-ing in the air. We all know that Nietzsche took it up again in *Zarathustra,* as the transformation into the superman; but he brought the superman into dangerously close proximity with the man-in-the-street. By so doing he inevitably called up all the latter's reserves of anti-Christian resentment, for his superman is the overweening pride, the hybris, of individual conscious-ness, which must necessarily collide with the collective power of Christianity and lead to the catastrophic destruction of the indi-vidual. We know just how, and in what an exceedingly charac-teristic form, this fate overtook Nietzsche, *tam ethice quam physice.* And what kind of an answer did the next generation give to the individualism of Nietzsche's superman? It answered with a collectivism, a mass organization, a herding together of the mob, *tam ethice quam physice,* that made everything that went before look like a bad joke. Suffocation of the personality and an impotent Christianity that may well have received its death-wound—such is the unadorned balance sheet of our time.

560   Faust's sin was that he identified with the thing to be trans-formed and that had been transformed. Nietzsche overreached himself by identifying his ego with the superman Zarathustra, the part of the personality that was struggling into consciousness. But can we speak of Zarathustra as a part of the personality? Was

he not rather something superhuman—something which man is not, though he has his share in it? Is God really dead, because Nietzsche declared that he had not been heard of for a long time? May he not have come back in the guise of the superman?

561 In his blind urge for superhuman power, Faust brought about the murder of Philemon and Baucis. Who are these two humble old people? When the world had become godless and no longer offered a hospitable retreat to the divine strangers Jupiter and Mercury, it was Philemon and Baucis who received the superhuman guests. And when Baucis was about to sacrifice her last goose for them, the metamorphosis came to pass: the gods made themselves known, the humble cottage was changed into a temple, and the old couple became immortal servitors at the shrine.

562 In a sense, the old alchemists were nearer to the central truth of the psyche than Faust when they strove to deliver the fiery spirit from the chemical elements, and treated the mystery as though it lay in the dark and silent womb of nature. It was still outside them. The upward thrust of evolving consciousness was bound sooner or later to put an end to the projection, and to restore to the psyche that which had been psychic from the beginning. Yet, ever since the Age of Enlightenment and in the era of scientific rationalism, what indeed was the psyche? It had become synonymous with consciousness. The psyche was "what I know." There was no psyche outside the ego. Inevitably, then, the ego identified with the contents accruing from the withdrawal of projections. Gone were the days when the psyche was still for the most part "outside the body" and imagined "those greater things" which the body could not grasp. The contents that were formerly projected were now bound to appear as personal possessions, as chimerical phantasms of the ego-consciousness. The fire chilled to air, and the air became the great wind of Zarathustra and caused an inflation of consciousness which, it seems, can be damped down only by the most terrible catastrophe to civilization, another deluge let loose by the gods upon inhospitable humanity.

563 An inflated consciousness is always egocentric and conscious of nothing but its own existence. It is incapable of learning from the past, incapable of understanding contemporary events, and incapable of drawing right conclusions about the future. It is

hypnotized by itself and therefore cannot be argued with. It inevitably dooms itself to calamities that must strike it dead. Paradoxically enough, inflation is a regression of consciousness into unconsciousness. This always happens when consciousness takes too many unconscious contents upon itself and loses the faculty of discrimination, the *sine qua non* of all consciousness. When fate, for four whole years, played out a war of monumental frightfulness on the stage of Europe—a war that *nobody* wanted —nobody dreamed of asking exactly who or what had caused the war and its continuation. Nobody realized that European man was possessed by something that robbed him of all free will. And this state of unconscious possession will continue undeterred until we Europeans become scared of our "god-almightiness." Such a change can begin only with individuals, for the masses are blind brutes, as we know to our cost. It seems to me of some importance, therefore, that a few individuals, or people individually, should begin to understand that there are contents which do not belong to the ego-personality, but must be ascribed to a psychic non-ego. This mental operation has to be undertaken if we want to avoid a threatening inflation. To help us, we have the useful and edifying models held up to us by poets and philosophers—models or *archetypi* that we may well call remedies for both men and the times. Of course, what we discover there is nothing that can be held up to the masses— only some hidden thing that we can hold up to ourselves in solitude and in silence. Very few people care to know anything about this; it is so much easier to preach the universal panacea to everybody else than to take it oneself, and, as we all know, things are never so bad when everybody is in the same boat. No doubts can exist in the herd; the bigger the crowd the better the truth—and the greater the catastrophe.

564   What we may learn from the models of the past is above all this: that the psyche harbours contents, or is exposed to influences, the assimilation of which is attended by the greatest dangers. If the old alchemists ascribed their secret to matter, and if neither Faust nor Zarathustra is a very encouraging example of what happens when we embody this secret in ourselves, then the only course left to us is to repudiate the arrogant claim of the conscious mind to be the whole of the psyche, and to admit that the psyche is a reality which we cannot grasp with our present

Ora
Lege Lege Lege Relege labora
et Invenies.

269. The artifex and his *soror mystica* making the gesture of the secret at the end of the work.—*Mutus liber* (1702)

means of understanding. I do not call the man who admits his ignorance an obscurantist; I think it is much rather the man whose consciousness is not sufficiently developed for him to be aware of his ignorance. I hold the view that the alchemist's hope of conjuring out of matter the philosophical gold, or the panacea, or the wonderful stone, was only in part an illusion, an effect of projection; for the rest it corresponded to certain psychic facts that are of great importance in the psychology of the unconscious. As is shown by the texts and their symbolism, the alchemist projected what I have called the process of individuation into the phenomena of chemical change. A scientific term like "individuation" does not mean that we are dealing with something known and finally cleared up, on which there is no more to be said.[3] It merely indicates an as yet very obscure field of research much in need of exploration: the centralizing processes in the unconscious that go to form the personality. We are dealing with life-processes which, on account of their numinous character, have from time immemorial provided the strongest incentive for the formation of symbols. These processes are steeped in mystery; they pose riddles with which the human mind will long wrestle for a solution, and perhaps in vain. For, in the last analysis, it is exceedingly doubtful whether human reason is a suitable instrument for this purpose. Not for nothing did alchemy style itself an "art," feeling—and rightly so—that it was concerned with creative processes that can be truly grasped only by experience, though intellect may give them a name. The alchemists themselves warned us: "Rumpite libros, ne corda vestra rumpantur" (Rend the books, lest your hearts be rent

[3] Cf. Jung, *Psychological Types*, Def. 29.

482

asunder), and this despite their insistence on study. Experience, not books, is what leads to understanding (fig. 269).

565　　In the foregoing study of dream-symbols I have shown how such an experience looks in reality. From this we can see more or less what happens when an earnest inquiry is turned upon the unknown regions of the soul. The forms which the experience takes in each individual may be infinite in their variations, but, like the alchemical symbols, they are all variants of certain central types, and these occur universally. They are the primordial images, from which the religions each draw their absolute truth.

270. The phoenix as symbol of resurrection.—Boschius, *Symbolographia* (1702)

BIBLIOGRAPHY

The items of the bibliography are arranged alphabetically under two headings: *A*. Ancient volumes containing collections of alchemical tracts by various authors; *B*. General bibliography, including cross-references to the material in *A*. Short titles of the ancient volumes are printed in capital letters.

BIBLIOGRAPHY

A. VOLUMES CONTAINING COLLECTIONS OF ALCHEMICAL WORKS BY VARIOUS AUTHORS

ARS CHEMICA, quod sit licita recte exercentibus, probationes doctissimorum iurisconsultorum . . . Argentorati [Strasbourg], 1566.

Contents quoted in this volume:

    i   Septem tractatus seu capitula Hermetis Trismegisti aurei [pp. 7–31; usually referred to as "Tractatus aureus"]

   ii   Tabula smaragdina [pp. 32–33]

  iii   Studium Consilii coniugii de massa solis et lunae [pp. 48–263; usually referred to as "Consilium coniugii"]

ARTIS AURIFERAE quam chemiam vocant . . . Basileae [Basel], [1593]. 2 vols.

Contents quoted in this volume:

VOLUME I

    i   Turba philosophorum [two versions: pp. 1–64, 65–139]

   ii   Allegoriae super librum Turbae [pp. 139–45]

  iii   Aenigmata ex visione Arislei et allegoriis sapientum [pp. 146–54; usually referred to as "Visio Arislei"]

   iv   In Turbam philosophorum exercitationes [pp. 154–82]

    v   Aurora consurgens, quae dicitur Aurea hora [pp. 185–246; Part II only]

   vi   Rosinus ad Sarratantam episcopum [pp. 277–319]

  vii   Maria Prophetissa: Practica . . . in artem alchemicam [pp. 319–24]

 viii   Kalid: Liber trium verborum [pp. 352–61]

   ix   Merlinus: Allegoria de arcano lapidis [pp. 392–96]

    x   Liber de arte chimica [pp. 575–631]

VOLUME II

   xi   Morienus Romanus: Sermo de transmutatione metallorum [pp. 7–54]

487

xii Rosarium philosophorum [pp. 204–384; contains a second
       version of "Visio Arislei" at pp. 246ff.]

*AUREUM VELLUS, oder Güldin Schatz und Kunstkammer . . .
von dem . . . bewehrten Philosopho Salomone Trismosino.*
Rorschach, 1598.

Contents quoted in this volume:

  i [Trismosin:] Splendor solis [Tract. III, pp. 3–59]
 ii Melchior, Cardinal Bishop of Brixen: Von dem gelben und
       rotten Mann [Tract. III, pp. 177–91]

For translations of this volume, see: *La Toyson d'or, ou La Fleur
des thresors . . .* Translated from German into French by L. I.
Paris, 1612. / "The Golden Fleece, or The Flower of Treasures."
Translated by William Backhouse, 1718. / In MS. Bodleian 7597,
Oxford.

MANGETUS, JOANNES JACOBUS (ed.). *BIBLIOTHECA CHEMICA
CURIOSA, seu Rerum ad alchemiam pertinentium thesaurus in-
structissimus . . .* Geneva, 1702. 2 vols.

Contents quoted in this volume:

VOLUME I

   i Hoghelande: De alchemiae difficultatibus [pp. 336–68]
  ii Hermes Trismegistus: Tractatus aureus de lapidis physici
        secreto [pp. 400–445]
 iii Turba philosophorum [pp. 445–65; another version, pp.
        480–94]
  iv Allegoriae sapientum supra librum Turbae philosophorum
        XXIX distinctiones [pp. 467–79]
   v Geber: Summa perfectionis magisterii [pp. 519–57]
  vi Lully: Compendium artis alchemiae et naturalis philoso-
        phiae secundum naturalem cursum [pp. 875–78]
 vii Lully: Codicillus, seu vade mecum aut Cantilena [pp. 880–
        911]
vii-a Mutus liber, in quo tamen tota philosophia hermetica,
        figuris hieroglyphicis depingitur [unpaged; bound into
        Mellon Alchemical Library copy]

VOLUME II

viii Bonus: Margarita pretiosa novella correctissima [pp. 1–80]
  ix Rosarium philosophorum [pp. 87–119]

488

x Ficinus [Marsilio Ficino]: Liber de arte chimica [pp. 172–83]

xi [Zadith] Senior: De chymia [pp. 198–235]

xii Ripley: Liber duodecim portarum [pp. 275–85]

xiii Sendivogius: Parabola, seu Aenigma philosophicum [pp. 474–75]

xiv Orthelius: Epilogus et recapitulatio in Novum lumen Sendivogii [pp. 526–30]

xv [Siebmacher:] Hydrolithus sophicus, seu Aquarium sapientum [pp. 537–58]

xvi Grasseus: Lilium inter spinas [pp. 596–600]

xvii [Espagnet:] Arcanum hermeticae philosophiae [pp. 649–61]

In hoc volumine DE ALCHEMIA continentur haec. Gebri Arabis . . . De investigatione perfectionis metallorum . . . Norimbergae [Nuremberg], 1541.

Contents quoted in this volume:

i Rosarius minor [pp. 309–37]

ii Tabula smaragdina Hermetis Trismegisti [p. 363]

iii Hortulanus: Super Tabulam smaragdinam commentarius [pp. 364–73]

MUSAEUM HERMETICUM reformatum et amplificatum . . . continens tractatus chimicos XXI praestantissimos . . . Francofurti [Frankfort], 1678. (For translation, see (*B*) WAITE, ARTHUR EDWARD.) (Also an edn. of 1625. See fig. 240.)

Contents quoted in this volume:

i [Hermes Trismegistus:] Tractatus aureus de lapide philosophorum [pp. 1–52]

ii Madathanus Aureum saeculum redivivum [pp. 53–72]

iii [Siebmacher:] Hydrolithus sophicus, seu Aquarium sapientum [pp. 73–144]

iv Melung: Demonstratio naturae [pp. 145–71]

v Flamel: Tractatus brevis sive Summarium philosophicum [pp. 172–79]

vi [Barcius (F. von Sternberg):] Gloria mundi, alias Paradysi tabula [pp. 203–304]

vii Lambspringk: De lapide philosophico figurae et emblemata [pp. 337–72]

489

viii [Maier:] Tripus aureus, hoc est, Tres tractatus chymici selectissimi [pp. 373–544]

ix Valentinus: Practica una cum duodecim clavibus [pp. 377–432; Duodecim claves, pp. 393–423]

x Norton: Crede mihi, seu Ordinale [pp. 433–532]

xi Cremer: Testamentum [pp. 533–44]

xii Sendivogius: Novum lumen chemicum e naturae fonte et manuali experientia depromptum [pp. 545–600]

xiii [Sendivogius:] Novi luminis chemici tractatus alter de sulphure [pp. 601–46]

xiv Philalethes: Introitus apertus . . . [pp. 647–700]

xv Philalethes: Metallorum metamorphosis [pp. 714–74]

xvi Philalethes: Fons chymicae veritatis [pp. 799–814]

THEATRUM CHEMICUM, praecipuos selectorum auctorum tractatus . . . continens. Ursellis [Ursel], 1602. 3 vols. (Vol. IV, Argentorati [Strasbourg], 1613; Vol. V, 1622; Vol. VI, 1661.)

Contents quoted in this volume:

quam patefacere . . . [p. 123; a table]

xiii   Quercetanus: Ad Jacobi Auberti Vendonis de ortu et causis
       metallorum contra chemicos explicationem [pp. 170–
       202]

xiv   Dee: Monas hieroglyphica [pp. 218–43]

xv   Ventura: De ratione conficiendi lapidis [pp. 244–356]

xvi   Richardus Anglicus: Correctorium alchymiae [pp. 442–66]

xvii Albertus Magnus: Super arborem Aristotelis [pp. 524–27]

VOLUME III

xviii [Melchior:] Addam et processum sub forma missae [pp.
       853–60]

VOLUME IV

xix   Von der Materi und Prattick des Steins [pp. 284–93]

xx   Aphorismi Basiliani sive Canones Hermetici [pp. 368–71]

xxi   Sendivogius: Dialogus Mercurii, alchymistae, et naturae
      [pp. 509–17]

xxii Arnaldus de Villanova: Carmen [pp. 614–15]

xxiii Guilhelmus Tecenensis: Lilium . . . de spinis evulsum [pp.
      1000–1027]

VOLUME V

xxiv   Turba philosophorum [pp. 1–57]

xxv   Allegoriae sapientum . . . supra librum Turbae [pp. 64–
       100]

xxvi   Tractatus Micreris suo discipulo Mirnefindo [pp. 101–13]

xxvii Liber Platonis quartorum . . . [pp. 114–208]

xxviii Tractatus Aristotelis alchymistae ad Alexandrum Mag-
       num de lapide philosophico [pp. 880–92]

xxix   Epistola ad . . . Hermannum archiepiscopum Colonien-
       sem de lapide philosophico [pp. 893–900]

VOLUME VI

xxx   Espagnet: Instructio . . . de arbore solari [pp. 163–94]

xxxi   Christopher of Paris: Elucidarius artis transmutatoriae
       metallorum [pp. 195–293]

xxxii Grasseus: Arca arcani . . . [pp. 294–381]

THEATRUM CHEMICUM BRITANNICUM. Containing Sev-
erall Poeticall Pieces of Our Famous English Philosophers, Who

491

Have Written the Hermetique Mysteries in Their Owne Ancient Language. Collected with annotations by Elias Ashmole. London, 1652.

Contents quoted in this volume:

  i Norton: The Ordinall of Alchimy [pp. 1–106]
 ii Liber patris sapientiae [pp. 195–212]
iii [Lully:] Hermes Bird [pp. 213–26]
 iv Verses Belonging to an Emblematicall Scrowle: Supposed to Be Invented by Geo: Ripley [pp. 375–79]

B. GENERAL BIBLIOGRAPHY

ABRAHAM LE JUIF. "Livre des figures hiéroglifiques." See Codices and MSS., xxxiv.

———. See also ELEAZAR, ABRAHAM.

ABU'L QĀSIM. See HOLMYARD.

ADOLPHUS SENIOR. See SENIOR, ADOLPHUS.

AEGIDIUS DE VADIS. "Dialogus inter naturam. . . ." See (A) *Theatrum chemicum,* xi.

AELIAN (Claudius Aelianus). *De natura animalium libri XVII.* Edited by R. Hercher. Leipzig, 1864–66. 2 vols.

AGRIPPA VON NETTESHEYM, HEINRICH (HENRICUS) CORNELIUS. *De incertitudine et vanitate omnium scientiarum et artium.* The Hague, 1653. English translation: *The Vanity of Arts and Sciences.* London, 1676.

ALBERTUS MAGNUS. *Philosophia naturalis.* Basel, 1650.

———. "Super arborem Aristotelis." See (A) *Theatrum chemicum,* xvii.

"Allegoriae sapientum supra librum Turbae." See (A) *Theatrum chemicum,* xxv, and *Artis auriferae,* ii.

ALLENDY, RENÉ FÉLIX. *Le Symbolisme des nombres.* Second edn., Paris, 1948.

AMMAN, JOST (illus.). *Ein neuw Thierbuch.* With verses by G. Schaller. Frankfort on the Main, 1569.

"Aphorismi Basiliani." See (A) *Theatrum chemicum,* xx.

APULEIUS, LUCIUS. *The Golden Ass. Being the Metamorphoses of Lucius Apuleius.* With an English translation by W. Adlington

492

(1566), revised by S. Gaselee. (Loeb Classical Library.) London and New York, 1915.

AQUINAS, THOMAS. See THOMAS.

"Arislei Visio." See (A) *Artis auriferae*, **iii** and **xii**.

[ARISTEAS.] *The Letter of Aristeas.* [Edited by H. G. Meecham.] Manchester, 1935. For translation, see: *The Oldest Version of the Bible: "Aristeas" on Its Traditional Origin.* Edited by Henry George Meecham. London, 1932.

ARISTOTLE. [*De coelo.*] . . . *On the Heavens.* With an English translation by W. K. C. Guthrie. (Loeb Classical Library.) London and Cambridge, Mass., 1939.

———. *Meteorologica.* Edited by Immanuel Bekker. Berlin, 1829.

ARISTOTLE, pseud. "Tractatus . . . alchymistae ad Alexandrum Magnum. . . ." See (A) *Theatrum chemicum*, **xxviii**.

ARNALDUS DE VILLANOVA. "Carmen." See (A) *Theatrum chemicum*, **xxii**.

ARNOBIUS. *Adversus gentes.* See MIGNE, *P.L.*, vol. 5, cols. 713–1290.

Atharva-Veda. See BLOOMFIELD.

AUGUSTINE, SAINT. *Tractatus in Joannis Evangelium.* Tract. XXXIV. See MIGNE, *P.L.*, vol. 35, cols. 1652–57. For translation, see: HENRY BROWNE (trans.). [Saint Augustine's] *Homilies on the Gospel According to Saint John, and His First Epistle.* (Library of Fathers of the Holy Catholic Church.) Oxford, 1848.

Aurea catena Homeri. Frankfort and Leipzig, 1723.

"Aurora consurgens." See (A) *Artis auriferae*, **v**; Codices and MSS., **xxxi** and **xlix**; FRANZ, M.-L. VON; RHENANUS, JOHANNES.

AVALON, ARTHUR (pseud. of Sir John George Woodroffe) (ed. and trans.). *The Serpent Power (Shat-cakra-nirūpana and Pādukāpanchaka).* (Tantrik Texts.) London, 1919.

BACON, ROGER. *The Mirror of Alchimy . . . with Certaine Other Worthie Treatises of the Like Argument.* London, 1597.

BALDUINUS, CHRISTIANUS ADOLPHUS. *Aurum superius et inferius aurae superioris et inferioris hermeticum.* Frankfort and Leipzig, 1675.

BARCHUSEN [BARKHAUSEN], JOHANN CONRAD. *Elementa chemiae.* Leiden, 1718.

BARNAUD, NICOLAS. *Triga chemica de lapide philosophico tractatus tres.* Leiden, 1599.

BATIFFOL, PIERRE. *Studia patristica.* Fasc. 1 and 2. Paris, 1889–90. ("Le Livre de la Prière d'Asenath," fasc. 1, pp. 1–37.)

BAYNES, CHARLOTTE AUGUSTA. *A Coptic Gnostic Treatise Contained in the Codex Brucianus—Bruce MS. 96, Bodleian Library, Oxford.* Cambridge, 1933.

BERNARD (OF CLAIRVAUX), SAINT. *Sermo IV de Ascensione Domini.* In: *Sermones de Tempore.* See MIGNE, *P.L.,* vol. 183, cols. 35–359.

BERNARD OF TREVISO [Bernardus Trevisanus]. "Liber de alchemia." See (*A*) *Theatrum chemicum,* **ix.**

BERNOULLI, RUDOLF. "Spiritual Development as Reflected in Alchemy and Related Disciplines," in *Spiritual Disciplines.* (Papers from the Eranos Yearbooks, 4.) New York (Bollingen Series 30) and London, 1960. (Orig. in *Eranos-Jahrbuch 1935.*)

BÉROALDE DE VERVILLE, FRANÇOIS (trans.). *Le Tableau des riches inventions couvertes du voile des feintes amoureuses, qui sont representees dans le Songe de Poliphile . . .* Paris, 1600. Contains the "Recueil stéganographique." For original, see COLONNA; for English paraphrase, see FIERZ-DAVID.

BERTHELOT, MARCELLIN. *La Chimie au moyen âge.* (Histoire des sciences.) Paris, 1893. 3 vols.

———. *Collection des anciens alchimistes grecs.* Paris, 1887–88. 3 vols.

———. *Les Origines de l'alchimie.* Paris, 1885.

Bible moralisée. See Codices and MSS., **xx.**

Biblia pauperum. (Gesellschaft der Bibliophilen.) Weimar, 1906. (After an edn. of 1471.)

BISCHOFF, ERICH (ed. and trans.). *Die Elemente der Kabbalah.* Berlin, 1913. 2 vols.

BLOOMFIELD, MAURICE (trans.). *Hymns of the Atharva-Veda.* (Sacred Books of the East, 42.) Oxford, 1897.

BOCK, HIERONYMUS. *Kräuterbuch.* Strasbourg, 1595.

BÖHME, JAKOB. *Des gottseligen, hocherleuchteten Jacob Böhmen Teutonici Philosophi alle Theosophische Schrifften.* Amsterdam, 1682. (A number of parts, separately paginated and variously bound up, the parts themselves being unnumbered. Referred to below as "Schrifften.")

————. *The Works of Jacob Behmen.* [Trans. and ed. by G. Ward and T. Langcake.] London, 1764–81. 4 vols. Referred to below as "Works."

————. *Aurora, oder Die Morgenröte in Aufgang.* See "Schrifften." For translation, see "Works," I ("Aurora").

————. *De signatura rerum.* See "Schrifften"; for translation, see CLIFFORD BAX (ed.). *The Signature of All Things, with Other Writings by Jacob Boehme.* Translated by John Ellistone. (Everyman's Library.) London and New York, 1912.

————. *Gespräch einer erleuchteten und unerleuchteten Seele.* See "Schrifften." For translation, see BAX, as previous entry.

————. *Hohe und tiefe Gründe von dem dreyfachen Leben des Menschen.* See "Schrifften." For translation, see "Works," II ("A High and Deep Search concerning the Threefold Life of Man").

————. *Vom irdischen und himmlischen Mysterium.* See "Schrifften." For translation, see *Six Theosophic Points and Other Writings.* Translated by John Rolleston Earle. London, 1919. ("On the Earthly and Heavenly Mystery," pp. 141–62.)

BONUS, PETRUS. *Pretiosa margarita novella de thesauro ac pretiosissimo philosophorum lapide . . .* Edited by Janus Lacinius. Venice, 1546. For translation see ARTHUR EDWARD WAITE (trans.). *The New Pearl of Great Price.* London, 1894. See also (*A*) *Bibliotheca chemica curiosa,* **viii.**

BÖRNER, C. G. [firm of booksellers, Leipzig.] *Auctions-Katalog 184.* Leipzig, 1914. (Catalogue of A. O. Meyer collection of drawings.)

BOSCHIUS, JACOBUS. *Symbolographia, sive De arte symbolica sermones septem.* Augsburg, 1702.

BOUSSET, WILHELM. *Hauptprobleme der Gnosis.* (Forschungen zur Religion und Literatur des Alten und Neuen Testaments, 10.) Göttingen, 1907.

BRANT, SEBASTIAN. *Hexastichon . . . in memorabiles evangelistarum figuras.* [No place of publication.] 1503.

BRAUN, JOSEPH. *Liturgisches Handlexikon.* Regensburg, 1922.

Brihadaranyaka Upanishad. See MAX MÜLLER.

BRUCHMANN, CARL FRIEDRICH HEINRICH (ed.). *Epitheta Deorum quae apud poetas Graecos leguntur.* (Ausführliches Lexikon der griechischen und römischen Mythologie. Supplement.) Leipzig, 1893.

BRUNO, SAINT, BISHOP OF WÜRZBURG. *Expositio psalmorum.* See MIGNE, *P.L.*, vol. 142, cols. 49–568.

BUBER, SALOMON (ed.). *Midrasch Tehillim.* The Buber text translated into German and edited by August Wünsche. Trier, 1892.

BUDGE, SIR E. A. WALLIS (ed.). *The Book of the Dead. Facsimiles of the Papyri of Hunefer, Anhai, Kerasher . . .* London, 1899.

———. *The Gods of the Egyptians.* London, 1904. 2 vols.

———. *Osiris and the Egyptian Resurrection.* London, 1911. 2 vols.

BÜHLER, JOHANN GEORG (trans.). *The Laws of Manu.* (Sacred Books of the East, 25.) London, 1886.

Bundahish. See WEST.

CARTARI, VINCENZO. *Le imagini de i dei de gli antichi.* Lyons, 1581. For French translation, see: *Les Images des dieux des anciens.* [Translated and enlarged by Antoine du Verdier.] Lyons, 1581.

CATELANUS, LAURENTIUS. *Ein schöner newer historischer Discurs, von der Natur, Tugenden, Eigenschafften, und Gebrauch dess Einhorns.* [Translated by Georgius Faber.] Frankfort on the Main, 1625.

CAUSSIN, NICOLAS. *De symbolica Aegyptiorum sapientia. Polyhistor symbolicus, Electorum Symbolorum, et Parabolarum historicarum stromata.* Paris, [1618] and 1631.

[CELLINI, BENVENUTO.] *The Life of Benvenuto Cellini.* Newly translated into English by John Addington Symonds. 4th edn., London, 1896.

CHAMPOLLION, JEAN FRANÇOIS. *Panthéon égyptien.* Paris, 1823–35.

CHARLES, ROBERT HENRY (ed.). *The Apocrypha and Pseudepigrapha of the Old Testament in English.* Oxford, 1913. 2 vols.

Chhandogya Upanishad. See MAX MÜLLER.

CHRISTOPHER OF PARIS (Christophorus Parisiensis). "Elucidarius artis transmutatoriae." See (*A*) *Theatrum chemicum*, **xxxi**.

CLEMEN, PAUL. *Die romanische Monumentalmalerei in den Rheinlanden.* (Gesellschaft für rheinische Geschichtskunde, 32.) Düsseldorf, 1916.

CLEMENT OF ALEXANDRIA. *Stromata.* See MIGNE, *P.G.*, vol. 8, col. 685

–vol. 9, col. 602. For translation, see WILLIAM WILSON (trans.). *The Writings of Clement of Alexandria.* (Ante-Nicene Christian Library, 4, 12.) Edinburgh, 1867, 1869. 2 vols.

CLEMENT OF ROME (Pope Clement I). *Homilia II.* See MIGNE, *P.G.*, vol. 2, cols. 77–112. For translation, see THOMAS SMITH, PETER PETERSON, and JAMES DONALDSON (trans.). *The Clementine Homilies and the Apostolical Constitutions.* (Ante-Nicene Christian Library, 17.) Edinburgh, 1870. (Pp. 32–56.)

Codices and Manuscripts.

i   Codex of Akhmim. See DIETERICH, *Nekyia.*

i-a   Aschaffenburg. Bibliothek. Codex 13 (earlier 3.) 13th cent. Evangeliary.

i-b   Berlin. Codex Berolinensis. See RUSKA, *Turba.*

i-c   Bingen. Abbey of St. Hildegarde. "Scivias." 12th cent.

ii   Chantilly. Musée Condé. Bibliothèque. MS. 1284. "Les Très Riches Heures du duc de Berry." 15th cent.

iii   Dresden. Sächsische Landesbibliothek. An old Mexican MS. (Codex Dresdensis.)

iv   Florence. Biblioteca Medicea-Laurenziana. MS. (Ashburnham 1166) "Miscellanea d'alchimia." 14th cent.

v   Leiden. Rijksuniversiteit Bibliotheek. Codex Vossianus 29. Thomas Aquinas, pseud. "De alchimia." 16th cent.

vi   London. British Museum. MS. Additional 1316. Emblematical Figures in red chalk, of the process of the Philosophers' Stone, with Latin interpretations. 17th cent.

vii   ———. ———. MS. Additional 5025. Four rolls drawn in Lübeck. 1588. (The "Ripley Scrowle.")

viii   ———. ———. MS. Additional 5245. Cabala mineralis Rabbi Simeon ben Cantara.

ix   ———. ———. MS. Additional 19352. Theodore Psalter, 1066. See also TIKKANEN.

x   ———. ———. MS. Harley 3469. Salomon Trismosin. "Splendor solis." 1582.

xi   ———. ———. MS. Harley 4751. "Historia animalium cum picturis."

xii   Lucca. Biblioteca governativa. Codex 1942. Saint Hildegarde of Bingen. "Liber divinorum operum." 12th cent.

xiii   Manuscripts in author's possession. "La Sagesse des anciens." 18th cent.

xiv   ———. "Figurarum Aegyptiorum secretarum . . ." 18th cent. See also **xxi, xxxiv.**

xv   Milan. Biblioteca Ambrosiana. Codex I.

xvi   Modena. Biblioteca. Codex Estensis Latinus 209. "De Sphaera." 15th cent.

xvii   Munich. Staatsbibliothek. Codex Germanicus 598. "Das Buch der heiligen Dreifaltigkeit und Beschreibung der Heimlichkeit von Veränderung der Metallen." 1420.

xviii   ———. ———. Codex Latinus 15713. *Perikopenbuch* or Lectionary. 12th cent.

xix   Oxford. Bodleian Library. MS. Bruce 96 (Codex Brucianus). See also BAYNES.

xx   ———. ———. MS. 270b. Bible moralisée. 13th cent.

xxi   Paris. Bibliothèque de l'Arsenal. MS. 973. "Explication des figures hiéroglifiques des Aegyptiens. . . ." 18th cent.

xxii   ———. ———. MS. 974. "De summa et universalis medicinae sapientiae veterum philosophorum." 18th cent.

xxiii   ———. ———. MS. 975. "Trésor des trésors." 17th cent.

xxiv   ———. ———. MS. 5061. Jean Thenaud. "Traité de la cabale." 16th cent.

xxv   ———. ———. MS. 5076. "Trésor de sapience." 15th cent.

xxvi   ———. ———. MS. 6577. "Traité d'alchimie." 17th cent.

xxvii   ———. Bibliothèque nationale. Codex Latinus 511. "Speculum humanae salvationis." 14th cent.

xxviii   ———. ———. Codex Latinus 512. "Speculum humanae salvationis." 15th cent.

xxix   ———. ———. Codex Latinus 7171. "Turba philosophorum." 16th cent.

xxx   ———. ———. MS. Latin 919. "Grandes heures du duc de Berry." 1413.

xxxi   ———. ———. MS. Latin 14006. "Aurora consurgens." 15th cent. See also "Aurora consurgens."

xxxii   ———. ———. MS. Français 116. "Roman de Lancelot du Lac." 15th cent.

xxxiii   ———. ———. MS. Français 594. Petrarch. "Les triomphes du poethe messire Françoys Pétrarche." 16th cent.

xxxiv ———. ———. MS. Français 14765. Abraham le Juif. "Livre des figures hiéroglifiques." 18th cent. (Contains also "Alchimie de Flamel, ecritte en chiffres en 12 clefs . . . par Denis Molinier," or "Pratique," pp. 204ff.)

xxxv ———. ———. MS. Français 14770. "Recueil de figures astrologiques." 18th cent.

xxxvi Preobrazhensk, Russia. Monastery of St. Nicholas. Codex 129. Khludov Psalter. 9th cent. See also TIKKANEN.

xxxvii Reims. Bibliothèque. "Recueil des fausses décrétales." 13th cent.

xxxviii Rome. Biblioteca Angelica. Codex 1474. Alcadini. "De balneis Puteolanis." 14th cent.

xxxix Tübingen. Universitätsbibliothek. MS. c. 1400.

xl Vatican. Biblioteca Vaticana. Codex Palatinus Latinus 412. Wynandi de Stega. "Adamas colluctancium aquilarum." 15th cent.

xl-a ———. ———. Codex Palatinus Latinus 413. "Speculum humanae saluacionis." 15th cent.

xli ———. ———. Codex Palatinus Latinus 565. Peregrinus, "Speculum virginum seu Dialogus cum Theodora virgine." 13th cent.

xlii ———. ———. Codex Reginensis Latinus 1458. 17th cent.

xliii ———. ———. Codex Urbanus Latinus 365. Dante. "Inferno," "Purgatorio," "Paradiso." 15th cent.

xliv ———. ———. Codex Urbanus Latinus 899. 15th cent.

xlv ———. ———. Codex Vaticanus Latinus 681. Peter Lombard. "De sacramentis." 14th cent.

xlvi ———. ———. Codex Vaticanus Latinus 7286. "Speculum veritatis." 17th cent.

xlvii Venice. Codex Marcianus. 11th cent. See also BERTHELOT, *Alchimistes grecs,* Introduction, p. 132.

xlviii Vienna. Nationalbibliothek. Codex Medicus Graecus 1. Dioscorides. "De materia medica." 16th cent.

xlix Zurich. Zentralbibliothek. Codex Rhenoviensis 172. "Aurora consurgens." 15th cent. See also **xxxi**.

l Zwiefalten Abbey. Breviary no. 128. 12th cent. See also LÖFFLER.

499

COLONNA, FRANCESCO. *Hypnerotomachia Poliphili* . . . Venice, 1499. For French translation, see BÉROALDE DE VERVILLE; for English paraphrase, see FIERZ-DAVID.

"Consilium coniugii." See (*A*) *Ars chemica*, **iii.**

CORNELL, JOHAN HENRIK. *The Iconography of the Nativity of Christ.* (Uppsala universitets årskrift 1924. Filosofi, språkvetenskap och historiska vetenskaper, 3.) Uppsala, 1924.

COSMAS. Χριστιανικὴ τοπογραφία. *Cosmae Aegyptii monachi Christiana topographia.* . . . (Bernard de Montfaucon, Collectio nova patrum et scriptorum Graecorum, 2.) Paris, 1706. For translation, see JOHN WATSON MCCRINDLE (trans.). Κοσμᾶ αἰγυπτοῦ μοναχοῦ χριστιανικὴ τοπογραφία. *The Christian Topography of Cosmas, an Egyptian Monk.* London, 1897.

CREMER, JOHN. "Testamentum." See (*A*) *Musaeum hermeticum*, **xi.**

CTESIAS (Ktesias). See MCCRINDLE.

CUMONT, FRANZ. *Textes et monuments figurés relatifs aux mystères de Mithra.* Brussels, 1894–99. 2 vols.

DARMSTAEDTER, ERNST. *Die Alchemie des Geber.* Berlin, 1922.

"De arte chimica." See (*A*) *Artis auriferae*, **x.**

DEE, JOHN. "Monas hieroglyphica." See (*A*) *Theatrum chemicum*, **xiv.**

DELACOTTE, JOSEPH. *Guillaume de Digulleville . . . Trois romans-poèmes du XIVᵉ siècle.* Paris, 1932.

DELACROIX. See GOETHE.

"De summa et universalis medicinae sapientiae veterum philosophorum." See Codices and MSS., **xxii.**

DEUSSEN, PAUL. *Allgemeine Geschichte der Philosophie.* Leipzig, 1906. 2 vols.

[DIDYMUS OF ALEXANDRIA.] *Physiologus Graecus.* See SBORDONE.

DIELS, HERMANN. *Die Fragmente der Vorsokratiker.* Berlin, 1912. 2 vols.

DIETERICH, ALBRECHT. *Nekyia: Beiträge zur Erklärung der neuentdeckten Petrusapokalypse.* Leipzig and Berlin, 1913.

——— (ed.). "Papyrus magica Musei Lugdunensis Batavi . . . ," *Jahrbücher für classische Philologie* (Leipzig), Supplement, XVI (1888), 747–829.

DIODORUS SICULUS. *Bibliotheca historica.* With an English translation by C. H. Oldfather. (Loeb Classical Library.) London and Cambridge, Mass., 1933–47. 10 vols.

DIOGENES LAERTIUS. *Lives of Eminent Philosophers.* With an English translation by R. D. Hicks. (Loeb Classical Library.) London and New York, 1925. 2 vols.

DIOSCORIDES "De materia medica." See Codices and MSS., **xlviii.**

DORN, GERHARD. "Congeries Paracelsicae chemicae de transmutationibus metallorum." See (*A*) *Theatrum chemicum*, **viii.**

———. "De spagirico artificio Trithemii sententia." See (*A*) *Theatrum chemicum*, **v.**

———. "Philosophia chemica ad meditativam comparata." See (*A*) *Theatrum chemicum*, **vii.**

———. "Philosophia meditativa." See (*A*) *Theatrum chemicum*, **vi.**

———. "Physica genesis." See (*A*) *Theatrum chemicum*, **iii.**

———. "Physica Trismegisti." See (*A*) *Theatrum chemicum*, **iv.**

———. "Speculativae philosophiae, gradus septem vel decem continens." See (*A*) *Theatrum chemicum*, **ii.**

DREYFUSS, J. *Adam und Eva nach der Auffassung des Midrasch.* Strasbourg, 1894.

[ECKHART, MEISTER.] *Meister Eckhart, by Franz Pfeiffer.* Translated . . . by C. de B. Evans. London, 1924. 2 vols.

EGGELING, JULIUS. See *Shatapatha-Brahmana.*

EHRENSTEIN, THEODOR (ed.). *Das Alte Testament im Bilde.* Vienna, 1923.

EISENSTEIN, JUDAH DAVID (ed.). *Ozar Midrashim.* New York, 1915.

EISLER, ROBERT. *Orpheus—the Fisher.* London, 1921.

ELEAZAR, ABRAHAM (Abraham le Juif). *Uraltes chymisches Werk,* Leipzig, 1760.

———. See also Codices and MSS., **xxxiv.**

[ELIEZER BEN HYRCANUS.] *Pirkê de Rabbi Eliezer.* Translated and edited by Gerald Friedlander. London and New York, 1916.

EMERSON, RALPH WALDO. *Essays: First Series.* (Complete Works, Centenary Edition, 2.) Boston and New York, 1903. [Jung's copy.]

Enoch, Book of. See CHARLES, *Apocrypha and Pseudepigrapha,* II, pp. 163ff. For Slavonic Book of Enoch, see ibid., pp. 425ff.

EPIPHANIUS. [*Panarium.*] *Contra octoginta haereses opus quod in-*

scribitur Panarium sive Arcula. See MIGNE, *P.G.,* vol. 41, col. 173 to vol. 42, col. 832.

"Epistola ad Hermannum." See (*A*) *Theatrum chemicum,* **xxix.**

Esdras, Second Book of. Included in Holy Bible, Apocrypha. See also CHARLES, *Apocrypha,* II, pp. 542–624, where it is called IV Ezra.

ESPAGNET, JEAN D'. "Arcanum hermeticae philosophiae." See (*A*) *Bibliotheca chemica,* **xvii.**

———. "Instructio . . . de arbore Solari." See (*A*) *Theatrum chemicum,* **xxx.**

EUCHERIUS OF LYONS. *Formularium spiritalis intelligentiae ad Uranium,* Lib. I. See MIGNE, *P.L.,* vol. 50, cols. 727–772.

EUSEBIUS OF ALEXANDRIA. "Constantini Oratio ad Sanctorum coetum." See MIGNE, *P.G.,* vol. 20, cols. 1233–1316.

EUSEBIUS OF CAESAREA. *Evangelica praeparatio.* See MIGNE, *P.G.,* vol. 21, cols. 853–64. For translation, see: EDWIN HAMILTON GIFFORD (ed.). *Eusebii Pamphili Evangelicae praeparationis libri XV.* Oxford, 1903. 4 vols.

EVOLA, J. *La tradizione ermetica.* Bari, 1931.

"Exercitationes in Turbam." See (*A*) *Artis auriferae,* **iv.**

FALKE, JAKOB VON. *Geschichte des deutschen Kunstgewerbes.* (Geschichte des deutschen Kunst, 5.) Berlin, 1888.

FECHNER, GUSTAV THEODOR. *Elemente der Psychophysik.* 2nd edn., Leipzig, 1889. 2 vols.

FERGUSON, JOHN. *Bibliotheca chemica.* Glasgow, 1906. 2 vols.

FERGUSON, JOHN C., and ANESAKI, MASAHARU. *Chinese and Japanese [Mythology].* (Mythology of All Races, ed. John Arnott McCulloch, 8.) Boston and London, 1928.

FICINO, MARSILIO. *Auctores Platonici.* Venice, 1497.

———. "Liber de arte chimica." See (*A*) *Bibliotheca chemica,* **x.**

[FIERZ-DAVID, LINDA.] *The Dream of Poliphilo.* Related and interpreted by Linda Fierz-David. Translated by Mary Hottinger. (Bollingen Series 25.) New York, 1950.

FIGULUS, BENEDICTUS. *Rosarium novum olympicum et benedictum.* Basel, 1608.

"Figurarum Aegyptiorum secretarum." See Codices and MSS., **xiv, xxi, xxxiv.**

FIRMICUS MATERNUS, JULIUS. *De errore profanarum religionum.* (Corpus scriptorum ecclesiasticorum latinorum, 2.) Vienna, 1867. See also MIGNE, *P.L.*, vol. 12, cols. 981–1050.

FLAMEL, NICOLAS. "Alchimie de Flamel . . ." See Codices and MSS., xxxiv.

———. "Tractatus brevis." See (*A*) *Musaeum hermeticum*, v.

FLAUBERT, GUSTAVE. *La Tentation de Saint Antoine.* Paris, 1874.

FLEISCHER, HEINRICH LIEBERECHT (ed.). *Hermes Trismegistus an die menschliche Seele.* Text in Arabic and German. Leipzig, 1870.

FLUDD, ROBERT. . . . *summum bonum.* . . . Frankfort on the Main, 1629.

———. *Utriusque cosmi maioris scilicet et minoris metaphysica, physica atque technica historia.* Oppenheim, 1617.

FÖRSTER, MAX. "Adams Erschaffung und Namengebung. Ein lateinisches Fragment des s.g. slawischen Henoch," *Archiv für Religionswissenschaft* (Leipzig), XI (1908), 477–529.

FOUCART, PAUL FRANÇOIS. *Les Mystères d'Eleusis.* Paris, 1914.

FRANCK, ADOLPHE. *La Kabbale.* Paris, 1843. For German translation, see: *Die Kabbala . . .* Translated by Ad. Gelinek. Leipzig, 1844.

FRANZ, MARIE-LOUISE VON (ed.). *Aurora Consurgens: A Document Attributed to Thomas Aquinas on the Problem of Opposites in Alchemy.* Translated by R. F. C. Hull and A. S. B. Glover. New York (Bollingen Series) and London, 1966.

FROBENIUS, LEO. *Das Zeitalter des Sonnengottes.* Berlin, 1904.

GAUGLER, ERNST. "Das Spätjudentum." In: *Mensch und Gottheit in den Religionen.* Bern, 1942. (Pp. 277–313.)

GEBER (Jābir ibn Hayyān). *De alchimia libri tres.* Strasbourg, 1529.

———. "Livre de la miséricorde." See BERTHELOT, *La Chimie au moyen âge,* III, pp. 163–90.

———. *Summa perfectionis de alchimia.* Strasbourg, 1529, 1531. See also (*A*) *Bibliotheca chemica,* v. For translation, see: WILLIAM SALMON. *Medicina practica; or, Practical Physick.* London, 1692.

Geheime Figuren der Rosenkreuzer, aus dem 16ten und 17ten Jahrhundert. Altona, 1785–88. 2 vols.

GEISBERG, MAX (ed.). *Die Kupferstiche des Meisters E.S.* Berlin, 1924.

GILLEN, OTTO. *Ikonographische Studien zum Hortus deliciarum der Herrad von Landsberg.* (Kunstwissenschaftliche Studien, 9.) Berlin, 1931.

GLANVILLE, BARTHOLOMEW DE. *Le Propriétaire des choses.* [Translated from *Liber de proprietatibus rerum* by Jean Corbichon.] Lyons, 1482.

"Gloria mundi." See (*A*) *Musaeum hermeticum,* **vi.**

GNOSIUS, DOMINICUS. See HERMES TRISMEGISTUS.

GOETHE, JOHANN WOLFGANG VON. *Dichtung und Wahrheit.* See *Sämtliche Werke,* vols. 22–25. For translation, see: MINNA STEELE SMITH (trans.). *Poetry and Truth, from My Own Life.* London, 1908. 2 vols.

————. *Sämtliche Werke.* Jubilee edition, edited by Eduard von der Hellen. Stuttgart and Berlin, 1902–7. 40 vols.

————. *Faust; A Tragedy.* In a modern translation by Alice Raphael. With plates after the lithographs of Eugène Delacroix. New York, 1939.

————. *Faust, Part One.* Translated by Philip Wayne. (Penguin Classics.) Harmondsworth and Baltimore, 1949. 6th impression.

————. *Faust, Part Two.* Translated by Philip Wayne. (Penguin Classics.) Harmondsworth and Baltimore, 1959.

GOLDSCHMIDT, LAZARUS (ed.). *Der babylonische Talmud.* Berlin, 1929–36. 12 vols. For English translation, see Talmud.

GOURMONT, RENÉ DE. *Le Latin mystique.* Paris, 1913.

"Grandes heures du duc de Berry." See Codices and MSS., **xxx.**

GRASSEUS, JOHANNES (Grashoff, Johann). "Lilium inter spinas." See (*A*) *Bibliotheca chemica,* **xvi.**

————. "Arca arcani." See (*A*) *Theatrum chemicum,* **xxxii.**

GRENFELL, BERNARD PYNE; DREXEL, LUCY WHARTON; and HUNT, ARTHUR S. (eds.). *New Sayings of Jesus.* New York and London, 1904.

GUILHELMUS TECENENSIS. "Lilium de spinis evulsum." See (*A*) *Theatrum chemicum,* **xxiii.**

GUILLAUME DE DIGULLEVILLE. See DELACOTTE.

GYSIN, FRITZ. *Gotische Bildteppiche der Schweiz.* Basel, 1941.

HALL, MANLY PALMER. *Codex Rosae Crucis.* Los Angeles, 1938.

HALM, KARL FELIX VON (ed.). *Rhetores Latini minores.* Leipzig, 1863.

HAMBRUCH, PAUL (ed.). *Südseemärchen.* . . . Jena, 1916.

HAMMER-PURGSTALL, JOSEPH. *Mémoire sur deux coffrets gnostiques du moyen âge.* Paris, 1835.

HÄNDLER, OTTO. *Die Predigt.* Berlin, 1941.

HARNACK, ADOLF VON. *History of Dogma.* Translated [by Neil Buchanan] from the 3rd German edition. London, 1894–99. 7 vols. (Paperback reissue, with same pagination, New York, 1961. 7 vols. in 4.)

HARRISON, JANE ELLEN. *Themis: a Study of the Social Origins of Greek Religion.* Cambridge, 1912.

HASTINGS, JAMES (ed.). *Encyclopaedia of Religion and Ethics.* Edinburgh and New York, 1908–27. 13 vols.

HAUCK, ALBERT (ed.). *Realencyklopädie für protestantische Theologie und Kirche.* Leipzig, 1896–1913. 24 vols.

HEGEMONIUS. *Acta Archelai.* Edited by Charles Henry Beeson. Leipzig, 1906.

HENNING, WALTER. "Ein manichäisches Henochbuch," *Sitzungsberichte der preussischen Akademie der Wissenschaften* (Berlin), *Philosophisch-historische Klasse,* 1934, 27–35.

Hermaphroditisches Sonn- und Mondskind. Das ist: Des Sohns deren Philosophen natürlich-übernatürliche Gebährung, Zerstörung und Regenerierung. Mainz, 1752.

"Hermes Bird." See (*A*) *Theatrum chemicum Britannicum,* **iii.**

HERMES TRISMEGISTUS. *An die menschliche Seele.* See FLEISCHER.

———. *Tractatus vere aureus, de lapidis philosophici secreto . . . cum scholiis Dominici Gnosii.* ("Tractatus aureus.") Leipzig, 1610. See also (*A*) *Ars chemica,* **i** (this version gives the main points only); (*A*) *Musaeum hermeticum,* **i**; (*A*) *Bibliotheca chemica curiosa,* **ii.**

———. See also "Tabula smaragdina."

HERODOTUS. [*Histories.*] Translated by J. Enoch Powell. Oxford, 1949. 2 vols.

HERRAD OF LANDSBERG. *Hortus deliciarum.* See KELLER and STRAUB.

HERRLIBERGER, DAVID. *Heilige Ceremonien oder Religionsübungen der abgöttischen Völcker der Welt.* Zurich, 1748.

505

HERRMANN, PAUL. *Nordische Mythologie in gemeinverständlicher Darstellung.* Leipzig, 1903.

HESIOD. *Theogony.* In: *The Homeric Hymns and Homerica.* With translation by Hugh G. Evelyn-White. (Loeb Classical Library.) London and New York, 1915.

HILDEGARDE OF BINGEN, SAINT. "Liber divinorum operum." See Codices and MSS., **xii.**

————. "Scivias." MS. (12th cent.), Abbey of St. Hildegarde, Bingen. In: M. BÖCKELER (ed.). *Wisse die Wege; Scivias.* Salzburg, 1954.

HIPPOLYTUS. *Elenchos.* (*Hippolytus' Werke.* Edited by Paul Wendland. Vol. III.) Leipzig, 1916. For translation, see: FRANCIS LEGGE, (trans.). *Philosophumena; or, The Refutation of All Heresies.* London and New York, 1921. 2 vols.

HOGHELANDE, THEOBALD DE. "Liber de alchemiae difficultatibus." See (*A*) *Theatrum chemicum,* **i;** (*A*) *Bibliotheca chemica curiosa,* **i.**

HOLMYARD, ERIC JOHN (ed. and trans.). *Kitāb al-'ilm al-muktasab fi zinā'at adhdhahab* [Book of knowledge acquired concerning the cultivation of gold]. [By Abu'l Qāsim Muhammad ibn Ahmad al-'Irāqī.] Paris, 1923.

HOLTZMANN, ADOLF. *Indische Sagen.* Edited by Moriz Winternitz. Jena, 1921.

HOMER. *The Odyssey.* With an English translation by A. T. Murray. (Loeb Classical Library.) London and New York, 1919. 2 vols.

HONORIUS OF AUTUN. *Speculum ecclesiae.* See MIGNE, *P.L.,* vol. 172, cols. 807–1108.

[HORAPOLLO NILIACUS.] *Hori Apollinis Selecta hieroglyphica, sive Sacrae notae Aegyptiorum, et insculptae imagines.* Rome, 1597. For translation, see: GEORGE BOAS (trans. and ed.). *The Hieroglyphics of Horapollo.* (Bollingen Series 23.) New York, 1950.

HORTULANUS, pseud. (Joannes de Garlandia). "Commentarius in Tabulam Smaragdinam Hermetis Trismegisti." See (*A*) *De alchemia,* **iii.** See also RUSKA, *Tabula smaragdina,* pp. 180ff. For translation, see: "A Briefe Commentarie upon the Smaragdine Table of Hermes of Alchemy," in BACON, *The Mirror of Alchimy,* q.v.

IAMBLICHUS. *De mysteriis Aegyptiorum, Chaldaeorum, Assyriorum.*

. . . Venice, 1491. For translation, see: THOMAS TAYLOR (trans.). *Iamblichus on the Mysteries of the Egyptians.* 2nd edn., London, 1895.

IGNATIUS OF LOYOLA, SAINT. [*Exercitia spiritualia.*] *The Spiritual Exercises of St. Ignatius Loyola, with a Continuous Commentary.* 2nd edn. New York and London, 1923.

INMAN, THOMAS. *Ancient Pagan and Modern Christian Symbolism Exposed and Explained.* New York, 1879.

IRENAEUS, SAINT. *Contra* [or *Adversus*] *haereses libri quinque.* See MIGNE, *P.G.,* vol. 7, cols. 433–1224. For translation, see JOHN KEBLE (trans.). *Five Books of S. Irenaeus . . . against Heresies.* Oxford, 1872.

ISIDORE OF SEVILLE, SAINT. *Liber etymologiarum.* See MIGNE, *P.L.,* vol. 82, cols. 73–728.

IZQUIERDO, SEBASTIAN. *Praxis exercitiorum spiritualium P.N.S. Ignatii.* Rome, 1695.

JACOBI, JOLANDE. *The Psychology of C. G. Jung.* Translated by Ralph Manheim. 6th edn., New Haven and London, 1962.

JAMES, MONTAGUE RHODES (ed. and trans.). *The Apocryphal New Testament.* Oxford, 1924.

JAMES, WILLIAM. *Pragmatism: A New Name for Some Old Ways of Thinking.* London and Cambridge, Mass., 1907.

JAMSTHALER, HERBRANDT. *Viatorium spagyricum. Das ist: Ein gebenedeyter spagyrischer Wegweiser.* Frankfort on the Main, 1625.

[Jatakas.] *The Jataka; or, Stories of the Buddha's Former Births.* Edited and translated by Edward Byles Cowell. Cambridge, 1895–1913. 6 vols.

JOHANNES A MEHUNG (Jean de Meung). "Demonstratio naturae." See *(A) Musaeum hermeticum,* **iv.**

JOSEPH BEN GORION (pseud. of Micha Jozef Berdyczewski). *Die Sagen der Juden.* Collected and revised by M. J. bin Gorion. The text translated into German by R. Ramberg-Berdyczewski. Edited by Rahel and Emanuel bin Gorion [i.e., R. and E. Berdyczewski]. Frankfort on the Main, 1913–27. 5 vols.

JOSEPHUS, FLAVIUS. *Antiquitates Judaicae.* In: *Josephus.* With an English translation by H. St J. Thackeray. (Loeb Classical Library.) London and New York, 1926–43. 7 vols.

Jung, Carl Gustav. *Aion. Collected Works,** Vol. 9, ii.

————. "The Archetypes of the Collective Unconscious." In: *Collected Works,** Vol. 9, i.

————. "Basic Postulates of Analytical Psychology." In: *Collected Works,** Vol. 8.

————. "Concerning Mandala Symbolism." In: *Collected Works,** Vol. 9, i.

————. "Concerning Rebirth." In: *Collected Works,** Vol. 9, i.

————. *Memories, Dreams, Reflections.* Recorded and edited by Aniela Jaffé. Translated by Richard and Clara Winston. New York and London, 1963. (Edns. separately paginated.)

————. *Mysterium Coniunctionis. Collected Works,** Vol. 14.

————. "Paracelsus as a Spiritual Phenomenon." In: *Collected Works,** Vol. 13.

————. "Paracelsus the Physician." In: *Collected Works,** Vol. 15.

————. *Psychological Types. Collected Works,** Vol. 6. Alternative source: Translation by H. G. Baynes. New York and London, 1923.

————. "The Psychology of the Child Archetype." *Collected Works,** Vol. 9, i.

————. "Psychology and Religion." In: *Collected Works,** Vol. 11.

————. "Psychology of the Transference." In: *Collected Works,** Vol. 16.

————. "The Relations between the Ego and the Unconscious." In: *Collected Works,** Vol. 7.

————. "The Spirit Mercurius." In: *Collected Works,** Vol. 13.

————. *Symbols of Transformation. Collected Works,** Vol. 5. (A translation of *Symbole der Wandlung,* Zurich, 1951. For the translation of the superseded version, *Wandlungen und Symbole der Libido,* see: *Psychology of the Unconscious.* Translated by Beatrice M. Hinkle. New York, 1916; London, 1917; new edn., 1921.)

————. "The Transcendent Function." In: *Collected Works,** Vol. 8.

————. "Transformation Symbolism in the Mass." In: *Collected Works,** Vol. 11.

————. "The Visions of Zosimos." In: *Collected Works,** Vol. 13.

* For details of the *Collected Works of C. G. Jung,* see announcement at end of this volume.

————. See also WILHELM.

JURAIN, ABTALA. *Hyle und Coahyl.* Translated from Ethiopian into Latin and from Latin into German by Johannes Elias Müller. Hamburg, 1732.

JUSTIN [MARTYR], SAINT. *Dialogus cum Tryphone Judaeo.* See MIGNE, *P.G.,* vol. 6, cols. 471–800. For translation, see: MARCUS DODS, GEORGE REITH, and B. P. PRATTEN (trans.). *The Writings of Justin Martyr and Athenagoras.* (Ante-Nicene Christian Library, 2.) Edinburgh, 1867.

KALID (Khalid ibn Jazid ibn Muawiyah). "Liber trium verborum." See (*A*) *Artis auriferae*, **viii.**

KELLER, G., and STRAUB, A. (trans.). *Herrad von Landsberg Hortus deliciarum.* Strasbourg, 1879–99 (1901).

KELLEY, EDWARD. *Tractatus duo egregii, de Lapide philosophorum.* Hamburg and Amsterdam, 1676.

KERÉNYI, KAROLY [or C.]. *Die griechisch-orientalische Romanliteratur in religionsgeschichtlicher Beleuchtung.* Tübingen, 1927.

Khludov Psalter. See Codices and MSS., **xxxvi.**

KHUNRATH, HEINRICH CONRAD. *Amphitheatrum sapientiae aeternae solius verae, Christiano-kabalisticum, divino-magicum . . . Tertriunum, Catholicon.* Hanau, 1609.

————. *Von hylealischen, das ist, pri-materialischen catholischen, oder algemeinem natürlichen Chaos.* Magdeburg, 1597.

KING, CHARLES WILLIAM. *The Gnostics and their Remains, Ancient and Mediaeval.* London, 1864.

KNORR VON ROSENROTH, CHRISTIAN. *Kabbala denudata seu Doctrina Hebraeorum.* Sulzbach, 1677–84. 2 vols.

KNUCHEL, EDUARD FRITZ. *Die Umwandlung in Kult, Magie und Rechtsbrauch.* Basel, 1919.

KOEMSTEDT, R. *Vormittelalterliche Malerei.* Augsburg, 1929.

KOPP, HERMANN. *Die Alchemie in älterer und neuerer Zeit.* Heidelberg, 1886. 2 vols.

Koran, The. Translated from the Arabic by the Rev. J. M. Rodwell. (Everyman's Library, 380.) London and New York, 1909.

KOSMAS. See COSMAS.

KRAMP, JOSEPH. *Die Opferanschauungen der römischen Messliturgie.* Regensburg, 1924.

[Krates.] "The Book of Krates." See Berthelot, *La Chimie au moyen âge*, III, pp. 44–75.

Lactantius, Firmianus. *Opera omnia*. Edited by Samuel Brandt and Georg Laubmann. (Corpus scriptorum ecclesiasticorum latinorum.) Vienna, 1890–97. 3 vols. For translation, see: William Fletcher (trans.). *The Works of Lactantius*. (Ante-Nicene Christian Library, 21–22.) Edinburgh, 1871. 2 vols.

Laignel-Lavastine, Maxime (ed.). *Histoire générale de la médecine*. Paris, 1936–49. 3 vols.

Lajard, Jean Baptiste Félix. "Mémoire sur une représentation figurée de la Vénus orientale androgyne," *Nouvelles annales de l'Institut archéologique* (Paris), I (1836).

Lambspringk. "De lapide philosophico figurae et emblemata." See (*A*) *Musaeum hermeticum*, **vii.**

Lang, Joseph Bernhard. *Hat ein Gott die Welt erschaffen?* Bern, 1942.

La Légende latine de S. Brandaines. . . . Edited by Achille Jubinal. Paris, 1836.

Leisegang, Hans. *Die Gnosis*. Leipzig, 1924.

———. *Der heilige Geist*. Leipzig, 1919.

Lenormant, Charles, and Witte, Jean Joseph Antoine Marie, Baron de. *Élite des monuments céramographiques*. Paris, 1844–61. 8 vols.

Libavius, Andreas. *Alchymia . . . recognita, emendata, et aucta*. Frankfort on the Main, 1606.

"Liber patris sapientiae." See (*A*) *Theatrum chemicum Britannicum*, **ii.**

[Li-Chi.] *The Li-Ki*. In: *The Texts of Confucianism*, Vol. III. Translated by James Legge. (Sacred Books of the East, 27.) Oxford, 1885.

Lippmann, Edmund O. von. *Entstehung und Ausbreitung der Alchemie*. Berlin, 1919–54. 3 vols.

Löffler, Karl. *Schwäbische Buchmalerei in romanischer Zeit*. Augsburg, 1928.

Lombardus, Petrus. See Petrus.

Lüders, Horstmann. *Nachrichten von der königlichen Gesellschaft der Wissenschaften zu Göttingen. Geschäftliche Mittheilungen aus dem Jahre 1897.* Göttingen, 1897.

LULLY, RAYMOND. "Codicillus." See (*A*) *Bibliotheca chemica curiosa,* **vii.**

————. "Compendium artis alchemiae. . . . See (*A*) *Bibliotheca chemica curiosa,* **vi.**

LYDUS, JOANNES. *De mensibus.* Edited by Richard Wünsch. Leipzig, 1898.

McCRINDLE, JOHN WATSON (trans.). *Ancient India, as Described by Ktesias . . .* Being a translation of the abridgement of his "Indika" by Photios. Calcutta, 1882.

————. See also COSMAS.

MACKENNA, STEPHEN (trans.). *Plotinus: The Enneads.* Second edn., revised by B. S. Page. London, 1956. (Porphyry's *Life of Plotinus* is translated on pp. 1–20.)

MADATHANUS, HENRICUS. "Aureum saeculum redivivum." See (*A*) *Musaeum hermeticum,* **ii.**

MAIER, MICHAEL. *De circulo physico quadrato.* Oppenheim, 1616.

————. *Secretioris naturae secretorum scrutinium chymicum.* Frankfort on the Main, 1687. (Usually called *Scrutinium chymicum.*)

————. *Symbola aureae mensae duodecim nationum.* Frankfort on the Main, 1617.

————. *Tripus aureus, hoc est, Tres tractatus chymici selectissimi.* Frankfort on the Main, 1618. See also (*A*) *Musaeum hermeticum,* **viii.**

————. *Viatorium, hoc est, De montibus planetarum septem seu metallorum.* Rouen, 1651.

MAIURI, AMEDEO. *La villa dei misteri.* Rome, 1931. 2 vols.

MANGET, JEAN JACQUES. See (*A*) *Bibliotheca chemica curiosa.*

MARIA PROPHETISSA (Maria the Jewess). "Practica. . . ." See (*A*) *Artis auriferae,* **vii.**

MAROLLES, MICHEL DE. *Tableaux du temple des muses.* Paris, 1655.

MASPERO, GASTON CAMILLE CHARLES. *Études de mythologie et d'archéologie égyptiennes.* Paris, 1893–1913. 7 vols.

MAX MÜLLER, FRIEDRICH (trans.). *The Upanishads.* Parts I and II. (Sacred Books of the East, I and XV.) Oxford, 1879 and 1884.

MEHUNG. See JOHANNES A MEHUNG.

MELCHIOR, CARDINAL BISHOP OF BRIXEN. "Von dem gelben und rotten Mann." See (*A*) *Aureum vellus*, **ii.**

MELCHIOR, NICHOLAS, OF HERMANNSTADT (Cibinensis) (Nicolaus Melchior Szebeni). "Addam et processum . . ." See (*A*) *Theatrum chemicum*, **xviii.**

———. *Symbolum*. In MAIER, *Symbola* . . . , q.v. (pp. 507–52).

MELITO OF SARDIS. *De baptismo*. See PITRA, *Analecta sacra*, II, pp. 3–5.

MERLINUS. "Allegoria de arcano lapidis." See (*A*) *Artis auriferae*, **ix.**

MERZ, WALTHER (ed.). *Die Wappenrolle von Zürich*. Zurich, 1930.

MEYRINK, GUSTAV. *Der Golem*. Leipzig, 1915. For translation, see: MADGE PEMBERTON (trans.). *The Golem*. London, 1928.

——— (ed.). *Thomas Aquinas: Abhandlung über den Stein der Weysen*. Munich, 1925.

MICHELSPACHER, STEFFAN. *Cabala, speculum artis et naturae, in alchymia*. Augsburg, 1654.

MICRERIS. "Tractatus Micreris." See (*A*) *Theatrum chemicum*, **xxvi.**

Midrash Tehillim. See BUBER.

MIGNE, JACQUES PAUL. *Dictionnaire des sciences occultes*. Paris, 1846–48. 2 vols.

———. (ed.). *Patrologiae cursus completus*.
　　[*P.L.*] Latin series. Paris, 1844–64. 221 vols.
　　[*P.G.*] Greek series. Paris, 1857–66. 166 vols.
　　(These works are referred to in the text as "Migne, *P.L.*" and
　　　"Migne, *P.G.*" respectively. References are to columns, not to
　　　pages.)

MOLSDORF, WILHELM. *Christliche Symbolik der Mittelalterlichen Kunst*. Leipzig, 1926.

MORIENUS ROMANUS. "Sermo de transmutatione metallorum." See (*A*) *Artis auriferae*, **xi.**

MUELLER, NIKOLAUS. *Glauben, Wissen und Kunst der alten Hindus.* . . . Mainz, 1822.

Munich Lectionary (*Perikopenbuch*). See Codices and MSS., **xviii.**

Mutus liber in quo tamen tota philosophia hermetica, figuris hiero-

glyphicis depingitur. La Rochelle, 1677. See also (*A*) *Bibliotheca chemica curiosa,* **vii-a** (for illustrations in present work).

MYLIUS, JOHANN DANIEL. *Philosophia reformata.* Frankfort on the Main, 1622.

NAZARI, GIOVANNI BATTISTA. *Della tramutatione metallica sogni tre.* Brescia, 1599.

NIERENSTEIN, M., and CHAPMAN, P. F. "Enquiry into the Authorship of the *Ordinall of Alchimy,*" *Isis* (Bruges), XVIII:53 (Oct. 1932), 290–321.

NIETZSCHE, FRIEDRICH WILHELM. *Thus Spake Zarathustra.* Translated by Thomas Common. London, 1932.

[NILUS, SAINT.] *Anonymi vita S. Nili.* In MIGNE, *P.G.,* vol. 120, cols. 9–166.

NORTON, SAMUEL. *Catholicon physicorum, seu Modus conficiendi tincturam physicam et alchymicam.* Frankfort on the Main, 1630.

———. *Mercurius redivivus, seu Modus conficiendi lapidem philosophicum tum album, quam rubeum e Mercurio.* Frankfort on the Main, 1630.

NORTON, THOMAS. *The Ordinall of Alchimy.* A facsimile reproduction from the *Theatrum chemicum Britannicum,* with annotations by Elias Ashmole. Edited by Eric John Holmyard. London, 1928. See also (*A*) *Theatrum chemicum Britannicum,* **i;** (*A*) *Musaeum hermeticum,* **x.**

OPPENHEIM, GUSTAV. *Fabula Josephi et Asenathae apocrypha.* . . . Berlin, 1886.

ORIGEN. *Homiliae in Jeremiam.* See MIGNE, *P.G.,* vol. 13, cols. 255–544.

ORTHELIUS. "Epilogus et recapitulatio." See (*A*) *Bibliotheca chemica curiosa,* **xiv.**

PARACELSUS (Theophrastus Bombast of Hohenheim). See: JOHANN HUSER (ed.). *Aureoli Philippi Theophrasti Bombasts von Hohenheim Paracelsi . . . Opera Bücher und Schrifften.* Strasbourg, 1589–91. 10 parts. Reprinted 1603, 1616. 2 vols. See also: KARL SUDHOFF and WILHELM MATTHIESSEN (ed.). *Theophrast von Hohenheim genannt Paracelsus Sämtliche Werke.* First section. *Medizinische Schriften.* Munich and Berlin, 1922–33, 14 vols.

———. *Auslegung der Figuren, so zu Nürenberg gefunden seind worden, gefürt in grunt der Magischen Weissagung, durch Doctorem Theophrastum von Hohenheim.* [Fastenmess,] 1569.

———. *Das Buch Azoth seu De ligno vitae.* See HUSER, Vol. 2, or SUDHOFF, Vol. 14, pp. 547ff.

———. *De vita longa.* See SUDHOFF, Vol. 3, pp. 247ff.

———. *Ein ander Erklärung der gantzen Astronomie.* See HUSER, Vol. 2, or SUDHOFF, Vol. 12, pp. 447ff.

———. *Philosophia ad Athenienses.* See SUDHOFF, Vol. 13, pp. 387ff.

———. *Theoretica schemata seu Typi.* See HUSER, Vol. 1, pp. 670–82.

PATRIZI, FRANCESCO. *Nova de universis philosophia.* Venice, 1593.

PENOTUS, BERNHARDUIS GEORGIUS (Bernardus à Portu). "Philosophi potius . . ." (a table). See (*A*) *Theatrum chemicum,* **xii.**

PEREGRINUS. "Speculum virginum." See Codices and MSS., **xli.**

[PETRARCH.] "Les triomphes du poethe messire Françoys Pétrarche." See Codices and MSS., **xxxiii.**

PETRONIUS ARBITER. [*Works.*] With an English translation by Michael Heseltine. (Loeb Classical Library.) London and New York, 1913.

PETRUS LOMBARDUS (Peter Lombard). "De sacramentis." See Codices and MSS., **xlv.**

PHILALETHES, EIRENAEUS, *Erklärung der Hermetisch poetischen Werke Herrn Georgii Riplaei.* Hamburg, 1741. (A translation of the following.)

———. *Ripley Reviv'd; or, An Exposition upon Sir George Ripley's Hermetico-Poetical Works.* London, 1678.

———. "Fons chymicae veritatis." See (*A*) *Musaeum hermeticum,* **xvi.**

———. "Introitus apertus." See (*A*) *Musaeum hermeticum,* **xiv.**

———. "Metallorum metamorphosis." See (*A*) *Musaeum hermeticum,* **xv.**

PHILO. [*Works.*] Translated by Francis Henry Colson and George Herbert Whitaker. (Loeb Classical Library.) London and Cambridge, Mass., 1929– . 10 vols. (in progress).

PHILOSTRATUS. *The Life of Apollonius of Tyana.* . . . Translated by Frederick Cornwallis Conybeare. (Loeb Classical Library.) London and New York, 1912. 2 vols.

PHOTIUS. *Bibliotheca.* Edited by J. Bekker. Berlin, 1824–25. 2 vols.

For French translation, see: *Bibliothèque*. Edited and translated by René Henry. Paris, 1959–62. 3 vols.

Physiologus. See SBORDONE.

PICINELLI, PHILIPPUS. *Mundus symbolicus*. Cologne, 1680–81.

PIGNATELLI, JACOBUS. *Consultationes canonicae*. Geneva, 1700. 11 vols.

Pirkê de Rabbi Eliezer. See ELIEZER BEN HYRCANUS.

Pistis Sophia. Translated (into German) by Carl Schmidt. Leipzig, 1925. English trans. by George William Horner. London, 1924.

PITRA, JEAN BAPTISTE (ed.). *Analecta sacra* . . . Paris, 1876–91. 8 vols. (II, pp. 3–5, contains Melito of Sardis, *De baptismo*.)

———. *Spicilegium solesmense*. Paris, 1852–58. 4 vols.

PLATO. *The Collected Dialogues*. Edited by Edith Hamilton and Huntington Cairns. (Bollingen Series 71.) New York, 1961. (*Phaedrus*, pp. 475–525; *Philebus*, pp. 1086–1150; *Timaeus*, pp. 1151–1211.)

PLATO, pseud. "Liber Platonis quartorum." See (*A*) *Theatrum chemicum,* **xxvii.**

PLINY. [*Historia naturalis.*] *Natural History*. With an English translation by H. Rackham. (Loeb Classical Library.) London, 1938–45. 11 vols.

POMMET, P. *Histoire générale des drogues*. Paris, 1694.

PORPHYRY. See MACKENNA.

PORTA, GIAMBATTISTA DELLA. *De distillationibus libri IX*. Strasbourg, 1609.

PREISENDANZ, KARL (ed.). *Papyri Graecae magicae*. Leipzig and Berlin, 1928–31. 2 vols.

PRINZ, HUGO. *Altorientalische Symbolik*. Berlin, 1915.

PRISCILLIAN. [*Opera*] *Priscilliani quae supersunt*. Edited by Georg Schepss. (Corpus scriptorum ecclesiasticorum latinorum, 18.) Vienna, 1889.

PRZYWARA, ERICH. *Deus semper major*. Freiburg im Breisgau, 1938. 3 vols.

PUËCH, HENRI CHARLES. "The Concept of Redemption in Manichaeism," in *The Mystic Vision*. (Papers from the Eranos Yearbooks, 6.) New York (Bollingen Series 30) and London, 1968. (Orig. in *Eranos-Jahrbuch 1936*.)

QUERCETANUS, JOSEPHUS. "Ad Jacobi Auberti Vendonis de ortu. . . ." See (A) *Theatrum chemicum*, **xiii.**

RABANUS MAURUS. *Allegoriae in universam sacram scripturam.* See MIGNE, *P.L.*, vol. 112, cols. 849–1088.

"Recueil des fausses décrétales." See Codices and MSS., **xxxvii.**

"Recueil de figures astrologiques." See Codices and MSS., **xxxv.**

REITZENSTEIN, RICHARD. "Alchemistische Lehrschriften und Märchen bei den Arabern." In: *Heliodori carmina quattuor.* (Religionsgeschichtliche Versuche und Vorarbeiten, XIX, 2.) Giessen, 1923. (Pp. 63–86.)

————. *Die hellenistischen Mysterienreligionen.* Leipzig, 1910.

————. *Poimandres: Studien zur griechisch-ägyptischen und frühchristlichen Literatur.* Leipzig, 1904.

REUSNER, HIERONYMUS. *Pandora: Das ist, die edelst Gab Gottes, oder der Werde und heilsame Stein der Weysen.* Basel, 1588.

REYMANN, LEONHARD. *Nativität-Kalender.* 1515. See STRAUSS.

RHENANUS, JOHANNES. *Solis e puteo emergentis sive dissertationis chymotechnicae libri tres.* Frankfort on the Main, 1613.

———— (ed.). *Harmoniae inperscrutabilis chymico-philosophicae Decades duae.* Frankfort on the Main, 1625. (A text of "Aurora consurgens" is given in Decas II, pp. 175ff.)

RICHARDUS ANGLICUS (Richard of Wendover). "Correctorium alchymiae." See (A) *Theatrum chemicum*, **xvi.**

RIPLEY, GEORGE. "Cantilena Riplaei." See *Opera*, below. For translation, see: JUNG, *Mysterium Coniunctionis*, ch. IV, 4.

————. *Opera omnia chemica.* Kassel, 1649.

————. "Liber duodecim portarum." See (A) *Bibliotheca chemica curiosa*, **xii.**

————. "Verses Belonging to an Emblematicall Scrowle." See (A) *Theatrum chemicum Britannicum*, **iv;** Codices and MSS., **vii.**

"Roman de Lancelot du Lac." See Codices and MSS., **xxxii.**

Rosario dela gloriosa vergine Maria. Venice, 1524. See INMAN.

Rosarium philosophorum. Secunda pars alchimiae de lapide philosophico vero modo praeparando. . . . Cum figuris rei perfectionem ostendentibus. (Vol. 2 of *De alchimia*.) Frankfort on the Main, 1550. See also (A) *Artis auriferae*, **xii;** (A) *Bibliotheca chemica curiosa*, **ix.**

"Rosarius minor." See (*A*) *De alchemia*, **i.**

ROSCHER, WILHELM HEINRICH (ed.). *Ausführliches Lexikon der griechischen und römischen Mythologie.* Leipzig, 1884–1937. 6 vols.

———. *Hermes der Windgott.* Leipzig, 1878.

ROSENCREUTZ, CHRISTIAN. *Chymische Hochzeit.* Reprinted from a Strasbourg 1616 edition. Edited by F. Maack. Berlin, 1913. For translation, see: *The Hermetick Romance, or The Chymical Wedding.* Translated by E. Foxcroft. London, 1690.

RULAND, MARTIN. *Lexicon alchemiae, sive Dictionarium alchemisticum.* Frankfort on the Main, 1612. For translation, see: *A Lexicon of Alchemy.* London, 1892.

RUPERT, SAINT. *De trinitate et operibus ejus.* See MIGNE, *P.L.,* vol. 167, cols. 199–1828.

RUPESCISSA, JOANNES DE. *La Vertu et propriété de la quinte essence.* Lyons, 1581.

RUSKA, JULIUS FERDINAND. "Die Vision des Arisleus." See SUDHOFF, *Historische Studien.*

———. "Die siebzig Bücher des Gabir ibn Hajjan." See the following, pp. 38–47.

——— (ed.). *Studien zur Geschichte der Chemie.* Memorial volume to Edmund O. von Lippmann on his seventieth birthday. Berlin, 1927.

———. *Tabula Smaragdina: ein Beitrag zur Geschichte der hermetischen Literatur.* Heidelberg, 1926.

———. *Turba Philosophorum: ein Beitrag zur Geschichte der Alchemie.* (Quellen und Studien zur Geschichte der Naturwissenschaften und der Medizin, 1.) Berlin, 1931.

"Sagesse des anciens, La." See Codices and MSS., **xiii.**

SALZER, ANSELM, *Die Sinnbilder und Beiworte Mariens in der deutschen Literatur und lateinischen Hymnen-Poesie des Mittelalters.* Linz, 1893.

SANCHEZ, THOMAS. *Opus morale in praecepta decalogi, sive Summa casuum conscientiae.* Paris, Antwerp, 1615–22. 2 vols.

SBORDONE, F. (ed.). *Physiologus.* Milan, Genoa, Rome, Naples, 1936.

SCALIGER, PAULUS. [*Explanatio imaginum.*] *P. Principis de la Scala primi tomi Miscellaneorum de rerum caussis.* . . . Cologne, 1570.

SCHEDEL, HARTMANN. *Das Buch der Chroniken.* Nuremberg, 1493.

SCHEFTELOWITZ, ISIDOR. "Das Hörnermotiv in den Religionen," *Archiv für Religionswissenschaft* (Leipzig), XV (1912), 451–87.

SCHMIDT, CARL (ed. and trans.). "Gnostische Schriften in koptischer Sprache aus dem Codex Brucianus herausgegeben," *Texte und Untersuchungen der altchristlichen Literatur* (Leipzig), VIII (1892), 1–692.

SCHMIEDER, KARL CHRISTOPH. *Geschichte der Alchemie.* Halle, 1832.

SCHRADER, EBERHARD. "Die Vorstellung vom μονόκερως und ihr Ursprung," *Sitzungsberichte der königlichen preussischen Akademie der Wissenschaften* (Berlin), 1892, 573–81.

SCHULTZ, WOLFGANG. *Dokumente der Gnosis.* Jena, 1910.

SCOTT, WALTER (ed.). *Hermetica.* Oxford, 1924–36. 4 vols.

SENDIVOGIUS, MICHAEL (Michal Sendiwoj). "Dialogus Mercurii . . ." See (A) *Theatrum chemicum,* **xxi.**

———. "Novi luminis chemici tractatus alter de sulphure." See (A) *Musaeum hermeticum,* **xiii.**

———. "Novum lumen chemicum." See (A) *Musaeum hermeticum,* **xii.**

———. "Parabola. . . ." See (A) *Bibliotheca chemica curiosa,* **xiii.**

SENIOR (Zadith ben Hamuel). *De chemia Senioris antiquissimi philosophi libellus.* Strasbourg, 1566. See also (A) *Bibliotheca chemica curiosa,* **xi.**

———. *Tabula chymica.* In: *Philosophiae chymicae IV. vetustissima scripta.* Frankfort on the Main, 1605.

SENIOR, ADOLPHUS. *Azoth, sive Aureliae occultae philosophorum . . .* Frankfort on the Main, 1613.

Shatapatha-Brahmana. Part I, Books I and II. Edited and translated by Julius Eggeling. (Sacred Books of the East, 12.) Oxford, 1882.

[Shêng Chi-t'u.] *The Life of Confucius, Reproduced from a Book entitled Shêng Chi-t'u, being Rubbings from the Stone "Tablets of the Holy Shrine."* Shanghai [1934?].

SHEPARD, ODELL. *The Lore of the Unicorn.* London and Boston, 1930.

Sibylline Oracles. See CHARLES, *Apocrypha,* Vol. II, pp. 368–406.

SIEBMACHER, JOHANN AMBROSIUS. "Hydrolithus sophicus." See (A) *Bibliotheca chemica curiosa*, **xv**; *Musaeum hermeticum*, **iii.**

SILBERER, HERBERT. *Problems of Mysticism and Its Symbolism.* Translated by Smith Ely Jelliffe. New York, 1917.

Slavonic Book of Enoch. See CHARLES, *Apocrypha*.

Speculum humanae salvationis. (i) . . . *cum Speculo S. Mariae Virginis.* Augsburg, 1480. (ii) Codices and MSS., **xxvii; xxviii; xl-a.**

"Speculum veritatis." See Codices and MSS., **xlvi.**

SPITTELER, CARL. *Prometheus and Epimetheus.* Translated by James Fullarton Muirhead. London. 1931.

"Splendor solis." See TRISMOSIN.

SPRINGER, ANTON HEINRICH. *Handbuch der Kunstgeschichte.* 7th edn., Leipzig, 1902–4. 4 vols.

STAPLETON, HENRY ERNEST and HUSAIN, M. HIDAYAT (eds.). *Three Arabic Treatises on Alchemy, by Muhammad ibn Umail.* (Asiatic Society of Bengal: Memoirs, XII, 1.) Calcutta, 1933.

STEEB, JOANNES CHRISTOPHORUS. *Coelum sephiroticum* . . . Mainz, 1679.

STEINSCHNEIDER, MORITZ. *Die europäischen Übersetzungen aus dem arabischen bis Mitte des 17. Jahrhunderts.* (Sitzungsberichte der kaiserlichen Akademie der Wissenschaften in Wien, Philosophisch-historische Klasse, 149, 151.) Vienna, 1904 5. 2 parts.

STEVENSON, JAMES. "Ceremonial of Hasjelti Dailjis and Mythical Sand Painting of the Navajo Indians," *Eighth Annual Report of the Bureau of Ethnology to the Secretary of the Smithsonian Institution 1886–87* (Washington, 1891), 229–85.

STOBAEUS, JOANNES. *Eclogarum physicarum et ethicarum libri duo.* Edited by T. Gainsford. Oxford, 1850. 2 vols.

STOLCIUS DE STOLCENBERG, DANIEL. *Viridarium chymicum figuris cupro incisis adornatum et poeticis picturis illustratum* . . . Frankfort on the Main, 1624.

STRAUSS, HEINZ ARTUR. *Der astrologische Gedanke in der deutschen Vergangenheit.* Munich, 1926.

[SUDHOFF, KARL, ed.] *Historische Studien und Skizzen zur Natur- und Heilwissenschaft.* Memorial volume presented to Georg Sticker upon his seventieth birthday. Berlin, 1930.

"Tabula smaragdina" ("The Emerald Table of Hermes Trismegistus"). See (i) RUSKA; (ii) (A) *Ars chemica*, ii; (iii) (A) *De Alchemia*, ii; (iv) for translation, BACON, *The Mirror of Alchimy*, q.v.

[Talmud.] *The Babylonian Talmud*. Translated into English under the editorship of I. Epstein. London, 1935–48. 34 vols. See also GOLDSCHMIDT.

TAYLOR, F. SHERWOOD. "A Survey of Greek Alchemy," *Journal of Hellenic Studies* (London), L (1930), 109–39.

TECENENSIS. See GUILHELMUS TECENENSIS.

TERTULLIAN [Quintus Septimius Clemens Tertullianus]. *Apologeticus adversus Gentes pro Christianis*. See MIGNE, *P.L.*, vol. 1, cols. 257–536. For translation, see: SYDNEY THELWALL (trans.). *The Writings of . . . Tertullianus*. (Ante-Nicene Christian Library, 11, 15, 18.) Edinburgh, 1869–70. 3 vols. Vol. I, pp. 53–140.

———. *De carne Christi*. See MIGNE, *P.L.*, vol. 2, cols. 751–92. For translation see: THELWALL (as above), Vol. II, pp. 163–214.

———. *Liber adversus Judaeos*. See MIGNE, *P.L.*, vol. 2, cols. 595–642. For translation, see: THELWALL (as above), Vol. III, pp. 201–88.

THENAUD, JEAN. "Traité de la cabale." See Codices and MSS., **xxiv.**

THEODORE PSALTER. See Codices and MSS., **ix.**

THOMAS AQUINAS, pseud. "De alchimia." See Codices and MSS., **v.**

———. See also MEYRINK.

THURNEISSER ZUM THURN, LEONHART. *Quinta essentia, das ist die höchste Subtilitet, Krafft und Wirkung, beider der fürtrefflichen (und menschlichem Geschlecht den nutzlichsten) Künsten der Medicina, und Alchemia*. Leipzig, 1574.

TIKKANEN, JOHAN JAKOB. *Die Psalterillustration im Mittelalter*. (Acta Societatis Scientiarum Fennicae, XXXI, 5.) Helsingfors, 1903.

Toyson d'Or, La. See (A) *Aureum vellus*.

Tractatus aureus. See HERMES TRISMEGISTUS.

"Tractatus rhythmicus novus vom Stein der Weysen." See FIGULUS (pp. 58–70).

"Très Riches Heures du duc de Berry." See Codices and MSS., **ii.**

"Trésor de sapience." See Codices and MSS., **xxv.**

"Trésor des trésors." See Codices and MSS., **xxiii.**

TRISMOSIN, SALOMON. "Splendor solis." See Codices and MSS., **x**. See also: *Splendor solis: Alchemical Treatises of Solomon Trismosin*. With explanatory notes by J. K. London, 1920.

——. *La Toyson d'or*. See (A) *Aureum vellus*.

Turba philosophorum. See (A) *Theatrum chemicum*, **xxiv**; (A) *Artis auriferae*, **i**; (A) *Bibliotheca chemica curiosa*, **iii**; Codices and MSS., **xxix**; RUSKA.

——. *Auriferae artis . . . sive Turba philosophorum*. Basel, 1572. 2 vols.

Tz'u-yuan [Chinese lexicon]. 26th edn., Shanghai, 1930.

Upanishads. Translated by F. Max Müller. (Sacred Books of the East, 1, 15.) Oxford, 1879 and 1884. 2 vols.

——. See also Brihadaranyaka Upanishad; Chhandogya Upanishad.

VALENTINUS, BASILIUS. *Chymische Schriften*. Hamburg, 1700.

——. "Practica una. . . ." See (A) *Musaeum hermeticum*, **ix**.

VALLI, LUIGI. "Die Geheimsprache Dantes und der Fedeli d'Amore," *Europäische Revue* (Berlin), VI Jahrgang: 1 Halbband (January-June, 1930), 92–112.

Vedic Hymns. Part I: Hymns to Maruts . . . Part II: Hymns to Agni . . . Translated by F. Max Müller and Hermann Oldenberg. (Sacred Books of the East, 32, 46.) Oxford, 1891 and 1897. 2 vols.

VENTURA, LAURENTIUS. *De ratione conficiendi lapidis philosophici*. Basel, 1571. See also (A) *Theatrum chemicum*, **xv**.

VIRGIL. [*Works*.] Translated by H. Rushton Fairclough. (Loeb Classical Library.) London and New York, 1929. 2 vols.

Viridarium chymicum. See STOLCIUS.

VOLLERS, KARL. "Chidh r," *Archiv für Religionswissenschaft* (Leipzig), XII (1909), 234–84.

"Von der Materi und Prattick des Steins." See (A) *Theatrum chemicum*, **xix**.

VREESWYCK, GOOSEN VAN. *De Groene Leeuw*. Amsterdam, 1672.

WAITE, ARTHUR EDWARD. *The Hermetic Museum Restored and Enlarged*. London, 1893. 2 vols. Repr., 1953. A translation of (A) *Musaeum hermeticum*.

————. *The Secret Tradition in Alchemy. Its Development and Records.* London, 1926.

————. See also BONUS; *Musaeum hermeticum.*

Wasserstein der Weysen, das ist, Ein chymisch Tractätlein. Frankfort on the Main, 1619.

[WEI PO-YANG.] "An Ancient Chinese Treatise on Alchemy Entitled Ts'an T'ung Ch'i, written by Wei Po-yang about 142 A.D. Now translated . . . by Lu-ch'iang Wu," *Isis* (Bruges), XVIII:53 (Oct., 1932), 210–89.

WESSELY, CARL. "Griechische Zauberpapyrus von Paris und London," *Denkschriften der kaiserlichen Akademie der Wissenschaften* (Vienna), *Philosophisch-historische Classe,* XXXVI (1888), 2, 27–208.

WEST, EDWARD WILLIAM (trans.). *Pahlavi Texts.* (Sacred Books of the East, 5.) Oxford, 1880. (Contains the Bundahish.)

WILHELM, RICHARD. *Kung-Tse, Leben und Werk.* (Frommanns Klassiker der Philosophie, 25.) Stuttgart, 1925.

————. *The Secret of the Golden Flower; a Chinese Book of Life.* Translated [into German] and explained . . . with a foreword and commentary by C. G. Jung. Translated into English by Cary F. Baynes. New and revised edn. London and New York, 1962.

WILKEN, ULRICH. *Urkunden der Ptolemäerzeit.* Berlin, 1927.

WIRTH, ALBRECHT. *Aus orientalischen Chroniken.* Frankfort on the Main, 1894.

WOLFF, TONI. "Einführung in die Grundlagen der komplexen Psychologie." In: *Studien zu C. G. Jungs Psychologie.* Zurich, 1959. (Pp. 15–230.)

WOLFRAM VON ESCHENBACH. *Parsifal und Titurel.* Edited by Karl Bartsch. (Deutsche Classiker des Mittelalters, 9–11.) Leipzig, 1875–77. 3 vols.

WOODROFFE, SIR JOHN GEORGE. *Shakti and Shakta.* Madras, 1920.

————. See also AVALON.

ZACHARIUS, DIONYSIUS. "Opusculum philosophiae. . . ." See (*A*) *Theatrum chemicum,* **x.**

ZADITH SENIOR. See SENIOR.

ZELLER, EDUARD. *Die Philosophie der Griechen in ihrer geschichtlichen Entwicklung dargestellt.* Tübingen, 1856. 3 vols.

ZIMMER, HEINRICH. *Myths and Symbols in Indian Art and Civilization.* Edited by Joseph Campbell. (Bollingen Series 6.) New York, 1946.

ZÖCKLER, OTTO. "Probabilismus." See HAUCK, *Realencyklopädie,* XVI, pp. 66ff.

ZOSIMOS. "Rosinus ad Sarratantam episcopum." See (*A*) *Artis auriferae,* **vi.**

ZUNZ, LEOPOLD. *Die gottesdienstlichen Vorträge der Juden, historisch entwickelt.* Berlin, 1932. (First published 1832.)

Zwiefalten Abbey Breviary. See Codices and MSS., l. See also LÖF-FLER.

INDEX

The following subjects are indexed under collective entries: ANIMALS (including birds, insects, reptiles, etc., and fabulous beasts), BIBLE, CODICES & MSS., COLOURS (including alchemical terms), and NUMBERS. The references to illustrations, by *"fig.,"* indicate data included in the List of Illustrations (pp. xv*ff*) as well as in the text captions. For references to "names of individual authors and treatises" in alchemical collections, see the Bibliography, part *A* (pp. 487*ff*), where these are listed. Italic type is used for all literary titles, whether MS. or printed, except in the case of papers under the entry for Jung, whose titles appear in quotation marks.

INDEX

A

abaissement du niveau mental, 89, 333
ablutio, 231; *see also* bath
Abraham/Abram, 206, 322
Abraham le Juif, *see* Eleazar
absurd, the, 15
Abu'l Qāsim, 387, 433, 460
ace of clubs, 76, 169
acetum fontis, 74
Acheron, 430
Acta Archelai, 365n, 380n, 383n
active imagination, *see* imagination
actor, 185
Adam, 115, 151n, 246, 327, 358, 391,
    450f, 460; as Anthropos, 362ff, 368,
    370, 392; creation of, 145, 221n, *fig.*
    71; earthly/spiritual, 362ff, 370, 392;
    as *prima materia,* 319&n, *fig.* 131;
    quaternity of, 363, 368; second, 392
Addam et processum (Melchior), 396n
Adech, 115, 161n, 456n
Ademarus, 171n
Ad Jacobi Auberti Vendonis (Querce-
    tanus), 239n
Adolphus Senior, 76n
adoption, rite of, 415
Aegidius de Vadis, 127n, 319n, 325n,
    371n
Aelian, 442n, 447n
Aenesidemus, 299n
aenigma regis, 112, 186, *fig.* 54
*Aenigmata ex Visione Arislei et alle-
    goriis sapientum, see Visio Arislei*
aeon, *fig.* 7
Aesculapius, 180, *fig.* 77
affects, 143, 190
Agathodaimon, 379
aggression, 89
Agrippa, Heinrich Cornelius, 206, 314n
Ahasuerus, 123

Ahijah, 461
Ahmed ibn-Tulun, mosque of, 118
air/aer, 126n, 178, 205, 229, 263f, 280ff,
    285f, 363, 392, 394, *fig.* 211; lead of
    the, 340; as *prima materia,* 299n,
    301n, 317
airplane, 113, 117
Alain of Lille, 398n
albedo, see COLOURS
Albertus Magnus, 370, 376, 386n, 398f,
    401n, 445f, *fig.* 117
alchemist, 243ff, 258, 267, 278, 289, 291f,
    352ff, 477f, 481f, *figs.* 2, 124, 133, 137,
    143, 144; and Church, 35, 353; mysti-
    fication by, 73, 243f, 289, 316; psy-
    chology of, 251f; as redeemer, *see*
    opus alchymicum, as work of re-
    demption; solitary life of, 35, 314;
    see also artifex
alchemy, aberration of, 279, 431; alle-
    gorical aspect, 34; Arabic, 266, 290,
    387, 458f; as "art," 482; black art,
    67, 80; and chemistry, 23, 34, 37, 227f,
    239, 242ff, 245, 270, 288f, 423, 432;
    Chinese, 76, 357, 428; Christian, 26,
    368; and Christianity, 23f, 33ff; and
    Christian sacraments, 306ff, 350ff,
    396ff, 424f, 426f, 428f, 476f; classical,
    228, 476; downfall of, 37, 227, 423;
    goal of, 232ff, 260, 267, 272; and
    heresy, 34, 74, 112; and individua-
    tion, 3, 35, 346, 475; and Mani-
    cheism, 380n; obscurity of, 34, 35, 227,
    244, 288f, 424; pagan, 26; as philos-
    ophy, 24, 131, 227, 290, 423, 471; and
    projection, *q.v.;* psychological signifi-
    cance, 23, 228; redemption in, *q.v.;*
    symbolism of, *q.v.;* task of, 306; and
    transformation, *q.v.;* two parts of,
    228, 242f, 270, 289ff, 423
alcheringa, 131

childishness, 59*f*, 150

ch'i-lin (Chinese unicorn), *see* ANIMALS

China, 22, 107, 129, 150, 330*n*, 357; unicorn in, 465*f*, figs. 259, 260

Chnuphis, 237*n*; serpent, *fig.* 203

Christ, 12, 17*ff*, 23, 84, 184*f*, 206*f*, 353*f*, 391, 394, 419, *figs.* 18, 101, 197; Adam as, 365; allegories of, 17; androgyny of, 19, 22, 464; as Anthropos, 304, 368, 392, *fig.* 64; archetype, 17, 19; as bridegroom, 389; as bull, 440; *coniunctio* on mountain, 160; descent to hell, 53*n*, 339, 354; dogmatic, 17*f*, 185; esoteric, 120; as *filius macrocosmi*, 425; as *filius philosophorum*, 389, *fig.* 234; as fire, 120, 196, 353*f*, *fig.* 58; gnostic, 368; historicity of, 35, 185; as *homo philosophicus*, 392; as horn, 445; identity with calendar, 206; imitation of, 7, 22, 32, 35, 308, 354; as *lapis, q.v.*; as living water, 390*n*; as Logos/Nous, 304; and Mass, 308*ff*; as Mercurius, 438; as microcosm, 392; Pantokrator, 133; as pelican, *figs.* 89, 256; as phoenix, 419; pre-Christian, 185; as Redeemer, 184, 306, 308*f*, 354*f*, 358, *fig.* 182; risen, 422, *figs.* 177, 234; in rose, 108*n*; sacrificial death, 306, 308*f*, 353; as second Adam, 392; in sepulchre, *fig.* 170; as serpent, 144; as sun, 84, 208, 417; symbol of self, 18*f*, 208, 355; symbol in mandala, 129, *fig.* 62; as transforming substance, 434; as unicorn, 438*ff&n*, 444*f*, 463; as vine, 394; yoke of, 21*n*, 22

Christianity, 7*f*, 11*f*, 15*ff*, 20*ff*, 33*f*, 143, 355; and alchemy, 23, 33*f*, 352*f*, 428*ff*, 476; good and evil in, 22; and modern mentality, 150; and paganism, 11; world religion, 19

Christianos, 159, 315*n*

Christopher of Paris, 340

χρυσάνθεμον, 76*n*

chthonic: bear, 187; = dark, 175*f*; femininity of unconscious, 23*f*; gods, 158, 329*n*; Mercurius, 65; prison, 190;

serpent, 292; trinity, 460; underworld, 25

Ch'un-ts'iu, fig. 260

Church, 4, 17, 27*f*, 30*ff*, 73, 138*ff*, 210, 308*ff*; alchemist and, 35, 353; Fathers, 17*f*, 386, *fig.* 197; return to, 4, 33; seven churches, 379; schism of, 424

chymical wedding, 37, 232, 402*n*, 436, 463

cibatio, 239

Cibinensis, *see* Melchior

Cienfuegos, Alvarez, 309*n*

circle, 42*n*, 54, 81, 95*f*, 104, 118, 124*f*, 128*&n*, 174, 191*f*, 209*f*, 325, 382; with centre, allegory of God, 106*f*; divided into four, 106, 128*n*, 150, 164, 191, 197; magic, 42*n*, 54, 95, 106, 118, 148, 167; movement in a, 103*f*, 180, 188, 192; —, opus as, 293, 381*f*, 386; and *rotatio*, 165; squared, 169; squaring of, 96, 124, 127, 128*n*, 167, figs. 59, 60

circulatio/circulation, 164, 172, 186, 191, 192*f*, 197

circumambulatio / circumambulation, 28, 108*n*, 127, 128*n*, 145, 148, 174, 179*n*, 180, 190, 206

cista, 157

citrinitas, see COLOURS

city, 107, 126*n*; of Brahma, 108; with four gates, 108*f*; as *rotundum*, 127*n*; as *temenos*, 107, *fig.* 31

civilization, Christian, hollowness of, 12

Clement, of Alexandria, 109*n*; of Rome, 380

Cleopatra, 120*n*, 401

clock, cosmic, 105; pendulum, 104*ff*, 112, 120, 181; world, 203*f*

cloud(s), 248, 250, 285*f*; as *prima materia*, 317

clover, 164, 169

coagulatio/coagulation, 239, 285*f*

coal, 218

CODICES AND MSS. (*boldface numerals refer to Bibliography*)

Akhmim, **i**, 53*n*

Aschaffenburg: *Evangeliary*, **i-a**, *fig.* 109

U

THE COLLECTED WORKS OF

C. G. JUNG

EDITORS: SIR HERBERT READ, MICHAEL FORDHAM, AND GER-
HARD ADLER; *EXECUTIVE EDITOR*, WILLIAM McGUIRE. *TRANS-
LATED BY* R.F.C. HULL, EXCEPT WHERE NOTED.

IN THE FOLLOWING LIST, dates of original publication are given in pa-
rentheses (of original composition, in brackets). Multiple dates indicate
revisions.

(continued)

The Theory of Psychoanalysis (1913)
General Aspects of Psychoanalysis (1913)
Psychoanalysis and Neurosis (1916)
Some Crucial Points in Psychoanalysis: A Correspondence between Dr. Jung and Dr. Loÿ (1914)
Prefaces to "Collected Papers on Analytical Psychology" (1916, 1917)
The Significance of the Father in the Destiny of the Individual (1909/1949)
Introduction to Kranefeldt's "Secret Ways of the Mind" (1930)
Freud and Jung: Contrasts (1929)

5. SYMBOLS OF TRANSFORMATION ([1911–12/1952] 1956; 2nd edn., 1967)

PART I
Introduction
Two Kinds of Thinking
The Miller Fantasies: Anamnesis
The Hymn of Creation
The Song of the Moth

PART II
Introduction
The Concept of Libido
The Transformation of Libido
The Origin of the Hero
Symbols of the Mother and of Rebirth
The Battle for Deliverance from the Mother
The Dual Mother
The Sacrifice
Epilogue
Appendix: The Miller Fantasies

6. PSYCHOLOGICAL TYPES ([1921] 1971)

A revision by R.F.C. Hull of the translation by H. G. Baynes

Introduction
The Problem of Types in the History of Classical and Medieval Thought
Schiller's Ideas on the Type Problem
The Apollinian and the Dionysian
The Type Problem in Human Character
The Type Problem in Poetry
The Type Problem in Psychopathology

(*continued*)

(*continued*)

(continued)

16. (*continued*)

The Psychology of the Transference (1946)
Appendix: The Realities of Practical Psychotherapy ([1937] added 1966)

17. THE DEVELOPMENT OF PERSONALITY (1954)
Psychic Conflicts in a Child (1910/1946)
Introduction to Wickes's "Analyses der Kinderseele" (1927/1931)
Child Development and Education (1928)
Analytical Psychology and Education: Three Lectures (1926/1946)
The Gifted Child (1943)
The Significance of the Unconscious in Individual Education (1928)
The Development of Personality (1934)
Marriage as a Psychological Relationship (1925)

18. THE SYMBOLIC LIFE (1954)
Translated by R.F.C. Hull and others

Miscellaneous writings

19. COMPLETE BIBLIOGRAPHY OF C. G. JUNG'S WRITINGS (1976; 2nd edn., 1992)

20. GENERAL INDEX TO THE COLLECTED WORKS (1979)

THE ZOFINGIA LECTURES (1983)
Supplementary Volume A to The Collected Works. Edited by William McGuire, translated by Jan van Heurck, introduction by Marie-Louise von Franz

PSYCHOLOGY OF THE UNCONSCIOUS ([1912] 1992)

A STUDY OF THE TRANSFORMATIONS AND SYMBOLISMS OF THE LIBIDO.
A CONTRIBUTION TO THE HISTORY OF THE EVOLUTION OF THOUGHT

Supplementary Volume B to the Collected Works. Translated by Beatrice M. Hinkle, introduction by William McGuire

Related publications:

THE BASIC WRITINGS OF C. G. JUNG
Selected and introduced by Violet S. de Laszlo

C. G. JUNG: LETTERS
Selected and edited by Gerhard Adler, in collaboration with Aniela Jaffé.
Translations from the German by R.F.C. Hull.
VOL. 1: 1906–1950
VOL. 2: 1951–1961

C. G. JUNG SPEAKING: Interviews and Encounters
Edited by William McGuire and R.F.C. Hull

C. G. JUNG: Word and Image
Edited by Aniela Jaffé

THE ESSENTIAL JUNG
Selected and introduced by Anthony Storr

THE GNOSTIC JUNG
Selected and introduced by Robert A. Segal

PSYCHE AND SYMBOL
Selected and introduced by Violet S. de Laszlo

Notes of C. G. Jung's Seminars:

DREAM ANALYSIS ([1928–30] 1984)
Edited by William McGuire

NIETZSCHE'S *ZARATHUSTRA* ([1934–39] 1988)
Edited by James L. Jarrett (2 vols.)

ANALYTICAL PSYCHOLOGY ([1925] 1989)
Edited by William McGuire